GROWTH AND
MATURATION FACTORS

GROWTH AND MATURATION FACTORS

Volume 2

GORDON GUROFF

Editor
Section on Growth Factors
National Institute of Child Health and Human Development
National Institutes of Health

A Wiley-Interscience Publication

JOHN WILEY & SONS

New York ● Chichester ● Brisbane ● Toronto ● Singapore

Library of Congress Cataloging in Publication Data:

(Revised for volume 2)
Main entry under title:

 Growth and maturation factors.

 "A Wiley-Interscience publication."
 Includes bibliographical references and indexes.
  I. Growth promoting substances.   2. Nerve growth
factor.   I. Guroff, Gordon, 1933-

QP84.G76 1983   612'.6   82-17598
ISBN 0-471-09709-8 (v. 1)
ISBN 0-471-09708-X (v. 2)

Printed in the United States of America

10 9 8 7 6 5 4 3 2 1

CONTRIBUTORS

Michael P. Czech, Department of Biochemistry, University of Massachusetts Medical School, Worcester, Massachusetts

Luis Jimenez de Asua, Department of Biochemistry, St. George's Hospital Medical School, Cramer Terrace, London, England. Formerly Friedrich Miescher Institute, Basel, Switzerland

Allen Fenselau, Miami Heart Institute, Miami, Florida

Robert C. Gallo, Laboratory of Tumor Cell Biology, National Cancer Institute, National Institutes of Health, Bethesda, Maryland

David W. Golde, Division of Hematology–Oncology, Department of Medicine, UCLA School of Medicine, Los Angeles, California

Eugene Goldwasser, Department of Biochemistry, University of Chicago, Chicago, Illinois

C. Ronald Kahn, Brigham and Women's Hospital, Harvard Medical School, Boston, Massachusetts

George L. King, Brigham and Women's Hospital, Harvard Medical School, Boston, Massachusetts

Michael Klagsbrun, Children's Hospital Medical Center, Boston, Massachusetts

Aldons J. Lusis, Division of Hematology–Oncology, Department of Medicine, UCLA School of Medicine, Los Angeles, California

George J. Markelonis, Department of Anatomy, University of Maryland, School of Medicine, Baltimore, Maryland

Tae H. Oh, Department of Anatomy, University of Maryland, School of Medicine, Baltimore, Maryland

Catherine L. Oppenheimer, Department of Biochemistry, University of Massachusetts Medical School, Worcester, Massachusetts

Angela M. Otto, Department of Biochemistry, St. George's Hospital Medical School, Cramer Terrace, London, England. Formerly Friedrich Miescher Institute, Basel, Switzerland

Marjorie Robert-Guroff, Laboratory of Tumor Cell Biology, National Cancer Institute, National Institutes of Health, Bethesda, Maryland

M. G. Sarngadharan, Department of Cell Biology, Litton Bionetics, Inc., Kensington, Maryland

Yuen W. Shing, Harvard Medical School, Children's Hospital Medical Center, Boston, Massachusetts

Christina Smith, Friedrich Miescher Institute, Basel, Switzerland

Carol A. Westbrook, Division of Hematology-Oncology, Department of Medicine, UCLA School of Medicine, Los Angeles, California

Gary Van Zant, Malline Krodt Institute of Radiology, Division of Radiation Oncology, St. Louis, Missouri

To my mother, with love and admiration

SERIES PREFACE

Since the first identifiable experiments on growth factors were done more than 30 years ago, the literature on the subject has expanded at a steady pace. Nevertheless, the expansion has been undisciplined. Growth factors appear and many disappear. Conditioned-medium factors and serum factors abound, but the vast majority remain uncharacterized. Of the dozens that have been reported, only a few have been described in any detail. Indeed, despite a large body of work on a few factors, the exact mechanism by which any one of the factors works, in a molecular sense, remains unknown. Even more, there is still a very real question about whether any of these factors, with the possible exception of nerve growth factor, has a role in the normal growth and development of the individual.

Despite the rather primitive state of our current understanding of these materials, the vistas for them are immense. They appear to impinge on the most fundamental processes of life. They influence the rate of cell division, the course of differentiation, and the characteristics of the immune system. They could have roles in clinical problems as diverse as atherosclerosis, sensory deficits, and cancer. Their actions are of concern to scientists in every area of biology.

There is, at present, no continuing source of information about growth factors. Papers appear in all contemporary journals, and reviews are found in virtually every compendium. It would seem useful to have a single set of volumes that would present the unfolding information in this area from several points of view. Reviews of the information concerning specific growth factors should appear, of course, but also there should be discussions of methods applicable to all factors, chapters on growth factors of clinical interest, and coverage of the effects of several factors on specific organs or organ systems. The present series is intended to satisfy this need for a collection of reviews of what appears to be a rapidly expanding field but one still in its infancy.

GORDON GUROFF

Bethesda, Maryland
February 1983

PREFACE

The rapidity with which the field of growth factors is moving can be illustrated by simply mentioning the signal advances which have taken place in the short time since the publication of Volume 1. These include the identification of the genes for mouse and human nerve growth factor and for mouse and human epidermal growth factor. During the same span of weeks came the remarkable finding that platelet-derived growth factor is virtually identical to the product of the onc gene, *cis*, from simian sarcoma virus-transformed cells. These studies—the first providing powerful new tools, the second opening astounding new conceptual frontiers—have extended the provinces of growth factor research.

In this second volume I have tried to continue the systematic coverage of specific growth factors begun in Volume 1. Thus, there are major chapters on Erythropoietin, Sciatin, and T-Cell Growth Factor. In addition, I have tried to incorporate information on factors which may not be so well characterized as yet, but which impinge on important aspects of development. Accordingly, I have included chapters on Erythroid-Potentiating Activity, Angiogenesis Factors, and the Factors in Milk. The chapter on Insulin should help to sort out what has become a somewhat controversial subject and the information provided in the chapter on Prostaglandin will hopefully allow the reader a firm foundation from which to enter the increasing literature on this subject. Finally, the chapter on Affinity Labeling should provide an introduction to a methodology useful for studies on any of the growth factors.

Clearly it is impossible in a series such as this to provide comprehensive coverage in each volume. It is equally impossible, writing and publishing time constraints being what they are, to have such a volume contain the absolute latest findings. Nevertheless, the first volume did provide a background, and an up-to-date one at that, for the understanding of the most recent findings in nerve growth factor, epidermal growth factor, and platelet-derived growth factor research mentioned above. Hopefully the chapters contained herein will also provide the backdrop for equally exciting findings to come in the near future.

Bethesda, Maryland   GORDON GUROFF
March 1984

CONTENTS

1

ERYTHROPOIETIN AND ITS TARGET CELLS

Gary Van Zant
Eugene Goldwasser

CONTENTS

Abbreviations

epo	Erythropoietin
CSF	Colony-stimulating factor
CFU-E	Colony-forming unit-erythroid
BFU-E	Burst-forming unit-erythroid
BFU-E-3	Burst-forming unit-erythroid, 3-day colonies
CFU-S	Colony forming unit, pluripotent stem cells
CFU-GM	Colony-forming unit, granulocyte-macrophage
BPA	Burst-promoting activity
BFA	Burst-feeder activity
Gy	Gray
CSF-1	Macrophage colony-stimulating factor
AMS	Anemic mouse serum

1. INTRODUCTION

There is abundant evidence that normal red cell production in mammals is regulated by the glycoprotein hormone, erythropoietin (epo). Much of this evidence, derived from experiments on whole animals and from clinical observations, was extensively reviewed in the monograph by Krantz and Jacobson (1) published in 1967. Our original intent for this review was to survey the pertinent literature for the past 10 years, but a quick search revealed that in the past 3 years there have been 540 papers on epo and erythropoiesis published, making the task too formidable for a review of this type. In addition, there have been several fairly recent reviews (2–9) on the subject of epo, so we could restrict our attention to two topics: the biochemistry of epo and its cell biology as studied *in vitro*. The important and fascinating question of the role of epo in the differential expression of the non-α globin genes has been discussed in recent published symposia and is not treated in this review.

In considering the effects of epo on cells in culture we make the tacit assumption that information gained from studies *in vitro* may represent artifacts due to culturing cells in an artificial environment and must eventually be verified in whole animals before a comprehensive and plausible model of erythroid cell differentiation can be developed. In this context we should once again point out some of the advantages and disadvantages of using the differentiation of erythrocytes as a model for the general study of cell differentiation.

In the adult mammal, red cells are derived from pluripotent hemopoietic stem cells (hereafter called "stem cells"); some of the biological properties of these precursor cells are known but there is no detailed information about their physical and chemical characteristics. There is a specific molecular marker, hemoglobin, for late cells in the erythroid cell lineage. The pathway culminating in red cells is under the direct influence of epo which acts at some point before hemoglobin synthesis is detectable. The precise cellular locus of epo action is not yet defined and is discussed later. The evidence, however, is clear: with epo present normal erythropoiesis occurs; without epo it does not.

The vast amount of information available about the structure of hemoglobin, its chemistry, biosynthesis, genetics, and molecular biology make it a very useful marker of the later stages of the erythroid pathway. The ability to study erythropoiesis *in vitro* also provides a decided advantage in this research, although not having a pure population of epo target cells is a major disadvantage. Another drawback which is discussed later is the extremely limited supply of pure epo available for study.

2. THE CHEMISTRY OF EPO

2.1. Original Purification

Although the purification of sheep plasma epo (potency: 8000 units* per mg of protein) was described in 1971 (10), there was too little available to determine more than the barest few of its properties. It was evident that epo was a very minor constituent of the plasma proteins† even under conditions that maximized its concentration. It was also evident that an alternative large-scale source was needed. Espada and Gutnisky had obtained a preparation of human epo, derived from the urine of anemic patients, with about the same potency as the purified sheep epo, and determined some of its properties (12, 13). The advantage of using urine was that most of the plasma protein had already been removed by the kidneys, and it would not be necessary to go through a one million-fold purification as was the case for plasma. However, as indicated in the following, this preparation was only about 11% pure and the properties ascribed to it cannot be taken as characteristic of epo. Urine from patients with the appropriate kind of anemia might, nevertheless, be the needed source.

Miyake et al. (14), working with concentrates of urine from patients with aplastic anemia, succeeded in preparing epo that was homogeneous and that had a potency of about 70,000 units per mg of protein, about 8–10 times higher than that prepared by Espada and Gutnisky or that found for the sheep plasma preparation. This epo preparation is homogeneous by several criteria: a single component is found on nondenaturing gel electrophoresis, a single component is seen under denaturing and reducing conditions, and there is a single N-terminal amino acid residue, alanine (15).

2.2. Molecular Forms

In the final step of purification of urinary epo, chromatography on hydroxylapatite, there were two fractions of equal potency, but with differing chromatographic properties and differing electrophoretic mobilities under nondenaturing conditions. The first component eluted from the column, termed α epo, has a slower mobility than the second, the β form. On denaturing gels the two forms were indistinguishable and appear to have the same molecular size as well as the same biological activity, reactivity

---

* A unit of epo is arbitrarily defined as the amount of biological activity equivalent to one-tenth the content of an ampoule of WHO, International Reference Preparation which is a crude human urinary epo (11).

† The concentration of epo in normal human serum is about 0.02 μ/ml; this is equivalent to 1.4×10^{-11} M or 3.5×10^{-7}% of the plasma protein.

toward an antiserum, amino acid composition, and N-terminal amino acid. They differ appreciably in percent carbohydrate and in content of two of the carbohydrate constituents, N-acetylglucosamine and sialic acid (16). The difference in sialic acid does not explain the difference in electrophoretic mobility at pH 8, inasmuch as the α form would be expected to move more quickly in the electric field at pH 9 because of its higher sialic acid content. At this stage of incomplete data we can only invoke a possible difference in amino acid amidation to account for the difference in mobility between the two forms. It does not appear to be an important problem.

2.3.   Amino Acid Composition

Although the amino acid composition indicates that there are three cysteine residues per molecule (17), more recent data (18) using alkylation with labeled N-ethyl maleimide show that there are four cysteines. These are in two internal disulfide bridges that appear to be inaccessible except under denaturing conditions and may be buried in the hydrophobic structure of epo. This finding confirms the suggestion (19) that epo has critical disulfide bridges. Alkylation of the cysteines after denaturation results in loss of biological activity but we do not yet know whether the inactivation is due to the denaturation, or to a requirement for one or both disulfide bonds. The data of Espada et al. obtained with crude material suggest that denaturation *per se* does not inactivate epo (19).

Using pure human epo we have shown that iodination (most likely of a single tyrosine residue) results in loss of biological activity (17) and of binding to target cells. The same result is obtained when free amino groups are alkylated with the Bolton–Hunter reagent. This reagent does not distinguish between α and ε amino groups so we do not know whether the N-terminal alanine or the lysines (or both) are included in the active site. Studies with crude epo suggest that one or more tryptophan residues may also be at, or near, the site inasmuch as hydroxynitrobenzyl bromide causes loss of biological activity (20). Similar studies indicate that periodate oxidation also results in loss of biological activity (19). Study of the effects of a wide variety of proteases, again with crude epo, showed that whereas trypsin, pepsin, chymotrypsin A, elastase, papain, ficin, and bromelin caused inactivation, carboxypeptidase A and leucine aminopeptidase did not (19).

2.4.   Molecular Weight

The early estimate of the molecular weight of pure epo, based on electrophoresis in reducing sodium dodecylsulfate-containing gels, was 39,000

(14); we have since accumulated data indicating that 34,000 may be closer to the true value.

2.5. Carbohydrate Content

Epo is a glycoprotein with a single polypeptide chain; the α form has about 31% carbohydrate and the β about 24% (16). The carbohydrate composition is consistent with there being several complex, N-linked oligosaccharide chains but we have insufficient evidence as yet to determine how many. It will require considerably more pure epo than is now available to determine the number of oligosaccharide chains and the sequences of sugars in them.

The role of terminal sialic acids has been studied in some detail. Lowy et al. first showed that sialidase treatment inactivated crude epo (21); this was followed by the finding of Lukowsky and Painter (22) that asialo epo regained activity after oxidation with galactose oxidase. These data indicated that asialo epo was inactive because the liver lectin described by Ashwell and his colleagues (23) removed it from the circulation. Further evidence for this conclusion came from work by Goldwasser et al. (24) who showed that the asialo form was active *in vivo* if the assay animal had been pretreated with a large amount of asialoorosomucoid or the galactose terminal tetra-saccharide, stachyose. They further showed that asialo epo was active on target cells of marrow in culture. In fact, it was considerably more active than the native, sialated form. These data together show that neither the sialic acid termini nor the penultimate galactose residues are required for the intrinsic biological activity of epo although the carbohydrate may be needed for stability *in vivo*. Additional data reinforced the idea that epo is stabilized by sialic acid; the asialo form is less stable to heat than the native form and more rapidly inactivated by trypsin (24).

More recently Dordal and Goldwasser (16) have succeeded in removing about 85% of the carbohydrate by hydrolysis with mixed glycosidases prepared from *S. pneumoniae*. The largely deglycosylated epo retained about 60% of its biological activity when assayed *in vitro* and 40% of its immunological activity when assayed by radioimmunoassay, but was devoid of activity when assayed in whole animals. The residual biological activity measured by the rat marrow cell culture method is, however, a minimal estimate because there is considerable aggregation of epo after deglycosylation and the aggregate has little or no biological activity. The 60% of the biological activity found for the deglycosylated epo, then, represents largely the activity of the nonaggregated material, which must be more active, per unit of protein, than the native epo, inasmuch as 85–90% of the epo protein is in the aggregate form.

3. PURIFICATION OF EPO

3.1. Use of Lectins

Important innovations in purification techniques have been introduced into this field in recent years. The use of immobilized plant lectins by Sieber (25) and Spivak and colleagues (26–28) takes advantage of the presence of carbohydrate to permit the adsorption of epo from crude mixtures and the subsequent elution of epo with a more or less specific sugar. The use of immobilized wheat germ agglutinin which adsorbs epo, and from which epo can be eluted in good yield will undoubtedly become routine in the purification.

Inasmuch as most urine concentrates contain significant amounts of colony-stimulating factor (CSF) that can markedly alter the response of cells *in vitro* to epo (29), it is useful to use immobilized concanavalin A to remove most of the CSF at an early step in purification (25). In addition to yielding an epo preparation almost free of a troublesome contaminant, the use of this lectin also permits the recovery of the CSF.

3.2. Hydrophobic Chromatography

Another important advance in purification techniques came from the work of Lee-Huang who introduced the use of hydrophobic chromatography in the successful purification of epo (30). Previous studies had shown that binding of epo activity to aliphatic chains (e.g., octyl Sepharose) was apparently irreversible (27); Lee-Huang showed that binding of epo at high ionic strength to phenyl Sepharose was essentially quantitative, as was elution at high pH, low salt, and 4 M guanidine, in the presence of 20% ethylene glycol. Surprisingly, epo is stable to 10 mM NaOH under these conditions. This method yields a stable concentrate of epo that can be used for further fractionation.

The seven-step purification method reported by Miyake et al. (14), which has an overall yield of about 20%, can, no doubt, be significantly improved with respect to yield by use of some of the newer techniques, and by modification of the more conventional methods. For example, the published yield using sulfopropyl Sephadex was 50% with a purification factor of 6 (31). By incorporation of 20% ethylene glycol in the eluting buffers, the yield increased to 90% with a purification factor of 5. Another potentially important purification technique, the use of specific immunoaffinity columns, should be developed soon now that two laboratories have reported success in producing anti-epo monoclonal antibodies (32, 33).

3.3.   Removal of Proteases

One problem with the use of urine concentrates as a source of epo derives from the presence of protease and sialidase activities. One method of removal of these destabilizing enzymes involves the treatment of the concentrate with phenol and p-aminosalicylate (34). Mok and Spivak reported that the same effect could be achieved by heating to 80°C for 5 minutes (35), and Lee-Huang reported that the 4 M NaCl used for adsorption to phenyl Sepharose prevented proteolysis (30). Our own experience suggests that there is a fair degree of variability in both the level of enzymes in the various urine concentrates and the effectiveness of methods to remove the hydrolases. Any method chosen should be tested with a particular batch of urine concentrate to ensure the stability of the epo and/or the inactivation of the enzymes.

3.4.   Alternate Sources

One clearly obvious need in this field is a large-scale, reliable source of epo; without such a source, information about its chemistry, the relationship between its structure and its function, and its clinical efficacy is going to continue to be agonizingly slow in accumulating. Even if newer techniques in processing urine can be used to increase the yield, there will still be a shortage inasmuch as the maximum increase can only be fivefold and the supply of urine from suitably anemic patients is severely limited. Because there is no clear, immediate alternative, efforts should continue to be made to extend the availability of epo by increasing its yield from present sources while other sources are being sought. There is undoubtedly a vast amount of active urine not being collected, but the feasibility of worldwide collection and concentration seems to be questionable.

One possible alternative source may be the culture media of cells that produce epo *in vitro*. Despite much effort, neoplastic cells from patients with erythrocytosis, cells from fetal liver, macrophages, and normal kidney mesangial cells (36–42) grown *in vitro* produce disappointingly small amounts of epo activity. Because of the present cost of culturing cells it may not be economically feasible to use cells with minimal epo secretion for large-scale production. As an example, if a culture could be made to yield 0.1 U/ml it would require 14,000 liters to get 10 mg of epo protein at a yield of 50%.

The direct extraction of epo from, for example, fresh beef kidney, if it could be accomplished on a vast scale, might provide a moderate amount of epo. We have found that about 0.2 units of epo can be extracted from a gram of fresh tissue (43), and if the potency of pure beef epo were the same as that of human epo, it would require about 7000 kg to yield 10 mg of epo if the yield, again optimistically, were 50%.

There seem to be only two realistic longer range alternatives: finding a method to increase greatly the amount of epo secreted by cultured cells, perhaps by the use of a particularly active tumor hybridized with an immortalized cell. If such a cell were under the same kind of control as that found *in vivo*, it might be possible to increase the synthesis and secretion by use of hypoxic conditions, anabolic steroids, or cobaltous salts in the medium. The other possibility is cloning the epo gene so that it could be produced in a rapidly (and cheaply) growing cell. If the gene were recombined with a strong, active promoter the organism might synthesize epo in amounts large enough to meet the need.

This strategy would entail either cloning the epo gene in a cell that could glycosylate it or finding a method of keeping aglycoepo active, stable, and nonaggregated. The problems in this area of research will, no doubt, be studied for some time to come.

4. THE MOLECULAR MODE OF ACTION OF EPO

4.1. Early Studies

A fair amount of information about the biochemical effects of epo on target cells has been accumulated and reviewed in the years since a biochemical effect of epo, *in vitro*, was first described (44). Unfortunately, most of those investigations were, of necessity, done with very impure epo and there is no *a priori* way to determine which of the observed effects were due to epo and which to impurities. For example, crude epo preparations were shown to have an early effect on transcription by either adult marrow (45, 46) or fetal liver cells (47, 48); we now know that some epo preparations contain CSF and that CSF also has an effect on transcription (49). The effects on transcription may, therefore, reflect the actions of a non-epo factor or of two or more factors. It is also well known that epo is frequently contaminated with endotoxin (50, 51, 52), that endotoxin itself can have an effect on hemopoietic cells (53), and that endotoxin can induce the formation of CSF in animals (54). The various details of epo action will have to be restudied with pure epo before we can be confident that effects previously attributed to it are truly due to epo. In one paper, Weiss and Goldwasser (55) showed that some of the effects of pure, endotoxin-free epo on rat and mouse cells were the same as those previously reported using crude epo. These effects included the induction of hemoglobin synthesis, the stimulation of total transcription, and the appearance of the marrow cytoplasmic mediator protein that acts to increase transcription in isolated nuclei.

One area of epo action on hemopoietic cells, the induction of hemoglobin synthesis, may be less affected by the use of impure epo than others inasmuch as hemoglobin synthesis is a specific marker of erythroid differentiation and not likely to be affected, in a primary, positive sense, by other factors. It can, however, be materially decreased by CSF (29), and perhaps by other specific substances. Because it is well established that red cell formation, and hence hemoglobin synthesis, *in vivo* is dependent on epo and that pure epo *in vitro* can induce the synthesis of hemoglobin, it is reasonable to accept the findings of the effects of crude preparations on stimulation of globin synthesis as truly reflecting the action of epo.

Two kinds of *in vitro* systems have been used to study the mechanisms by which epo regulates hemoglobin synthesis: adult bone marrow cells and fetal liver cells. Each has both advantages and disadvantages. Marrow is a very heterogeneous collection of cells, most of which are not affected by epo. It contains, however, both early pluripotent cells and late erythroid precursor cells and, because of that, it may be possible to study the important question of whether epo has an instructive role in cell differentiation; that is, whether it acts on the step committing cells to the erythroid pathway or acts solely as a mitogen for committed cells. Fetal liver cells, on the other hand, comprise a more uniform population containing both early and late erythroid precursors and hepatocytes plus some other cells. In some cases an immune lysis method has been useful to deplete selectively the population of the more mature erythroid cells. One disadvantage of this system derives from the capacity of some of the cells in fetal liver to make and/or release epo into the medium (39), making it impossible to dissect out the effect of exogenously supplied epo. It also makes for great difficulty in studying the temporal relationships among the various epo effects since the time of initiation cannot be known with any precision.

4.2.   Effects on Transcription

It is established now that pure endotoxin-free epo does cause an increase in the rate of marrow cell transcription (55). This suggests that at least some of the effects on transcription reported earlier with crude epo can be accepted as indicating that the early action on hemopoietic cells is on RNA synthesis. There are considerable data showing an effect of epo (not pure) on DNA synthesis (48, 56, 57), and some of these data have been interpreted as indicating that the effect of epo is on proliferation of cells committed to the erythroid pathway. The effect on transcription is, in this view, secondary to the action on proliferation and dependent on the pre-established program of erythroid function. It is quite certain that epo does have an effect on the proliferation of late erythroid cells which seem to have only two alternatives: to die if not acted on by epo, or in the presence of epo to go through the rest of the maturation pathway and become, after several divisions, mature red cells. If that is the only action of epo, and we believe it is not, then the effect of epo on DNA synthesis is mediated through an effect on RNA synthesis, inasmuch as inhibition of the former does not affect the rapid action on transcription (48, 57, 58, 59). The reciprocal experiment, however, shows that inhibition of transcription does prevent the action of epo on DNA replication (57). The experiments on thymidine incorporation will all have to be repeated, however, because they were not carried out with pure epo, and as indicated previously, other factors may be responsible for increased DNA synthesis, perhaps by cells not in the erythroid pathway.

4.3. Effects on Hemoglobin Synthesis

Even with impure epo it seems clear that there is an effect on the transcription of the globin genes. Work with fetal liver cells *in vitro* (60) indicated that epo causes an increase in the amount of RNA hybridizable to globin cDNA, and translatable to yield globin within about 10 hours of addition. There was, in addition, a significant increase in the same hybridizable globin messenger RNA without any added epo, possibly due to epo production by the cells. There was no increase in the calculated number of molecules of globin message per cell due to epo, but the increased amount of message appeared to be accounted for by the increase in cell number. The question remains open: is the epo-induced increase in globin message a result of the increase in cells or does epo have an effect on globin gene transcription that persists in the subsequent cells that arise because of the additional effect on proliferation?

Studies of the content of mature, translatable, globin message in rat marrow cells show that there is a rapid increase in message that starts very soon after epo is added *in vitro* (61). These cells, from suppressed rats (rats that have been made artificially polycythemic and have a very low rate of hemoglobin synthesis), also show a time-dependent increase in globin message when no epo is added. Both of the time courses (plus and minus epo) extrapolate to zero time, suggesting that stimulation of globin gene transcription and processing of the transcript may be some of the primary actions of epo before any cell division has had time to occur.

4.4. Intracellular Mediator Protein

Since globin gene transcription is a nuclear event and since there is some indirect evidence that epo binds to a protein receptor (62) on the outside surface of the target cell, one may ask about the nature of signal to the nucleus. We have verified with pure epo (55) an earlier finding that, in the absence of protein synthesis, epo acts to generate a cytoplasmic protein mediator that can act on nuclei to effect an increase in the rate of transcription (63).

The tentative picture derived from these findings is that the interaction of epo with specific external receptors results in the appearance, on the cytoplasmic side of the membrane, of a protein that can interact with the transcriptional system in the nucleus to increase the rate of RNA synthesis. There are some data suggesting that this mediator protein can affect at least three nuclear components: RNA polymerases I + III, RNA polymerase II, and DNA (template activity) (64). At least one key question about this system still awaits an answer: Is there any specificity with respect to the transcripts formed as a result of this activity? The system at present relies on the use of isolated nuclei for the assay of the mediator protein activity and there is enough nuclease action to cause large-scale breakdown of the transcripts. The problem is still being studied.

4.5.   Action on Nuclear Processes

In experiments that combined the *in vivo* and *in vitro* approaches, the effect of epo on the enzymes of RNA synthesis was shown clearly (65). Within ½ hour after injection of epo, the level of mouse spleen RNA polymerase II was elevated; by 2 hours it was back to baseline. At 3 hours the activity of polymerase I had increased, reaching a maximum at 12 hours, at which time a secondary increase in polymerase II activity had occurred. Even though these experiments were done with a crude epo preparation, the likelihood of the effect being due to epo is good since the same preparation of epo with the sialic acid removed had no effect on the spleen polymerases and inasmuch as there was no effect of unmodified epo on the RNA polymerases of liver. There is still the possibility that some sialo glycoprotein other than epo was acting specifically on spleen cells, but it seems reasonable to accept these findings as effects of epo.

In a similar type of experiment, crude epo caused an increase in the synthesis of all five of the major histones and most of the nuclear non-histone proteins of the spleen (66). These effects were observed considerably later than those found for RNA polymerase, but were seen prior to the appearance of any morphologically detectable erythroid cells. Once again, there was no effect of this epo preparation on the nuclear proteins of liver and no effect of the asialo epo preparation on spleen.

In a third experiment of this type, the activities of splenic acetyl and methyl transferases, using chromosomal proteins as acceptors, were studied

(67). The conclusion from this experiment was that the effect of epo on transcription could not be explained by a prior action on either acetylation or methylation of chromosomal proteins. ·

4.6.   Effects on Membrane Constituents

Study of the synthesis of red cell membrane constituents, using cultured human or rat cells, has shown some interesting effects of impure epo which should be confirmed with the pure inducer. Fukuda and Fukuda (68) found that human erythroblasts obtained from cultured precursor cells contained barely detectable amounts of bands 3 and 4.5, some glycophorins, and two glycoproteins with apparent molecular weights 105,000 and 95,000. They also found significant differences between fetal or neonatal red cells and adult red cells. Tong and Goldwasser (69) found that marrow cells from polycythemic animals showed stimulated synthesis of glycophorin and band 3 when cultured with crude epo. There was also a transient effect on proteins found in marrow membranes but not on those in mature erythrocytes.

4.7.   Role of Cyclic Nucleotides

The role of cyclic nucleotides in epo action *in vitro* has been studied in some detail. An interesting species difference was found; marrow from mice, rats, and guinea pigs showed decreased hemoglobin synthesis due to dibutyrylcyclic AMP whereas marrow from sheep, rabbit, dogs, and humans showed an increase (70). The end result of several detailed studies is that the cyclic nucleotides, some steroids (71, 72, 73), and β adrenergic agonists (74) modulate the effect of epo on marrow cells *in vitro* but do not seem to play an important role in the primary action.

The observation that rat fetal liver cells respond to epo by a marked increase in cyclic GMP (75) had to be corrected when it was found that it was the endotoxin contaminant that caused the effect, not epo (76). This is clearly one of the findings that make it essential to verify previous effects attributed to epo by use of the endotoxin-free, pure material.

Despite the plethora of literature, and perhaps because of the difficulty in obtaining sufficiently pure epo, we are still not in possession of enough basic observations to understand the molecular mechanisms by which epo regulates the production of red cells. What is needed, besides more pure epo, is a pure population of early progenitor cells. It has become possible, recently, to study the mechanism of epo action on colony-forming unit-erythroid (CFU-E) since those precursor cells can be obtained in pure form (77, 78). This will undoubtedly yield important information about the mode of action of epo on cells already committed to erythroid differentiation, but it will not relate directly to the important problem of how cells become committed. Although it may be possible that epo action on cells earlier than CFU-E will follow essentially the same molecular pattern that is found for CFU-E, one cannot rely on that without confirmatory evidence. If, as discussed later in detail, epo is directly involved in the commitment events (i.e., epo has an instructive mode of action), it will be necessary to study its molecular effects on cells earlier than CFU-E and those are not yet available for investigation.

An approach to the problem of working with purified early erythroid precursor cells may be provided by the findings of Koury et al. (79) who showed that mouse marrow cells infected with the anemia strain of the Friend virus can yield colonies of proliferating cells that do not contain hemoglobin. When epo is added to such colonies, hemoglobin synthesis is initiated resulting in benzidine-positive bursts 56 hours later.

5. CELL BIOLOGY OF ERYTHROPOIETIN

5.1. Progenitor Cells

The single most important development in the study of erythropoietin action at the cellular level during the past decade has been the advent of new tissue culture techniques. One technique, originally developed by Dexter et al. (80), and discussed in detail later, allows for continuous proliferation and differentiation of hemopoietic cells *in vitro* over several months, thus providing an important system for the *in vitro* study of erythropoiesis. A second type of culture technique permits the clonal development of hemoglobin-containing cells from discrete precursor populations. By immobilizing single cell suspensions of hemopoietic tissue in a fibrin clot, in agar, or in a viscous solution of methylcellulose, investigators have identified erythroid colonies derived from at least three precursors. These cells lack hemoglobin; however, during the course of their subsequent differentiation, cells synthesizing hemoglobin arise. The most well-differentiated precursor population, the CFU-E, was first identified by Stephenson et al. (81) in plasma clot cultures of mouse fetal liver cells. The colonies consisted of 8–64 erythroblasts and developed within 2 days of plating. Three years later, Axelrad et al. (82) reported the growth of large colonies consisting of several thousand erythroblasts. These colonies frequently appear multifocal and have clusters of erythroblasts similar to colonies derived from CFU-E scattered around the periphery, often at some distance from the main body of the colony. This morphology prompted the discoverers to name the colonies "bursts"; hence the progenitor cell became known as the burst-forming unit-erythroid (BFU-E). Studies in which mixtures of male and female cells were cultured at low concentrations showed that cells in a burst were of either male or female origin and not a mixture, a finding consistent with the clonal origin of a burst (83). The development of colonies from CFU-E has been studied by time-lapse cinematography and their single-cell origin has been documented (84).

Bursts develop in 6–14 days, depending on the culture technique used and on the species, and we have found that hemoglobin synthesis in the majority of mouse bursts is maximal between 7 and 8 days (29, 85). In contrast with the 3–5 divisions required for the generation of a colony from CFU-E, the BFU-E progenitor cells are capable of many more divisions and thus possess considerably more proliferative potential. The BFU-E probably gives rise to the CFU-E during the course of its developmental program.

Gregory (86) discovered a third progenitor cell with a proliferative potential between those of the BFU-E and the CFU-E. The colonies derived from this cell developed in 3 or 4 days and consisted of several clusters of erythroblasts resembling scattered CFU-E-derived colonies. These colonies are referred to as BFU-E-3, the "3" indicating the day at which they are at their zenith. According to this nomenclature, the more primitive burst form is designated BFU-E-8, but throughout this chapter BFU-E will be used to designate the day-8 colonies. During the development of large, day-8 erythroid bursts, CFU-E and BFU-E-3 present in the culture along with the BFU-E yield colonies at 2 and 3 days, respectively. Rather than persisting in the culture dish, however, the colonies disappear shortly after cells reach the later erythroblast or reticulocyte stages (86). Apparently, conditions in culture are not adequate for terminal differentiation of erythrocytes and the arrested erythroid cells undergo cytolysis. Most BFU-E follow the same pattern and disappear from the culture plate after about 10 days (29).

This lineage of erythroid precursors was first described for mouse hemopoietic cells, but subsequent studies have shown that homologous populations can be grown from hemopoietic tissues of humans (87) and sheep (88). Human cells, as might be expected given that cell cycle times of erythroid cells are longer (89, 90), require more time to develop; human CFU-E-derived colonies require 7 days to grow and bursts require 14 days or more to reach maximal size (87). Not all species, however, have been amenable to this type of analysis. Attempts to grow erythroid bursts from rat bone marrow, for example, have been unsuccessful despite extensive experimentation with culture conditions (91).

As one would expect in a developmental lineage characterized by a great deal of amplification, the primitive precursors are less abundant than the more differentiated ones. Thus, between 10 and 20 CFU-E are found in mouse marrow for every BFU-E (86, 92, 93).

5.2.   Genetic Influences

Similarly, the developmental age of erythroid progenitors is correlated with their proliferative activity. When the BFU-E, BFU-E-3, and CFU-E populations that synthesize DNA were determined, numerous workers found that the S phase fraction increased with developmental age (92, 94–98). About 30% of BFU-E and approximately 75% of CFU-E were killed by hydroxyurea or tritiated thymidine with high specific activity. A note of caution, however, must be sounded here because Suzuki and Axelrad (99) have recently shown that a single pair of alleles at the Fv-2 locus apparently regulates the proliferative activity in the BFU-E population but not in other erythroid progenitors. In mice congenic at the Fv-2 locus and possessing the dominant "s" allele, originally described as determining sensitivity to Friend leukemia virus, about 50% of the BFU-E population is in S phase. Mice with the Fv-2^{rr} genotype, and hence resistant to infection by leukemia virus, are phenotypically characterized by a BFU-E population in which few, if any, cells are killed by tritiated thymidine. Axelrad et al. (100) have found that mice with the Fv-2^{rr} genotype produce a negative regulator of BFU-E cycling. When Fv-2^{rr} marrow cells were washed prior to exposure to tritiated thymidine, about the same fraction of BFU-E were killed as in Fv-2^{s-} mice (i.e., about 50%). They also found that a medium conditioned by Fv-2^{rr} cells diminished the DNA-synthesizing fraction of BFU-E from Fv-2^{s-} mice; removal of the conditioned medium reversed the inhibition.

Inbred mouse strains commonly used in the study of erythropoiesis are known to differ with respect to genotype at the Fv-2 locus. Therefore, those with an "s" genotype might be expected to have rapidly proliferating BFU-E populations. This prediction has been borne out in the inbred strains tested so far (99, 101) and DBA/2 (Fv-2^{ss}) is a good example; the BFU-E population is reduced by about 60% after a short exposure to tritiated thymidine or hydroxyurea. Given that DBA/2 and C57BL/6 mice have similar red blood cell counts and the lifespans of their red cells are similar (102), it is difficult to understand how the cell cycle kinetics of their BFU-E populations could be so different. The only reasonable explanation at the moment is that other homeostatic mechanisms must operate in these mouse strains between the levels of the BFU-E and the red cell resulting in comparable production rates.

5.3.   Developmental Correlations

Other evidence important in establishing the developmental relationships of the erythroid progenitors has come from a statistical analysis of frequencies of the cells in individual spleen colonies. Gregory and Henkelman (103)

have systematically analyzed large numbers of individual spleen colonies and determined correlative indices for every combination of erythroid precursors, spleen colony-forming or pluripotent stem cells (CFU-S), and granulocyte-macrophage precursors (CFU-GM). The results show that incidences of CFU-S, BFU-E, and CFU-GM are highly positively correlated, whereas numbers of CFU-E and any of the former populations are poorly correlated. These results suggest that CFU-S, BFU-E, and CFU-GM are closely related developmentally and that a series of randomizing events intervene in the erythroid pathway between the BFU-E and CFU-E stages. Comparisons between BFU-E-3 and stem cells yield intermediate correlative indices.

5.4. Role in Cell Survival

A central consideration in this discussion of erythroid precursors is the role of epo in the developmental biology of this lineage. There is little question that epo is required for the terminal stages in erythroid development. Growth of colonies derived from CFU-E in serum-free media has been shown to be strictly dependent on epo (although there may be an exception that is discussed later). Furthermore, epo is apparently crucial to the survival of CFU-E and maintenance of the compartment by influx from the preceding stage, perhaps the BFU-E-3; if epo is added to marrow cultures at successively later times, colonies derived from CFU-E decline dramatically after only a few hours of epo deprivation (104). Iscove (105) found that culture of mouse marrow for 24 hours in the absence of epo resulted in almost a complete loss of CFU-E when epo was subsequently added. These findings were corroborated *in vivo* under conditions where erythropoiesis was perturbed following bleeding or hypertransfusion. During the anemia resulting from bleeding, Iscove (97) found that the marrow content of CFU-E increased dramatically and, conversely, that during the polycythemia following transfusion, CFU-E numbers declined. Others have obtained similar results under conditions where erythropoiesis was either stimulated or suppressed (92, 95, 106, 107). These results suggest that CFU-E population size is regulated by epo inasmuch as epo titers are known to increase after bleeding or during and immediately following hypoxia, and conversely, to decrease during polycythemia (1).

A second finding of these *in vivo* studies was that BFU-E numbers were not dramatically affected by either induced anemia or polycythemia, although a small and transient increase was observed when mice were rendered polycythemic (105, 106). These results imply that BFU-E population size is not tightly regulated by epo. As a part of these studies, Iscove (97) and Wagemaker (108) determined the fraction of cells synthesizing DNA within each of the colony-forming cell populations by measuring the loss of colony-forming cells after exposure to tritiated thymidine or hydroxyurea. They found that neither anemia nor polycythemia altered the fraction of BFU-E in S phase of the cell cycle. At the same time, CFU-E proliferative activity as measured by this method increased during anemia and declined during polycythemia. In contrast with these findings, Peschle et al. (109) found that both BFU-E and CFU-E populations had smaller fractions synthesizing DNA during the first 24 hours after transfusion. The CFU-E population did not regain its normal proliferative activity for the next 2 days; however, the BFU-E population had returned to normal by the third day, the time at which Iscove and Wagemaker determined the S phase component of these populations in their studies. In addition, Peschle et al. (109) found that epo injection caused an immediate increase in the DNA-synthesizing fractions of the BFU-E and the CFU-E populations. The response of the BFU-E population was transient and cell cycle kinetics returned to normal within 24 hours, possibly explaining why Iscove and Wagemaker found that bleeding or hypoxia had no effect after 2–3 days. In accord with these findings, Peschle et al. (110) have reported that the size of the marrow BFU-E population within the first 24 hours after transfusion or epo administration is indirectly correlated with epo levels (i.e., the population size decreased after epo and increased after transfusion). Inasmuch as only population sizes in the marrow were studied, the changes may reflect migration of BFU-E from the marrow to the spleen after epo injection. Hara and Ogawa have found that BFU-E follow this migration pathway after erythropoietic stimulation (95, 111).

One of the most striking differences between CFU-E and BFU-E is the amount of epo required by each for colony growth *in vitro*. The development of CFU-E-derived colonies is maximally stimulated by 0.3–0.5 units/ml of epo whereas burst growth, as originally described by Axelrad, requires approximately tenfold higher concentrations (82, 86, 93). This striking difference in epo sensitivity *in vitro* raises serious questions about the physiological role of epo in regulating early stages of erythroid differentiation inasmuch as normal serum titers of epo are well below those required for burst growth *in vitro*.

5.5. Influence of BPA or BFA

One explanation for this discrepancy may be that the culture medium lacks important, but not essential, ingredients whose absence can be offset, at least partially, by higher epo concentrations. Iscove (105) found that media from spleen cell cultures stimulated with pokeweed mitogen, when added to bone marrow cells in methylcellulose-containing media, reduced the concentration of epo required for burst growth by as much as tenfold. This material, called burst-promoting activity (BPA), caused two to three times as many bursts to grow at plateau levels of epo as in its absence. Inasmuch as BPA affected neither the sensitivity of CFU-E to epo nor the plating efficiency of CFU-E, its action is apparently restricted to more primitive developmental steps. When Iscove delayed the addition of epo to burst cultures he found that, as the period of epo deprivation increased, the number of bursts which subsequently developed decreased; in the presence of BPA, however, burst development did not decline as the period of epo deprivation lengthened (up to 5 days). Iscove (105) also reported that the addition of epo to cultures on the fifth day resulted in bursts on the tenth day with the same morphology and size as those bursts grown for the entire 10 days with epo. These results suggest that the early phases of burst development may occur in the absence of epo, provided BPA is present, and that epo is only absolutely required for events occurring during the later stages.

Wagemaker (112) found that a similar activity was produced by a subpopulation of bone marrow cells. When irradiated marrow cells were included in burst cultures, the sensitivity of BFU-E in the unirradiated population increased (the dose-response curve was shifted to the left) and the number of bursts formed on the plateau increased threefold. This activity (termed burst-feeder activity or BFA) was apparently produced by marrow cells that were more radioresistant than BFU-E. The latter population had a D_0 of 0.73 Gy, whereas BFA produced by irradiated cells was not diminished by as much as 20 Gy (112). Wagemaker et al. (113) fractionated marrow cells by velocity sedimentation and density and demonstrated that BFU-E and cells producing BFA had different modal peaks although they overlapped considerably with respect to both size and density.

A refinement of culture techniques has made it possible to define more clearly the growth requirements for CFU-E and CFU-GM. By including transferrin, selenite, albumin, and selected lipids, Iscove et al. (114) were able to eliminate serum completely from the culture medium used for CFU-E. Colony formation in this medium is completely dependent on epo. Similarly, the serum content required for CFU-GM growth can be reduced to 1% without affecting colony number. In contrast, it has not been possible to eliminate serum from BFU-E culture media. The fact that the serum requirement can also be decreased, but not completely replaced, by BPA suggests that the activity in both sources may be the same.

Eliason and Van Zant (115) have found that there are clear differences, however, between the activities of BPA and BFA. First, the enhancement of burst formation by BPA is independent of the serum content, whereas enhancement by BFA is directly proportional to serum content. Second, we found that optimal concentrations of BPA permitted burst growth at lower epo concentrations than did optimal concentrations of BFA. Third, the number of bursts formed at optimal concentrations was higher with BPA than with BFA. Finally, we found that BPA, but not BFA, permitted complete survival of BFU-E when epo was withheld from cultures for 3 days. In the presence of BFA, the number of bursts counted on day 10 progressively declined in the absence of epo. Furthermore, we found that the reduced number of bursts, which developed after epo deprivation in the presence of BFA, reached maturity at progressively later times, indicating that an epo-dependent series of developmental steps was triggered. On the other hand, BPA not only allowed all BFU-E to survive epo deprivation, but also caused BFU-E to undergo the early steps in burst development in the absence of added epo.

Attempts to purify BPA from mitogen-stimulated spleen cells and BFA from bone marrow cell media have to date been only partially successful. Both are apparently glycoproteins since they bind to concanavalin A-Sepharose; estimates of the molecular weight of BPA vary from 24,000 to 35,000 (108, 116). Besides BPA activity, spleen cell-conditioned medium contains a complex mixture of hemopoietic growth activities. For example, it has been shown to contain megakaryocyte, eosinophil, and granulocyte-macrophage colony-forming activities (116). Attempts to separate the various activities using a variety of biochemical techniques have not yet been successful. In addition to the activities already mentioned, mitogen-stimulated spleen cells are the source of a family of growth factors called interleukins which play important roles in lymphocyte differentiation and growth. The fact that the separate activities cannot be separated biochemically raises the possibility that one pleiotropic chemical species may be responsible for several kinds of activity. Medium conditioned by the mouse myelomonocytic cell line WEHI-3 has been shown to be another source of BPA.

Iscove et al. (117), using a variety of chromatographic techniques, were unable to separate the hemopoietic growth activities in WEHI-3 media on the basis of size, hydrophobicity, or net charge; they found that the several activities had an apparent molecular weight of 33,000.

As further evidence of its role in regulating the population size of primitive hemopoietic cells, BPA was shown to cause a net increase in BFU-E and CFU-GM numbers during 8-day cultures of mouse marrow in liquid media (117). Cerny (118) found that the T cells in spleen cell cultures stimulated with phytohemagglutinin were responsible for the production of an activity increasing the proliferative activity of CFU-S. Similarly, Wagemaker (119) found that BPA (from spleen cells) caused a larger fraction of BFU-E populations in normal marrow to become sensitive to tritiated thymidine cytocide, thus suggesting that proliferative activity was increased. Iscove et al. (105,

117) have proposed a model of hemopoietic differentiation incorporating these findings regarding BPA. According to their model, the substance operationally called BPA regulates the early phases of hemopoietic differentiation and proliferation, whereas lineage-specific hormones such as epo and macrophage colony-stimulating factor (CSF-1) regulate the more distal stages of each of the developmental lines culminating in the formation of each of the blood cell types. This two-factor model implies that BPA is a normal physiological regulator *in vivo*. To date, this important point has not been experimentally verified. In this regard, Wagemaker (112) has found that epo-dependent burst formation is potentiated by serum from (a) mice made anemic by phenylhydrazine injection alone, (b) mice given phenylhydrazine and sublethal irradiation, or (c) mice polycythemic after hypoxia.

Serum from (a) and (b) may also be expected to contain elevated epo titers, but serum from (c) might be expected to manifest suppressed levels of epo. Whether the serum activities are the same from all three sources remains to be demonstrated. Our knowledge of similarities between BPA and these activities is at the moment limited to their common capacity to potentiate burst formation. The only other evidence that BPA may exert a physiological control *in vivo* is its elevated level in the urine of patients with aplastic anemia (120, 121).

5.6. Role in Differentiation

Johnson and Metcalf (122) were the first to report that mitogen-stimulated spleen cell-conditioned media caused the growth (in 7 days) of colonies containing cells of several lineages, including erythroid cells. Furthermore, they found that pure and mixed erythroid bursts could grow without the addition of exogenous epo. The only possible source of epo in these cultures, aside from a subpopulation of fetal liver cells known to produce epo (39), was the fetal calf serum in the medium, yet a bioassay able to detect as little as 0.05 units revealed none. These findings suggested two important concepts: first, that pluripotent stem cells could be assayed *in vitro* and, second, that at least under some conditions epo was not required for even the terminal stages of erythroid growth. The first point has been verified in subsequent studies in both the mouse and human (123), thus marking the advent of the first assay for multipotent stem cells *in vitro*. Humphries et al. (124) found that cells derived from long-term mouse marrow cell cultures formed macroscopic mixed-lineage colonies in semisolid media in the presence of epo and BPA. When these colonies were harvested and the cellular contents injected into lethally irradiated hosts, the entire hemopoietic system of the host was repopulated (125, 126). Similarly, when primary colonies were harvested and replated, secondary colonies of the same type developed.

These results provide strong evidence that hemopoietic stem cells not only differentiated to give rise to mixed-lineage colonies *in vitro*, but also replicate themselves within the colony.

The studies of Johnson and Metcalf (122) were initially carried out with primary explants of fetal liver cells but the same authors subsequently used adult bone marrow cells to obtain qualitatively similar results, that is, the formation of erythroid and mixed-erythroid colonies in the absence of any detectable epo (127). It now appears (128) that the lack of an epo requirement is peculiar to certain strains of mice including the CBA strain used by Johnson and Metcalf, and might be due to a high degree of sensitivity to the small amount of epo in the fetal calf serum.

Recently, Fagg (129) has shown that spleen-conditioned media caused CFU-E-derived erythroid colony formation from bone marrow or fetal liver cells of DBA/2 mice in the absence of epo. These colonies were indistinguishable from those grown using epo; however, maximal numbers of colonies obtained with the spleen medium ranged between 40% and 80% of the number obtained with optimal epo concentrations. Johnson and Metcalf (122) found that the addition of epo to their cultures of CBA cells did not significantly change the numbers of erythroid colonies, but did increase the erythroid component within the mixed colonies. These results then suggest that, with CBA and DBA/2 mice, the components in spleen-conditioned media are sufficient to cause complete erythroid differentiation. Fagg (129) showed that this activity was biochemically separable from epo. These data also demonstrate that cells from these mouse strains retain responsiveness to epo and thus may possess a dual regulatory mechanism. Krystal (130) has recently reported that a factor in normal mouse and human serum, separable from epo, acts synergistically with epo to enhance hemoglobin synthesis in erythroblasts. In widely used strains of mice including C57BL/6 and the F_1 hybrid of C57BL/6 and DBA/2, B6D2F1, spleen-conditioned medium cannot be substituted for epo to cause CFU-E differentiation. Results obtained with B6D2F1 mice suggest that the genetic component is inherited in a recessive pattern. Johnson (128) reported that the epo dependence of C57BL/6 mice was dominant when they were crossed with CBA mice and moreover that the majority, but not all, of the F_2 generation exhibited the phenotype of the C57BL/6 parental strain. A 3:1 ratio of the F_2 phenotype would strongly suggest that a single pair of alleles following a completely dominant pattern of inheritance is responsible.

McLeod et al. (131) and Vainchenker et al. (132) have found that epo or epo plus BPA is capable of inducing erythroid bursts containing megakaryocytes. Using mixed cultures of male and female C57BL/6 marrow cells, McLeod et al. (131) showed that the erythroid cells and the megakaryocytes in any one burst always had the same complement of sex chromosomes, suggesting that these cells have a common lineage. However, they rarely found macrophages or granulocytes present in the "megaerythro bursts" even after the addition of CSF and, therefore, these investigators felt that the burst-forming cell was bipotent rather than multipotent. Regardless of the number of cell lineages present in a burst, it is now clear that the BFU-E compartment is heterogeneous and the original belief that BFU-E represented a cell committed solely to the erythroid pathway must be modified.

Greenberger (133) has recently derived several permanent cell lines from long-term (Dexter) cultures of marrow cells. Two of these lines, derived from C57BL/6SUtA and C57BL/6JUt mouse strains, consist of cells arrested in development at a point intermediate between hemopoietic pluripotency and unipotency. The cell lines do not protect lethally irradiated mice from hemopoietic death, nor do they cause spleen colonies in such hosts; they are not malignant. They do, however, respond to epo, CSF, and lectin-stimulated spleen-conditioned media to form erythroid bursts, neutrophil colonies, and basophil or mast cell colonies in semisolid media. Attempts to promote differentiation along the B lymphocyte, megakaryocyte, or macrophage pathways have been unsuccessful, suggesting that the developmental capacities of these cells have been restricted to specific lineages. It is interesting to note that developmental potentials for what are thought to be closely related blood cell lineages apparently did not co-segregate in these cell lines. For example, the cells are capable of differentiating along the erythroid pathway but not the megakaryocytic line, and are capable of forming neutrophils but not macrophages. The cell lines may, therefore, be important in establishing the requirements for specific inducers in particular lines of differentiation.

5.7. Sources of BPA

Although little convincing evidence points to an important role for BPA *in vivo*, the observation that colonies of mixed cell lineages can be grown *in vitro* in the presence of spleen cell medium or BPA lends credence to the idea that BPA is a lineage-independent hemopoietic regulator. Inasmuch as BPA is the subject of another chapter in this volume we discuss its sources only briefly. In the mouse, as we have already mentioned, lectin or alloantigen-stimulation of spleen cells is the most potent source of the activity. The specific cell type responsible for its production is not known, although T cells and monocytes-macrophages are generally believed to be responsible (134–136). The myelomonocytic mouse cell line WEHI-3 has been shown to be a rich source of activity (117). Recently, it has been found that these cells may be more similar to lymphocytes than to monocytes making their designation as myelomonocytic questionable (137). Kurland et al. (136) found that peritoneal macrophages were the source of activity potentiating the effect of epo on both CFU-E and BFU-E *in vitro*.

The cellular source of BPA in the human system has been the subject of controversy. Convincing evidence favors both monocytes and T cells as potent sources of activity and at least part of the controversy may be due to contamination of lymphocyte preparations with monocytes-macrophages and vice versa (138–143). It seems possible that coordinate responses of both cell types may be required for BPA production. The most commonly used source of human BPA has been media conditioned by mitogen-stimulated peripheral blood leukocytes (140), although unstimulated human marrow cells have also been used as a source (144, 145). Recently, several human cell lines have been identified as potent sources of BPA. For example, Golde et al. (146) have described a T lymphoblast cell line (Mo) secreting not only BPA but substance(s) capable of generating multilineage colonies and human granulocyte-macrophage colonies. Unlike most sources of mouse BPA, human sources potentiate both CFU-E and BFU-E. Such is the case of Mo cell medium, and Lusis et al. (147) report that BPA from this source potentiated mouse BFU-E growth but not CFU-E growth. It would appear that the human and mouse CFU-Es are not strictly analogous from a developmental standpoint; the effects of BPA on mouse CFU-E, however, must be interpreted cautiously in light of the demonstrated differences between mouse strains. Ascensao et al. (148) recently found that a human monocytic cell line (U-937) produces a BPA that potentiates both CFU-E and BFU-E growth in humans. Unlike most sources, however, U-937 does not elaborate activity stimulating granulocyte-macrophage colonies; in fact, the medium suppresses granulocyte-macrophage colony formation.

Chemical identities of BPA activities from different human sources are not known, but it is possible that a common family of glycoproteins is responsible. Sharkis et al. (149) have shown that T lymphocytes, as determined by the presence of Thy 1 cell surface markers, are capable of suppressing murine burst formation at low concentrations and, at higher concentrations, enhancing burst growth. Recently, Sieber and Sharkis (150) showed that the opposing activities were due to different subpopulations in the thymus characterized by different densities of the cell markers; cells enhancing burst growth had the higher content of Thy 1 markers. Similarly, Torok-Storb and Hansen (151) found that functionally separate populations in both human marrow and blood enhanced and suppressed burst formation. The subpopulation limiting growth was characterized by an Ia-like antigen identified by a monoclonal antibody 7.2.

5.8. The Dexter System

A valuable model system with which to study hemopoiesis *in vitro* is the Dexter system, named after its developer (80). In this system mouse marrow cells in suspension culture form a monolayer morphologically characterized by cells containing lipid vacuoles, endothelial cells, and macrophages. This microenvironment fosters the proliferation and differentiation of stem cells over a period of several months. If the stem cells released into the liquid phase of the culture are removed, a wave of stem cell proliferation restores the population; thus, in its maintenance of population homeostasis, this culture system mimics hemopoiesis *in vivo*. Complete development along the granulocyte-macrophage and megakaryocyte cell lines occurs *in vitro* to give rise to granulocytes, macrophages, and platelet-shedding mega-karyocytes, respectively. On the other hand, erythropoiesis is arrested at the primitive BFU-E stage and no BFU-E-3 or CFU-E are detected. Eliason et al. (152) found that addition of epo to long-term cultures caused complete differentiation to anucleate erythrocytes provided that cell attachment was prevented. They subsequently found that the addition of BPA to B6D2F1 marrow cells in this developmental system stimulated the generation of BFU-E-3 but not of CFU-E, whereas epo addition caused the appearance of both BFU-E and CFU-E. These results suggest that, at least with this mouse strain, differentiation of BFU-E to BFU-E-3 is stimulated by both BPA and epo, whereas epo is uniquely capable of stimulating further de-velopmental steps. In further studies (153) the number of CFU-E generated was directly related to the epo concentration; however, generation of BFU-E-3 was not epo dose-dependent. Generation of the latter progenitor in this system was dependent on the dose of BPA added, suggesting a role for BPA in the precise regulation of this population. Dexter et al. (154) recently reported that complete erythroid differentiation could be induced by the addition of serum from mice made anemic by a combination of irradiation and phenylhydrazine treatment. The effect of the serum on erythropoiesis in long-term cultures in which no steps were taken to prevent cell attachment was highly concentration-dependent with a narrow range of activity found in some, but not all, serum batches. Erythropoiesis was also stimulated in this system by the addition of normal mouse serum plus epo. Inasmuch as neither component had this effect when added alone, it seems likely that they each contributed a requirement for erythropoiesis. Whether the required serum component is BPA remains to be shown, although it should be noted that Wagemaker (112) found that serum from mice subjected to the same treatment contained elevated BPA levels. Dexter (155) also found that the production of granulocytes declined as erythropoiesis increased after the addition of anemic mouse serum (AMS). Moreover, the number of CFU-

GM decreased in these cultures, suggesting a competition between the erythroid and granulocytic lines of differentiation. Changes in hemopoietic differentiation after the addition of AMS were accompanied by changes in the cell monolayer supporting hemopoiesis; addition of AMS resulted in a decline in the areas characterized by many fat cells and endothelial cells usually associated with granulopoiesis. In contrast, the resulting increase in erythropoiesis was associated with monocytes in the monolayer, and Dexter found clusters of erythroblasts surrounding and in intimate contact with monocytes, a configuration closely resembling the erythropoietic islets described *in vivo* in bone marrow.

5.9. Relation to CSF

Numerous studies *in vivo* have shown that accelerated differentiation into the erythroid or granulocytic pathways is accompanied by diminished differentiation into the other pathway (156–159). However, it has not been possible to identify the mechanisms by which these inverse changes occur *in vivo*. We have examined the simultaneous effects of epo and CSF on hemopoietic differentiation *in vitro* and have found that the two inducers have competitive effects on marrow target cells (29, 160). CSF caused a dose-dependent suppression of epo-stimulated burst formation and, conversely, epo caused a dose-dependent suppression of CSF-induced granulocyte-macrophage colony formation. Because we found that CSF did not suppress the formation of CFU-E-derived colonies, we concluded that it did not cause erythroid suppression by interfering with the terminal stages of erythropoiesis but rather that its effects were manifested on a more primitive multipotent cell capable of differentiation into either the red cell or the granulocytic/macrophage pathways.

Steinberg et al. (161), in a study in which they employed diffusion chambers implanted intraperitoneally in rats, have similarly found that stimulation of erythropoiesis was accompanied by a decline in granulopoiesis. They induced erythroid colony and burst formation in plasma clots within the diffusion chambers by injecting the hosts with phenylhydrazine. Conversely, when they injected endotoxin they stimulated granulocytic colony formation at the expense of erythroid colonies and bursts.

Colony-stimulating activity has been obtained from a variety of tissues and cell types and it is resident in factors with diverse biochemical characterics. Two of these have been purified and characterized. CSF-1 has been obtained from L-cell medium and has been reported to stimulate solely macrophage colony development (162). It is a glycoprotein consisting of two identical subunits with molecular weights of 35,000 each; the subunits lack biological activity. CSF from mouse lung cells causes both granulocyte and macrophage colony formation *in vitro* and this GM-CSF is a single peptide chain glycoprotein with a molecular weight of 23,000 (163). Both purified CSF-1 and GM-CSF have specific activities of about 5×10^7 units/ mg of protein; a unit is the amount sufficient to cause one colony to develop in a culture of 7.5×10^4 marrow cells from C57BL/6 mice. Thus picogram quantities of these preparations are biologically active.

We found that purified GM-CSF had two qualitatively different and dose-dependent effects on epo-stimulated methylcellulose cultures of B6D2F1 marrow cells (29). At concentrations of less than 50 units/ml it significantly potentiated erythroid burst formation at 8 days; at higher concentrations it caused progressive suppression.

Metcalf and Johnson (164), in studies using CBA fetal liver cells, purified GM-CSF, and purified epo, found no competitive effects between these two inducers but they did confirm our finding that the two together potentiated erythroid growth. Because of these contradictory results using the same preparations of inducers, a closer examination of these studies is warranted. In our experiments the epo and GM-CSF were added simultaneously to marrow cells in methylcellulose cultures containing fetal calf serum but without an exogenous source of BPA. Metcalf and Johnson used an agar culture medium containing serum, human serum for fetal liver cell cultures, and a mixture of fetal calf and horse sera for adult bone marrow cells. In one set of experiments they preincubated C57BL/6 bone marrow cells and CBA fetal liver cells for 6 hours with a concentration of GM-CSF 250 times the concentration required for maximal granulocyte-macrophage colony formation. Cells were subsequently washed free of GM-CSF and plated at low cell density in agar with BPA. They found no reduction in the number of erythroid colonies after preincubation. Metcalf and Johnson (164) did not find any erythroid colony growth in cultures of CBA marrow or fetal liver cells stimulated with 4 units/ml of epo in the absence of spleen-conditioned media or GM-CSF. We found maximal stimulation of burst growth (20–30 BFU-E/10^5 B6D2F1 marrow cells) at 3–5 units of epo/ml (29). The disparity in results obtained with epo alone makes comparable studies impossible and interpretation of our two sets of results difficult.

Mitchell and Adamson (165) found that a 2-hour preincubation of rat marrow cells with CSF did not affect the number of CFU-E colonies caused by epo after the cells were washed and cultured in a plasma clot. Similarly, the simultaneous addition of epo and CSF (medium conditioned by rat peripheral blood leukocytes) had no effect on the number of CFU-E colonies developing in the presence of epo alone. These results are consistent with our findings that CSF does not suppress erythroid colony formation from CFU-E. However, in contrast with our results showing that epo suppressed CSF-stimulated granulocyte-macrophage colony formation, Mitchell and

Adamson found no evidence of competition either when the two inducers were added simultaneously and/or the cells were preincubated with epo. It should be noted that Mitchell and Adamson plated marrow cells at a concentration of 7.5×10^4/ml in their CFU-GM assay.

Iscove (97) found no evidence of competition between epo and CSF using an experimental design and culture system similar to the one we used. Simultaneous addition of CSF in mouse kidney cell-conditioned medium and 6 units/ml of epo to cultures of 4×10^4 B6D2F1 marrow cells had no effect on the numbers of erythroid bursts or granulocyte-macrophage colonies obtained with epo or CSF added individually.

A possible explanation for the discrepancy between our results (29) and those of Iscove (97) and of Mitchell and Adamson (165) is the concentration at which cells were cultured. In a systematic study of the effects of cell number we found that competitive effects of epo and CSF occurred only at cell concentrations above 1×10^5/ml and the suppression of epo-stimulated erythroid burst formation caused by a fixed concentration of CSF increased with increasing cell concentration in the range between 10^5 and 10^6 cells/ml (29, 166). Conversely, we found that suppression of CSF-stimulated granulocyte-macrophage colony formation caused by epo was similarly dependent on cell concentration; no suppression was found below a concentration of about 1×10^5 nucleated cells/ml and suppression increased with cell concentration. It is known that monocytes and macrophages are rich sources of CSF and inasmuch as these cells are present in the marrow, it is possible that at higher cell concentrations the increased numbers of monocytes and macrophages augmented the exogenous CSF concentration in the medium. Because suppression of burst formation was found to be dependent on the CSF concentration, greater suppression might be expected to result. In support of this idea we have found that the addition of peritoneal macrophages to cultures of marrow cells at 1×10^5/ml resulted in suppression of burst formation. An analogous hypothesis to explain the effect of cell number on suppression of granulocyte-macrophage colony formation caused by epo would argue that a subpopulation of marrow cells was producing epo. Rich et al. (167) have recently reported that bone marrow macrophages produce or secrete epo as well as CSF, thus making this hypothesis plausible. However, this line of reasoning leads to the conclusion that macrophages are ultimately responsible for the competitive effects we observed and the relative concentrations of exogenously added epo and CSF somehow modulate macrophage activity. There is no solid evidence at present to support this hypothesis. Macrophages have been shown to be the source of a number of hemopoietic growth regulators and Kurland and Moore (168) have shown that two macrophage products, prostaglandin E and CSF, exert negative and positive effects, respectively, on CFU-GM proliferation and differentiation. When we added exogenous prostaglandin E to marrow cultures containing epo and a burst-suppressive concentration of CSF, the suppression due to CSF was almost completely abrogated (166). The explanation of these results that we favor is consistent with our other results, namely, that a common target cell for epo and CSF exists. When the action of a suppressive concentration of CSF was blocked by prostaglandin, epo-stimulated burst formation was restored.

An alternative explanation for the effects of cell number holds that colony growth *in vitro* was restricted by depletion of cell nutrients or release of nonspecific inhibitors of cell growth, perhaps by dying cells. Although it is difficult to rule out this possiblity completely, we have results from two types of experiments that make this explanation highly unlikely (166). First we fed cultures with fresh media twice during the 8-day culture period and found that we did not modify the suppression of burst growth caused by CSF. Second, we cultured marrow cells at increasing concentrations under conditions where both erythroid bursts and granulocyte-macrophage colonies developed. The presence of large numbers of granulocyte-macrophage colonies did not affect the size of bursts and the relationship between burst number and the number of cells plated remained linear. This result is not surprising because erythropoiesis and granulopoiesis *in vivo* occur simultaneously and in close proximity within the bone marrow. The concentration of bone marrow cells in the rat is in the order of 10^9 cells per ml of bone marrow volume (169).

We have found that CSF preparations derived from human embryonic kidney cells, serum from endotoxin-injected mice, purified CSF-1 from L cells, and purified GM-CSF from mouse lung cells all cause suppression of epo-induced burst formation. In addition we have found that the human kidney cell preparation and GM-CSF from mouse lung cells cause erythroid burst potentiation at low doses. We don't understand this latter phenomenon as yet, but it is a further piece of evidence corroborating the hypothesis that a common cell is responsive to both epo and CSF. Potentiation of burst growth is, of course, the operational definition of BPA; therefore, these two sources of CSF at low concentrations behave like BPA.

Metcalf et al. (170) have found that GM-CSF had an additional characteristic of BPA. Although GM-CSF did not directly stimulate the formation of erythroid and mixed-erythroid colonies, as spleen-conditioned medium did, it, like BPA, permitted the survival of the erythroid colony-forming cells from CBA fetal liver when they were incubated for 2 days with GM-CSF. The latter was not as effective in this regard as was spleen-conditioned medium (21 colonies versus 58 colonies surviving), but in the absence of either one, no colony-forming cells survived. Metcalf and Johnson (164) also found that GM-CSF and epo individually did not cause erythroid colony formation in their culture system but when they were added together erythroid colonies developed. In their hands GM-CSF was like BPA in that it was requisite for erythroid colony growth.

We have obtained further evidence that epo plays a role in the early steps of erythropoiesis. This evidence has been derived from experiments in which mouse marrow was cultured in a liquid medium for up to 13 days in the presence or absence of epo (171). At various intervals cells were harvested and CFU-S were assayed by the spleen colony assay in lethally irradiated hosts. Two significant findings emerged. The first finding was that the numbers of CFU-S recovered at time points between 5 and 10 days were always higher in cultures containing epo; the increment was greatest in the 7-day cultures. The second finding resulted from the use of polycythemic mouse hosts in which erythroid spleen colonies failed to develop, presumably because of diminished epo titers. By comparing colony counts obtained from spleens of normal and polycythemic hosts receiving an inoculum of the same cells we were able to determine if exposure of CFU-S to epo altered their probability of forming erythroid colonies. We found that epo increased the number of erythroid spleen colonies and concomitantly decreased the number of nonerythroid colonies. We have subsequently confirmed these findings by direct histological examination of spleen colonies (172). These results do not support the concept that commitment of stem cells to a particular differentiation pathway is a stochastic event as has been proposed (173, 174). They do, however, support the concept that epo plays a role in the early steps of erythroid differentiation.

6. SUMMARY

In summary, we are left with two bodies of evidence pointing to separate and seemingly irreconcilable conclusions. One points to the fact that epo regulates only the later stages of erythropoiesis. The early events in erythroid differentiation, according to this conclusion, are regulated by BPA. The most direct evidence supporting this can be summarized as follows:

1. BFU-E are maintained in culture, and probably stimulated to proliferate and differentiate, by BPA. In the presence of epo, but in the absence of BPA, BFU-E progressively decline in number and those that survive do not undergo further developmental steps.

2. The epo dose-response curve for BFU-E is shifted to the left by BPA suggesting that the sensitivity of BFU-E to epo is increased. Possible mechanisms for this change remain speculative but include the possibility that epo receptors are increased in number or in affinity for its ligand.

3. BPA increases the number of bursts formed by a maximally stimulating dose of epo. This result is consistent with either of two possible effects of

BPA. The first is that it increases the plating efficiency of BFU-E by contributing a culture factor that permits expression of more of the pre-existing BFU-E. The second is that BPA increases the number of BFU-E expressed by causing influx from a more primitive compartment. Enhanced self-replication of BFU-E would also result in the growth of more bursts provided that the daughter cells could migrate through the semisolid medium to form separate bursts. The possibilities included under this second point are made more likely by the findings that BPA increases the proliferative activity of BFU-E and CFU-S.

The second conclusion is that epo plays a role in regulating erythropoiesis at several steps; one of these steps involves the differentiation of multipotent cells into the erythroid lineage. The data supporting this conclusion can be summarized as follows:

1.   Epo increases the number of CFU-S in cultures of marrow cells. Furthermore, it causes these cultured CFU-S to form erythroid spleen colonies at the expense of nonerythroid colonies.
2.   Epo competes with CSF *in vitro* for target cells in bone marrow. These data suggest that commitment of at least a bipotent cell to either granulocyte-macrophage differentiation or erythroid differentiation is directly or indirectly regulated by the appropriate lineage-specific inducer. Numerous studies *in vivo* have shown that accelerated differentiation into either of these developmental lines is often accompanied by a diminished rate of differentiation into the other line.

At present the only way to reconcile these two bodies of conflicting evidence is to assume that both, at least in part, are correct. A dual regulatory mechanism in the early stages of erythropoiesis may include both epo and BPA*; each may be capable of causing stem cell proliferation and the early events in erythropoiesis. The fact that BPA can regulate even the terminal stages of erythropoiesis in some strains of mice, but not in others where epo is a strict requirement, supports the concept of dual regulation. Moreover, these findings suggest that the importance of epo or BPA in regulating erythropoiesis, at least in mice, may be under tight genetic control and it is possible that only one locus is responsible. If true in humans, a disease such as polycythemia vera may involve a diminished importance of epo in erythropoiesis and an increased reliance on BPA. In this example it is assumed that regulation of erythroid differentiation by BPA is abnormal and over-production of red cells results.

---

* For an alternate view of the role of epo, see Chapter 2.

ACKNOWLEDGMENTS

We gratefully acknowledge the skill and patience of Kathy McDonald during the preparation of this chapter and we thank Mary Jo Tillman for proofreading the galleys.

REFERENCES

1. Krantz, S. B., and Jacobson, L. O., *Erythropoietin and the Regulation of Erythropoiesis*, University of Chicago Press, Chicago, 1967.
2. Goldwasser, E., *Fed. Proc.*, **34**, 2285 (1976).
3. Ogle, J. W., Lange, R. D., and Dunn, C. D., *In Vitro*, **14**, 945 (1978).
4. Cline, M. J., and Golde, D. W., *Blood*, **53**, 157 (1979).
5. Dunn, C. D., and Lange, R. D., *Exp. Hematol.*, **8**, 231 (1980).
6. Erslev, A. J., Caro, J., Miller, O., and Silver, R., *Ann. Clin. Lab. Sci.*, **10**, 250 (1980).
7. Spivak, J. L., and Graber, S., *Johns Hopkins Med. J.*, **146**, 311 (1980).
8. Heilman, E., *Folia Haematol.*, **197**, 817 (1980).
9. Peschle, C., *Ann. Rev. Med.*, **32**, 143 (1981).
10. Goldwasser, E., and Kung, C. K.-H., *Proc. Natl. Acad. Sci. USA*, **68**, 697 (1971).
11. Annable, L., Cotes, P. M., and Mussett, M. V., *Bull. WHO*, **117**, 99 (1972).
12. Espada, J., and Gutnisky, A., *Acta Physiol. Lat. Am.*, **20**, 122 (1970).
13. Espada, J., Langton, A. A., and Dorado, M., *Biochim. Biophys. Acta*, **285**, 427 (1972).
14. Miyake, T., Kung, C. K.-H., and Goldwasser, E., *J. Biol. Chem.*, **252**, 5558 (1977).
15. Goldwasser, E., Paul, C., and Hood, L., unpublished.
16. Dordal, M. S., and Goldwasser, E., *Exp. Hematol.*, **10**, 133 (1982).
17. Goldwasser, E., in D. Cunningham, E. Goldwasser, J. Watson, and C. F. Fox, Eds., *Control of Cellular Division and Development Part A*, Alan R. Liss, New York, 1981.
18. Wang, F. F., Kung, C. K.-H., and Goldwasser, E., unpublished.
19. Espada, J., Brandan, N. L., and Dorada, M., *Acta Physiol. Lat. Am.*, **23**, 193 (1973).
20. Lowy, P. H., and Keighly, G., *Biochim. Biophys. Acta*, **160**, 413 (1968).
21. Lowy, P. H., Keighly, G., and Borsook, H., *Nature*, **185**, 102 (1968).
22. Lukowsky, W. A., and Painter, R. N., *Can. J. Biochem.*, **50**, 909 (1972).
23. Morell, A. G., Gregoriadis, G., Scheinberg, I. H., Hickman, J., and Ashwell, G., *J. Biol. Chem.*, **246**, 1461 (1971).
24. Goldwasser, E., Kung, C. K.-H., and Eliason, J. F., *J. Biol. Chem.*, **249**, 4202, (1974).
25. Sieber, F., *Biochim. Biophys. Acta*, **496**, 146 (1977).
26. Spivak, J. L., Small, D., and Hollenberg, M. D., *Proc. Natl. Acad. Sci. USA*, **74**, 4633 (1977).
27. Spivak, J. L., Small, D., Shaper, J. H., and Hollenberg, M. D., *Blood*, **52**, 1178 (1978).
28. Spivak, J. L., and Hollenberg, M. D., *Biomedical Applications of the Horseshoe Crab (limulidae)* Alan R. Liss, New York, 1979.
29. Van Zant, G., and Goldwasser, E., *Blood*, **53**, 946 (1979).
30. Lee-Huang, S., *Blood*, **56**, 620 (1980).
31. Kung, C. K.-H., and Goldwasser, E., unpublished.
32. Lee-Huang, S., *Fed. Proc.*, **41**, 520 (1982).
33. Weiss, T. L., Kavinsky, C. J., and Goldwasser, E., *Proc. Natl. Acad. Sci. USA*, **79**, 5465 (1982).

34. Chiba, S., Kung, C. K.-H., and Goldwasser, E., *Biochem. Biophys. Res. Commun.*, **47**, 1372 (1972).

35. Mok, M., and Spivak, J. L., *Exp. Hematol.*, **10**, 300 (1982).

36. Keio Ogawa, S., *J. Med.*, **16**, 193 (1967).

37. McDonald, T. P., Martin, D. H., Simmons, L. L., and Lange, R. D., *Life Sci.*, **8**, 949 (1969).

38. Burlington, H., Cronkite, E. P., Reincke, U., and Zanjani, E. D., *Proc. Natl. Acad. Sci. USA*, **69**, 3547 (1972).

39. Zucali, J. R., Stevens, V., and Mirand, E. A., *Blood*, **46**, 85 (1975).

40. Sherwood, J. B., and Goldwasser, E., *Endocrinology*, **99**, 504 (1976).

41. Rich, I. N., Heit, W., and Kubanek, B., *Blut*, **40**, 297 (1980).

42. Kurtz, A., Jelkmann, W., and Bauer, C., *FEBS Lett.*, **137**, 129 (1982).

43. Sherwood, J. B., and Goldwasser, E., *Endocrinology*, **103**, 866 (1978).

44. Krantz, S. B., Gallien-Lartigue, O., and Goldwasser, E., *J. Biol. Chem.*, **238**, 4085 (1963).

45. Gross, M., and Goldwasser, E., *Biochemistry*, **8**, 1795 (1969).

46. Gross, M., and Goldwasser, E., *J. Biol. Chem.*, **246**, 2480 (1971).

47. Paul, J., Conkie, D., and Burgos, H., *J. Embryol. Exp. Morph.*, **29**, 453 (1973).

48. Djaldetti, M., Preisler, H., Marks, P. A., and Rifkind, R. A., *J. Biol. Chem.*, **247**, 731 (1972).

49. Ross, D. D., Groth, D. P., and Kinkade, J. M., *J. Biol. Chem.*, **250**, 8829 (1975).

50. Fumarola, D., *Blood*, **50**, 548 (1977).

51. Spivak, J. L., and Levin, J., *Blood*, **50**, 549 (1977).

52. Zuckerman, K. S., Quesenberry, P. J., Levin, J., and Sullivan, R., *Blood*, **54**, 146 (1979).

53. Udupa, K. B., and Reissmann, K. R., *J. Lab. Clin. Med.*, **89**, 278 (1977).

54. Metcalf, D., *Immunology*, **21**, 427 (1971).

55. Weiss, T. L., and Goldwasser, E., *Biochem. J.*, **198**, 17 (1981).

56. Paul, J., and Hunter, J. A., *J. Mol. Biol.*, **42**, 31 (1969).

57. Gross, M., and Goldwasser, E., *J. Biol. Chem.*, **245**, 1632 (1970).

58. Datta, M. C., and Dukes, P. P., *Biochem. Biophys. Res. Commun.*, **69**, 489 (1976).

59. Bedard, D. L., and Goldwasser, E., *Exp. Cell Res.*, **102**, 376 (1976).

60. Ramirez, F., Gambino, R., Maniatis, G. M., Rifkind, R. A., Marks, P. A., and Bank, A., *J. Biol. Chem.*, **250**, 6054 (1975).

61. Sahr, K., and Goldwasser, E., *The Regulation of Hemoglobin Synthesis*, Elsevier, New York, in press.

62. Chang, S. C., Sikkema, D., and Goldwasser, E., *Biochem. Biophys. Res. Commun.*, **57**, 399 (1974).

63. Chang, S. C., and Goldwasser, E., *Dev. Biol.*, **34**, 246 (1973).

64. Goldwasser, E., and Inana, G., in D. Golde, M. Cline, D. Metcalf, and C. F. Fox, Eds., *Hematopoietic Cell Differentiation*, Academic, New York, 1978.

65. Piantadosi, C. A., Dickerman, H. W., and Spivak, J. L., *J. Clin. Invest.*, **57**, 20 (1976).

66. Spivak, J. L., *Blood*, **47**, 581 (1976).

67. Spivak, J. L., and Peck, L., *Am. J. Hematol.*, **7**, 45 (1979).

68. Fukuda, M., and Fukuda, M. N., *J. Supramol. Struct. Cell Biochem.*, **17**, 313 (1981).

69. Tong, B. D., and Goldwasser, E., *J. Biol. Chem.*, **256**, 1266 (1981).

70. Brown, J. E., and Adamson, J. W., *Br. J. Haematol.*, **35**, 193 (1977).

71. Singer, J. W., Samuels, A. J., and Adamson, J. W., *J. Cell. Physiol.*, **88**, 127 (1976).

72. Singer, J. W., and Adamson, J. W., *Blood*, **48**, 55 (1976).

73. Golde, D. W., Bersch, N., and Cline, M. J., *J. Clin. Invest.*, **57**, 57 (1976).

74. Brown, J. E., and Adamson, J. W., *J. Clin. Invest.*, **60**, 70 (1977).

75. Graber, S. E., Bomboy, J. B., Salmon, W. D., and Krantz, S. B., *J. Lab. Clin. Med.*, **90**, 162 (1977).

76. Graber, S. E., Bomboy, J. D., Salmon, W. D., and Krantz, S. B., *J. Lab. Clin. Med.*, **93**, 25 (1979).

77. Nijhof, W., Nierenga, P. K., and Goldwasser, E., *Exp. Hematol.*, **10**, 36 (1982).

78. Nijhof, W., and Nierenga, P. K., *Exp. Hematol.*, **10**, 170 (1982).

79. Koury, M. J., Bondurant, M. C., Duncan, D. T., Krantz, S. B., and Hankins, W. D., *Proc. Natl. Acad. Sci. USA*, **79**, 635 (1982).

80. Dexter, T. M., Allen, T. D., and Lajtha, L. G., *J. Cell. Physiol.*, **91**, 335 (1977).

81. Stephenson, J. R., Axelrad, A. A., McLeod, D. L., and Shreeve, M. M., *Proc. Natl. Acad. Sci. USA*, **68**, 1542 (1971).

82. Axelrad, A. A., McLeod, D. L., Shreeve, M. M., and Heath, D. S., in W. A. Robinson, Ed., *Hemopoiesis in Culture*, U.S. Government Printing Office, Washington, D.C., 1974.

83. Strome, J. E., McLeod, D. L., and Shreeve, M. M., *Exp. Hematol.*, **6**, 461 (1978).

84. Cormack, D., *Exp. Hematol.*, **4**, 319 (1976).

85. Eliason, J. F., Van Zant, G., and Goldwasser, E., *Blood*, **53**, 940 (1979).

86. Gregory, C. G., *J. Cell. Physiol.*, **89**, 289 (1976).

87. Gregory, C. G., and Eaves, A. C., *Blood*, **49**, 855 (1977).

88. Barker, J. E., Pierce, J. E., and Nienhuis, A. W., *J. Cell Biol.*, **71**, 715 (1976).

89. Dörmer, P., *Prog. Histochem. Cytochem.*, **6**, 1 (1973).

90. Dörmer, P., Militzer, H., Dahr, P., Jr., and Ruppett, W., *Cell Tissue Kinet.*, **15**, 295 (1982).

91. Van Zant, G., Eliason, J. F., and Goldwasser, E., unpublished.

92. Gregory, C. J., McCulloch, E. A., and Till, J. E., *J. Cell. Physiol.*, **81**, 411 (1973).

93. Iscove, N. N., and Sieber, F., *Exp. Hematol.*, **3**, 32 (1975).

94. Gregory, C. G., and Eaves, A. C., *Blood*, **51**, 527 (1978).

95. Hara, H., and Ogawa, M., *Exp. Hematol.*, **5**, 141 (1977).

96. Wagemaker, G., and Visser, J., *Cell Tissue Kinet.*, **13**, 505 (1980).

97. Iscove, N. N., *Cell Tissue Kinet.*, **10**, 323 (1977).

98. Adamson, J. W., Torok-Storb, B., and Lin, N., *Blood Cells*, **4**, 89 (1978).

99. Suzuki, S., and Axelrad, A. A., *Cell*, **19**, 225 (1980).

100. Axelrad, A. A., Croizat, H., and Eskinazi, D., *Cell*, **26**, 233 (1981).

101. Van Zant, G., unpublished.

102. Crispens, C. G., Jr., *Handbook on the Laboratory Mouse*, Charles C. Thomas, Springfield, Ill., 1975.

103. Gregory, C. G., and Henkelman, R. M., in S. J. Baum and G. D. Ledney, Eds., *Experimental Hematology Today*, Springer-Verlag, New York, 1977.

104. Kennedy, W. L., Alpen, E. L., and Garcia, J. F., *Blood Cells*, **4**, 143 (1978).

105. Iscove, N. N., in D. W. Golde, M. J. Cline, D. Metcalf, and C. F. Fox, Eds., *Hematopoietic Cell Differentiation*, Academic, New York, 1978.

106. Wagemaker, G., Ober-Kieftenburg, V. E., Brouwer, A., and Peters-Slough, M. F., in S. J. Baum and G. D. Ledney, Eds., *Experimental Hematology Today*, Springer-Verlag, New York, 1977.

107. Axelrad, A. A., McLeod, D. L., Suzuki, S., and Shreeve, M. M., in B. Clarkson, P. A. Marks, and J. E. Till, Eds., *Differentiation of Normal and Neoplastic Hematopoietic Cells*, Cold Spring Harbor Laboratory, New York, 1978.

108. Wagemaker, G., in S. J. Baum, G. D. Ledney, and D. W. van Bekkum, Eds., *Experimental Hematology Today 1980*, S. Karger, Basel, 1980.

109. Peschle, C., Cillo, C., Migliaccio, G., and Lettieri, E., *Exp. Hematol.*, **8**, 96 (1980).

110. Peschle, C., Cillo, C., Rappaport, I. A., Magli, M. C., Migliaccio, G., Pizzella, F., and Mastroberardino, G., *Exp. Hematol.*, **7**, 87 (1979).

111. Hara, H., and Ogawa, M., *Am. J. Hematol.*, **1**, 453 (1976).

112. Wagemaker, G., in M. J. Murphy, Jr., Ed., *In Vitro Aspects of Erythropoiesis*, Springer-Verlag, New York, 1977.

113. Wagemaker, G., Peters, M. F., and Bol, S. J. L., *Cell Tissue Kinet.*, **12**, 521 (1979).

114. Iscove, N. N., Guilbert, L. J., and Weyman, C., *Exp. Cell Res.*, **126**, 121 (1980).

115. Eliason, J. F., and Van Zant, G., *Cell Tissue Kinet.*, **16**, 65 (1983).

116. Burgess, A. W., Metcalf, D., Russell, S. H. M., and Nicola, N. A., *Biochem. J.*, **185**, 301 (1980).

117. Iscove, N. N., Roitsch, C. A., Williams, N., and Guilbert, L. J., *J. Cell. Physiol., Suppl.*, **1**, 65 (1982).

118. Cerny, J., *Nature*, **249**, 63 (1974).

119. Wagemaker, G., in G. Stamatoyannopoulos and A. W. Nienhuis, Eds., *Hemoglobins in Development and Differentiation*, Alan R. Liss, New York, 1981.

120. Nissen, C., Iscove, N. N., and Speck, B., in S. J. Baum and G. D. Ledney, Eds., *Experimental Hematology Today 1979*, Springer-Verlag, New York, 1979.

121. Okamoto, T., Kanamaru, A., Hara, H., and Nagai, K., *Exp. Hematol.*, **10**, 844 (1982).

122. Johnson, G. R., and Metcalf, D., *Proc. Natl. Acad. Sci. USA*, **74**, 3879 (1977).

123. Fauser, A. A., and Messner, H. A., *Blood*, **52**, 1243 (1978).

124. Humphries, R. K., Eaves, A. C., and Eaves, C. J., *Blood*, **53**, 746 (1979).

125. Humphries, R. K., Jacky, P. B., Dill, F. J., Eaves, A. C., and Eaves, C. J., *Nature*, **279**, 718 (1979).

126. Humphries, R. K., Eaves, A. C., and Eaves, C. J., *Proc. Natl. Acad. Sci. USA*, **78**, 3629 (1981).

127. Johnson, G. R., *J. Cell. Physiol.*, **103**, 371 (1980).

128. Johnson, G. R., in G. Stamatoyannopoulos and A. W. Nienhuis, Eds., *Hemoglobins in Development and Differentiation*, Alan R. Liss, New York, 1981.

129. Fagg, B., *Nature*, **289**, 184 (1981).

130. Krystal, G., *Exp. Hematol.*, **11**, 649 (1983).

131. McLeod, D. L., Shreeve, M. M., and Axelrad, A. A., *Blood*, **56**, 318 (1980).

132. Vainchenker, W., Bouquet, J., Guichard, J., and Breton-Gorius, J., *Blood*, **54**, 940 (1979).

133. Greenberger, J. S., Sakakeeny, M. A., Humphries, R. K., Eaves, C. J., and Eckner, R. J., *Proc. Natl. Acad. Sci. USA*, **80**, 2931 (1983).

134. Kanamaru, A., Durban, E., Gallagher, M. T., Miller, S. C., and Trentin, J. J., *J. Cell. Physiol.*, **104**, 187 (1980).

135. Meytes, D., Ma, A., Ortega, J. A., Shore, N. A., and Dukes, P. P., *Blood*, **54**, 1050 (1979).

136. Kurland, J. I., Meyers, P. A., and Moore, M. A. S., *J. Exp. Med.*, **151**, 839 (1980).

137. Ihle, J. N., Peppersack, L., and Rebar, L., *J. Immunol.*, **126**, 2184 (1981).

138. Zuckerman, K. S., *J. Clin. Invest.*, **67**, 702 (1981).

139. Lipton, J. M., Reinberg, E. L., Kudisch, M., Jackson, P. L., Schlossman, S. F., and Nathan, D. G., *J. Exp. Med.*, **152**, 350 (1980).

140. Aye, M. T. *J. Cell. Physiol.*, **91**, 69 (1977).

141. Tsang, R. W., and Aye, M. T., *Exp. Hematol.*, **7**, 383 (1979).

142. Magnan, K. F., and Desforges, J. F., *Exp. Hematol.*, **8**, 717 (1980).

143. Nathan, D. G., Chese, L., Hillman, D. G., Clarke, B., Brerard, J., Merler, E., and Housman, D. E., *J. Exp. Med.*, **147**, 324 (1978).

144. Porter, P. N., Ogawa, M., Leary, A. G., *Exp. Hematol.*, **8**, 83 (1980).

145. Porter, P. N., and Ogawa, M., *Blood*, **59**, 1207 (1982).

146. Golde, D. W., Bersch, N., Quan, S. G., and Lusis, A. J., *Proc. Natl. Acad. Sci. USA*, **77**, 593 (1980).

147. Lusis, A. J., Quan, D. H., and Golde, D. W., *Blood*, **57**, 13 (1981).

148. Ascensao, J. L., Kay, N. E., Earenfight-Engler, T., and Zanjari, E. D., in G. Stamatoyannopoulos and A. W. Nienhuis, Eds., *Hemoglobins in Development and Differentiation*, Alan R. Liss, New York, 1981.

149. Sharkis, S. J., Wiktor-Jedrzejczak, W., Ahmed, A., Santos, G. W., McKee, A., and Sell, K. W., *Blood*, **52**, 802 (1978).

150. Sieber, F., and Sharkis, S. J., *Blood*, **60**, 845 (1982).

151. Torok-Storb, B., and Hansen, J. A., *Nature*, **298**, 473 (1982).

152. Eliason, J. F., Testa, N. G., and Dexter, T. M., *Nature*, **281**, 382 (1979).

153. Eliason, J. F., Dexter, T. M., and Testa, N. G., *Exp. Hematol.*, **10**, 444 (1982).

154. Dexter, T. M., Testa, N. G., Allen, T. D., Rutherford, T., and Scolnick, E., *Blood*, 58, 699 (1981).

155. Dexter, T. M., *J. Cell. Physiol. Suppl.*, **1**, 87 (1982).

156. Harris, P. F., Harris, R. S., and Kugler, J. H., *Br. J. Haematol.*, **12**, 419 (1966).

157. Bradley, T. R., Robinson, W., and Metcalf, D., *Nature*, **214**, 511 (1967).

158. Hellman, S., and Grate, H. E., *Nature*, **216**, 65 (1967).

159. Hellman, S., and Grate, H. E., *J. Exp. Med.*, **127**, 605 (1968).

160. Van Zant, G., and Goldwasser, E., *Science*, **198**, 733 (1977).

161. Steinberg, H. N., Handler, E. S., and Handler, E. E., *Blood*, **47**, 1041 (1976).

162. Stanley, E. R., and Heard, P. M., *J. Biol. Chem.*, **252**, 4305 (1977).

163. Burgess, A. W., Camakaris, J., and Metcalf, D., *J. Biol. Chem.*, **252**, 1998 (1977).

164. Metcalf, D., and Johnson, G. R., *J. Cell. Physiol.*, **99**, 159 (1979).

165. Mitchell, B. S., and Adamson, J. W., in K. Nakao, J. W. Fisher, and F. Takaku, Eds., *Erythropoiesis*, University Park Press, Baltimore, 1975.

166. Van Zant, G., and Goldwasser, E., in S. J. Baum and G. D. Ledney, Eds., *Experimental Hematology Today 1979*, Springer-Verlag, 1979.

167. Rich, I. N., Heit, W., and Kubanek, B., *Blood*, **60**, 1007 (1982).

168. Kurland, J., and Moore, M. A. S., *Exp. Hematol.*, **5**, 357 (1977).

169. Crafts, R. C., and Meincke, H. A., *Ann. N.Y. Acad. Sci.*, **77**, 501 (1959).

170. Metcalf, D., Johnson, G. R., and Burgess, A. W., *Blood*, **55**, 138 (1980).

171. Van Zant, G., and Goldwasser, E., *J. Cell. Physiol.*, **90**, 241 (1977).

172. Wolf, N., Van Zant, G., and Goldwasser, E., unpublished.

173. Eaves, C. J., Humphries, R. K., and Eaves, A. C., in G. Stamatoyannopoulos and A. W. Nienhuis, Eds., *Hemoglobins in Development and Differentiation*, Alan R. Liss, New York, 1981.

174. Nakahata, T., Gross, A. J., and Ogawa, M., *J. Cell. Physiol.*, **113**, 455 (1982).

2

ERYTHROID-POTENTIATING ACTIVITY

David W. Golde
Carol A. Westbrook
Aldons J. Lusis

CONTENTS

Abbreviations

epo	Erythropoietin
CSF	Colony-stimulating factor
BPA	Burst-promoting activity
EPA	Erythroid-potentiating activity
CFU-E	Colony-forming unit-erythroid
BFU-E	Burst-forming unit-erythroid
CFU-S	Colony-forming unit-pluripotent stem cells
PHA	Phytohemagglutinin
HTLV	Human T-cell leukemia-associated virus
CFU-GM	Colony-forming unit-granulocyte-macrophage
CFU-DG	Colony-forming unit-diffusion chamber

1. INTRODUCTION

Hematopoiesis involves a coordinated process of cellular proliferation and differentiation along specific lineages. Stem cell differentiation results in restriction of potentiality whereby a stem cell can no longer differentiate along multiple pathways, but is constrained (committed) to a single line of development. The committed precursor cells undergo a series of replicative and maturational steps, ultimately leading to the production of large numbers of mature blood cell elements.

The regulation of pluripotent stem cell proliferation and differentiation has been difficult to analyze. Important regulatory influences, however, relate to interactions with the stromal microenvironment, cellular interactions with mature blood cell elements, and humoral regulators (1). The best-studied humoral regulators are the primary hemopoietins, erythropoietin (epo) and colony-stimulating factor (CSF) (2, 3). CSF acts on a committed precursor cell inducing proliferation and maturation along the granulocyte and monocyte pathway. Epo acts very late in erythropoiesis at the most mature precursor cell level (4, 5). What regulates the earliest steps of erythropoiesis and what hormonal factors are physiologically important in regulating multipotent stem cells? The answers to these questions are incomplete and studies in this field are presently at a relatively rudimentary level. Nonetheless, hormonal activities have been identified which are strong candidates for a "general hemopoietin." These hormonal activities have been referred to as burst-promoting activity (BPA) and erythroid-potentiating activity (EPA) (4, 6–8).

2. ERYTHROID COLONIES

Red cell precursors may be detected *in vitro* by their ability to give rise to colonies in plasma clot or methylcellulose culture (9–12). Several general classes of erythroid progenitors have been distinguished by the time course of colony formation and the characteristics of the colonies produced (13). Although there is a continuum with respect to the maturity of erythroid colony-forming cells, the most mature of these is generally referred to as colony-forming unit-erythroid (CFU-E), giving rise to relatively small colonies consisting of 8 to 64 hemoglobinized cells (Fig. 1a–d). The CFU-E are normally enumerated after 48 hours in murine systems, and 7 days in cultures of human hematopoietic cells. The burst-forming unit (BFU-E) is a more primitive erythroid progenitor of which there may be three subtypes with respect to proliferative potential (Fig. 1b,c). The BFU-Es require more time to mature than CFU-Es and they can give rise to very large colonies containing up to thousands of cells with multiple subcolonies. Until recently, pluripotent hematopoietic stem cells could only be assayed *in vivo* using the mouse spleen colony assay (14). Culture conditions have now been developed whereby multipotent stem cells from mice and humans can be cloned *in vitro* with systems similar to those used for growing erythroid progenitors (15–17).

3. CELLULAR INTERACTIONS WITH PLURIPOTENT STEM CELLS

Relatively little is known about the factors influencing proliferation of pluripotent stem cells (CFU-S) or their commitment to a single line of differentiation. Under normal circumstances CFU-S do not actively proliferate; however, with increased demand for hematopoiesis, such as after subtotal irradiation, the pluripotent stem cell compartment expands. A relationship between lymphocytes and pluripotent hematopoietic stem cell activation has long been known (1). Cerny and his colleagues showed that the number of CFU-S increased in spleen cell suspensions treated with phytohemagglutinin (PHA) or with conditioned medium from PHA-treated lymphocytes (18, 19). Thus T-lymphocytes are known to influence the activity of the pluripotent stem cell and to have important interactions in regulating erythropoiesis (20–23).

Several *in vivo* studies have suggested that epo does not affect the pluripotent hematopoietic stem cell or its commitment to erythroid differentiation (24, 25). These investigations also indicated that early precursor cells committed to erythropoiesis are not responsive to epo. In 1977 Iscove postulated

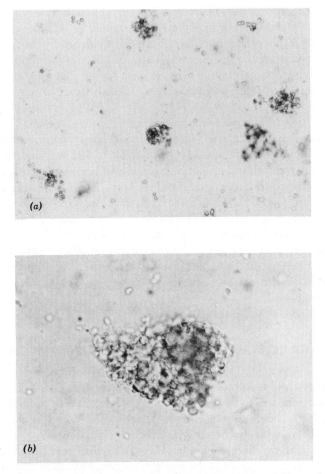

Figure 1. Erythroid colonies grown in methylcellulose culture. (*a*) Human bone marrow CFU-E (7 days); (*b*) small human bone marrow BFU-E (10 days).

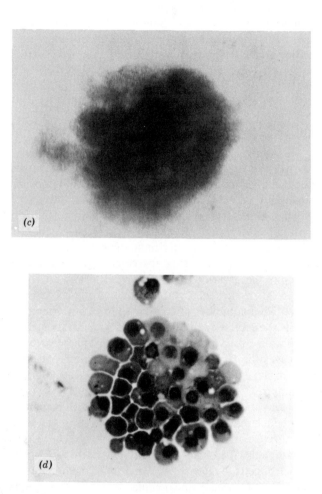

Figure 1 (continued). (*c*) large human peripheral blood BFU-E (17 days); (*d*) normoblasts containing hemoglobin comprising mouse CFU-E (2 days).

the existence of an independent modulator of multipotent stem cells and early, committed erythroid cells (24). Subsequent observations have supported this view and have provided evidence that the independent modulator is a hormone or hormones collectively referred to as burst-promoting activity (BPA) or erythroid-potentiating activity (EPA).

4. SOURCES OF ERYTHROID-POTENTIATING ACTIVITIES

In 1976 Aye demonstrated that conditioned medium from human peripheral blood leukocytes enhanced the growth of erythroid colonies *in vitro* (26). He referred to this activity as erythroid-enhancing activity. Stimulatory activity for burst proliferation *in vitro* has variously been referred to as burst-promoting activity, burst-feeder activity, burst-potentiating activity, erythroid-potentiating activity, and "regulatory protein" (4, 6, 8, 27–30). Although it is clear that there is extensive biologic and biochemical heterogeneity among these various factors and activities, for convenience we refer to them in this review as erythroid-potentiating activities (EPA). EPA may be derived from a number of cellular sources but often there has been little biochemical characterization of the molecules responsible for the observed potentiation of erythroid colony growth. Therefore, it is possible that in some cases the stimulatory activities measured are not strictly due to hormonal activity but may be related to the addition of nutrient factors, compounds important for cell growth which do not act as hormones (e.g., sulfhydryl reagents), and other biologic materials which may improve culture conditions but which may not properly be referred to as regulatory molecules. Although stimulators of *in vitro* erythropoiesis have been obtained from embryonic fibroblasts (31), the common sources for EPA are peripheral blood mononuclear cells, bone marrow-conditioned media, urine from anemic patients, serum, and normal and neoplastic cells of T-lymphocyte and mononuclear phagocyte lineage. Table 1 lists various sources of EPA as well as activities stimulating the proliferation of multipotent stem cells *in vitro*.

The most widely used source of EPA is lectin-stimulated lymphocytes. Media conditioned by PHA, concanavalin-A, and pokeweed mitogen-stimulated lymphoid populations consistently contain EPA (4, 8, 15, 37, 42–44). Erythroid-potentiating activity is also released by lymphoid cells responding to antigen (22, 33). It is most likely that in these circumstances the EPA is being elaborated by activated T-lymphocytes (44). The same material is most commonly used to stimulate the growth of mixed cell colonies (multipotent stem cells) *in vitro* (15, 16). Cells of the mononuclear phagocyte system also elaborate EPA, although they may release inhibitory

**Table 1. Humoral Factors Stimulating Erythroid Colony Formation
*in Vitro***

STAGE OF PROGENITOR STIMULATED	SOURCE (DESIGNATION)	REFERENCES
Committed, early (BFU-E)[a]	Human peripheral leukocytes (erythroid-enhancing activity)	26, 32
	Mouse embryonic fibroblasts	31
	Mitogen-stimulated mouse spleen cells (burst-promoting activity)	4, 15
	Antigen-stimulated mouse spleen cells	22, 33
	Mouse serum and bone marrow (burst-feeder activity)	27
	Human urine from anemic patients (regulatory protein)	28, 29
	Human bone marrow (burst-promoting activity)	34, 35
	Human T-lymphoblast cell lines (erythroid-potentiating activity)	6, 8, 36
	Phytohemagglutinin-stimulated human peripheral blood mononuclear cells	37
	Human monocyte cell lines (erythroid-enhancing activity) (erythroid-potentiating factor)	30, 38, 39
	Mouse monocyte cell line	Cited in 40
	Mouse peritoneal macrophages	41
Uncommitted (give rise to mixed myeloid colonies)	Mitogen-stimulated mouse spleen cells	15
	Mitogen-stimulated human leukocytes	17
	Human T-lymphoblast cell line	42

[a] Many of these factors stimulate CFU-E as well as BFU-E *in vitro*.

materials as well (41, 45–47). The cells responsible for the production of EPA from bone marrow-conditioned media have not been identified.

Conditioned media from heterogeneous cell populations have proved useful for biologic studies of the action of EPA; however, these materials have not been highly suitable for biochemical investigations. For this reason, the search for cell lines producing EPA has been actively pursued. Several cell lines are known to produce EPA. In general, human T-cell lines composed of mature helper T cells, which elaborate other lymphokines, produce EPA (6, 36). Most of these cell lines harbor a human T-cell leukemia-associated virus (HTLV) which must be considered a potential biohazard. Undifferentiated T-cell lines, which are widely used in studies of T-cell function, do not appear to produce EPA (48). Two human monocyte-like cell lines elaborate EPA. The GCT cell line elaborates both CSF and EPA (38); however, the monocyte-like cell line, U-937, constitutively produces EPA but no CSF (39). The murine WEHI-3 line produces both EPA and CSF (2, 40). These cell lines offer the possibility of obtaining large amounts of serum-free conditioned media which may then be used for biochemical characterization and purification. In general, the two prominent cell sources for EPA suggest that these modulators fall in the family of lymphokines and monokines.

5.   ASSAY OF EPA

One of the main problems in the study of EPA is the complexity of the assay systems used. As previously noted, there are several classes of erythroid progenitors, and various semisolid culture systems are used to grow the colonies. Most systems employ fetal bovine serum and some also use horse serum, beef embryo extract, and plasma. The presence of high concentrations of bovine serum may confound the assay system because serum itself contains EPA. On the other hand, the use of serum-free or serum-limited culture systems can introduce an excessive sensitivity to interfering factors of both a stimulatory and an inhibitory nature. Serum-free or serum-limited culture systems containing additives such as bovine serum albumin, transferrin, ferric chloride, and sodium selenite provide more useful assay systems (6) because these additives tend to maximize the culture conditions and limit the stimulation by extraneous substances in conditioned media. The serum-free culture conditions, however, are only useful for assaying EPA in serum-free conditioned medium. If a medium containing fetal bovine serum is added, predictable augmentation of erythroid colony growth will occur as a general response to the increased serum concentration. Inasmuch as many steroid and polypeptide hormones are known to augment erythropoiesis *in vitro*, they can also tend to confound assay results when serum is used in the culture medium. At present, there is no "standard" assay system for EPA. The *in vitro* bioassays are notoriously variable and unreliable. Improvement in assay technology will largely depend on biochemical purification of EPA, leading to the development of specific heterologous or monoclonal antibodies.

In our laboratory, we generally test conditioned media for EPA in either a serum-free, a 3%, or a 20–30% fetal bovine serum-containing system (depending on the material to be assayed), culturing human BFU-E from light density, nonadherent peripheral blood mononuclear leukocytes or unseparated buffy coat cells (6, 8). The cells are plated in 0.8% methylcellulose (Dow E4M premium) in the presence of 0.5–1.0 units/ml of partially purified human urinary epo (1140 units per mg protein, containing no CSF or EPA) using Iscove's medium (Irvine Scientific) with α-thioglycerol, transferrin, selenium, and ferric chloride (6, 49), adding bovine serum albumin to the serum-free cultures. The cultures are established in 100 μl wells (microtiter) to conserve materials, and erythroid colonies are scored at 10–14 days of culture (50, 51). Many conditioned media containing EPA also have high concentrations of CSF, and the growth of granulocyte-macrophage colonies in these cultures can lead to difficulties in assaying EPA, particularly if bone marrow cells are used as targets. Recently, a sensitive method for quantitating hemoglobin synthesis in human BFU-E cultures has been developed and this system may provide a more reliable assay for EPA (52).

6. EPA FROM THE Mo T-CELL LINE

We derived a T-lymphoblast cell line (Mo) from a patient with an unusual variant of hairy-cell leukemia. The patient's disease was phenotypically characteristic of hairy-cell leukemia (pancytopenia, splenomegaly, and bone marrow infiltration with mononuclear cells); however, the neoplastic lymphocytes rosetted with sheep erythrocytes, responded to PHA, and had no surface membrane immunoglobulin (53). The cell line was derived from spleen cells obtained at therapeutic splenectomy (53, 54). The Mo cells grow in suspension culture as individual cells and in clumps. They exhibit a normal male karyotype, and they contain the tartrate-resistant isozyme 5 of acid phosphatase characteristic of hairy-cell leukemia. The Mo cells are lysed by heterologous anti-T-cell antibodies with complement; they do not produce immunoglobulin, and they lack markers of Epstein–Barr virus infection. Monoclonal antibody typing indicates that 90% of the cells react with the Leu-1 antibody (Becton–Dickinson) defining a "common" T-cell antigen. Almost all of the cells react with the Leu-3a (Becton–Dickinson) and OKT-4 (Ortho), defining a subpopulation of T cells associated with helper or inducer function. There is no reaction with monoclonal antibodies OKT-8 and Leu-2a which identify suppressor T-lymphocytes. Ninety percent of the Mo cells react with anti-DR antibody (Ia-like) and recently the cells have been shown to harbor a strain of human T-cell leukemia virus (HTLV) different from that previously reported to be associated with T-cell leukemias and lymphomas in this country and in Japan (55). The Mo cells may be maintained for short periods of time in serum-free medium and in this way serum-free-conditioned media may be obtained. The Mo cells produce a number of lymphokines including a CSF for human granulocyte and monocyte colonies (56). Other virus-infected lymphokine-producing human T-cell lines also elaborate CSF and EPA (36).

We found that the crude Mo-conditioned medium caused approximately a twofold increase in BFU-E and CFU-E at optimal concentrations of between 3 and 5%. The degree of stimulation varied greatly with culture conditions; other laboratories have observed a similar effect of the Mo-conditioned medium (52). Stimulation is seen at epo concentrations up to 2 units/ml and the EPA in crude Mo-conditioned medium is found to be stable at refrigerator temperatures. Heat stability curves constructed for CSF and EPA in crude serum-free Mo-conditioned medium indicate that Mo EPA is unusually heat stable. The activity can usually withstand immersion in a boiling water bath for several minutes. The marked difference in the heat stability curves for CSF and EPA provided evidence that these activities reside in distinct molecules, a conclusion subsequently corroborated by biochemical studies (6, 8). Recently, EPA activity in conditioned medium from PHA-treated human spleen cells and Mo cells was found to be partially associated with membrane vesicles shed from the cell surfaces (57).

7. BIOCHEMICAL PROPERTIES OF EPA

The molecular and biochemical characteristics of EPA have not been extensively studied and there are clear differences in the physical characteristics of EPA obtained from various cellular sources. In general, the activities that have been characterized appear to be glycoproteins of molecular weight 30,000 to 45,000. The reported heat stabilities have varied considerably. The EPA from the GCT cell line has been difficult to separate from the CSF also produced by that cell line. The two activities were not separable by ion exchange chromatography or gel permeation chromatography, and the CSF and EPA eluted at an apparent molecular weight of 30,000 (30). Recently, Abboud and colleagues (38) have used hydrophobic adsorption chromatography to separate EPA from CSF (38). The EPA from pokeweed mitogen or concanavalin-A-stimulated mouse spleen cells has been partially purified by concanavalin-A-Sepharose affinity chromatography and gel filtration on Sephadex G-150 (4). The material has an apparent molecular weight of 35,000. The EPA from human bone marrow-conditioned medium has been purified approximately 300-fold by ion exchange chromatography and adsorption chromatography on hydroxy-apatite-agarose gel. This partially purified material did not have CSF activity and is not prominently heat stable (35). Dukes and colleagues (28, 29) separated an EPA in human urine from epo and CSF by chromatography on QAE-Sephadex A-50, gel filtration on Sephadex G-25, and hydroxy-apatite chromatography. They refer to this EPA as regulatory protein and they found that the partially purified material increased murine burst formation *in vitro* and stimulated murine CFU-S.

We undertook a partial purification of EPA from serum-free Mo-conditioned medium (Table 2; 8). The medium (1.8 liters) had a protein concentration of approximately 100 μg/ml. The material was concentrated by adsorption to and elution from calcium phosphate gel. The eluate was dialyzed against buffer and subjected to flat-bed isoelectric focusing. The bulk of the EPA activity was present primarily in acidic fractions ranging in pH from 3.5–4.8. The fractions with highest EPA specific activity were pooled, concentrated, and subjected to gel exclusion chromatography, using Ultrogel AcA 44. Peak EPA activity eluted in fractions corresponding to a molecular weight of approximately 40,000. We arbitrarily defined 1 unit of EPA activity as the amount required to stimulate human peripheral blood BFU-E by 50% in the presence of 0.5 units/ml human epo. The final product had a specific activity of about 51,000 units/mg protein, representing about a 250-fold purification with an overall yield of 20%. The partially purified EPA contained little or no CSF as judged by stimulation of colony formation in colony-forming unit-granulocyte-macrophage (CFU-GM) cultures. CSF and EPA in crude serum-free Mo-conditioned medium could be partially separated in a single step by gel filtration chromatography (Fig. 2). The weight of evidence from several systems, therefore, indicates that CSF and EPA are attributable to separate molecules.

Table 2. Partial Purification of EPA from Mo-Conditioned Medium

FRACTION	ACTIVITY[a] (UNITS × 10^{-2})	PROTEIN (mg)	SPECIFIC ACTIVITY (UNITS/mg × 10^{-2})	YIELD (%)
Mo-conditioned medium	360	180	2.0	100
Isoelectric focusing	140	21	6.7	39
Gel exclusion chromatography	72	0.14	514.0	20

[a] Activity was determined using stimulation of human BFU-E. One unit stimulates colony formation by 50% in the presence of 0.5 units human erythropoietin/ml.

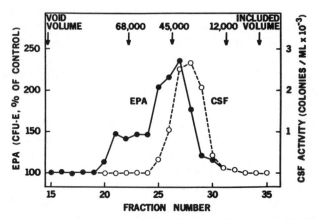

Figure 2.   Gel permeation chromatography of conditioned medium from the Mo T-lymphoblast cell showing partial separation of CSF and EPA.

The partially purified EPA from Mo-conditioned media stimulated both human CFU-E and BFU-E (Fig. 3). This material only stimulated BFU-E in a murine system and had little or no effect on mouse CFU-E (Fig. 4). Thus the effects of EPA on various classes of erythroid progenitors have a certain species dependence. In summary, then, EPA from the Mo cell line is an acidic glycoprotein hormone with a molecular weight of about 40,000.

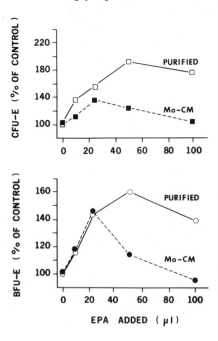

Figure 3.   Stimulation of human CFU-E and BFU-E by partially purified EPA and crude Mo-conditioned media. Assays performed in 1-ml plates with media containing 30% fetal bovine serum. Reprinted with permission from A. J. Lusis and D. W. Golde, in G. Stamatoyannopoulos and A. W. Nienhuis, Eds. *Hemoglobins in Development and Differentiation*, Alan R. Liss, Inc., New York, 1981.

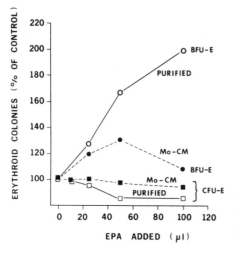

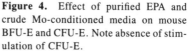

Figure 4. Effect of purified EPA and crude Mo-conditioned media on mouse BFU-E and CFU-E. Note absence of stimulation of CFU-E.

The partially purified EPA stimulated erythroid colonies in nanogram/ml quantities and we estimate that the homogeneous EPA hormone would stimulate erythroid colony formation at concentrations below 0.1 nM.

8. BIOLOGIC PROPERTIES OF EPA

Inasmuch as EPA has not been purified to homogeneity and the assay for EPA is complex and highly variable, it is not possible to draw firm conclusions regarding its biologic properties. Nonetheless, a number of inferences can be drawn on the basis of the data at hand. EPA appears to be the primary stimulator of BFU-E growth *in vitro* but will also stimulate CFU-E under appropriate circumstances (4, 6, 8, 15, 32, 33, 39, 58). Many of the materials containing EPA also have the ability to stimulate multipotent stem cells as assayed in the murine spleen colony assay *in vivo* or by the mixed colony assay *in vitro* (16, 17, 19, 29, 59). Thus lectin-treated lymphocyte populations are the usual source for multipotent stem cell stimulators. Partially purified EPA from the Mo cell line stimulated the growth of human mixed colonies *in vitro* (42). Both the *in vivo* and *in vitro* evidence to date suggests that EPA is an important regulator of multipotent stem cells, BFU-E, and perhaps to a lesser extent, CFU-E. The schema shown in Fig. 5 may require some modification when purified EPA is available; however, the general concept of epo regulating the terminal steps in erythropoiesis and EPA being important

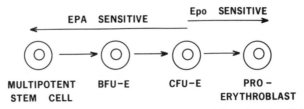

Figure 5.   Schema of erythropoiesis showing relative roles of EPA and epo in cellular regulation. There may be substantial overlap in cellular targets for these modulators.

for the earlier steps seems a reasonable conclusion at present.* The findings to date have supported Iscove's early hypothesis regarding the relative roles of EPA and epo (4, 24).

Conditioned media from lectin-treated lymphocytes have also been used to stimulate the growth of human leukemic cells (60). Conditioned media from the Mo cell line stimulate myeloid leukemic cell colony formation *in vitro* (61) although this effect may be due to the presence of both EPA and CSF. We have recently shown that colony growth of the pluripotent human cell line, K-562, is also enhanced *in vitro* by partially purified EPA from the Mo cells (43). Stimulatory activity for K-562 cell colony formation *in vitro* co-purified with EPA through gel filtration chromatography, isoelectric focusing, and heat denaturation procedures. A species dependence was noted in the effect of various EPA activities on the human K-562 cells. Conditioned medium from the GCT cell line, from normal lymphocytes exposed to PHA, and regulatory protein from human urine stimulated K-562 colony formation, whereas mouse spleen cell-conditioned medium and a preparation of EPA from mouse bone marrow did not (43). On the other hand, colony formation by the murine Friend erythroleukemia cell line was stimulated by both human and murine sources of EPA. These results suggest that EPA can modulate the growth of leukemic cells; they also provide evidence for some species specificity in the action of this hormone. BFU-E from Friend virus-infected mice also require an EPA for their growth *in vitro* (62).

EPA may also be an important modulator of the progenitor cell forming granulocyte and macrophage colonies in diffusion chambers (CFU-DG) implanted in mice (63). The cell forming this colony is believed to be a progenitor of CFU-GM, which may be unresponsive to CSF. In experiments with Mo-conditioned medium slowly released by a mini-osmotic pump (Alza) into the peritoneal cavities of mice containing diffusion chambers loaded with human bone marrow, stimulation of CFU-DG appeared to reside pri-

* For an alternate view of the role of epo, see Chapter 1.

marily in the fraction co-purifying with EPA. The weight of evidence to date supports the idea that EPA is an important modulator of the early steps of hematopoiesis.

There is little information regarding the role of EPA in man. Nissen et al. measured this activity in the serum of patients with acquired aplastic anemia (40). They found high levels of both CSF and EPA in the serum of these patients as compared to the low activities observed in sera from healthy volunteers and from patients with anemias of diverse origin. The high EPA activity returned to normal in the patients with aplastic anemia who achieved complete remission after treatment. This provocative report and the finding of EPA in human urine (29) lend support to the idea that EPA may be a primary humoral regulator of the early steps of hematopoiesis in man.

9.   EFFECT OF EPA ON HEMOGLOBIN SYNTHESIS

Because EPA stimulates erythropoiesis, it also causes an increase in hemoglobin synthesis *in vitro* (52, 64). EPA has been noted to alter the ratios of hemoglobin A and F synthesized in BFU-E *in vitro* (64–66). Under certain circumstances EPA may increase the proportion of hemoglobin F synthesized by adult human BFU-E, whereas it increases the proportion of hemoglobin A synthesized in cord blood BFU-E (66). The effect of EPA on hemoglobin synthesis by erythroid cells *in vitro* may depend heavily on culture conditions. It is not certain whether EPA directly affects globin gene expression or if its major effect is on stimulating precursor cells programmed for adult or fetal hemoglobin synthesis. Lastly, it is not known if the effects observed *in vitro* are ascribable solely to the EPA molecule.

ADDENDUM

Interleukin 3 (IL-3) is a glycoprotein mediator which has been identified in the conditioned medium of EL-4 mouse lymphoma cells and mouse mye-lomonocytic cells of the line WEHI-3 (1–3). This hormone has a molecular weight of 28,000 daltons and stimulates the growth of multipotent hema-topoietic precursors in semisolid culture and long-term hematopoietic cultures (4, 5). Similarly, Iscove and co-workers have purified BPA from lectin-stimulated mouse spleen cells and from the WEHI-3 cell line and showed that these molecules stimulated multipotent hematopoietic stem cells as well as early precursor cells committed to erythropoiesis (6). Thus, it appears that IL-3 or the hematopoietic cell growth factor produced by WEHI-3 cells or lectin-treated lymphocytes is analogous to human BPA or EPA. We have recently purified human EPA from the Mo line to homogeneity using a combination of lectin affinity chromatography, gel filtration chromatography, and reversed phase high-pressure liquid chromatography (7). The purified protein has a molecular weight of 28,000 daltons and appears as a single polypeptide chain. The homogeneous EPA stimulates human peripheral blood and bone marrow bursts, bone marrow CFU-E, and K-562 cells in picomolar concentrations.

REFERENCES

1. Cline, M. J., and Golde, D. W., *Nature*, **277**, 177 (1979).
2. Burgess, A. W., and Metcalf, D., *Blood*, **56**, 947 (1980).
3. Miyake, T., Kung, C. K.-H., and Goldwasser, E., *J. Biol. Chem.*, **252**, 5558 (1977).
4. Iscove, N. N., in D. W. Golde, M. J. Cline, D. Metcalf, and C. F. Fox, Eds., *Hematopoietic Cell Differentiation. ICN-UCLA Symposia on Molecular and Cellular Biology*, Academic, New York, Vol. 10, 1978.
5. Lipton, J. M., Kudisch, M., and Nathan, D. G., *Exp. Hematol.*, **9**, 1035 (1981).
6. Golde, D. W., Bersch, N., Quan, S. G., and Lusis, A. J., *Proc. Natl. Acad. Sci. USA*, **77**, 593 (1980).
7. Iscove, N. N., and Guilbert, L. J., in M. J. Murphy, Jr., C. Peschle, A. S. Gordon, and E. A. Mirand, Eds., *In Vitro Aspects of Erythropoiesis*, Springer, New York, 1978.
8. Lusis, A. J., and Golde, D. W., in G. Stamatoyannopoulos and A. W. Nienhuis, Eds., *Hemoglobins in Development and Differentiation*, Alan R. Liss, New York, 1981.
9. Stephenson, J. R., Axelrad, A. A., McLeod, D. L., and Shreeve, M. M., *Proc. Natl. Acad. Sci. USA*, **68**, 1542 (1971).
10. Axelrad, A. A., McLeod, D. L., Shreeve, M. M., and Heath, D. S., in W. A. Robinson, Ed., *Hemopoiesis in Culture*, U.S. Government Printing Office, Washington, D.C., 1974.
11. Iscove, N. N., Sieber, F., and Winterhalter, K. H., *J. Cell. Physiol.*, **83**, 309 (1974).
12. McLeod, D. L., Shreeve, M. M., and Axelrad, A. A., *Blood*, **44**, 517 (1974).
13. Eaves, C. J., and Eaves, A. C., *Blood*, **52**, 1196 (1978).
14. Abramson, S., Miller, R. G., and Phillips, R. A., *J. Exp. Med.*, **145**, 1567 (1977).
15. Johnson, G. R., and Metcalf, D., *Proc. Natl. Acad. Sci. USA*, **74**, 3879 (1977).
16. Fauser, A. A., and Messner, H. A., *Blood*, **52**, 1243 (1978).
17. Fauser, A. A., and Messner, H. A., *Blood*, **53**, 1023 (1979).
18. Cerny, J., *Nature*, **249**, 63 (1974).
19. Cerny, J., Waner, E. B., and Rubin, A. S., *J. Immunol.*, **115**, 513 (1975).
20. Lipton, J. M., and Nathan, D. G., *Br. J. Haematol.*, **53**, 361 (1983).
21. Wiktor-Jedrzejczak, W., Sharkis, S., Ahmed, A., Sell, K. W., and Santos, G. W., *Science*, **196**, 313 (1977).
22. Schreier, M. H., and Iscove, N. N., *Nature*, **287**, 228 (1980).
23. Nathan, D. G., Chess, L., Hillman, D. G., Clarke, B., Breard, J., Merler, E., and Housman, D. E., *J. Exp. Med.*, **147** 324 (1978).

24. Iscove, N. N., *Cell Tissue Kinet.*, **10**, 323 (1977).
25. Udupa, K. B., and Reissmann, K. R., *Blood*, **53**, 1164 (1979).
26. Aye, M. T., *J. Cell. Physiol.*, **91**, 69 (1977).
27. Wagemaker, G., in M. J. Murphy, Jrs., C. Peschle, A. S. Gordon and E. A. Mirand, Eds., *In Vitro Aspects of Erythropoiesis*, Springer, New York, 1978.
28. Dukes, P. P., Meytes, D., Ma, A., DiRocco, G., Ortega, J. A., and Shore, N. A., in D. W. Golde, M. J. Cline, D. Metcalf, and C. F. Fox, Eds., *Hematopoietic Cell Differentiation. ICN-UCLA Symposia on Molecular and Cellular Biology*, Academic, New York, Vol. 10, 1978.
29. Dukes, P. P., Ma, A., and Meytes, D., *Exp. Hematol.*, **8** (Suppl. 8), 128 (1980).
30. Abboud, C. N., DiPersio, J. F., Brennan, J. K., and Lichtman, M. A., *J. Supramol. Struct.*, **13**, 199 (1980).
31. Ghio, R., Bianchi, G., Löwenberg, B., Dicke, K. A., and Ajmar, F., *Exp. Hematol.*, **5**, 341 (1977).
32. Tsang, R. W., and Aye, M. T., *Exp. Hematol.*, **7**, 383 (1979).
33. Fagg, B., *Nature*, **289**, 184 (1981).
34. Porter, P. N., Ogawa, M., and Leary, A. G., *Exp. Hematol.*, **8**, 83 (1980).
35. Porter, P. N., and Ogawa, M., *Blood*, **59**, 1207 (1982).
36. Tarella, C., Ruscetti, F. W., Poiesz, B. J., Woods, A., and Gallo, R. C., *Blood*, **59**, 1330 (1982).
37. Meytes, D., Ma, A., Ortega, J. A., Shore, N. A., and Dukes, P. P., *Blood*, **54**, 1050 (1979).
38. Abboud, C. N., Brennan, J. K., Barlow, G. H., and Lichtman, M. A., *Blood*, **58**, 1148 (1981).
39. Ascensao, J. L., Kay, N. E., Earenfight-Engler, T., Koren, H. S., and Zanjani, E. D., *Blood*, **57**, 170 (1981).
40. Nissen, C., Iscove, N. N., and Speck, B., in S. J. Baum and G. D. Ledney, Eds., *Experimental Hematology Today 1979*, Springer, New York, 1979.
41. Kurland, J. I., Meyers, P. A., and Moore, M. A. S., *J. Exp. Med.*, **151**, 839 (1980).
42. Fauser, A. A., Messner, H. A., Lusis, A. J., and Golde, D. W., *Stem Cells*, **1**, 73 (1981).
43. Gauwerky, C. E., Lusis, A. J., and Golde, D. W., *Blood*, **59**, 300 (1982).
44. Metcalf, D., and Johnson, G. R., *J. Cell. Physiol.*, **96**, 31 (1978).
45. Rinehart, J. J., Zanjani, E. D., Nomdedeu, B., Gormus, B. J., and Kaplan, M. E., *J. Clin. Invest.*, **62**, 979 (1978).
46. Lipton, J. M., Link, N. A., Breard, J., Jackson, P. L., Clarke, B. J., and Nathan, D. G., *J. Clin. Invest.*, **65**, 219 (1980).
47. Zuckerman, K. S., *J. Clin. Invest.*, **67**, 702 (1981).
48. Kubota, K., Preisler, H. D., and Minowada, J., *Exp. Hematol.*, **10**, 130 (1982).
49. Guilbert, L. J., and Iscove, N. N., *Nature*, **263**, 594 (1976).
50. Urabe, A., and Murphy, M. J., Jr., in M. J. Murphy, Jr., C. Peschle, A. S. Gordon and E. A. Mirand, Eds., *In Vitro Aspects of Erythropoiesis*, Springer, New York, 1978.
51. Hunt, R. E., Moffat, K., and Golde, D. W., *J. Biol. Chem.*, **256**, 7042 (1981).
52. Clarke, B. J., Brickenden, A. M., Ives, R. A., and Chui, D. H. K., *Blood*, **60**, 346 (1982).

53. Saxon, A., Stevens, R. H., and Golde, D. W., *Ann. Intern. Med.*, **88**, 323 (1978).

54. Saxon, A., Stevens, R. H., Quan, S. G., and Golde, D. W., *J. Immunol.*, **120**, 777 (1978).

55. Kalyanaraman, V. S., Sarngadharan, M. G., Robert-Guroff, M., Miyoshi, I., Blayney, D., Golde, D., and Gallo, R. C., *Science*, **218**, 571 (1982).

56. Lusis, A. J., Quon, D. H., and Golde, D. W., *Blood*, **57**, 13 (1981).

57. Dainiak, N., and Cohen, C. M., *Blood*, **60**, 583 (1982).

58. Johnson, G. R., and Metcalf, D., *J. Cell. Physiol.*, **94**, 243 (1978).

59. Wagemaker, G., and Peters, M. F., *Cell Tissue Kinet.*, **11**, 45 (1978).

60. Buick, R. N., Minden, M. D., and McCulloch, E. A., *Blood*, **54**, 95 (1979).

61. Minden, M. D., Buick, R. N., and McCulloch, E. A., *Blood*, **54**, 186 (1979).

62. Kreja, L., and Seidel, H.-J., *Stem Cells*, **1**, 367 (1981).

63. Niskanen, E., Oki, A., Cline, M. J., and Golde, D. W., *Blood*, **60**, 368 (1982).

64. Ogawa, M., Porter, P. N., Terasawa, T., and Brockbank, K. G. M., *Exp. Hematol.* **8** (Suppl. 8), 90 (1980).

65. Terasawa, T., Ogawa, M., Porter, P. N., Golde, D. W., and Goldwasser, E., *Blood*, **56**, 1106 (1980).

66. Testa, U., Vainchenker, W., Guerrasio, A., Beuzard, Y., Breton-Gorius, J., Rosa, J., Lusis, A. J., and Golde, D., *J. Cell. Physiol.*, **110**, 196 (1982).

REFERENCES TO THE ADDENDUM

1. Ihle, J. N., Pepersack, L., and Rebar, L., *J. Immunol.*, **126**, 2184 (1981).

2. Ihle, J. N., Rebar, L., Keller, S., Lee, J. C., and Hapel, A. J. *Immunol. Rev.*, **63**, 5 (1982).

3. Hapel, A., Lee, J. C., Farrar, W. L., and Ihle, J. N., *Cell*, **25**, 179 (1981).

4. Garland, J. M., *Immunol. Today*, **3**, 208 (1982).

5. Garland, J. M., and Dexter, T. M., *Lymphokine Res.*, **2**, 13 (1983).

6. Iscove, N. N., Roitsch, C. A., Williams, N., and Guilbert, L. J., *J. Cell. Physiol.*, (Suppl. 1), 65 (1982).

7. Westbrook, C. A., Gasson, J. C., Gerber, S., Selsted, M. E., and Golde, D. W., submitted.

3

SCIATIN (TRANSFERRIN) AND OTHER MUSCLE TROPHIC FACTORS

Tae H. Oh

George J. Markelonis

CONTENTS

Abbreviations

RMP   Resting membrane potential
TTX   Tetrodotoxin
ACh   Acetylcholine
AChE   Acetylcholinesterase
PBS   Phosphate-buffered saline
ALD   Anterior latissimus dorsi
PLD   Posterior latissimus dorsi
α-Btx   α-Bungarotoxin
PAP   Peroxidase-antiperoxidase
APB   Anti-protease buffer
EE   Embryo extract
NGF   Nerve growth factor
EGF   Epidermal growth factor
MTF   Myotrophic factor
GFAP   Glial fibrillary acidic protein

1. INTRODUCTION

Numerous *in vivo* experiments have shown that spinal motor nerves exert trophic influences on the morphological, physiological, and biochemical properties of skeletal muscle (see reviews, 1–3). For example, denervation produces a variety of degenerative changes in fetal and adult muscle. In fetal muscle these changes include a slowing of morphological maturation, the retardation of further differentiation, and muscle atrophy and degeneration (4–9). In adult muscle, there is a decrease in resting membrane potential (RMP; 10), the appearance of both tetrodotoxin (TTX)-resistant potentials (11, 12) and extrajunctional acetylcholine (ACh) sensitivity (13–15), loss of acetylcholinesterase (AChE; 16), and muscle atrophy and degeneration (17). Although the mechanism by which the motor nerve regulates the properties of the muscle is not fully understood, three hypotheses have been proposed to account for this phenomenon: (i) muscle activity (18–20), (ii) ACh transmission (21, 22), and (iii) neurohumoral trophic substances (1–3). Recent evidence indicates that such trophic influence is mediated in part by muscle activity and in part by diffusible, trophic substances carried by axonal transport (23).

Evidence for the trophic roles of neurally derived substances has been obtained from studies on amphibian regeneration and from tissue culture experiments. The findings of these experiments can be summarized as follows: (i) infusion of nerve extracts into denervated newt limbs prevents the decrease in protein synthesis that otherwise occurs after denervation (24, 25), (ii) addition of nerve extracts to the culture medium of denervated newt limb muscles in organ culture delays the loss of muscle AChE activity (26, 27), (iii) extracts of spinal cord, but not of non-neural tissues, prevent the appearance of TTX-resistant potentials and the decrease in RMP, and partially reverse the changes in membrane properties of denervated muscle in organ culture (28, 29), (iv) substances released from nerves by electrical stimulation reverse the loss of muscle AChE activity in denervated muscle in organ culture (30), and (v) nerve extracts enhance growth and development of aneural muscle cells in culture and stimulate ACh receptor synthesis in these cells in the absence of innervation (31–34). The active principles in all of these extracts appear to be proteins of various molecular weights (27, 31–34).

Using chick muscle cultures, we demonstrated that muscle AChE activity is increased by the presence of spinal cord explants regardless of whether these explants are allowed to form functional synapses with the muscle (35). Also, the addition of extracts of chick brain and spinal cord increased muscle AChE activity in the absence of innervation (35, 36). Because our results indicated that trophic regulation of muscle AChE might well be mediated by a diffusible substance released from neural tissues, we initiated experiments to attempt to isolate and purify the bioactive agent. Our initial study demonstrated that the trophic agent was present in peripheral nervous tissue inasmuch as addition of extracts of adult chicken sciatic nerves enhanced the morphological maturation of aneural muscle cells in culture and increased protein synthesis and AChE activity of muscle cultures in the absence of innervation (37). Furthermore, noninnervated muscle cultures survived for several months in the presence of these extracts, whereas control cultures underwent atrophy and degeneration after only a few weeks *in vitro*. Further studies suggested that the active agent in the extracts was a protein of fairly high molecular weight (38–40). Recently, we have purified a bioactive protein from sciatic nerves which exerts trophic effects on muscle (41, 42). This myotrophic protein, which we have termed *sciatin* (59), is a glycoprotein with a native molecular weight of 86,400.

In this review, we summarize our data regarding sciatin. We also review other muscle trophic factors that have been characterized and partially purified. For earlier studies on trophic interactions between nerve and muscle, the reader is referred to several thorough reviews on the subject (1–3, 43).

2.   SCIATIN

2.1.   Isolation of Sciatin

The original purification scheme for sciatin utilized ion-exchange chromatography on DEAE-cellulose followed by gel filtration on Sephadex G-100 superfine (41, 42). This purification scheme suffered several disadvantages in terms of the rapidity with which sciatin could be purified. Subsequently, we developed a more rapid fractionation procedure for sciatin which takes advantage of the fact that sciatin, a glycoprotein, binds to immobilized concanavalin A (44; Fig. 1). Sciatin was purified 24-fold from sciatic nerve extracts by affinity chromatography on concanavalin A-agarose followed by ion-exchange chromatography on DEAE-cellulose. The purity of sciatin was greater than 97% as estimated by densitometric integration of SDS gels and represented over 70% of the sciatin present in sciatic nerve extracts as determined by rocket immunoelectrophoresis. Sciatin purified by this procedure retained full biological activity. This purification procedure using affinity chromatography provides a more rapid and convenient method for the isolation of sciatin.

2.2.   Chemical and Physical Properties of Sciatin

Sciatin migrated as a single polypeptide chain of molecular weight 84,000 on SDS-gel electrophoresis (Fig. 2). The native molecular weight of sciatin as estimated by sedimentation equilibrium centrifugation was 86,400 (42). Amino acid analysis revealed that sciatin is relatively deficient in methionine,

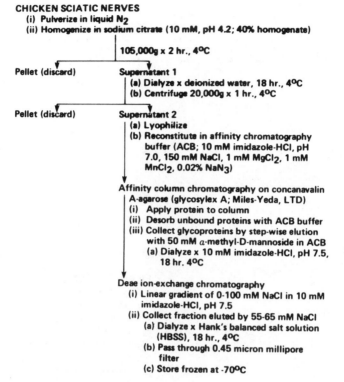

CHICKEN SCIATIC NERVES
(i) Pulverize in liquid N_2
(ii) Homogenize in sodium citrate (10 mM, pH 4.2; 40% homogenate)

105,000g x 2 hr., 4°C

Pellet (discard)   Supernatant 1
                       (a) Dialyze x deionized water, 18 hr., 4°C
                       (b) Centrifuge 20,000g x 1 hr., 4°C

Pellet (discard)   Supernatant 2
                       (a) Lyophilize
                       (b) Reconstitute in affinity chromatography
                           buffer (ACB; 10 mM imidazole-HCl, pH
                           7.0, 150 mM NaCl, 1 mM $MgCl_2$, 1 mM
                           $MnCl_2$, 0.02% NaN_3)

Affinity column chromatography on concanavalin
A-agarose (glycosylex A; Miles-Yeda, LTD)
(i) Apply protein to column
(ii) Desorb unbound proteins with ACB buffer
(iii) Collect glycoproteins by step-wise elution
      with 50 mM α-methyl-D-mannoside in ACB
      (a) Dialyze x 10 mM imidazole-HCl, pH 7.5,
          18 hr. 4°C

Deae ion-exchange chromatography
(i) Linear gradient of 0-100 mM NaCl in 10 mM
    imidazole-HCl, pH 7.5
(ii) Collect fraction eluted by 55-65 mM NaCl
     (a) Dialyze x Hank's balanced salt solution
         (HBSS), 18 hr., 4°C
     (b) Pass through 0.45 micron millipore
         filter
     (c) Store frozen at -70°C

Figure 1.   Purification scheme for sciatin.

but enriched in glutamic acid, glycine, aspartic acid, and lysine (45). Amino acid sequence analysis also revealed that sciatin is composed of a single polypeptide chain inasmuch as only one NH_2-terminal amino acid was detected (alanine; 45). Carbohydrate determination showed that sciatin is composed of 11% sugar by weight with no detectable N-acetylneuraminic acid residues. Sedimentation velocity centrifugation studies revealed an $S_{20,w}^0$ of 5.11 with a frictional coefficient of 1.31 (Table 1). Finally, sciatin had no detectable protease or AChE activity.

2.3.   Biological Activies of Sciatin *in Vitro*

2.3.1.   Morphological Maturation and Maintenance

Addition of sciatin to chick muscle cultures enhanced the rate and degree of morphological maturation (41). Muscle cultures treated with sciatin dif-

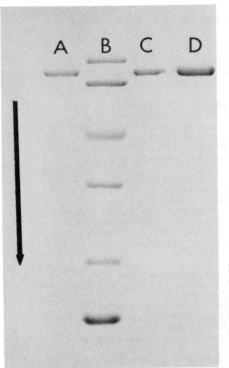

Figure 2. SDS-gel electrophoresis of sciatin. Lanes A and C, 5 μg of sciatin; Lane D, 10 μg of sciatin; Lane B, molecular weight standards; from top, phosphorylase b, 94,000; albumin, 67,000; ovalbumin, 43,000; carbonic anhydrase, 30,000; trypsin inhibitor, 20,100; lactalbumin, 14,400. Reproduced from reference 42 with permission.

ferentiated into cross-striated myotubes by six days *in vitro* (Fig. 3). By contrast, control cultures with inactive sciatic nerve protein or with phosphate-buffered saline (PBS) were composed of immature thin myotubes at 6 days *in vitro* and did not develop cross striations until 10 days in culture. For several days thereafter, the control cultures maintained their structural integrity, but then began to undergo muscle atrophy and degeneration; cross striations disappeared and the myotubes became thinner and shorter. Addition of sciatin to these degenerating, control cultures prevented or reversed the degenerative process. In the presence of sciatin, well-differentiated myotubes were maintained for more than 1 month, a time when control muscle cultures had completely degenerated (Fig. 3). If sciatin was withdrawn from these treated cultures, myotubes began to degenerate within 3–5 days indicating that the continuous presence of the protein was essential for the long-term maintenance of muscle cells in culture.

2.3.2. Protein Synthesis

Sciatin was added to postmitotic myotube cultures of chick embryonic muscle in order to determine the effect of sciatin on protein turnover (46).

Table 1.   Molecular Parameters of Sciatin

Molecular weight	
Sedimentation analysis	86,400
SDS-gel electrophoresis	84,000
Sedimentation coefficient (S)	5.1
Diffusion constant (10^{-7} cm^2 s^{-1})	5.60
Axial ratio (f/f_{min})	1.31
Isoelectric point (pI)	5.75[a]
Carbohydrate composition (%)	11

Source: Modified from reference 45 with permission.
[a] Major peak.

At a concentration of 25 μg/ml, sciatin selectively stimulated the rate of incorporation of [^{14}C]leucine into muscle protein without affecting the rate of protein degradation. The increased [^{14}C]leucine incorporation was linear up to 8 hours after addition of the isotope, but began to decelerate somewhat over the next 16 hours. The stimulatory effect of sciatin upon the rate of incorporation was not due to a differential increase in the intracellular pool of free [^{14}C]leucine inasmuch as sciatin failed to alter significantly the level of trichloroacetic acid-soluble [^{14}C]leucine in treated muscle cultures. Evidence obtained from experiments using the protein synthesis inhibitors actinomycin D and cycloheximide, or from labeling experiments with [^{3}H]uridine indicated that sciatin evoked a nonspecific increase in the rate of protein synthesis which involved the synthesis of RNA as well. The presence of TTX (0.1 μg/ml), an agent which abolishes spontaneous muscle contractions, had no effect upon sciatin-stimulated protein synthesis, suggesting that this action of sciatin does not require muscle activity. Stimulation of protein synthesis by sciatin did not appear to be mediated by the level of cyclic nucleotides inasmuch as neither theophylline (an inhibitor of phosphodiesterase) nor imidazole (an inhibitor of adenyl cyclase) affected its action. Furthermore, the rate of protein degradation in cultures pretreated with sciatin, TTX, or the combination of sciatin and TTX was not appreciably different than that in untreated controls.

2.3.3.   Acetylcholinesterase

Sciatin also regulated muscle AChE activity in culture (39). In differentiating aneural cultures of myoblasts, AChE activity increased markedly during the fusion of myoblasts, but the AChE activity subsequently decreased rapidly as muscle maturation progressed. By the sixth to eighth day, the

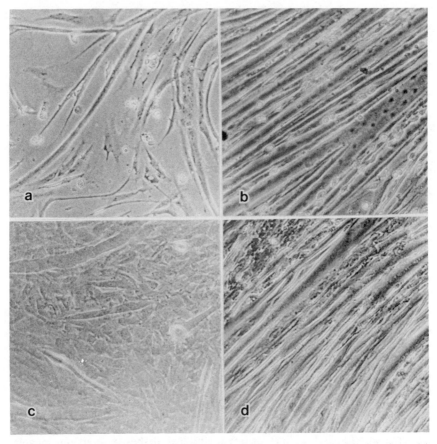

Figure 3. Phase contrast photomicrographs of chick embryonic muscle cells in culture. (*a*) Control culture grown for 6 days in the standard culture medium. (*b*) Muscle culture grown for 6 days in the presence of sciatin. (*c*) Control culture maintained for 5 weeks in the standard culture medium. (*d*) Muscle culture maintained for 5 weeks in the presence of sciatin. Reproduced from reference 41.

cultures had reached the *late myotube* stage and exhibited cross striations and spontaneous contractions. AChE decreased moderately between 8 and 11 days in culture (Table 2). Addition of sciatin to these cross-striated muscle cultures prevented a further decrease in muscle AChE activity (Table 2).

In order to determine whether this phenomenon resulted from enzyme induction, cycloheximide or actinomycin D was added to muscle cultures immediately after the addition of sciatin (39). After 24 hours in the presence

Table 2. Effects of Sciatin on Acetylcholinesterase (AChE) and Creatine Kinase (CK) Activities of Cultured Chick Muscle Cells[a]

Treatment	Days in Culture	AChE[b]	CK[c]
Control	8	1.94 ± 0.06	1.03 ± 0.01
Control	11	1.15 ± 0.05[d]	0.83 ± 0.06
Sciatin	11	1.87 ± 0.10	1.61 ± 0.16[d]

Source: Modified from reference 40, with permission.
[a] Each value is the mean ± S.E. of 12 dishes.
[b] Units are μmoles acetylthiocholine hydrolyzed/hour/mg protein.
[c] Units are μmoles NADPH formed/minute/mg protein.
[d] Significantly different from control (8-day), $p < 0.02$.

of protein synthesis inhibitors, AChE activity of muscle cultures was determined. Cycloheximide caused a significant decrease in AChE levels as compared to the inhibitor-free cultures. By contrast, actinomycin D caused a "superinduction" of AChE as evidenced by a significant increase in AChE activity. The results seem to indicate that the maintenance of AChE levels by sciatin is regulated by a post-transcriptional mechanism (47–49).

Since adult muscles in organ culture lose muscle AChE activity as a result of denervation (26, 50), we investigated whether sciatin would maintain the AChE activity of cultured muscle (39). The decrease of muscle AChE was retarded significantly when sciatin was added to media in which adult chicken anterior latissimus dorsi (ALD) and posterior latissimus dorsi (PLD) muscles were cultured. The results indicate that sciatin mimics the maintenance effect of innervation on muscle AChE activity *in vivo*.

2.3.4. Acetylcholine Receptors

Factors present in extracts of neural tissues have been shown to increase the number of ACh receptors in muscle cultures (33, 34). We therefore investigated the effect of sciatin on ACh receptors in cultures of chick embryonic muscle (51). Sciatin caused a significant increase in the number of ACh receptors/dish as determined by the binding of [^{125}I]α-bungarotoxin (α-Btx) and in AChE activity/dish in differentiating muscle cells (Fig. 4). The increase in ACh receptors elicited by sciatin was due solely to receptor synthesis and incorporation. The rate of ACh receptor synthesis in sciatin-treated muscle cultures was as much as five times the control rate and was significantly reduced by cycloheximide. ACh receptor degradation was un-

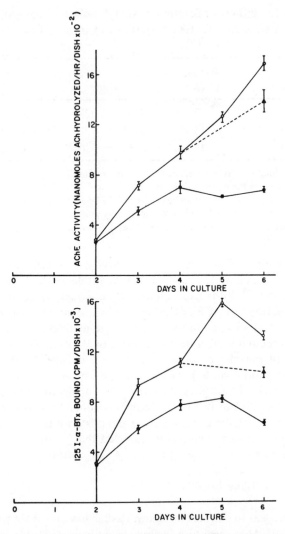

Figure 4. Effects of sciatin and sciatin withdrawal on ACh receptors and AChE during muscle differentiation. Myogenic cells were plated and maintained in the standard culture medium in the presence or absence of sciatin (25 μg/dish). At each time point, the cells were washed and labeled with $[^{125}I]\alpha$-Btx. Labeled cells were then washed, dissolved in 1.0 ml Tris, pH 7.2–1% Triton X-100, and an aliquot was counted in a γ counter. AChE activity was determined on a separate aliquot. Each point represents the mean ± SE of four determinations (●) Control, (○) sciatin, (▲) sciatin withdrawal after four days. Reproduced from reference 51 with permission.

affected by sciatin. Although the number of ACh receptors/dish was increased by sciatin during myogenesis, ACh receptor specific activity, expressed as fmoles of $[^{125}I]\alpha$-Btx bound/mg cell protein was only transiently increased by sciatin. This contrasted with AChE specific activity in sciatin-treated cultures which remained elevated throughout differentiation. Autoradiographs of $[^{125}I]\alpha$-Btx-labeled cultures showed that sciatin caused an increase in the number and size of ACh receptor clusters (Fig. 5) and maintained the integrity of these clusters in muscle cultures for up to 5 weeks in the absence of innervation. At this time, control cultures had completely degenerated. The mechanism by which sciatin enhanced the synthesis of ACh receptors appeared to be distinct from that of TTX, an agent which abolishes muscle contractions. The results suggested that sciatin may be related to the diffusible factor from motor neurons described by others which has trophic effects on ACh receptors.

2.4. Physiological Aspects of Sciatin

2.4.1. Concentration in Neural Tissues

Using the rocket immunoelectrophoretic technique (52), we have determined the concentrations of sciatin in adult chicken neural tissues. White

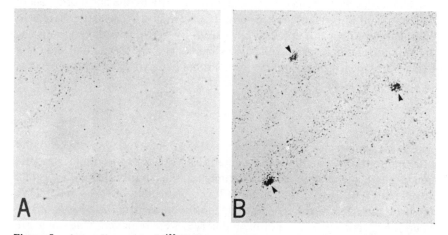

Figure 5. Autoradiography of $[^{125}I]$ACh receptor clusters in 5-day old cultures. Myogenic cells were maintained in the standard culture medium in the presence or absence of sciatin (25 μg/ml). After 5 days in culture, myotubes were washed, labeled with $[^{125}I]\alpha$-Btx, washed, and fixed in 4% paraformaldehyde–0.1% glutaraldehyde in cacodylate buffer, pH 7.2. Autoradiography was performed using NTB-2 emulsion for 5 days. (a) Control culture. (b) Sciatin-treated culture. Note the size, number, and density of hot spots (arrow heads) in the sciatin-treated culture. Reproduced from reference 51 with permission.

Leghorn chickens (28 weeks old) were killed by decapitation, and the cerebral hemispheres, spinal cord, and sciatic nerves were removed immediately. The tissues were homogenized in PBS (pH 7.2) containing protease inhibitors (10 µg/ml leupeptin, 2 TIU/ml aprotinin, 100 µg/ml antipain, and 10 mM EGTA). The homogenates were centrifuged at 40,000 g and the supernatants were assayed for sciatin by rocket immunoelectrophoresis. An average concentration of sciatin in the sciatic nerve, spinal cord, and cerebral hemisphere was 4.62, 2.38, and 0.44 µg/mg protein, respectively.

2.4.2. Localization

Using anti-sciatin serum, we investigated the distribution of sciatin in embryonic and adult chicken tissues by an unlabeled peroxidase-antiperoxidase (PAP) method (53) at the light microscopic level. The antiserum exclusively stained adult chicken neural tissues and cultured embryonic neurons (54). Staining was most intense in the cell bodies of ventral horn cells and the axoplasm of sciatic nerves (Fig. 6 and 7). Cerebral cortical neurons were stained weakly by the antiserum. No staining was apparent in oligodendrocytes, astrocytes, or Schwann cells. Non-neural tissues such as skeletal muscle, cardiac muscle, and liver were unstained by the antiserum. Cultured spinal cord neurons, cerebral cortical neurons, and sensory neurons from chick embryos were stained immunocytochemically by the antiserum. There was no reaction product seen in glial cells which were usually present in neuronal cultures or in cultured cells from liver, kidney, skeletal muscle, smooth muscle, and cardiac muscle. The results demonstrate that sciatin is exclusively localized in spinal cord neuronal perikarya and their processes *in vivo* and *in vitro*.

2.4.3. Axonal Transport and Release

White Leghorn chickens (28 weeks old) were anesthetized with Ketamine (100 mg/kg body weight) and the sciatic nerve was exposed under aseptic conditions. One sciatic nerve (experimental) was tightly tied with surgical silk thread (no. 5-0) at the midthigh level. The contralateral sciatic nerve (control) was left intact. At varying postoperative time intervals (6–24 hours), both control and experimental nerves were removed. One-cm nerve segments were taken proximal and distal to the ligature, and equivalent nerve segments were obtained from the corresponding control, contralateral sciatic nerves. The nerve segments were homogenized in PBS containing EGTA and protease inhibitors. The homogenates were centrifuged and the supernatants were assayed for sciatin by rocket immunoelectrophoresis. An average concentration of sciatin in control nerve segments was 25 µg per

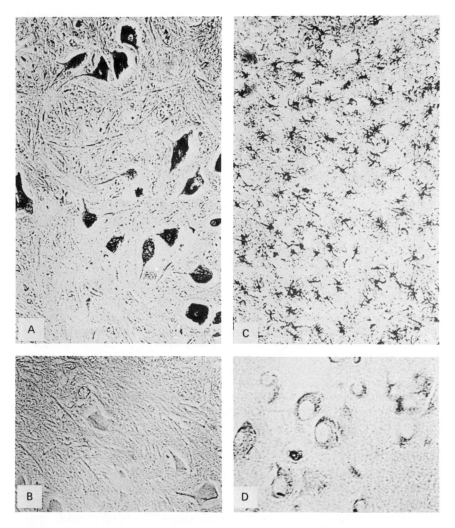

Figure 6. Light micrographs of sectioned neural tissues from adult chickens incubated with anti-sciatin serum or anti-human glial fibrillary acidic protein (GFAP) serum. (*a*) Motor neurons in the anterior horn of an ethanol-fixed spinal cord section incubated with 1:5000 rabbit anti-sciatin serum. Nomarski optics. (*b*) Control spinal cord section incubated with 1:1000 antiserum absorbed with excess sciatin. Nomarski optics. (*c*) Astrocytes in gray matter of an ethanol-fixed spinal cord incubated with 1:100 anti-GFAP serum. Nomarski optics. (*d*) Cerebral cortical neurons fixed in ethanol and incubated with 1:1000 anti-sciatin serum. Nomarski optics. Bar = 20 μm. Copyright 1981 by The Histochemical Society, Inc. Reproduced from reference 54 with permission.

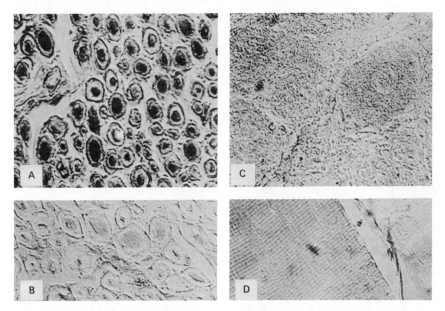

Figure 7. Light micrographs of sectioned tissues from adult chickens incubated with anti-sciatin serum. (*a*) Sciatic nerve fixed in aldehyde and incubated with 1:1000 anti-sciatin serum preabsorbed with chicken plasma acetone powder. Nomarski optics. (*b*) Control sciatic nerve incubated with 1:1000 preimmune serum. Nomarski optics. (*c*) Dorsal root ganglion neurons fixed in ethanol and incubated with 1:500 anti-sciatin serum preabsorbed with chicken plasma acetone powder. Nomarski optics. (*d*) Posterior latissimus dorsi muscle fixed in aldehyde and incubated with 1:1000 anti-sciatin serum. Nomarski optics. Bar = 10 μm. Copyright 1981 by The Histochemical Society, Inc. Reproduced from reference 54 with permission.

segment. Sciatin increased with time in both proximal and distal nerve segments close to the point of ligation. After 24 hours of nerve ligation, the concentration of sciatin was significantly increased in proximal nerve segments (652% of control; Fig. 8). The accumulation of sciatin in the distal nerve segments increased up to 12 hours (304% of control), but decreased slightly thereafter. Assuming that the linear rate of accumulation in the proximal nerve segments is a measure of net axonal transport and that sciatin is 100% mobile, the apparent rate of anterograde transport was estimated to be 59.8 mm/day.

A second group of adult chickens was killed by decapitation and the PLD muscles with their nerves were dissected and placed in 10 ml of oxygenated (95% O_2 and 5% CO_2) chicken Ringer solution. The nerve was stimulated supramaximally through platinum electrodes at 7–8 Hz for 15 minutes; the preparation was then allowed to rest for 5 minutes. The cycle of stimulation and rest was repeated at least three to four times. The contralateral PLD muscles were treated identically except that the nerve was not stimulated. The Ringer solutions conditioned by neurally stimulated and unstimulated PLD muscles were assayed for sciatin. In the solutions conditioned with stimulated and unstimulated PLD muscles, sciatin levels were 138 and 102 μg/muscle, respectively (55). The results suggest that sciatin may be released from presynaptic terminals by electrical stimulation.

2.5. Mechanism of Action of Sciatin on Muscle

2.5.1. Cyclic Nucleotides

Inasmuch as cyclic AMP has been known to regulate ACh receptors in muscle cultures (56), we investigated whether sciatin might act to regulate ACh receptors by increasing the intracellular concentration of cAMP (51). As shown in Table 3, both sciatin and theophylline, an inhibitor of phosphodiesterase, increased ACh receptors in treated muscle cultures. The concentration of cAMP was not significantly increased in cells treated with either sciatin or theophylline 3 days after treatment was initiated. However, the media conditioned by these cells did show a significant increase in the release of cAMP. Because the concentration of cAMP in conditioned media reflects the level of cAMP which is synthesized by and diffuses from the treated cells, sciatin must either increase the intracellular synthesis or decrease the degradation of cAMP. The results indicate that sciatin appears to influence the synthesis of ACh receptors by regulating the level of cyclic nucleotides

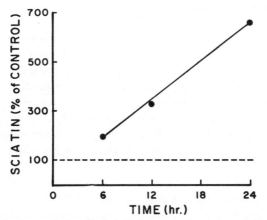

Figure 8. Relative accumulation of sciatin in the proximal segments of chicken sciatic nerves as a function of time (hours) after ligation. Sciatin was determined by rocket immunoelectrophoresis. Values represent the mean of four determinations.

Table 3.   Effect of Sciatin on cAMP and ACh Receptors

TREATMENT (DAY 4)	[^{125}I]α-Btx BOUND[a]	cAMP (DAY 7)	
		CELLS[b]	RELEASED INTO MEDIUM[c]
Control	3.8 ± 0.2	9.9 ± 0.8	2.8 ± 0.3
Sciatin (30μg)	5.4 ± 0.1[d] (+44)	12.4 ± 1.0	6.3 ± 0.5[d]
Theophylline (10^{-3} M)	4.7 ± 0.4 (+22)	9.2 ± 0.3	8.3 ± 0.7[d]

Source: From reference 51, with permission.

Cells were grown in standard culture medium for 4 days and sciatin or theophylline were added to cultures at this time. [^{125}I]α-Btx binding and cAMP were determined 72 hours later. All values represent the mean ± SE of 3 determinations.

[a] Expressed as CPM bound × 10^{-3}/dish. Values in parentheses indicate percentage increase over the control.

[b] Expressed as pmoles cAMP/dish.

[c] Expressed as pmoles cAMP accumulated/72 hours/ml conditioned culture medium.

[d] Value represents a significant increase ($p < 0.05$) over the control value.

in muscle cells. Recent evidence, however, showed that stimulation of protein synthesis by sciatin was not affected by theophylline (46). From these results, we conclude that although sciatin may increase ACh receptor synthesis by regulating cAMP, this action is not sciatin's only mechanism for regulating trophic responses in cultured muscle.

2.5.2.   Immunocytotoxicity

Sciatin has trophic effects similar to those of the trophic group of growth factors which includes nerve growth factor (NGF) and epidermal growth factor (EGF). One characteristic of this group of growth factors is that they mediate their trophic effects on their target tissues by binding to high affinity receptors located on the plasma membrane (57). Inasmuch as sciatin appears to be closely related to this group of growth factors, it is possible that it too elicits its trophic effects by binding to a membrane receptor. Our preliminary results suggest the presence of sciatin receptors on cultured muscle cells.

The reaction of specific antibody with antigens on the cell surface in the presence of complement may cause the death of the cell. When anti-sciatin serum was added to muscle cultures in the presence of complement, the muscle cells rapidly underwent degeneration (Fig. 9). This seems to suggest that anti-sciatin antibody binds to sciatin which is, in turn, bound to a

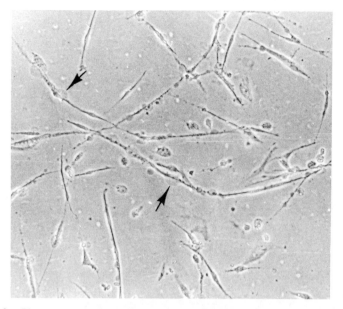

Figure 9. Phase contrast micrograph of muscle culture treated with anti-sciatin serum plus complement. Muscle culture (3-day-old) was treated with anti-sciatin serum (100 μl/dish) plus guinea pig complement (Miles, 1:10 diluted, 100 μl/dish) at 37°C for 30 minutes. Note extensively damaged muscle cells. Arrows indicate membrane blebs in young myotubes.

receptor. Thus it is this antibody–sciatin–receptor complex which is involved in the complement-mediated cytotoxicity.

2.5.3. Role in Myogenesis

By using antiserum against sciatin, we investigated the role of sciatin in myogenesis *in vitro* (58). Sciatin was found, using a double immunodiffusion assay, to be a component of chick embryo extract (EE), a constituent of culture medium required for differentiation of chick myogenic cells *in vitro*. The presence of sciatin in EE was further demonstrated by SDS-gel electrophoresis. When EE was separated into protein constituents by SDS-gel electrophoresis, the resulting gels showed the presence of a protein with an R_f identical to that of sciatin purified from adult sciatic nerves (Fig. 10). Furthermore, the protein precipitated from EE by anti-sciatin serum also migrated in a position identical to that of sciatin (Fig. 10).

Muscle cultures grown in the absence of EE showed no myotube formation and consisted of mononucleated myoblasts. The removal of sciatin from EE by immunoprecipitation with anti-sciatin serum also completely inhibited

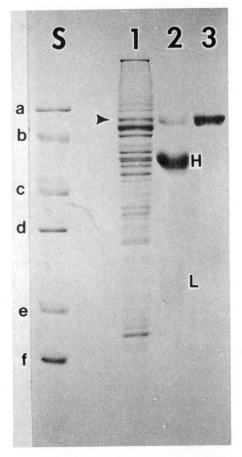

Figure 10. SDS-gel electrophoresis of chick embryo extract (EE), precipitated antigen–antibody complexes, and purified sciatin. Arrowhead indicates the position of sciatin. Lane 1, EE (25 μg). Lane 2, precipitated antigen–antibody complexes (23 μg) obtained by mixing EE and anti-sciatin serum (vol/vol); H, heavy chains of IgG (MW 50,000); L. light chains of IgG (MW 25,000). Lane 3, purified sciatin (5 μg). Lane S, molecular weight standards: (a) phosphorylase B (94,000); (b) albumin (67,000); (c) ovalbumin (43,000); (d) carbonic anhydrase (30,000); (e) trypsin inhibitor (20,100); (f) α-lactalbumin (14,400). Reproduced from 59.

myogenesis (Fig. 11). By contrast, muscle cultures grown in media in which EE had been absorbed with preimmune serum exhibited mature my-otubes. Furthermore, when sciatin was added to the sciatin-absorbed culture medium, normal myogenesis ensued. Finally, myogenic cells underwent normal myogenesis in the absence of EE if sciatin was added to the culture medium. These results demonstrate that sciatin is the component of EE required for myogenesis and that this myotrophic protein influences the initial differentiation of chick myogenic cells *in vitro*.

2.5.4. Phosphorylation

The phosphorylation of certain muscle proteins by endogeneous kinases appears to be under neural control. Denervation causes a significant decrease in the phosphorylation of the H2A histone subfraction in the regenerating forelimb of the newt (59). Inasmuch as sciatin has been shown to cause an increase in muscle cAMP (51), and cAMP produces many, if not all, of its effects by stimulating the phosphorylation of cell proteins (60), it may be that sciatin influences muscle phenotypic expression by controlling protein phosphorylation.

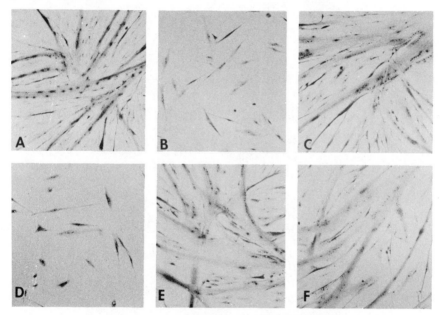

Preliminary results indicate that muscle cultures treated with sciatin phosphorylate a protein of molecular weight 35,000 which is not apparent in muscle cells grown in the absence of the myotrophic protein (61). Therefore, it appears that sciatin may selectively promote the *de novo* synthesis and/or phosphorylation of a cytosolic protein. The function of this protein is as yet unknown.

2.5.5.   Antibodies in Muscle Development

Inasmuch as sciatin has been shown to promote the morphological maturation and maintenance of aneural muscle cells in culture in the absence

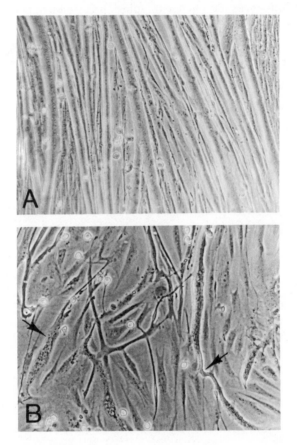

Figure 12.   Effects of complement-free anti-sciatin serum on muscle culture. (*A*) Nine-day-old muscle culture treated 48 hours with preimmune serum (diluted 1:100). (*B*) Nine-day old muscle culture treated 48 hours with anti-sciatin serum (diluted 1:100). Arrows indicate degenerated myotubes.

of innervation, we investigated whether anti-sciatin antibodies could produce degeneration of muscle *in vitro*. The anti-sciatin serum was added to cross-striated myotube cultures and the cultures were observed daily under a phase-contrast Zeiss Invertoscope. After 48 hours of incubation, control muscle cultures and cultures treated with preimmune serum showed no morphological abberations (Fig. 12). By contrast, muscle cultures treated with antiserum showed degenerated myotubes; cross striations disappeared, and myotubes became thinner and shorter (Fig. 12).

We also investigated the effect of anti-sciatin antibodies on muscle development *in ovo* (62). Goat anti-sciatin immunoglobulin G (IgG) was applied daily to the chorioallantoic membrane through an opening in the shell of 6-day old Peking duck embryos. Each injection contained 1 mg IgG dissolved in 100 μl of sterile saline. Control embryos were injected daily with equal amounts of preimmune goat IgG. On day 15–23 of incubation, embryonic motility and total body weight were determined in the anti-sciatin-treated and the preimmune-treated control embryos. Embryonic motility was measured by counting spontaneous movement for 5 minutes.

As shown in Table 4, the total body weight of the anti-sciatin-treated embryos was greatly reduced as compared to that of the control embryos. However, weights of individual organs (e.g., brain and liver) in the anti-sciatin-treated embryos were not significantly different from those of the control embryos (data not shown). Inasmuch as skeletal muscle is considered to be the largest tissue in the embryos, the decreased total body weight may reflect a decrease in the muscle of the anti-sciatin-treated embryos. Table 4 also shows that embryonic motility was markedly reduced in the anti-sciatin-treated embryos as compared to that in the controls. Furthermore, the survival rate of the anti-sciatin-treated embryos was significantly lower by 30% as compared to that of the controls (62).

Table 4.   Effects of Anti-Sciatin Antibodies on Duck Embryos[a]

TREATMENT	IgG DOSES OF DAILY INJECTION (mg)	TREATMENT INTERVALS	TOTAL BODY WEIGHT (g)[b]	SPONTANEOUS MOTILITY (LEG MOVEMENTS/ MINUTE)[c]
Preimmune IgG	1	6–22	27.8	18.1
Anti-sciatin IgG	1	6–22	22.1 (79)	12.8 (71)

Source: Previously unpublished data by G. S. Sohal, T. H. Oh, and G. J. Markelonis.
[a] Indicates mean of 10 embryos. Values in parentheses indicate percentage of control value.
[b] Determined on day 23.
[c] Determined on day 15.

Preliminary electron microscopic examinations revealed that anti-sciatin-treated muscles were composed in large proportion of mononucleated myoblasts and myotubes whereas control muscles were composed primarily of myofibers although a few myotubes were seen. These observations indicate that anti-sciatin antibodies prevent or delay muscle development and that sciatin plays an important role in the differentiation of muscle cells *in vivo*.

2.6.   Relationship of Sciatin to Serum Transferrin

2.6.1.   Structure

As sciatin was found to have certain structural similarities to chicken serum transferrin, we have further investigated the physicochemical characteristics of sciatin in order to determine the relationship between these two proteins (45). Using the purification procedure developed for sciatin, we purified transferrin from chicken serum and found that it migrated to a position identical to that of sciatin on SDS-gel electrophoresis (Fig. 13). Sciatin was found to be strikingly similar to serum transferrin in amino acid composition (Table 5). The biggest differences between sciatin and

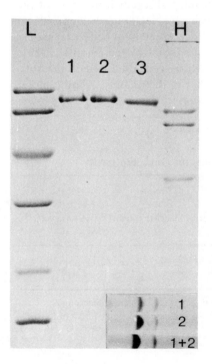

Figure 13.   SDS-gel electrophoresis of serum transferrin, ovotransferrin, and sciatin. Lane 1, sciatin (10 μg). Lane 2, serum transferrin (10 μg). Lane 3, ovotransferrin (10 μg). Lane H and L, high and low molecular weight standards (Pharmacia). (*Inset*) Isoelectric focusing of sciatin and serum transferrin. Lane 1, sciatin. Lane 2, serum transferrin. Lane 1 + 2, sciatin plus serum transferrin. The major peak has an isoelectric point (pI) of 5.75.

Table 5. Amino Acid Compositions of Chicken Serum Transferrin and Sciatin

	RESIDUES/MOLECULE	
AMINO ACID	SCIATIN[a]	SERUM TRANSFERRIN[a]
Lysine	56	56
Histidine	11	11
Arginine	33	34
Aspartic acid	77	76
Threonine	35	36
Serine	50	45
Glutamic acid	64	68
Proline	26	29
Glycine	54	52
Alanine	53	52
Half-cystine	28[b]	27[b]
Valine	32	43
Methionine	8	7
Isoleucine	30	17
Leucine	49	45
Tyrosine	14	20
Phenylalanine	20	24
Tryptophan[c]	ND	ND
Total	640	642

Source: Modified from reference 45, with permission.
[a] Values represent nearest integers to the average of duplicate 24- and 72-hour determinations. Calculations based on a molecular weight of 74,000.
[b] Determined as cysteic acid.
[c] Not determined (ND).

serum transferrin were found in the number of valine and tyrosine residues. Both were present in sciatin in only 60% the amount found in the transferrin molecule. This probably cannot be explained by experimental variations alone. Other differences, such as those found with serine or isoleucine, are also probably significant. In addition, in the presence of bicarbonate, sciatin bound approximately 2 mol of ferrous iron/mol protein. From these data, we conclude that sciatin is a growth-promoting polypeptide closely related structurally to serum transferrin.

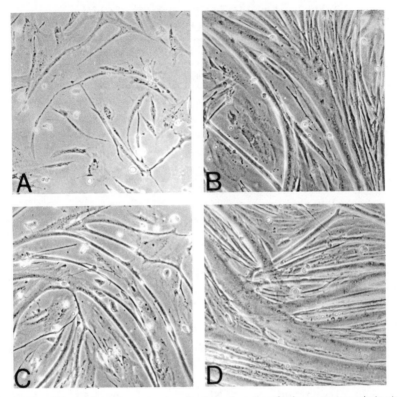

Figure 14. Effects of sciatin, serum transferrin, and ovotransferrin on myogenesis *in vitro*. For the first 24 hours, all cultures were maintained in standard culture medium. Thereafter, cultures were grown in a medium containing no chick embryo extract (EE) but supplemented with proteins for four days. (*A*) Muscle culture grown in the absence of EE. (*B*) Muscle culture grown in the absence of EE but supplemented with sciatin (30 μg/ml). (*C*) Muscle culture grown in the absence of EE but supplemented with ovotransferrin (30 μg/ml). (*D*) Muscle culture grown in the absence of EE but supplemented with serum transferrin (30 μg/ml).

2.6.2. Immunological Reactivity

Structural similarities between sciatin and serum transferrin were further demonstrated by immunological reactivity. Chicken serum transferrin cross reacted with anti-sciatin serum upon either rocket immunoelectrophoresis (45) or double immunodiffusion (64). Human transferrin, chicken albumin, chicken immunoglobulin G, and chicken hemoglobin failed to cross react with anti-sciatin serum.

2.6.3. Biological Activities

Inasmuch as sciatin is structurally related to serum transferrin, we investigated the muscle growth-promoting activity of transferrin on cultured chick muscle cells. Purified serum transferrin had myotrophic effects identical to those of sciatin when added to muscle cultures (63). Both sciatin and serum transferrin caused a significant increase in the level of protein synthesis, the number of ACh receptors, and AChE activity in treated muscle cultures. When chick embryo extract (a constituent normally required for myogenesis) was omitted from culture media, either serum transferrin or sciatin promoted myogenesis in culture (Fig. 14). By contrast, commercially obtained ovo-transferrin (conalbumin) or $FeSO_4$ (100 μM) were unable to fully support myogenesis of muscle cells *in vitro* if embryo extract was omitted from the culture medium. From these results, we conclude that sciatin is both structurally and biologically related to serum transferrin. Furthermore, we suggest that sciatin may represent a neuronal form of this iron-transport protein.

3. OTHER MUSCLE TROPHIC FACTORS

There is evidence that a variety of substances are conveyed throughout the length of nerve axons by axonal transport. It has been postulated that one or more of these substances may be released to muscle and may exert trophic influences (64). Various substances, including neuronal proteins are released into the medium during nerve stimulation of nerve–muscle preparations (65). The suggestion that substances transported by axonal flow might have trophic activity on muscle has been derived primarily from experiments using two different approaches: (i) chronic application of colchicine (a drug known to block axonal transport) to motor nerves causes denervationlike changes in muscle membranes without affecting ACh transmission and consequent muscle activity (66–68), and (ii) substances moved by axonal transport and released by nerve stimulation increase muscle AChE activity in organ culture (30). Furthermore, substances that increase muscle AChE activity appear to be released from synaptic vesicles along with ACh.

Inasmuch as trophic effects are long-term interactions influencing many properties of the muscle, the existence of a single trophic substance seems unlikely. In the past several years, in fact, many trophic substances have been isolated and partially purified (Table 6). These trophic substances appear to be proteins with various molecular weights.

Lentz et al. (69) have identified and partially purified a basic protein from rat brains which has a trophic effect on muscle AChE activity. Addition of the protein to adult newt muscle in organ culture increases muscle AChE activity. This basic protein has a molecular weight of 34,000 daltons. Rathbone et al. (70) have also reported a small protein (molecular weight < 20,000) from chick embryo brains which has an identical trophic effect on muscle AChE activity in newt muscle cultures.

Table 6. Muscle Trophic Factors

Source	Molecular Weight	Target Muscle Culture	Trophic Activity	References
Rat brain	34,000	Adult newt	AChE activity	69
Chicken brain and liver	$\geq$ 5,000	Chick embryo	DNA synthesis	32
Chicken ischiatic-peroneal nerve	80,000	Chick embryo	DNA synthesis	71
Chicken serum	80,000	Chick embryo	Myogenesis	81
Chicken brain	< 20,000	Adult newt	AChE activity	70
Mouse spinal cord	< 10,000	Adult mouse	TTX sensitivity	72
Chicken brain and spinal cord	< 2,000	Chick embryo	ACh receptor synthesis and clusters	34
Rat embryo spinal cord	100,000	Rat L_6 clone	ACh receptors and clusters	33
Conditioned medium from neuroblastoma-glioma cells	> 150,000	Rat embryo	ACh receptor aggregation	77
Conditioned medium from rat embryo spinal cord cultures	> 50,000	Rat embryo	ACh receptor aggregation	78

Jabaily and Singer (32) found that chick embryonic brain and liver extracts are most effective in promoting proliferation of chick myogenic cells in culture. They also found the presence of two proteins in these extracts, one of high molecular weight ($>$ 5000) and one of low molecular weight ($<$ 5000), both of which must be present to produce full mitogenic activity. Recently, Popiela and Ellis (71) have identified and partially purified an 80,000 dalton protein from chicken ischiatic-peroneal nerves which has a mitogenic effect on chick muscle cells in culture. Considering the tissue source as well as the molecular size of the protein, it may be that this protein is similar to sciatin. However, whether this protein is identical to sciatin which is similar to serum transferrin is yet to be determined.

Kuromi and Hasegawa (28, 29) have shown that mouse spinal cord extracts reverse the postdenervation decrease in TTX sensitivity of action potentials in organ-cultured mouse muscle. The active agent in the extract is a protein with a molecular weight of less than 10,000 (72). Furthermore, this protein promotes the development of TTX-sensitive sodium channels in cultured rat embryo muscle (73). Kano et al. (74) also reported that crude nerve extracts from chick embryos promote the development of TTX-sensitive channels in chick embryonic muscle cells in culture.

Factors present in neural extracts or in media conditioned by neurons have been shown to increase both the number of ACh receptors and the number of receptor clusters in cultures of embryonic muscle. Cohen and Fischbach (75) demonstrated that spinal cord explants release a diffusible factor into the culture medium which increases the density of $[^{125}I]\alpha$-Btx binding sites on co-cultured myotubes. The increase in ACh receptors occurs in a gradient fashion with the highest density of receptors occurring on myotubes located close to the spinal cord explant. Podleski et al. (33) reported that extracts of rat embryo spinal cord increase the number of ACh receptors and receptor clusters in the rat L_6 line of cloned muscle cells. They partially characterized a diffusible factor and found it to be a protein with a molecular weight of approximately 100,000. Jessell et al. (34) also demonstrated that extracts of chick embryo brain and spinal cord increase the number of ACh receptors and receptor clusters in chick muscle cultures. The active component of the extracts appears to be a small peptide with an estimated molecular weight of 2000. Medium conditioned by hybrid neuroblastoma-glioma cells increases the aggregation of ACh receptors into definable clusters on mouse, rat, or chick muscle cells in culture (76). The factor produced by these cells is a protein with a molecular weight greater than 150,000 daltons (77). Schaffner and Daniels (78) also reported a protein with a molecular weight greater than 50,000 released by cultured spinal cord neurons of rat embryos which increases receptor aggregation in rat muscle cultures. Recently, Kalcheim et al. (79) demonstrated that extracts of rat embryonic brain contain a factor that stimulates the aggregation of ACh receptors, as well as synthesis, secretion, and conversion of collagen in cultured rat muscle cells. Thus it is possible that collagen accumulation induced by factors present in neural extracts or released by cultured neurons may be involved in the induction of ACh receptor aggregation in cultured muscle cells.

Hagiwara et al. (80) have recently purified a protein of molecular weight 80,000 from chicken serum which has growth-promoting effects upon cultured chick muscle cells. This serum protein, myotrophic factor (MTF), was shown to be serum transferrin, as evidenced by its co-migration with transferrin on SDS-gel electrophoresis, by immunological cross reactivity of anti-MTF serum with transferrin, and by iron-binding studies (81). Furthermore, Hasegawa et al. (82) reported that ferric iron (10–100 μM) also could duplicate the growth-promoting activity of transferrin on myogenesis *in vitro*. Although our results on the myotrophic effects of chicken serum transferrin are consistent with the findings of Kimura et al. (81), we found that $FeSO_4$ (100 μM) could not simply duplicate the effect of either transferrin or sciatin on myogenesis *in vitro* in the absence of chick embryo extract (63).

4.   CONCLUDING REMARKS

We have isolated and purified sciatin from chicken sciatic nerves. This glycoprotein exerts many trophic effects on cultured chick muscle cells. This myotrophic protein is structurally very similar to serum transferrin. Recent immunocytochemical studies revealed that sciatin is localized in the cell bodies of spinal cord neurons and the axoplasm of sciatic nerves. Immunoprecipitation studies demonstrate that sciatin plays an important role in the normal differentiation of chick muscle *in vitro* as well as *in vivo*. Preliminary studies indicate that sciatin is transported by anterograde axonal flow in chicken sciatic nerves and is released from chicken nerve–muscle preparations by electrical stimulation. In view of its pronounced biological effects on muscle and its structural relationship to serum transferrin, sciatin appears to be related to the "trophic" group of growth factors which include NGF and EGF. Furthermore, sciatin may represent a neuronal form of the iron-transport protein, transferrin.

Although we have clearly demonstrated the trophic effects of sciatin on cultured muscle and its presence in the motor nerve, we still have not demonstrated that this protein has similar physiological functions *in vivo*. For example, whether sciatin is transported to the muscle and then serves trophic functions is not yet known. This may prove to be a difficult problem to approach experimentally. However, this step is essential for the definitive proof of the "trophic substances" hypothesis.

As regards other muscle trophic factors, several neurally derived substances, unrelated to impulse activities, have been shown to regulate many properties of muscle including AChE activity, ACh receptors, and differentiation. However, the biochemical characterization of these putative trophic substances has not been fully accomplished. As Gutmann (2) has noted, until these substances are purified and characterized completely, our understanding of the nature of trophic influence will be incomplete.

ACKNOWLEDGMENTS

This work was supported by the National Institutes of Health (NS 15013, T.H.O.; NS 16076, G.J.M.) and the Muscular Dystrophy Association (T.H.O.). The authors thank Ms. F. Spaven, Mr. G. Holm, and Ms. T. Dion-Guidera for technical assistance and Mrs. E. DeLong for preparation of the manuscript.

REFERENCES

1. Guth, L., *Physiol. Rev.*, **48**, 645 (1968).
2. Gutmann, E., *Ann. Rev. Physiol.*, **38**, 177 (1976).
3. Singer, M., *Am. Zool.*, **18**, 829 (1978).
4. Zelena, J., in E. Gutmann, Ed., *The Denervated Muscle*, Publ. House Czechoslovak Academy of Science, Prague, 1962.
5. Engel, W. K., and Karpati, G., *Dev. Biol.*, **17**, 713 (1968).
6. Schafiq, S. A., Siedu, S. A., and Milhorat, A. T., *Exp. Neurol.*, **35**, 529 (1972).
7. Hanzlikova, V., and Schiaffino, S., *Z. Zellforsch.*, **147**, 75 (1973).
8. Sohal, G. S., and Holt, R. K., *Cell Tissue Res.*, **210**, 383 (1980).
9. Popiela, H., *Exp. Neurol.*, **53**, 214 (1976).
10. Albuquerque, E. X., Schuh, F. T., and Kauffman, F. C., *Pflug. Arch.*, **328**, 36 (1971).
11. Albuquerque, E. X., and Thesleff, S., *Acta Physiol. Scand.*, **73**, 471 (1968).
12. Redfern, P., Lundh, H., and Thesleff, S., *Eur. J. Pharmacol.*, **11**, 263 (1970).
13. Axelsson, J., and Thesleff, S., *J. Physiol. (Lond.)*, **149**, 178 (1959).
14. Miledi, R., *J. Physiol. (Lond.)*, **151**, 24 (1960).
15. Hartzell, H. C., and Fambrough, D. M., *J. Gen. Physiol.*, **60**, 248 (1972).
16. Guth, L., Albers, R. W., and Brown, W. C., *Exp. Neurol.*, **10**, 236 (1964).
17. Gutmann, E., and Zelena, J., in E. Gutmann, Ed., *The Denervated Muscle*, Publ. House Czechoslovak Academy of Science, Prague, 1961.
18. Fischbach, G. D., and Robbins, N., *J. Neurophysiol.*, **34**, 562 (1971).
19. Lomo, T., and Rosenthal, J., *J. Physiol. (Lond.)*, **221**, 439 (1972).
20. Drachman, D. B., and Witzke, F., *Science*, **176**, 514 (1972).
21. Thesleff, S., *J. Physiol. (Lond.)*, **151**, 598 (1960).

22. Drachman, D. B., *Ann. N.Y. Acad. Sci.*, **228**, 160 (1974).
23. Guth, L., and Albuquerque, E. X., in A. Mauro, Ed., *Muscle Regeneration*, Raven, New York, 1979.
24. Lebowitz, P., and Singer, M., *Nature (Lond.)*, **225**, 824 (1970).
25. Singer, M., *Ann. N.Y. Acad. Sci.*, **228**, 308 (1974).
26. Lentz, T. L., *Science*, **171**, 187 (1971).
27. Lentz, T. L., *Exp. Neurol.*, **45**, 520 (1974).
28. Kuromi, H., and Hasegawa, *Brain Res.*, **100**, 178 (1975).
29. Hasegawa, S., and Kuromi, H., *Brain Res.*, **119**, 133 (1977).
30. Younkin, S. G., Brett, R. S., Davey, B., and Younkin, L. H., *Science*, **200**, 1292 (1978).
31. Popiela, H., *Exp. Neurol.*, **62**, 405 (1978).
32. Jabaily, J., and Singer, M., *Dev. Biol.*, **64**, 189 (1978).
33. Podleski, T. R., Axelrod, D., Ravdin, P., Greenberg, I., Johnson, M. M., and Salpeter, M. M., *Proc. Natl. Acad. Sci. USA*, **75**, 2035 (1978).
34. Jessell, T. M., Siegel, R. E., and Fischbach, G. D., *Proc. Natl. Acad. Sci. USA*, **76**, 5397 (1979).
35. Oh, T. H., Johnson, D. D., and Kim, S. U., *Science*, **178**, 1298 (1972).
36. Oh, T. H., *Exp. Neurol.*, **46**, 432 (1975).
37. Oh, T. H., *Exp. Neurol.*, **50**, 376 (1976).
38. Markelonis, G. J., and Oh, T. H., *Exp. Neurol.*, **58**, 285 (1978).
39. Oh, T. H., and Markelonis, G. J., *Science*, **200**, 337 (1978).
40. Oh, T. H., and Markelonis, G. J., in A. Mauro, Ed., *Muscle Regeneration*, Raven, New York, 1979.
41. Markelonis, G. J., and Oh, T. H., *Proc. Natl. Acad. Sci. USA*, **76**, 2470 (1979).
42. Markelonis, G. J., Kemerer, V. F., and Oh, T. H., *J. Biol. Chem.*, **255**, 8967 (1980).
43. Drachman, D. B., in A. M. Goldberg and I. Hanin, Eds., *Biology of Cholinergic Function*, Raven, New York, 1976.
44. Markelonis, G. J., and Oh, T. H., *J. Neurochem.*, **37**, 95 (1981).
45. Markelonis, G. J., Bradshaw, R. A., Oh, T. H., Johnson, J. L., and Bates, O. J., *J. Neurochem.*, **39**, 315 (1982).
46. Markelonis, G. J., Oh, T. H., and Derr, D., *Exp. Neurol.*, **70**, 598 (1980).
47. Goodwin, B. C., and Sizer, I. W., *Science*, **148**, 242 (1965).
48. Tomkins, G. M., Gelehrter, T. D., Granner, D., Martin, D., Jr., Samuels, H. H., and Thompson, E. B., *Science*, **166**, 1474 (1969).
49. Tomkins, G. M., Levinson, B. B., Baxter, J. D., and Dethlefsen, L., *Nature (New Biol.)*, **239**, 9 (1972).
50. Max, S. R., and Oh, T. H., *Exp. Neurol.*, **55**, 493 (1977).
51. Markelonis, G. J., Oh, T. H., Eldefrawi, M. E., and Guth, L., *Dev. Biol.*, **89**, 353 (1982).
52. Laurell, C. B., *Anal. Biochem.*, **15**, 45 (1966).
53. Sternberger, L. A., *Immunocytochemistry*, 2nd ed., Wiley, New York, 1979.
54. Oh, T. H., Sofia, C. A., Kim, Y. C., Carroll, C., Kim, H. H., Markelonis, G. J., and Reier, P. J., *J. Histochem. Cytochem.*, **29**, 1205 (1981).
55. Oh, T. H., Pumplin, D. W., and Markelonis, G. J., unpublished data.

56. Blosser, J. C., and Appel, S. H., *J. Biol. Chem.*, **255**, 1235 (1980).

57. Bradshaw, R. A., *Ann. Rev. Biochem.*, **47**, 191 (1978).

58. Oh, T. H., and Markelonis, G. J., *Proc. Natl. Acad. Sci. USA*, **77**, 6922 (1980).

59. Kelly, C. M., and Singer, M., *Dev. Biol.*, **81**, 366 (1981).

60. Greengard, P., *Science*, **199**, 146 (1978).

61. Markelonis, G. J., Johnson, D. D., and Oh, T. H., unpublished data.

62. Sohal, G. S., Oh, T. H., and Markelonis, G. J., unpublished data.

63. Oh, T. H., and Markelonis, G. J., *J. Neurosci. Res.*, **8**, 535 (1982).

64. Ochs, S., *Science*, **176**, 252 (1972).

65. Musick, J., and Hubbard, J. I., *Nature (Lond.)*, **237**, 279 (1972).

66. Albuquerque, E. X., Warnick, J. E., Tasse, J. R., and Sansone, F. M., *Exp. Neurol.*, **37**, 607 (1972).

67. Hofmann, W. W., and Thesleff, S., *Eur. J. Pharmacol.*, **20**, 256 (1972).

68. Warnick, J. E., Albuquerque, E. X., and Guth, L., *Exp. Neurol.*, **57**, 622 (1977).

69. Lentz, T. L., Addis, J. S., and Chester, J., *Exp. Neurol.*, **73**, 542 (1981).

70. Rathbone, M. P., Vickers, J. D., and Logan, D. M., *J. Exp. Zool.*, **210**, 463 (1979).

71. Popiela, H., and Ellis, S., *Dev. Biol.*, **83**, 266 (1981).

72. Kuromi, H., Gonoi, T., and Hasegawa, S., *Brain Res.*, **175**, 109 (1979).

73. Kuromi, H., Gonoi, T., and Hasegawa, S., *Dev. Brain Res.*, **1**, 369 (1981).

74. Kano, M., Suzuki, N., and Ozima, H., *J. Cell. Physiol.*, **99**, 327 (1979).

75. Cohen, S. A., and Fischbach, G. D., *Dev. Biol.*, **59**, 24 (1977).

76. Christian, C. N., Daniels, M. P., Sugiyama, H., Vogel, Z., Jacques, L., and Nelson, P. G., *Proc. Natl. Acad. Sci. USA*, **75**, 4011 (1978).

77. Bauer, H. C., Daniels, M. P., Pudimat, P. A., Jacques, L., Sugiyama, H., and Christian, C. N., *Brain Res.*, **209**, 395 (1981).

78. Schaffner, A. E., and Daniels, M. P., *J. Neurosci.*, **2**, 623 (1982).

79. Kalcheim, C., Vogel, Z., and Duksin, D., *Proc. Natl. Acad. Sci. USA*, **79**, 3077 (1982).

80. Hagiwara, Y., Kimura, I., and Ozawa, E., *Dev. Growth Different.*, **23**, 249 (1981).

81. Kimura, I., Hasegawa, T., Miura, T., and Ozawa, E., *Proc. Japan Acad.*, **57**, 200 (1981).

82. Hasegawa, T., Saito, K., Kimura, I., and Ozawa, E., *Proc. Japan Acad.*, **57**, 206 (1981).

4

TUMOR AND RELATED ANGIOGENESIS FACTORS

Allan Fenselau

CONTENTS

Abbreviations

CAM	Chorioallantoic membrane
PA	Plasminogen activator
LIA	Lymphocyte-induced angiogenesis
GVH	Graft-versus-host
PDGF	Platelet-derived growth factor
EGF	Epidermal growth factor
PG	Prostaglandin
FGF	Fibroblast growth factor
ECM	Extracellular matrix

1. INTRODUCTION

Tumor angiogenesis, or the process by which solid malignancies induce new vessel growth from surrounding host tissues, is well documented and universally accepted as another vital marker of the neoplastic state. Less well understood are the mechanistic and biochemical details of this process. Although tumor angiogenesis factor(s) no longer deserves to be placed in quotation marks, questions about its(their) identity and mode(s) of action still remain. This review seeks to provide a basis for examining these questions, whose answers will permit control of this process and, consequently, tumor growth and spread.

The focus of this review is on the chemical and cellular participants in angiogenesis—tumor-related and unrelated. The reason for failing to make a critical discrimination between tumor angiogenesis and other, nontumor angiogenesis is that presently it is debatable whether tumor angiogenesis occurs by means of its own unique pathway or merely utilizes existing physiological pathways, such as are found in inflammation and wound repair. Unclear is whether tumor angiogenesis factors operate directly on host endothelium to produce neovascularization or indirectly by first recruiting bona fide angiogenic cells which, in turn, direct their own factors to producing neovascularization. Possibly both of these mechanisms are involved simultaneously. The number and kind of angiogenesis factors derived from a given tumor as well as their relation to comparable factors from other tumors or cells also are still matters of conjecture. Given these uncertainties it seems appropriate to review tumor angiogenesis factors in as broad a context as possible.

The topics discussed in this review include, first, a brief overview of tumor angiogenesis with emphasis on the importance of better understanding this process. Then the distinct stages of angiogenesis are outlined, in order to introduce the various bioassays now in use for identifying cellular and specific chemical mediators of the process. Finally, angiogenic roles are examined for cells that can interact with tumor or tumor-derived materials and for chemical factors from tumor and nontumor sources. Other perspectives on tumor angiogenesis can be obtained from several recent and excellent reviews (1–8), all of which attest to the considerable gains in the understanding of this process that have occurred during the past decade.

2. HISTORY AND SIGNIFICANCE OF TUMOR ANGIOGENESIS

The foundations for the present advances in tumor angiogenesis were put in place by so vast a number of investigators that only the efforts of a few can be highlighted. The earliest published observations on tumor vasculature date to the midnineteenth century and described the altered and characteristic vascular network about solid malignancies (9–11). At the turn of the twentieth century separate studies by Ribbert (12), Goldmann (13), and Russell (14) detailed the irregular and tortuous vessel pattern about the tumor and in the adjacent tissue. Such findings found subsequent value as an indication of the presence of a tumor. At that time Goldmann also came to the profound conclusion that tumors can promote vessel growth and that the new vasculature correspondingly promotes tumor growth (13).

The validity of these reciprocally related concepts was repeatedly confirmed by later experimental studies on the dynamics of this interaction between solid malignancies and host vasculature. Direct observation of angiogenesis under controlled conditions, followed up by histologic examination, was first afforded by the use of the transparent chamber technique in a variety of animal models (15). From this prototype have evolved the present-day angiogenesis assays, which are described in detail later. Of interest now are the results of these earlier studies that documented the role of vessel growth and the resulting vasculature in controlling tumor growth and spread. These findings justify the present efforts to determine the mechanisms for tumor control of vessel growth.

Algire and his co-workers (16–20), by quantitating the vascular level about tumors whose growth could be observed in a transparent chamber on a mouse skin flap, concluded that "the rapid growth of tumor transplants is dependent upon the development of a rich vascular supply" (16). The vascular supply to the various mouse mammary gland carcinomas and sarcomas used in these studies was continuously elicited beginning within 3 days of implantation and was characterized by its higher vessel density (compared to surrounding connective tissue) and its poor state of differentiation. These conclusions have been verified in similar studies with rats (21, 22), hamsters (23, 24), and rabbits (25, 26).

However, studies on spontaneous tumors (17, 27) and more slowly growing tumor implants (18) in experimental animals revealed that tumor vascular density need not exceed that seen in the surrounding connective tissue. In fact, when tumors are categorized according to type and vasculature, a spectrum of tumors is found, ranging from the highly vascularized (*endothelial-rich*) glioblastomas to the poorly vascularized (*endothelial-poor*) chondrosarcomas (28). The impression regarding the vascularity of tumor tissue seems to be similar to that for normal tissue: vascularity is directly proportional to metabolic activity. The increased metabolic needs of the faster growing tumor appear to be linked to an essential blood-borne nutrient, oxygen. Support for this comes from several studies, most notably Tannock's (29, 30), that find an excellent correlation between oxygen diffusion length of 85–210 μm and the distance between capillaries and the interface between live and dead tumor cells. The significance of oxygen in the angiogenic process is considered later.

The most graphic demonstrations of the ability of vessel growth to control tumor growth are those in which tumor neovascularization is prevented as a consequence of choice of implant site. Growth of tumor mass can be restricted to a spheroid of 2–3 mm diameter when tumor is implanted in soft agar (31), perfused thyroid or intestinal segments (32) (where new vessel growth has been compromised due to extensive degeneration of capillary endothelium), and avascular regions of the eye, the anterior (33) or vitreous (34) chambers. That these implants were suspended in a dormant, non-necrotic state was shown by histologic examinations of the spheroids and by transfer of the spheroids to sites where vascularization could occur. For example, in the eye studies placement of the dormant tumor mass in contact with the retina resulted in an explosive growth of the tumor (35). These results led Folkman to the concept of antiangiogenesis, or the inhibition of angiogenesis, as a plausible therapeutic approach to the treatment of solid malignancies (36).

Folkman and his colleagues tested the hypothesis of antiangiogenic control of tumor growth with two substances, a cartilage-derived factor (37, 38) and protamine (39). Regional infusion of the partially purified cartilage extract inhibited tumor growth in two implant systems: the V2 carcinoma in the rabbit cornea and the B16 melanoma on mouse subconjunctiva (38). Inasmuch as the cartilage extract did not alter the growth properties of either tumor cell type in cell culture, the effects are best understood in terms of an inhibition of angiogenesis. The protamine studies (39) both confirmed these observations on tumor angiogenesis and extended them to other types of angiogenesis. Protamine inhibited vessel growth during embryonic development on the chicken chorioallantoic membrane (CAM) or vessel growth induced in rabbit corneas by implants of inflammatory agents or lymph node fragments. Inhibition of tumor angiogenesis accounted for the retarded growth of lung metastases of Lewis lung carcinoma and B16 melanoma in mice, and of Walker 256 carcinoma in rat. On the other hand, subcutaneous implants of the mouse tumors were generally refractory to protamine treatment. These studies reveal the promise of antiangiogenesis therapy and, perhaps, have yielded a glimpse of its limitations. Whether antiangiogenic therapies will succeed in the treatment of all or only a few tumors and whether the correlation between vessel growth and tumor growth will hold in all cases are matters for which judgment is still pending. Clearly, growth of numerous tumors is controlled by the attending vasculature, in some instances in a most dramatic manner. These solid tumors, whose growth is most clearly linked to the attending vasculature, represent excellent candidates for testing antiangiogenic therapies.

A better understanding of tumor angiogenesis has implications for diagnosis as well as therapy. The most impressive diagnostic studies to date are those of Gullino and co-workers, who have demonstrated the value of the angiogenic capacity associated with mammary tissue in evaluating the risk for malignancy (40–43). Implants onto the rabbit iris of normal, hyperplastic, and neoplastic mouse mammary tissues revealed a range of angiogenic responses—from 90% positive responses for tumor implants to 6% for normal tissues (41). Implants from premalignant hyperplastic alveolar nodules elicited a neovascular response in 30% of the cases; however, outgrowths of these tissues with a high predicted incidence of tumors produced a considerably greater response than another strain with a predicted low incidence (76% versus 32%). When the angiogenic potential of corresponding human mammary tissues was examined (43), similar results pertained, revealing the value of angiogenesis as a marker of preneoplastic lesions of the human breast. Whether these human hyperplastic lesions carry the same risk for future neoplastic behavior as the corresponding murine lesions will be determined only by prospective clinical trials.

In another study an angiogenesis-related assay was used to determine if a screening of body fluids would detect the presence of cancerous tissue. Chodak et al. (44) examined the ability of various urine samples to stimulate the *in vitro* migration of capillary endothelial cells. Dialyzed and concentrated specimens collected from human subjects with grossly evident transitional-cell carcinomas of the bladder produced clearcut positive responses, whereas no response was observed with samples from normal subjects, patients with benign urologic or nonurologic diseases, patients with prostate cancer, and patients with a history of bladder cancer but with no recurrent tumors. Although the equivalence of *in vivo* angiogenesis with this *in vitro* cell migration assay is problematic, these promising results indicate the potential value of applying an angiogenesis assay to body fluids (using blood as well as urine) for detecting certain malignancies.

Tumor vascularization is also a critical step in the process of hematogenous metastasis (45). In a pertinent study the relationships of intravascular tumor cells, tumor vessels, and pulmonary metastases were determined following transplantation of a fibrosarcoma into the femoral region of a mouse (46). A linear relation was noted between the density of perfused vessels around the implant and the concentration of tumor cells in the perfusate. Agents capable of inhibiting vessel growth (as well as tumor cell intravasation into the existing vasculature) could have considerable antimetastatic potential. Taylor and Folkman (39) have reported that the antiangiogenic agent, protamine, appears to decrease the number of lung metastases from a primary tumor in the case of the mouse B16 melanoma but not in the Lewis lung carcinoma. In both instances tumor volume at the metastatic site was greatly reduced by systemically administered protamine. Based on these preliminary observations, control of metastatic spread might reasonably arise from control of tumor neovascularization.

Specific information on tumor vascularization, therefore, is needed in order to take advantage of this characteristic feature of solid tumors for the development of novel therapeutic and diagnostic procedures. Early studies again provided some insights into the cellular and chemical participants in the process. Clearly associated with tumor angiogenesis were tumor cells and the predominant cell type of the newly formed capillary, the endothelial cell. However, also present in the neovascularizing region were other cell types, such as pericytes, macrophages, mast cells, and lymphocytes. Questions about the angiogenic roles, if any, of these other cell types still remain and are considered subsequently.

The existence of a specific biochemical agent, presumably tumor-derived, was inferred by Ide et al. (25) during their early studies on the vascularization of the Brown–Pearce rabbit epithelioma. The tumor growth rate, the abundance of vessels around the tumor, and the greater anastomotic network at the tumor's growing edge as compared to its core were factors that led to the suggestion of a "blood vessel growth stimulating factor." Greenblatt and Shubik (47) first presented evidence supporting the existence of such a factor in their transfilter diffusion studies in the hamster cheek pouch. In this system neovascularization was seen in the connective tissue stroma that was separated from tumor fragments by a Millipore filter. Confirmation of the existence of a diffusible, chemical mediator was provided by several later studies using different tumors (48, 49).

Thus by 1970 the stage was set to begin biochemical studies on angiogenesis in general, and tumor angiogenesis in particular. The limitations of the pioneering techniques for observing angiogenesis were well recognized and new, revised *in vivo* model systems were developed. These systems have proved more useful because of their convenience for studies identifying and isolating angiogenic agents. In addition, a more detailed description of the mechanics of angiogenesis has come from these models. This, in turn, has led to the introduction of novel *in vitro* assays that examine specific aspects of the process, namely, degradation of basement membrane and endothelial cell migration and proliferation. These *in vivo* and *in vitro* assays, coupled with the *in situ* identification of various cell types that are intimately associated with pathologic or physiologic angiogensis, have opened up exploration for specific chemical factors that control angiogenesis.

3. OVERVIEW OF ANGIOGENESIS: MECHANICS AND MECHANISMS

Vascularization has been observed at the microscopic level in developing tissues (50–52), wound repair (52–54), and inflammation (55) as well as in implants of tumor (16–26, 56) and normal (57) tissue. From these diverse systems have come some general patterns regarding the pathways for vessel growth. The two most common pathways, capillary elongation and capillary sprouting, are described with emphasis on the three different steps that comprise these processes: endothelial matrix modification, endothelial cell migration, and proliferation. In addition to a description of endothelial events, these studies have identified other, nontumor cells that appear to participate in angiogenesis. These cell types are only mentioned in this section; a more substantive discussion of their possible angiogenic roles follows in a later section after the various bioassays for angiogenesis and its component steps have been described.

3.1. Capillary Elongation and Sprouting

Of the two processes by which new vessel growth can occur one, capillary sprouting, is encountered more frequently than the other, capillary elongation. However, capillary elongation has been observed in neovascularization occurring during the development of the chicken CAM (51), in rabbit iris induced by tumor implantation (58), in rat cornea following mild chemical injury (55), and in mouse skin after wounding (20). The mechanistic details for capillary elongation have not been unequivocally determined. Autoradiographic studies of the CAM vessels revealed uniform distribution of tritiated thymidine in labeled endothelial cells, suggesting vessel expansion had occurred by a general proliferation of these cells from the tips of existing capillaries (51). Directed growth of the new vessels, as in tumor-induced iris neovascularization (58), has not been completely elucidated. Presumably, vessel growth involves an increase in endothelial cell mitotic activity within a concentration gradient of an appropriate mitogen originating from some cellular (possibly tumor) source. Based on these assumptions, a component process of capillary elongation, amenable to independent analysis, is capillary endothelial cell proliferation.

Capillary sprouting as the only means of capillary proliferation was demonstrated using light microscopy first by Clark and Clark in their classic studies on wound vascularization in rabbit ear chambers (52). This pattern of growth has been described in greater detail by coupling light and electron microscopic techniques in examinations of rabbit ear (53) and human skin (54) wounds. Further confirmation of the existence of this process for vessel growth has arisen from studies with autografts of subcutaneous tissue in rabbit ears (57), with tumor transplants in mouse skin flaps (16) and hamster cheek pouch (56), and with wounds of rat cremaster muscle and rat cornea (where elongation also occurred) (55). The greatest detail on this process has come from the work of Yamagami (59) and of Ausprunk and Folkman (60). In these studies corneal neovascularization, induced either by cauterization (59) or by tumor implantation (60), was examined by light and electron microscopy (59, 60) as well as by thymidine labeling (60). The overall picture that emerged from these studies is that the process of sprouting from existing vessels is comprised of three coordinated steps: (a) loosening of endothelial cell junctions and rupture of membrane wall constraints, permitting formation of a new capillary bud; (b) migration of endothelial cells into the perivascular space, creating the advancing capillary tip; and (c) endothelial cell mitosis that occurs at a distance of several cells from the tip, producing a simple endothelial tube. Subsequently, the tube becomes invested with a basement membrane that increases structural stability and decreases vascular leakage. Thus capillary sprouting implicates two other biochemical processes not considered in the elongation process: matrix modification and cellular migration. The apparent precedence of cell migration before cell proliferation suggests that vessel growth directed to a specific site (e.g., to a tumor implant) is best explained in terms of a cellular response to a concentration gradient of chemoattractants. Each of these processes — matrix modification, endothelial cellular migration, and proliferation—has proved useful in devising *in vitro* assays for potential effectors of angiogenesis. Before proceeding to a consideration of the details of these assays, it is now worthwhile to consider the added insights from the *in vivo* studies that bear on possible chemical and cellular contributors to angiogenesis.

3.2. Cellular and Biochemical Aspects of Angiogenesis

Examination of tissue undergoing experimentally induced neovascularization reveals the occurrence of an early, common event, capillary closure. This observation has evoked two hypotheses for explaining vessel growth in biochemical terms. In the one case hypoxia produced by ischemia has been identified as the significant precondition for a neovascular response (61–64); in the other, the exudate from leaking vessels has been proposed to contain angiogenic stimuli (65). Hypoxia has been found in all major examples of neovascularization: ocular (61–64) and tumor (66, 67) neovascularization, wound repair (68, 69), and tissue grafting (57). For example, Remensnyder and Majno (68) in their studies of oxygen tension patterns in wounded rat cremasters found with 4-day wounds pO_2 values of 3–5 mm Hg at the center of the wound, 16–30 mm Hg at its edge, and 35–58 mm Hg in the surrounding normal tissue. The notion of a specific role for oxygen in angiogenesis gains further support from the aforementioned correlation between oxygen diffusion length and the distance between a capillary and the border separating viable and dead tumor cells (30, 31). The theory of hypoxia triggering angiogenesis inadequately describes the details for converting the signal of low oxygen tension into the various angiogenic events. In the case of ocular vascularization Ashton (62) associated retinal hypoxia with production by the viable but hypoxic tissue of a putative angiogenic factor(s), possibly a product(s) of cellular anaerobic metabolism. The recent demonstration of the existence of a retinal angiogenic factor(s) (70, 71) is the first evidence in support of this idea. However, significant questions relating to the production and release of this retinal factor in response to hypoxic conditions have yet to be answered.

The alternative proposal, consequently, deserves serious consideration, namely, that neovascularization is best associated with capillary leakage following ischemia and that the leaking materials contain angiogenic agents (65). This hypothesis shifts the focus on the search for angiogenic factors from the tissues undergoing new vessel growth to the circulating blood, which may contain active or activatable angiogenic factors of unknown origin. Leakage cannot explain all instances of neovascularization, inasmuch as neovascularization is not associated with hemorrhages. However, the concept may have validity in a number of situations, as in corneal, iris, and vitreal neovascularization, and forces a broader understanding of the role for blood and tissue (cellular) factors in angiogenesis.

Hypoxia and vessel structure also may help to explain the observation that vasoproliferation is most commonly associated with capillaries and venules. These vessels, unlike arterioles, have a simpler construction in terms of molecular and cellular matrix. Likewise, these vessels are subject to variable and reduced oxygen tensions. Thus capillary and venule endothelial cells need not be the only vascular cells capable of responding to angiogenic factors. Other vascular endothelial cells may be able to show similar responses; however, physical and physiological factors extrinsic to these cells' properties may govern their ability to respond *in situ*. This point becomes important in the later considerations for establishing *in vitro* models for angiogenesis.

Microscopic studies have indicated that fibrin, like oxygen and other blood-borne molecules, may play an angiogenic role. Clark and Clark (52) first reported in their rabbit ear wound studies the appearance of a fibrin network at the front of new capillary growth. This fibrin scaffold appears to provide clefts and lattices through which endothelial cells readily migrate (20, 52–55, 72). The close similarity in quantity and kinetics of neovascularization induced in guinea pigs by implants of fibrin gel-invested hepatocarcinomas and fibrin prompted Dvorak et al. (73) to propose that activation of the clotting and/or fibrinolytic systems may provide an adequate stimulus for angiogenesis. However, the authors also cautioned that inflammatory cells, present either with tumor implants or with the deposits of bovine fibrinogen and thrombin used to generate the subcutaneous fibrin clots, might contribute to the appearance of new vessels at the implant site. These observations on the association of fibrin with neovascularization, along with those on collagen degradation as an early step in capillary sprouting, underscore the importance of vessel matrix modification in angiogenesis.

Contributions to capillary growth by materials derived from nontumor cellular participants have also been inferred from microscopic studies. In wound repair studies macrophages and fibroblastlike cells, pericytes, have been found to dominate the vascularizing zone (53). Because of their appearance in the wound area immediately before the occurrence of the first neovascularizing events, macrophages were felt to be active participants in the angiogenic process, perhaps by producing angiogenic materials. Support for this was obtained by observing neovascularization in response to the presence of wound (74) and activated peritoneal (75) macrophages introduced into the avascular cornea. Pericytes, on the other hand, appeared to play a structural supporting role by insinuating themselves along the newly formed, fragile endothelial strands and thereupon elaborating a collagen-containing support matrix (76, 77). Their incorporation into the capillary matrix generally denoted the termination of capillary proliferation, which has led to a proposal for pericyte-endothelial contacts in inhibiting neovascularization (78).

Depending on the severity of the wounding process it is possible to observe involvement of inflammatory cells in angiogenesis. Polymorphonuclear leukocytic invasion of corneas, either following various treatments for inducing corneal vascularization *in situ* (79, 80) or corneal implantation into the hamster cheek pouch (81), seemed to precede any vascularizing response. Subsequent studies have demonstrated that intracorneal injections of polymorphonuclear leukocytes or leukocyte-derived materials were angiogenic (82). Lymphocyte-induced angiogenesis (8), as a manifestation of a graft-versus-host reaction, has been reported by several groups in several systems, which include implantation, either intradermally on mouse skin (83), onto the chicken CAM (84, 85), or into the mouse cornea (86) or hamster cheek pouch (87), of lymphoid tissue, specific lymphocytes or lymphocyte-derived materials (83–89). The preponderance of data supports the idea that the effector T-lymphocyte is the cell most responsible for evoking an angiogenic response.

Several studies using tumor implants in rat subcutaneous tissue (90), CAM (91), or rabbit cornea (61) have noted the paucity of inflammatory cells around the implant site. Although such cells are not completely missing, the display of a full-blown angiogenic effect indicates that in these cases inflammatory cells may play only a secondary role in tumor angiogenesis. In one study mast cells were found to concentrate around an implant of crude tumor-derived angiogenic material (92), an observation consistent with other findings regarding mast cell density in the infiltrating zones about tumors (93) or in psoriatic lesions (94), chronic inflammation (95), and immunologic rejection (96). However, based on their inability to produce neovascularization when placed directly on the CAM (92), mast cells have been assigned only an intermediary function in tumor angiogenesis.

Platelets, in the main due to their continual endothelial interaction and their contents of a growth factor for fibroblasts and smooth muscle cells, have been considered to play a part in maintaining endothelial integrity and possibly in controlling angiogenesis (97). Notwithstanding the lack of supporting evidence from microscopic studies, various *in vitro* studies suggest a possible association between platelet-derived materials and vascular endothelial cell migration and proliferation (98, 99).

Thus light and electron microscopic studies of healing tissue, and corneal and tumor vascularization have revealed the possibility of direct or indirect roles in angiogenesis for macrophages, leukocytes, lymphocytes, mast cells, and possibly platelets. These cells and their putative angiogenic agents in particular are considered in more detail later. In addition, angiogenesis has been claimed for various normal tissue implants: corpus luteum (100, 101), retina (70, 102), epidermis (103, 104), follicles (105), salivary glands (106), and fetal tissues (3, 84). Of these only the angiogenic materials from retina and salivary glands have been characterized to any extent and are detailed later.

4. ANGIOGENESIS AND RELATED ASSAYS

The assays that have proved most useful to date in studying angiogenesis and its controlling substances can be subdivided into *in vivo* and *in vitro* bioassays. The most commonly employed *in vivo* assays are the ocular implants and the chicken CAM methods, which examine bona fide angiogenesis induced by added tissue, cells, or water-soluble materials derived from these sources. The *in vitro* assays are based on a given feature of the angiogenic process; the assays for effects on vascular endothelial cell migration and proliferation have found greatest application so far in detecting potential angiogenic agents. The *in vitro* assays are preferred for survey and purification studies on potential angiogenic material, inasmuch as they generally require less sample and shorter test periods and are more facile, less expensive, and more manipulatable in terms of experimental parameters. However, until an absolute correlation is demonstrated between *in vitro* and angiogenic effects, any conclusions derived from *in vitro* studies need to be confirmed with an appropriate *in vivo* assay.

4.1 *In Vivo* Assays for Angiogenesis

4.1.1. Ocular Implant Assays

The assay systems using corneal (107) or iris (58) implants are probably the most reliable of the various angiogenic assays. The corneal assay is based on the fact that vessel growth from the limbal capillary plexus can be readily monitored when it is directed to the test material implanted in the avascular corneal stroma abutting the limbus. Iris implants, by comparison, are placed directly upon the surface of the iris, from which neovascularization occurs in a distinctive radial pattern. The surgical techniques are somewhat more complicated for iris implantation, in that an incision must be made through the cornea and the aqueous humor should be flushed out before inserting the implant on the iris. For corneal implantation a micropocket in the peripheral region of the cornea need only be fashioned surgically. However, surgical trauma to the corneal stroma must be kept to a minimum and placement of the bottom of the pocket at a distance of 2 mm from the limbal plexus is critical for obtaining reproducible results. The use of the corneal site for transplants, unlike the iris site, also affords the opportunity for topical administration of drugs or antiangiogenic agents by means of eye drops. The choice of experimental animal appears less limited for corneal transplants: rabbit (107), guinea pig (75), rat (108), and mouse (86) have been employed in corneal studies. Only rabbit has been used for iris implants (41, 58); presumably the greatest limitation is the size of the eye. In both corneal and iris implant techniques vessel growth is directly visualized by slit-lamp stereomicroscopy, which can be adapted to include an ocular micrometer for measuring vessel length. New vessels appear as a rule by days 4–5 after implantation in the cornea and by days 5–7 on the iris; the study is usually terminated by day 14 in both cases. The vascular response at any given time can be scored by measuring vessel density around the implant (such as by counting vessels) or, in the case of corneal studies, by measuring the length of specific capillaries at various times.

The choice of test materials influences the duration of the study and the quality of the neovascular response. When heterologous transplants are employed, a host immune response generally is mounted beginning by day 8, forcing an end to the study. In fact, if the tissue opacity, seen early in the test run and produced by edema around the wound, does not disappear, inflammation is indicated, negating any test results. When cell-free test materials (as dry solids from lyophilized salt-free aqueous solutions) are introduced by means of noninflammatory, slow-release polymeric pellets (109), a neovascular response can be seen as early as days 2–3. If desired, observation of the response can be extended past day 8 and up to day 14. The most valuable of the pellet polymers to date has been an ethylene-vinyl acetate copolymer (40% vinyl acetate by weight), called Elvax 40 (110). Elvax 40 is most satisfactory with respect to its release and noninflammatory properties. However, significant variability in the amounts of material placed on test arises from the problems in achieving uniform pellet size and from the need to use in the pellet-making process the organic solvent methylene chloride, in which water-soluble materials can only be homogeneously dispersed at best. Other materials, such as polyvinylalcohol and Hydron (a polmer of hydroxymethylacrylate), are better suited for water-soluble samples, but are more inflammatory than Elvax 40(109).

At various times in the course of the study the cornea or the iris can be removed for histologic examination. This protocol is clearly recommended in preliminary studies with new test materials. By ascertaining the cleanness of the angiogenic response, any suspicions about the involvement of host cells (e.g., inflammatory cells) in the observed angiogenesis can be effectively eliminated.

4.1.2. Chicken Chorioallantoic Membrane (CAM) Assay

The chorioallantoic membrane in fertilized, usually white Leghorn eggs affords a suitable table for observing neovascularization induced by extrinsic factors (91, 111). But unlike the ocular systems, the CAM system is undergoing considerable intrinsic neovascularization, which can produce artifactual findings (3). Most common of these is the angiogenesis induced by egg shell fragments. Hence considerable care must be exercised in CAM studies with regard to treatment of the eggs, use of appropriate controls, choice of the testing period, and the collection of a statistically significant number of observations. Also the CAM is subject to severe seasonal variability, which limits its usefulness. If the complexities of the technique are borne in mind, the CAM assay, based on considerations of convenience and economy, becomes a viable alternative to the ocular assays.

Neovascularization induced by test substances is distinguished on the CAM by the rapid (generally within 2 test days) and characteristic spokewheel appearance of new vessels at the implant site (3). Fertile eggs are prepared for testing by either of two procedures, the window or egg culture techniques. In both cases the eggs are initially maintained in a humidified incubator at 36–37°C and in a horizontal position with twice daily rotations. In the case of the window technique an air pocket is created in the egg, often by withdrawing albumen, and by the eighth day after fertilization a 1.5–2.5 cm^2 window is cut from the shell directly over the air pocket. The underlying shell membrane is carefully removed, exposing a CAM that is undamaged and free of any shell or shell membrane fragments. These operations are carried out under clean, but not necessarily sterile conditions.

For the egg culture method sterile techniques are employed in transferring the fertilized egg at day 3–4 to a petri dish containing a tissue culture medium and antifungal/antibacterial agents (112). Until the start-up of the test the egg cultures are incubated at 36–37°C in a humidified atmosphere containing 1–2% CO_2. The advantages of the culture method over the window method are the ready access to the CAM surface, including access for microscopic observation, and the availability of a larger surface for testing. However, balanced against these are (a) the increased expenses for dishes, media, and sterile hoods, (b) a need for more incubator space, and (c) a reduced survival for cultured eggs.

Tests are initiated between the eighth and tenth days after fertilization, which usually permits 4–5 days of observation. Embryo development and the appearance of an immune response limit the workable time frame. Artifactual angiogenesis has been suppressed by applying a water solution of hydrocortisone phosphate to the CAM before beginning the test (113). As was the case with the ocular assays, tissue implants or implants of inert carriers containing test agents can be placed upon the membrane and, particularly in the window technique, held in place by an overlaid plastic coverslip. In addition to Elvax 40 and Hydron, methyl cellulose pellets have been employed as carriers (39). The ability to employ aqueous solutions throughout the process and to form uniform pellets make this material attractive to use. Vessel growth can be monitored by means of a dissecting microscope in the window method or an inverted microscope in the culture method. Photomicrographic recording of the observations is generally simpler and of a higher quality with the latter system. Grading of the vascular response can be made on a scale of 0 to 4+ according to the criteria outlined by Folkman and Cotran (3). Most investigators prefer a simpler scale of 0–2+ ("yes, no, or maybe"). At the end of the test (or at other time points), the CAM, with or without india ink infusion of the vasculature, can be fixed in formalin for more detailed examination, including histologic study.

4.1.3. Miscellaneous In Vivo Assays

Four other assays have also been useful in studying angiogenesis: hamster cheek pouch assay (47), rat dorsal air sac assay (114), mouse intracutaneous assay (83), and mouse renal assay (115). Only the hamster cheek pouch assay has had considerable usage. Folkman and co-workers (114), in their early studies on the tumor angiogenic factor from the Walker rat adenocarcinoma, demonstrated activity by creating a subcutaneous air sac in the sacral region of a rat and inserting a transparent chamber to permit direct observation of angiogenic responses to test materials. Using this technique, Phillips and Kumar (116) were able to demonstrate the effectiveness of rabbit antiserum against preparations from the same rat tumor with angiogenic activity. Sidky and Auerbach (83) in their first report on lymphocyte-induced angiogenesis demonstrated this activity by injecting lymphocytes subdermally at various sites on mouse skin. Vascular branches around the injection site were examined microscopically and counted 2–3 days after the injection.

Increases in numbers of capillary endothelial cells effected by injection of various test substances were screened by McAuslan and co-workers (115) in various mouse organs. The most definitive results were seen on histologic examination of the intertubular spaces of the kidney. The early findings with this assay also produced an evocative and unexplained conclusion, namely, that the increase in endothelial cell content did not arise from cell division. Each of these assays suffers from a number of inadequacies, such as poor quantitation, difficult observation, and need for considerable amounts of test substances.

The hamster cheek pouch assay has similar limitations, but based on its historic role in angiogenesis studies the method deserves special mention. The transparent chamber technique, introduced by Sandison (15), was adapted to the hamster cheek pouch by Shubik and his colleagues in their pioneering studies on tumor angiogenesis (47, 56, 117–119). In brief, the technique consists of producing a stage for observing neovascularization in the hamster by stretching the delicate pouch membrane over a transparent plate. After removing nonvascular, muco-areolar tissue as a means for improving visualization, the test materials (tissue transplants or cell-free materials encased in Millipore filters) are placed on the membrane and then sealed in a clear plastic chamber. Vascular changes in the space surrounding the implant can be observed with a specially adapted light microscope and are scored subjectively. For more details of the instrumentation and surgical procedures, various publications can be consulted (119, 120).

4.2 *In Vitro* Assays for Angiogenic Agents

4.2.1. Endothelial Cell Proliferation

An *in vitro* assay for endothelial cell proliferation requires vascular endothelial cells in adequate amounts from an appropriate source, reproducible culture conditions which allow the cells to display differential growth responses to test materials included in the culture medium, and means for quantitating any growth effects. Several useful systems for monitoring growth effects with cultured endothelial cells are summarized in Table 1.

Capillary endothelial cells, because of their involvement in the *in vivo* process of angiogenesis, are the preferred cell for *in vitro* studies. However, the difficulty of obtaining them in quantity precluded their use until recently (127, 131). Consequently, endothelial cells from major vessel sources, such as bovine aorta (121) or human umbilical cord vein (125), were the first to be successfully employed in angiogenesis studies. The few cautionary publications on the use of noncapillary endothelial cells underscore the importance of attention to detail in the application of these cells to angio-

Table 1. Endothelial Cell Growth Assays for Potential Angiogenic Agents

CELL SOURCE	STIMULATORY MATERIAL	MONITORING TECHNIQUE	SPECIAL CONDITIONS	REFERENCE
Fetal bovine aorta	Tumor cell, lysates and purified material	Cell counts	*	(121, 123, 124)
	Fetal tissue, lysates	Thymidine labeling		(70, 71)
	Retinal extracts			
	Serum ultrafiltrates			(122)
Human umbilical cord vein	Tumor cell conditioned medium	Thymidine labeling	—	(125)
Porcine aorta	Tumor cells	Colony formation	—	(126)
Bovine brain capillary	Tumor-derived materials	Cell counts	Collagen substratum	(127)
			Platelet-derived materials	(185)
Fetal bovine aorta	Lymphocyte culture supernatants	Thymidine labeling	—	(129)
Bovine adrenal capillary				
Fetal bovine aorta	Tumor cell lysates	DNA content	—	(113)
Fetal bovine subclavian vein				
Bovine adrenal capillary				
Calf aorta				
Bovine aorta	Embryonic 3T3 adipocytes conditioned medium	Cell counts	—	(130)

genesis studies (128, 132). Commonly applied as controls for these studies are cultures of nonendothelial cells derived from the same sources if possible, such as vascular smooth muscle cells and fibroblasts. Selectivity of the model system is shown by the failure of these cell types to display a growth response to test substances.

Culture conditions for demonstrating growth effects need not be complex. With fetal bovine aortic endothelial cells Medium 199 can be used as the base medium for the test (121). Growth responses to test substances in the medium can be monitored in serumless media or media containing low levels of fetal bovine serum or dialysed (or ultrafiltered) fetal bovine serum. The use of dialysed or ultrafiltered serum derives from the generally poor growth but healthy appearance of the fetal bovine cells in media containing the serum (122). On the other hand, more complex conditions have been used to observe any growth effects with bovine brain capillary cells (127, 128). In this instance a matrix of rat tail collagen (type I versus type IV produced by capillary endothelium) was found necessary along with media containing human platelets from outdated blood (185). Results such as these reinforce the preceding conclusion regarding the care required for establishing viable conditions for the chosen assay system.

Growth effects can be monitored in a variety of ways. Determining the actual number of detached cells measured at the end of the test period should be considered the benchmark. Quantitation of incorporated tritiated thymidine (121, 124) or DNA content (113), provided that the results correlate well with actual cell counts, considerably simplifies the process. Another variation is to count endothelial cell colonies that have grown out from initially low cell platings (126).

The protocol employed by Fenselau and co-workers (70, 71, 121–124) demonstrates many of the features of the *in vitro* cell growth assays. Fetal bovine aortic endothelial cells are isolated by straightforward procedures and used for assays generally from passage 10 to 18 (generations 25 to 50). The cells are plated at moderate density ($7–12 \times 10^3$ cells/cm^2) into multiwell dishes (with wells of 2 cm^2), allowed to attach and, after 5–16 hours, subjected to test conditions. All tests are carried out in Medium 199 (1 ml/ well) either without serum or with low concentrations of untreated or dialysed (or ultrafiltered) fetal bovine serum. Test materials (as sterile aqueous solutions) are added directly to the medium. The dishes are incubated for 3 days at 37°C in a humidified atmosphere containing 5% CO_2. During this incubation period and at its termination the cells can be examined for gross effects under an inverted microscope. Quantitation of these effects is accomplished either by cell counting or tritiated thymidine pulse-labeling techniques. Radioisotopic labeling procedures are about twice as efficient as those using cell counts; however, at high cell densities the amount of thymidine label incorporated into the cells correlates poorly with actual cell number. Generally, results of preliminary studies are monitored by labeling techniques; key experiments are repeated using cell count measurements.

4.2.2. Endothelial Cell Migration

In vitro assays for factors affecting cell mobility may examine effects on either cell movement (chemokinesis) or cell migration (chemotaxis). Chemokinetic studies employ media with a uniform concentration of test materials; chemotaxis assays can use the experimental equivalence of a concentration gradient of these substances. Various studies to date are summarized in Table 2.

The procedures of Albrecht–Buehler (140) have been adapted by two groups to provide information on endothelial cell motility (133, 134). The movements of cells plated on a gold-coated surface can be visualized from the tracks that result from the ingestion of gold particles by the migrating endothelial cells. Track length or track surface area 24–72 hours after initiating the test can be measured as a function of the concentration of test material.

Cell migration from a region of high cell density (confluence) to an open area has been examined in two similar systems. In one case cells are plated in a well within an agarose gel (135, 136). Their migration beneath the agarose can be observed as a function of the contents of the medium over the cells. In the other case a scratch or wound is produced through a confluent cell culture and cell expansion into the wound are can be measured in media with varying concentrations of test materials (137). In both assays cell proliferation as an explanation for the observed results can be eliminated by prior irradiation of the cells, so that cell migration is the only means available for the appearance of cells into the open areas during the 2–3 day test period.

Cell migration in response to a concentration gradient of test materials can be examined with the aid of Boyden migration chambers (138, 139). Endothelial cells are plated into the upper well of the chamber and attach to the upper surface of a porous membrane, which separates the upper and lower wells of the chamber. Test materials at defined concentrations are placed in the lower wells and the chambers are incubated at 37°C in a humidified atmosphere containing 5% CO_2. At the end of the experiment (generally < 8 hours) the cells that have migrated through the 5 μm pores to the underside of the membrane are fixed and enumerated microscopically. Chemotaxis can be demonstrated by observing a dose dependency in the number of cells that migrate; chemokinetic effects are manifested when both upper and lower wells contain the same concentration of test materials.

Table 2. Endothelial Cell Migration Assays for Potential Angiogenic Agents

Cell Source	Stimulatory Material	Assay Type	Reference
Bovine aorta	Copper-containing materials	Chemokinesis	(133)
Bovine adrenal capillary	Tumor cell conditioned medium	Chemokinesis	(134)
Fetal bovine aorta	Lymphocyte culture supernatants	Chemokinesis	(129)
Human umbilical cord vein	Platelet-derived materials	Radial migration under agarose gel	(135)
Same	Same	Same	(136)
Same	Serum	Mechanical denuding ("wounding")	(137)
Fetal bovine aorta	Retina-derived materials	Chemotaxis	(138)
Calf aorta	Fibronectin	Chemotaxis	(139)

4.2.3. Endothelial Matrix Modification

Assays based on matrix modification by endothelial cells have not yet gained widespread use. However, once its credibility as a measure of angiogenic potential has become more delineated, this type of assay could find much greater application due to its ease of use and quantifiability. The rationale for this approach, enunciated by Rifkin et al. (141), is that capillary endothelial cells should produce specific proteases during angiogenesis in order to permit their escape from basement membrane constraints and then their penetration into and through the surrounding stroma. Two specific proteolytic activities, plasminogen activator (PA) and collagenase, were considered to be potential markers for endothelial cell invasiveness. When bovine capillary endothelial cells used for these studies were grown in the presence or absence of angiogenic substances, such as bovine retinal extracts or human hepatoma lysates, the proteolytic activities recovered from the treated cells were 3–10-fold higher for PA activity and 6–55-fold higher for collagenolytic activity than were recovered from the untreated cells (141). Bovine aortic endothelial cells failed to exhibit a comparable responsiveness, indicating a specificity of cell function that is consistent with the observed association between neovascularization and capillaries (as opposed to arterial vasculature).

Inasmuch as the basement membrane to be traversed by endothelial cells is composed primarily of type IV collagen, the substrate specificity of the collagenase assay could be an important consideration. The work from Rifkin's laboratory utilized type I collagen from guinea pig skin (142). A reasonable refinement to these procedures is the employment of a screen for activities with types I–V collagens as substrates, using procedures analogous to those reported by Liotta et al. (143) in their studies on the specificity of a collagenase derived from a metastatic mouse tumor. Other technical improvements might be envisioned, such as the use of nitrocellulose-bound collagens to facilitate data collection (144) or the use of amnion membranes to examine endothelial cell invasiveness *per se* (145).

4.2.4. Miscellaneous *in Vitro* Assays

The two following techniques have not been employed in angiogenic assays, but the potential to do so clearly exists. Both systems have considerable value in studying vascular morphogenesis and neoplastic intravasation as well as the biochemistry of vascularization. On the latter point these techniques should permit an unambiguous determination of direct and indirect angiogenic effects, inasmuch as the *in vitro* test conditions need only include soluble factors and can rigorously exclude specific cell types of the host defense system. Nicosia et al. (146) have reported conditions for observing angiogenesis *in vitro* using organ cultures of rat aorta. Aortic rings placed in a three-dimensional matrix of clotted chick plasma were grown in histophysiologic gradient culture. Endothelial cell sprouts from the rings could be observed by light microscopy on the second day of culture; by the end of the first week a vascular network had developed. Vessel growth in this system occurred in preference to intimal plaque formation, which is more commonly found in organ culture studies. Variations in the culture conditions, such as including possible angiogenic substances, were not reported in this first study.

Capillary tube formation and assembly into networks has been accomplished by Folkman and Haudenschild (147), starting not with tissue fragments but with cultures of capillary endothelial cells from several sources, including human foreskin. The cells, after plating on gelatin-coated plastic dishes, were maintained on a culture medium supplemented with various growth-promoting substances, such as endothelial cell growth supplement from bovine brain and growth factors present in conditioned media from tumor and aortic endothelial cells. Within 2–4 weeks capillary tubes formed generally in the zone of intermediate cell density within a cell colony. Tube extension and branching occurred slowly during the remaining time in culture. The results suggest that one cell type, the capillary endothelial cell, possesses all the information necessary for developing an entire capillary network *in vitro*. Tumor angiogenesis factor(s), on the basis of the requirement for tumor-conditioned medium, is postulated by Folkman and Haudenschild (147) to function in starting and directing capillary growth.

5.   CELLULAR PARTICIPANTS IN ANGIOGENESIS

5.1.   Cells Associated with Host Defense Mechanisms

5.1.1.   Macrophages

A role for macrophages in angiogenesis was intimated from various *in vivo* studies (53). At the outset of this discussion, however, it must be noted that macrophages need not be present in all instances for new vessel growth to occur. For example, no monocyte infiltration into skin lesions induced by thermal injury was observed in leukopenic rats, even though endothelial proliferation and vessel growth in the granulation tissue was similar for irradiated and nonirradiated animals (148). Nevertheless, macrophages — either activated peritoneal (75) or wound (74, 149) macrophages —have demonstrated the ability to elicit new vessel growth. Studies are now well underway in both instances to characterize the substances responsible for the angiogenic activity.

Polverini et al. (75) were able to show blatant corneal neovascularization in guinea pig eyes with activated peritoneal macrophages from autologous, isologous, and heterologous (mouse) sources. Control, nonactivated macrophages did not produce a comparable neovascular response. Conditioned media from cultures of the mouse macrophages were also successful in inducing corneal vasoproliferation. Martin et al. (150) have continued to study this material, finding that it stimulated the growth of cultured fibroblasts, vascular smooth muscle cells, and vascular endothelial cells. Following *in vitro* activation of the macrophages the growth-stimulatory activity in the conditioned medium increased when tested with all three cell types. Gel filtration of materials following dialysis and concentration of the conditioned media revealed that the growth-stimulatory activity had been fractionated; materials promoting fibroblast and smooth muscle growth eluted in the void volume, whereas endothelial cell growth was enhanced more by materials eluting later (with an estimated size <21K daltons). The angiogenic properties of these materials were not reported.

Wound macrophages stimulate vessel growth in rabbit cornea (74) and dead-space wounds (149). The macrophages were isolated from wound fluid from wound chambers, which had been implanted subcutaneously in rabbits 21 days earlier. The starting cell population, like that for the peritoneal macrophage work, was heterogeneous, but in all cases contained >80% macrophages (with lymphocytes and granulocytes being the major contaminants). When these macrophages were included in rabbit ear chambers under standardized wound conditions, the appearance of new vessels into the wound was hastened by about 2 days. The wound macrophages and their derived materials were next examined by Greenburg and Hunt (151) for their growth effects on cultured vascular smooth muscle and endothelial cells. Co-cultivation of macrophages with either of the vascular cell types led to a significant stimulation of vascular cell growth. Wound fluid or macrophage-conditioned media also enhanced endothelial cell and smooth muscle cell growth, particularly in the presence of 10% calf serum. Preliminary studies indicate that after acid dialysis of wound fluid, material with angiogenic activity in the corneal assay can be recovered in the dialysate (152). In addition, this low molecular weight material has chemokinetic activity with vascular endothelial cells and no mitogenic activity with these cells or with fibroblasts. Other low molecular weight material was found to be mitogenic for endothelial cells, but not angiogenic.

5.1.2. Leukocytes

Leukocytes, like macrophages, are angiogenic but are not obligatorily required for the occurrence of new vessel growth. Unlike the situation for macrophages, studies on leukocyte angiogenesis have so far been primarily descriptive (79–82), with no examination of the specific chemical factors at play in the phenomenon having been reported. Perhaps an exception to this statement is the report on the effects of leukocytes and leukocyte-derived materials on the growth of endothelial cells from human umbilical cord vein; only modest (<25%) increases in cell numbers were obtained with acid extracts of leukocyte lysosomes (153). Angiogenic effects were not investigated.

Klintworth, in studying corneal neovascularization with tissues implanted in the hamster cheek pouch (81), noted a correlation between the degree of leukocytic infiltration and the implant vascularity. These observations were extended to the eyes of rabbits and rats, where corneal neovascularization as an inflammatory response was induced by a variety of means (79, 80, 82). This system permitted an examination of the effects of whole body x-irradiation on corneal angiogenesis. In the absence of leukocytes vascular ingrowth to the cornea did not occur following cauterization (80). A vascular response could be induced when polymorphonuclear leukocytes isolated from glycogen-induced peritoneal exudates were injected intracorneally into leukopenic rats (82).

Contradictory results with leukopenic animals were subsequently reported by two groups. Sholley et al. (148) did not observe decreases in endothelial labeling of skin wounds when rats were made leukopenic by whole body x-irradiation. The same group studied corneal neovascularization induced by cauterization and found that vessel growth was depressed but not eliminated in rats depleted of leukocytes by radiation treatment and injections of antineutrophil serum (154). Eliason (155) reported similar findings in assessing vessel growth to corneal burns in normal and irradiated rabbits. The impression to be gained from these studies is that leukocytes can play a contributory but not necessarily principal role in angiogenesis, or at least in corneal angiogenesis.

5.1.3.   Lymphocytes

A correlation between lymphocyte-induced angiogenesis (LIA) and the graft-versus-host (GVH) reaction was evident in the first report on LIA (83). Later studies associated the same major antigenic stimulus, the I-region alloantigens, with both LIA and the GVH reaction (156). Thus from its conception LIA was recognized to involve not only lymphocytes as probable initiators of a neovascular response, but also other cells and chemical factors that collectively produce an inflammatory response. Untreated lymphoid cells from mouse spleen and lymph nodes (83, 88) as well as from human peripheral blood (88, 157) or mouse spleen cells activated with phytohemagglutinin (85, 87) displayed vessel growth stimulatory activities. The assay systems used for these various studies included subdermal injections into irradiated mice (83, 88, 89), hamster cheek pouch implants (87), corneal implants in rabbits (84) or mice (86), or chicken CAM implants (84, 85). Controls that were inactive in these tests were bone marrow cells and spleen cells from athymic donors.

The results of these studies strongly implicate an association between angiogenesis and activated T-lymphocytes. A soluble, lymphocyte-derived factor(s), possibly a lymphokine(s), may act as a mediator of this process. Some experimental support for this and for the possibility that such soluble factors may act directly on endothelium has been provided by the results from testing supernatants of mixed lymphocyte cultures in endothelial cell chemokinetic and mitogenic assays (129). The preliminary findings indicate that material with a size >12,000K daltons and with mitogenic and chemokinetic activity is present in these supernatants and that this material may differ from the lymphokine IL-2.

5.1.4. Mast Cells

Mast cells provide an object lesson on the problems encountered while trying to unravel the complex interactions among the cellular and chemical factors that comprise angiogenesis. Chicken CAM studies on the angiogenic effects of a tumor factor revealed that mast cells accumulated around the implant site before the ingrowth of new vessels (92). Similar observations have also been made regarding mast cell presence around tumors, conspicuously in the infiltrating zones (93). However, mast cells were not angiogenic in the CAM assay. Nevertheless, Azizkhan et al. (158) followed up on these observations by using mast cell preparations (conditioned media from mast cell cultures as well as lysates) in the chemokinesis assay. From these studies emerged the conclusion that heparin, a major product released by mast cells, can stimulate capillary endothelial cell migration, but cannot function as a mitogen for these cells or as an angiogenic factor. Within these constraints heparin has still found usefulness in the CAM assay by potentiating angiogenic effects induced by true stimuli (39).

5.1.5. Platelets

An angiogenic role for platelets has yet to be demonstrated, although retinal neovascularization in leukemic patients has been correlated with elevated blood platelet counts (159). Obscure in this observation is whether platelets are directly involved or whether other factors, such as the hyperviscosity of the patients' blood (which can lead to vaso-occlusion and ischemia) or the increased numbers of circulating leukocytes, account for the observed effects. The bulk of pertinent platelet studies relate to the effects of platelets or their derived materials on endothelial cell growth and migration. Presently unresolved is their activity in chemotaxis; claims that platelets increase migration of human umbilical cord vein endothelial cells (98, 99) are countered by contradictory claims (160).

Platelet effects on cell growth, however, appear to be less controversial. Saba and Mason (161) showed that platelet-stored substances, ADP and 5-hydroxytryptamine, enhance cell growth. Various other platelet substances, in particular the biogenic amines, were found by D'Amore (97) to support endothelial cell growth. Interestingly enough, earlier studies by Zauberman et al. (162) had revealed corneal angiogenesis induced by biogenic amines. Infusion of 1–2% solutions of acetylcholine, histamine, or serotonin produced an angiogenic response in approximately one third of the rabbit corneas tested. The fact that surface receptors for these vasoactive agents are present in vascular endothelium (163) suggests that these agents may act directly on endothelium.

The polypeptide, platelet-derived growth factor (PDGF), has also been examined for possible effects on endothelial cell growth. PDGF weakly stimulated the growth of human umbilical cord cells (164); this effect was potentiated by thrombin. On the other hand, bovine aortic (164) and bovine adrenal capillary (165) endothelial cells were unresponsive to PDGF, with or without thrombin. In sum, the need exists for more information on the possible relationship between angiogenesis and platelet-derived materials.

5.2. Normal Tissues

On the matter of the angiogenic capabilities of normal and neoplastic tissues there is general agreement that the vascularizing potential decreases in the order: solid tumors, embryonic and neonatal tissues, and normal adult tissues (3, 5, 7, 84). However, certain normal tissues, such as mammalian retina (70, 102), murine testes (166), bovine (100) and rabbit (101) corpora lutea, bovine and murine salivary glands (106), and rat follicles (105), have considerable angiogenic potency. Why tissue differences exist is unexplained at present and will only be understood as greater insights are gained into those biochemical factors that control neovascularization—the physiologic angiogenic and antiangiogenic factors. In the following, four examples of neovascularizing tissues are examined: epidermis, corpus luteum, salivary glands, and retina.

5.2.1. Epidermis

A cogent review by Ryan (167) on the factors influencing vessel growth in skin has provided an excellent basis for subsequent studies on epidermal angiogenesis. Nishioka and Ryan (103) were able to demonstrate the ability of Millipore filter-encased implants of epidermis from neonatal hamsters to induce neovascularization in the hamster cheek pouch. These observations were confirmed and extended by Wolf and Harrison (104) in angiogenesis studies with adult hamster epidermis and epidermal homogenates. The active materials in the homogenates were heat-labile, trichloroacetic acid-precipitable, and nondialyzable; further characterization of this putative epidermal angiogenic factor has not been reported. The angiogenic activities of various skin tumors, examined by Wolf and his colleagues (168–170), may involve the abnormal production of a factor similar to that found in normal skin.

5.2.2 Corpus Luteum

An extremely vigorous vasoproliferation is associated with implants of bovine corpus luteum in three angiogenesis assays using the chicken CAM, the mouse subcutaneous pouch, and the hamster cheek pouch (100) or with implants of rabbit corpus luteum in the rabbit corneal micropocket assay (101). The effects from the bovine implants required new vessel growth from the host (and not simply an outgrowth of preexisting vessels from the corpus luteum or an anastomosis to host capillaries). Neither Jakob et al. (100) nor Gospodarowicz and Thakral (101) detected any involvement of inflammatory or immune reactions. Extracts of bovine corpora lutea produced angiogenic effects similar to those with the tissue implants, which could be abolished by heating the extracts at 100°C for 5 minutes. Additions of crude extracts from rabbit corpora lutea in amounts of 1–10 μg/ml of culture medium stimulated the growth of cultured bovine vascular endothelial cells. The active ingredient(s) in these preparations has yet to be identified.

5.2.3. Salivary Glands

Evidence supporting the idea that salivary glands contain angiogenic materials was first adduced from the studies of Jeney and Torö (171), who observed vessel growth in chicken embryos after the injection of human saliva. Hoffman et al. (106) noted that crude extracts of bovine parotid glands and male mouse submaxillary glands, when injected into newborn or adult mice, induced a hypertrophic growth response from endothelium in numerous organs, especially the kidneys. Gel filtration of this material yielded three active fractions with molecular weights ranging from 3,000 to 80,000. From these various components an active substance(s) could be obtained with an apparent molecular weight of 210 (determined chromatographically), which contained copper as determined by spark source mass spectrometry (172). The angiogenic properties of cooper are considered in a later section.

Growth stimulation of cultured human umbilical cord vascular endothelial cells resulted from including extracts of male mouse submaxillary glands in the culture medium at concentrations of 100–300 ng protein/ml (173). Treatment of the extracts with antiserum to epidermal growth factor (EGF) eliminated their mitogenic activity; treatment with antiserum to nerve growth factor had no effect on activity. These results implicate EGF, or a closely related polypeptide, as an active component in these preparations. The angiogenic activities of these materials were not determined.

5.2.4. Retina

Retina as a source of angiogenic materials had been long suspected because of its association with a number of ocular neovascular disorders (61, 174), of which diabetic retinopathy is the most common example. However, only recently have these suspicions gained some experimental support. Retinas from various nondiseased animals produced a neovascular response in the chicken CAM assay (70). Implants of vascular autologous retinas into rabbit corneas induced neovascularization; similar implants of avascular peripheral retinas or boiled vascular retinas were inactive (102). When intraocular fluids from patients undergoing therapeutic vitrectomy for various ocular disorders were tested in the CAM assay and the endothelial cell assays for growth and migration, a good correlation was obtained between the assay results and the clinical findings of ocular neovascularization (175). These studies have presumed that the active factor(s) in the intraocular fluid is derived from retina; the test of this presumption awaits the identification of the retinal factor(s).

Characterization of retina-derived angiogenesis factors has to date been limited to one source, bovine retina, from which significant amounts of active materials can readily be extracted with minimal tissue damage. Activity in the crude and partially purified preparations, demonstrated by *in vivo* and *in vitro* bioassays, was associated with a proteinaceous substance with an apparent molecular weight of 50,000–100,000 (71). One scheme for the further purification of this material has employed the cell growth assay for routine analyses of active fractions; however, the final, apparently homogeneous product was tested with positive results in several assay systems (176). The combination of high pressure liquid chromatography using reducing and chaotropic agents and isoelectric focusing provided a purified retina-derived angiogenesis factor with an approximate molecular weight of 22,000 and a pI of 4.5–4.7. Angiogenic activity was displayed on both the chicken CAM and rabbit corneal pocket assays. The material, mitogenic for various vascular endothelial cells, was also active in the phagokinetic assay using capillary endothelial cells. These results suggest the existence of a relationship between this retinal angiogenesis factor and other nerve tissue-derived growth factors, such as fibroblast growth factor (177) and the endothelial cell growth stimulatory factor (178).

6. CHEMICAL ANGIOGENESIS FACTORS

This section contains a review of those specific chemical factors that have induced angiogenesis in any of the experimental systems. Presently the list is notably sparse, including only tumor-derived materials, prostaglandins, copper-containing materials, and polypeptide growth factors. However, additional angiogenic agents, representing novel classes of factors as well as new entries to the existing classes, will undoubtedly be discovered during the next few years as a consequence of the successes of presently ongoing work and the ultimate involvement of the pharmaceutical industry in these potentially commercially valuable substances.

6.1. Tumor-Derived Angiogenesis Factors

Considering the diversity of tumors that display angiogenic properties it is ironic that studies on the isolation and characterization of a specific tumor angiogenesis factor have centered on one tumor, the Walker 256 rat adenocarcinoma. Perhaps it is just as well that this is the case, because from this one tumor four apparently different chemical agents have been isolated and partially purified. The lead study was that reported by Folkman et al. (114), in which the isolation of the Walker 256 tumor angiogenesis factor was claimed. This material, purified by gel filtration and active in the rat dorsal sac assay, was composed of RNA (25%), protein (10%), carbohydrate (50%), and a remaining, presumably lipoidal portion. The activity was destroyed by various treatments, such as heating at 56°C for 1 hour or digestion with subtilisin or ribonuclease, but was unaffected by trypsin treatment. A later study from Folkman's laboratory documented the angiogenic activity in the rabbit corneal micropocket assay of the nonhistone proteins from the nuclear materials isolated from this same tumor as well as their mitogenic activity with cultured endothelial cells (174). No follow-up to these observations has been reported.

Weiss, Kumar, and co-workers (180) employed the Walker tumor material partially purified by gel filtration [according to the procedures of Folkman et al. (114)] in the eventual isolation of a low molecular weight (approximately 200) angiogenic substance. The critical step in their purification scheme was the application of affinity column chromatography utilizing rabbit antiserum raised against the crude rat tumor preparation (116, 181). The material eluted at pH 3.7 from this column was sized by gel filtration and assayed in the chicken CAM. This angiogenic substance also stimulated the growth of bovine brain capillary endothelial cells under carefully defined culture conditions that included the use of a collagen substratum (127). Although the precise nature of the isolated molecule(s) has yet to be determined, preliminary results indicate that it is not a prostaglandin, a protein or peptide, or a nucleic acid (180). Using essentially the same isolation techniques, the same or a similar substance has also been obtained from cat retina (182) and human synovial fluid (183).

McAuslan and Hoffman (115) began their purification using homogenates of Walker 256 tumor cells grown in culture, as opposed to using material isolated from rats as in the previous studies. The crude extracts were fractionated by Sephadex G100 chromatography at neutral pH into active components with approximate molecular weights of 80,000 and 3,000. Rechromatography of the 80,000 material yielded a 3,000 molecular weight material. This latter material when subjected to isoelectric focusing gave an active band with an isoelectric point of 4.0. The active substances could be eluted from a DEAE-cellulose column and purified further by Sephadex G10 chromatography, which was used to estimate the molecular weight of 210. Vascular activity was seen in the murine renal assay for endothelial hypertrophy. No growth stimulation with bovine aortic endothelial cells could be detected using the purified material, although crude tumor homogenates were found to be mitogenic. At the same time McAuslan's group showed that angiogenic materials from salivary glands and Balb/c 3T3 cells were similar in size and contained copper (172). The results imply that the purified Walker tumor factor contains copper that is essential for angiogenic activity; the way in which copper (atomic weight 63.546) is packaged in the purified factor (molecular weight 210) has not yet been specified. Copper-induced angiogenesis is considered in a later section.

The final procedure for purifying an angiogenesis factor from the Walker 256 rat tumor is the one described by Fenselau et al. (124). Unlike those in the other reports, this purification relied on the *in vitro* growth assay using fetal bovine aortic endothelial cells at each step in the process (121, 123); angiogenic activity was periodically confirmed using the CAM and cornea assays. The use of the cell culture assay afforded a measure of quantitation not possible with the *in vivo* assays, but still left unsettled the matter of how much of the original angiogenic activity was represented by the final isolate. Active material from homogenates of ascitic tumor cells appeared to have a high molecular weight when analyzed by gel filtration at neutral pH; however, at pH 4 activity was associated with materials of approximate molecular weight < 800. Purification of these materials was accomplished in high yields (over 50%) by repetitive silica gel chromatography of ethanol extracts obtained from lyophilized tumor cell homogenates. The purity of this material was assessed using both thin layer chromatography and high pressure liquid chromatography. This purified angiogenesis factor had an ultraviolet absorption maximum near 260 nm, did not contain copper when examined by atomic absorption spectroscopy, and was not composed of protein or peptides (184). An angiogenic factor with chromatographic and spectral properties similar to those for the tumor factor has been isolated from fetal bovine serum, which has significantly higher concentrations of this material than either calf or adult bovine serum (122).

Thus four laboratories may have succeeded independently in purifying three or possibly four different angiogenic agents from the Walker rat tumor. If the identification of nonhistone proteins (179) with angiogenesis activity remains firm in light of the subsequent studies that associate the Walker tumor angiogenic activity with low molecular weight materials, then these materials are unique. The low molecular weight substances of McAuslan and Hoffman (115) and of Fenselau et al. (124) appear to be distinctly different based on their copper content. The characterization of the material isolated by Weiss et al. (180) does not permit any comparisons with either of the other substances. A facet of every one of these studies that deserves further scrutiny is the association of activity in the partially purified preparations with a high molecular weight species. Whether these observation are due to artifacts produced during the isolation process or to the existence of specific binding or carrier macromolecules needs to be determined.

6.2. Prostaglandins (PG)

As a potential class of angiogenic agents prostaglandins (and leukotrienes as well) have considerable appeal based on their established chemoattractant abilities for various cell types. The first reports by BenEzra (186, 187) on the neovascularizing activity of certain prostaglandins have now been confirmed by other investigators (188, 189). The original observations were made with Elvax implants in rabbit corneas; similar results were later obtained on the CAM (188). BenEzra (186) demonstrated that PGE_1 was active at a dosage of 1 µg per pellet, whereas PGE_2 and $PGE_{2\alpha}$ at 5 µg and 20 µg, respectively, produced lesser vessel growth. Other prostaglandins, such as PGD_2, PGA_1, and $PGF_{1\alpha}$, were essentially inactive at 20 µg per implant.

Ziche et al. (189) determined that tumor interstitial fluids from two different rat carcinomas were angiogenic in the corneal assay. The fluids also contained levels of prostaglandins that were elevated relative to the subcutaneous fluids from nontumor-bearing rats. Dose-dependency tests with specific prostaglandins yielded results identical to those of BenEzra. Histologic examination of the cornea at various times after implantation revealed that inflammatory cells could not be detected at the implant site before the appearance of capillaries. When capillaries first invaded the cornea, leukocytes were in evidence; whether leukocytes brought in vessels or vice versa could not be determined. Administration of indomethacin to the rabbits, systemically before initiating the test and topically to the eye during the test, was found to eliminate corneal angiogenesis induced by Balb/c 3T3 fibroblasts. The angiogenic potential of these cells had been shown by Ziche and Gullino (190) to increase with subculture number. Although an explanation for these observations was not established, the presumption is that indomethacin inhibited prostaglandin production, which led to the block in angiogenesis.

6.3.   Copper

McAuslan and co-workers, in a series of studies, characterized angiogenic materials from such diverse sources as a rat carcinoma, bovine liver and parotid glands, and embryonic mouse fibroblasts (172, 191). The common denominator in their purified materials was a copper-containing substance with an approximate molecular weight of 210. In none of these purification schemes were yields presented as a means of determining the relative contribution these materials make to the cell or tissue-induced angiogenesis. Activity for the purified factor from bovine parotid gland was shown in the renal assay, the corneal micropocket assay, and the chemokinesis assay. Copper ions were also active in each of these assays, but apparently to a lesser degree than the parotid gland factor (191). The copper-containing serum protein, ceruloplasmin, considered as a possible physiological angiogenic factor, was also active in the corneal and chemokinetic assays (191). When this material, type III human ceruloplasmin, was subjected to isoelectric focusing, two active components were obtained. One of these with a pI of 7.8 and a molecular weight of 3000 appeared to be similar to the material purified from the bovine parotid glands. Still undetermined from this and related studies is the role(s) in angiogenesis, if any, for the larger, apparently inactive molecular species that are associated with the 210 dalton material.

Gullino and his co-workers (189) have marshalled additional experimental support for the angiogenic action of copper and also have probed into the possible relationship between PGE_1 production and copper concentration during angiogenesis. The copper content of corneal tissue was measured on the third day following implantation of test materials, before the occurrence of capillary invasion. The level of copper in the corneal stroma around the implant with PGE_1 (at a dosage sufficient to induce vessel growth) was 30% higher than that found in untreated controls or around the implants of an inactive prostaglandin, PGI_2. In addition, the PGE_1-induced corneal angiogenesis could be markedly decreased in rabbits maintained on a copper-deficient diet. A most intriguing finding in this study was that rabbit corneal neovascularization triggered by implants of ceruloplasmin (at 100 μg/implant) could be inhibited by employing the indomethacin treatments described under prostaglandin-induced angiogenesis. This observation suggested to Ziche et al. (189) that prostaglandin production probably precedes copper mobilization.

6.4. Polypeptide Growth Factors

Growth-stimulatory substances active *in vitro* at the cellular level, especially at the endothelial cell level, might be expected to display an *in vivo* activity on vessel growth. The retinal angiogenesis factor is one such example that has already been discussed. In actuality the first of the polypeptide growth factors to be associated with angiogenesis were fibroblast growth factor (FGF) and epidermal growth factor (EGF). BenEzra (185) reported a small, but significant, neovascularization when Elvax implants containing 10 μg of either growth factor were placed in rabbit corneas. Gospodarowicz et al. (192) obtained similar effects with FGF and EGF in the same system, determining that the optimal dosages for producing neovascularization in all test eyes were 10 μg of FGF/implant and 25 μg of EGF/implant. Furthermore, histologic examination of corneas during the period of greatest capillary proliferation (days 7–14 after implantation) revealed the absence of inflammation. Unlike inflammatory implants of bovine serum albumin, implants of FGF and EGF produced only minor infiltration of leukocytes and macrophages into the surrounding corneal stroma.

With both FGF and EGF the picture regarding their mitogenic activity with endothelial cells is presently confusing. Bovine arterial and human umbilical cord endothelial cells respond positively to bovine brain or pituitary FGF in some laboratories (173, 177) but in others show no effects (178). Whether EGF purified from mouse submaxillary gland is mitogenic for endothelial cells is also a controversial issue (165, 173, 192). In this context it would be of value to determine the angiogenic activities of a purified preparation of the endothelial cell mitogen from bovine hypothalamus (178) as well as the platelet-derived growth factor and of nerve growth factor, both of which are claimed to have little or no effect on endothelial cell growth (165, 173).

6.5. Miscellaneous Materials

Berman et al. (193) were able to observe a neovascular response by directly injecting a purified preparation of human urokinase into rabbit corneal stroma. Urokinase inactivated by previous treatment with an active site-directed inhibitor failed to elicit vessel growth. The capillary growth obtained by this injection technique differs from that seen in the implant technique in that a broad front of newly formed capillaries from the limbus is formed rather than a narrow front that is directed toward the implant. This situation can make it difficult to distinguish between neovascularization induced by test materials and inflammation (generally detected as a broad capillary front emanating from the limbus). When Elvax implants of urokinase were employed, the modest vascular responses were equivalent to the controls. Histologic examination of newly vascularized corneas revealed the presence of lymphocytes, macrophages, plasma cells, and leukocytes, the numbers of which decreased with the extent of vessel ingrowth.

The mechanism by which urokinase might act was not determined, although one of the possibilities considered was that the active species is plasmin generated from urokinase activation of plasminogen. Fenselau and Kaiser (194) observed an inhibition of fetal bovine aortic endothelial cell growth when various plasminogens and the corresponding plasmins (produced by treating the plasminogen with human urokinase) were included in the culture medium. Inactivation of plasmin by active site phosphorylation abolished the cell culture growth inhibition. Urokinase also had no effect on cell growth. Elvax implants of rabbit plasminogen or human urokinase only inhibited rabbit corneal vessel growth induced by implants of the rabbit V2 carcinoma. Similar results were obtained in the CAM assay, where neovascularization was produced by implants of partially purified angiogenic materials from the Walker rat tumor. Plasmin, from urokinase treatment of plasminogen, was inactive in both angiogenesis assays, presumably due to its instability from autolysis and inhibition by serum and tissue antiproteases. Thus based on these contradictory findings the role in angiogenesis of plasmin, plasminogen, and plasminogen activator/urokinase would appear at present to be undecided.

7.   ENDOTHELIAL CELL MATRIX FACTORS IN ANGIOGENESIS

Implicit in the intimate association between endothelial cells and basal lamina is the notion that this matrix can provide at least a permissive environment for endothelial growth. In addition, the tactile nature of the relationship between endothelial cells and certain components of basement membranes or fibrin-containing strands suggests that, were they freely diffusible, these components might be chemoattractants for the cells and possibly angiogenic. The progress in recent years in analyzing extracellular matrices (ECM) has allowed experimental examinations on these matters to proceed.

Gospodarowicz and his colleagues (195, 196) have shown that bovine or human vascular endothelial cells, which require FGF for growth on a plastic substratum, grow rapidly in the absence of FGF on a substratum of corneal endothelial cell ECM (195). Even though other factors, such as the nutrient composition of the culture medium, may contribute to the display of this *in vitro* growth effect (196), a role for ECM in permitting endothelial cell growth seems well established. The availability of the ECM system has also allowed better evaluation of defined media for endothelial cell proliferation. Bovine aortic endothelial cells maintained on the corneal endothelial cell ECM could be grown and subcultured in a serum-free Dulbecco's modified Eagle's medium that included only supplements of transferrin and high density lipoproteins (197). If these results on endothelial cell growth *in vitro* can be extrapolated to vessel growth *in vivo*, they tend to reinforce the views of Hayreh (65) on the contribution of blood components to inducing angiogenesis in ischemic tissues.

Studies on endothelial cell chemotaxis with specific matrix components have been few in number, but have revealed some promise for future development. Kadish et al. (198) examined the effects of fibrin clots on confluent cultures of vascular endothelial cells. Within 6 hours of contact with the clot, the cultures lost their normal cobblestone appearance, becoming disorganized by the apparent migration of individual cells into the clot. These reversible effects are localized to those cells in contact with the clot, which suggests that diffusible factors are not involved. Further investigation into the possible role in angiogenesis of fibrin or fibrin degradation products seems warranted based on these results along with those cited earlier on the vascularization of the fibrin-gel cocoon that invests certain tumors (73).

A more active role in angiogenesis for an endothelial matrix component, fibronectin, is indicated by the chemotaxis studies of Bowersox and Sorgente (139). Chemotaxis of bovine aortic endothelial cells, measured in blindwell chemotaxis chambers, was increased over fourfold by adding bovine plasma fibronectin at 100 μg/ml of medium. Such observations prompted the authors to hypothesize that a diffusible fibronectin produced by tumor or normal tissue could act as a chemotactic stimulus to capillary endothelial cells and, thereby, initiate capillary growth. The angiogenic properties of this material were not reported.

8. SUMMARY

Tumor angiogenesis appears to involve a host of factors. Some of these angiogenesis factors are actually produced by tumors; others, by cells of the host defense systems activated by the tumor's presence. Based on the present data these factors from tumor and nontumor sources differ with respect to size, chemical nature, and possible mode of action. At present the picture of tumor angiogenesis, and for angiogenesis in general, is only partially sketched. In the following are examined some areas that should provide significant details for improving the quality of the picture.

First there is a need to identify specific tumor angiogenesis factors. Only angiogenic copper has been identified from tumor-derived materials; in this case the matter is confused by the presence of at least two other angiogenic agents from the same Walker rat tumor. Thus the amounts of the factor present in the tumor itself need to be assessed, followed by analogous studies with other tumors. Correlations between the angiogenic potential of a tumor and its content of a specific mediator are necessary in order to effect rational means of therapeutic control. For example, an immunotherapy addressed to limiting the action of a polypeptide angiogenesis factor would obviously be impotent against angiogenic copper.

Studies with angiogenic materials from nontumor sources should proceed in parallel with these tumor studies. At least two objectives could be met: (i) delineating the uniqueness of any tumor angiogenesis factor and (ii) determining, particularly with cells of the immune system and the inflammatory process, the extent to which tumors can influence the production of other cell factors. In both cases the results will have bearing on devising antiangiogenic therapies. The latter studies will contribute to unraveling the issues regarding the mode of action of tumor angiogenesis factors — either a direct action on endothelium or an indirect one involving the recruitment of nontumor angiogenic cells.

These studies on angiogenesis factors from both tumor and nontumor tissues will also clarify other aspects of tissue vascularization. The relationship between tissue ischemia and neovascularization still needs a biochemical interpretation. The controls on tissue vascularity are poorly understood; tissue metabolic rate and the production of a tissue ischemic factor may be involved in signaling for vessel growth. On the other hand, specific inhibitors of angiogenesis, such as the cartilage-derived factor, may be elaborated under normal conditions, but their synthesis and/or release inhibited during angiogenesis. A better understanding of the situation between tissue angiogenesis and and antiangiogenesis factors has significant implication in tumor treatment.

Finally, the mechanistic details of angiogenesis require elucidation at the cellular and molecular level. The locus of action for any given angiogenesis factor, based on our present constructs of angiogenic events, can be at the level of endothelial matrix modification, endothelial cell migration, and/or proliferation. That one factor can act at all three loci seems as improbable as an action at one locus being sufficient to produce angiogenesis. Clearly, these matters will be resolved with the aid of appropriate *in vitro* model systems.

ACKNOWLEDGMENTS

I would like to express my deepest appreciation to the lifetime members of the Laboratory of Vascular Endothelial Research for their efforts on my behalf. The support of the National Institutes of Health (from grants CA 15381 and 31790) made this effort possible and is most gratefully acknowledged.

REFERENCES

1. Folkman, J., *Adv. Cancer Res.*, **19**, 331 (1974).
2. Folkman, J., *Sci. Am.*, **234**, 58 (1976).
3. Folkman, J., and Cotran, R., *Int. Rev. Exp. Pathol.*, **16**, 207 (1976).
4. Warren, B. A. in H.-I. Peterson, Ed., *Tumor Blood Circulation: Angiogenesis, Vascular Morphology and Blood Flow of Experimental and Human Tumors*, CRC Press, Inc., Boca Raton, Fla. 1979.
5. Ausprunk, D. H., in J. Houck, Ed., *Handbook of Inflammation I*, "*Chemical Messengers of the Inflammatory Process*," Elsevier/North-Holland, 1979.
6. Haudenschild, C. C., *Adv. Microcirc.* **9**, 226 (1980).
7. Gullino, P. M., in R. Baserga, Ed., *Handbook of Experimental Pharmacology*, Springer-Verlag, Berlin, Vol. 57, 1981.
8. Auerbach, R., *Lymphokines*, **4**, 69 (1981).
9. Van der Kolk, S., *Observationes Anatomico-Pathologici et Practici Argumenti*, G. G. Sulpke, Amsterdam, 1826.
10. Virchow, R., *Die krankhaften Geschwulste*, Hirschwald, Berlin, 1863.
11. Thiersch, C., *Der Epithelialkrebs, namentlich der Haut mit Atlas*, Leipzig, 1865.
12. Ribbert, H., *Dtsch. Med. Wochenschr.*, **30**, 801 (1904).
13. Goldmann, E., *Proc. R. Soc. Med.*, **1**, 1 (1907).
14. Russell, B. R. G., Imp. Cancer Res. Fund. 3rd Sci. Rept., 341 (1908).
15. Sandison, J. C., *Am. J. Anat.*, **41**, 447 (1928).
16. Algire, G. H., and Chalkley, H. W., *J. Natl. Cancer Inst.*, **6**, 73 (1945).
17. Algire, G. H., and Chalkley, H. W., in F. R. Moulton, Ed., *Mammary Tumors in Mice*, American Association for the Advancement of Science, Washington, D.C., 1945.
18. Algire, G. H., and Legallais, F. Y., *Cancer Res.*, **7**, 724 (1947).
19. Merwin, R. M., and Algire, G. H., *J. Natl. Cancer Inst.*, **17**, 23 (1956).
20. Chalkley, H. W., Algire, G. H., and Morris, H. P., *J. Natl. Cancer Inst.*, **6**, 363 (1946).
21. Yamaura, H., and Sato, H., in S. Garattini and G. Franchi, Eds., *Chemotherapy of Cancer Dissemination and Metastasis*, Raven Press, New York, 1973.

22. Yamaura, H., and Sato, H., *J. Natl. Cancer Inst.*, **53**, 1229 (1974).

23. Eddy, H. A., and Casarett, G. W., *Microvasc. Res.*, **6**, 63 (1973).

24. Sanders, A. G., and Shubik, P., *Isr. J. Exp. Med.*, **11**, 118 (1964).

25. Ide, A. G., Baker, N. H., and Warren, S. L., *Am. J. Roentgenol.*, **42**, 891 (1939).

26. Shivas, A. A., and Gillespie, W. J., *Br. J. Cancer*, **23**, 638 (1968).

27. Day, E. D., in M. J. Brennan and W. L. Simpson, Eds., *Biological Interactions in Normal and Neoplastic Growth*, Little, Brown, Boston, 1962.

28. Brem, S., Cotran, R., and Folkman, J., *J. Natl. Cancer Inst.*, **48**, 347 (1972).

29. Tannock, I. F., *Br. J. Cancer*, **22**, 258 (1968).

30. Tannock, I. F., and Steel, G. G., *J. Natl. Cancer Inst.*, **42**, 771 (1969).

31. Folkman, J., and Hochberg, M., *J. Exp. Med.*, **138**, 745 (1973).

32. Folkman, J., Cole, P., and Zimmerman, S., *Ann. Surg.*, **164**, 491 (1966).

33. Gimbrone, M. A., Jr., Leapman, S. B., Cotran, R. S., and Folkman, J., *J. Exp. Med.*, **136**, 261 (1972).

34. Brem, S., Brem, H., Folkman, J., Finkelstein, D., and Patz, A., *Cancer Res.*, **36**, 2807 (1976).

35. Patz, A., Brem, S., Finkelstein, D., Chen, C.-H., Lutty, G., Bennett, A., Coughlin, W. R., and Gardner, J., *Ophthalmology (Rochester)*, **85**, 626 (1978).

36. Folkman, J., *Ann. Surg.*, **175**, 409 (1972).

37. Sorgente, N., Kuettner, K. E., Soble, L. W., and Eisenstein, R., *Lab. Invest.*, **32**, 217 (1975).

38. Langer, R., Conn, H., Vacanti, J., Haudenschild, C., and Folkman, J., *Proc. Natl. Acad. Sci. USA*, **77**, 4331 (1980).

39. Taylor, S., and Folkman, J., *Nature*, **297**, 307 (1982).

40. Gullino, P. M., *Cancer*, **39**, 2697 (1977).

41. Gimbrone, M. A., Jr., and Gullino, P. M., *J. Natl. Cancer Inst.*, **56**, 305 (1976).

42. Maiorana, A., and Gullino, P. M., *Cancer Res.*, **38**, 4409 (1978).

43. Brem, S. S., Jensen, H. M., and Gullino, P. M., *Cancer*, **41**, 239 (1978).

44. Chodak, G. W., Scheiner, C. J., and Zetter, B. R., *N. Engl. J. Med.*, **305**, 869 (1981).

45. Wood, S., *Arch. Pathol.*, **66**, 550 (1958).

46. Liotta, L. A., Kleinerman, J., and Saidel, G. M., *Cancer Res.*, **34**, 997 (1974).

47. Greenblatt, M., and Shubik, P., *J. Natl. Cancer Inst.*, **41**, 111 (1968).

48. Ehrmann, R. L., and Knoth, M., *J. Natl Cancer Inst.*, **41**, 1329 (1968).

49. Gitterman, C. O., and Luell, S., *Proc. Am. Assoc. Cancer Res.*, **10**, 29 (1969).

50. Arey, L. B., in J. L. Orbison and D. E. Smith, Eds., *The Peripheral Blood Vessels*, Williams and Wilkins, Baltimore, 1963.

51. Ausprunk, D. H., Knighton, D. R., and Folkman, J., *Dev. Biol.*, **38**, 237 (1974).

52. Clark, E. R., and Clark, E. L., *Am. J. Anat.*, **64**, 251 (1939).

53. Cliff, W. J., *Phil. Trans. R. Soc.*, **246**, 305 (1963).

54. Branemark, P.-I., *Bibl. Anat.*, **7**, 9 (1964).

55. Schoefl, G. I., *Virchows Arch. Pathol. Anat.*, **337**, 97 (1963).

56. Warren, B. A., and Shubik, P., *Lab. Invest.*, **15**, 464 (1966).

57. Williams, R. G., *Anat. Rec.*, **133**, 465 (1959).

58. Gimbrone, M. A., Jr., Leapman, S. B., Cotran, R. S., and Folkman, J., *J. Natl. Cancer Inst.*, **50**, 219 (1973).

59. Yamagami, I., *Jap. J. Ophthalmol.*, **14**, 41 (1970).

60. Ausprunk, D. H., and Folkman, J., *Microvasc. Res.*, **14**, 53 (1977).

61. Patz, A., *Invest. Ophthalmol. Vis. Sci.*, **19**, 1133 (1980).

62. Ashton, N., *Trans. Ophthalmol. Soc. U.K.*, **100**, 359 (1980).

63. Wise, G. N., *Trans. Am. Ophthalmol. Soc.*, **54**, 720 (1956).

64. Goldberg, M. F., in J. R. Lynn, W. B. Snyder, and A. Vaisen, Eds., *Diabetic Retinopathy*, Grune and Stratton, New York, 1974.

65. Hayreh, S. S., *Int. Ophthalmol.*, **2**, 27 (1980).

66. Vaupel, P., *Microvasc. Res.*, **13**, 399 (1977).

67. Endrich, B., Hammersen, F., Gotz, A., and Messmer, K., *J. Natl. Cancer Inst.*, **68**, 475 (1982).

68. Remensnyder, J. P., and Majno, G., *Am. J. Pathol.*, **52**, 301 (1968).

69. Knighton, D. R., Silver, I. A., and Hunt, T. K., *Surgery*, **90**, 262 (1981).

70. Glaser, B. M., D'Amore, P. A., Michels, R. G., Patz, A., and Fenselau, A., *J. Cell Biol.*, **84**, 298 (1980).

71. D'Amore, P. A., Glaser, B. M., Brunson, S. K., and Fenselau, A. H., *Proc. Natl. Acad. Sci. USA*, **78**, 3068 (1981).

72. Ryan, T. J., in A. Jarrett, Ed., *The Physiology and Pathophysiology of the Skin*, Academic, New York, Vol. 2, 1973.

73. Dvorak, H. F., Dvorak, A. M., Manseau, E. J., Wiberg, L., and Churchill, W. H., *J. Natl. Cancer Inst.*, **62**, 1459 (1979).

74. Clark, R. A., Stone, R. D., Leung, D. Y. K., Silver, I., Hohn, D. D., and Hunt, T. K., *Surg. Forum*, **27**, 16 (1976).

75. Polverini, P. J., Cotran, R. S., Gimbrone, M. A., Jr., and Unanue, E. R., *Nature*, **269**, 804 (1977).

76. Cavallo, T., Sade, R., Folkman, J., and Cotran, R. S., *Am. J. Pathol.*, **70**, 345 (1973).

77. Burger, P. C., and Klintworth, G. K., *Lab. Invest.*, **45**, 328 (1981).

78. Crocker, D. J., Murad, T. M., and Geer, J. C., *Exp. Mol. Pathol.*, **13**, 51 (1970).

79. Fromer, C. H., and Klintworth, G. K., *Am. J. Pathol.*, **79**, 537 (1975).

80. Fromer, C. H., and Klintworth, G. K., *Am. J. Pathol.*, **81**, 531 (1975).

81. Klintworth, G. K., *Am. J. Pathol.*, **73**, 691 (1973).

82. Fromer, C. H., and Klintworth, G. K., *Am. J. Pathol.*, **82**,157 (1976).

83. Sidky, Y. A., and Auerbach, R., *J. Exp. Med.*, **141**, 1084 (1975).

84. Auerbach, R., Kubai, L., and Sidky, Y., *Cancer Res.*, **36**, 3435 (1976).

85. Pliskin, M. E., Ginsberg, S. M., and Carp, N., *Transplantation*, **29**, 255 (1980).

86. Muthukkaruppan, V., and Auerbach, R., *Science*, **205**, 1416 (1979).

87. Nishioka, K., and Katayama, I., *J. Pathol.*, **126**, 63 (1978).

88. Kaminski, M., Kaminska, G., and Majewski, S., *Folia Biol.(Praha)*, **24**, 105 (1978).

89. Kaminski, M., Majewski, S., Kaminska, G., Bem, W., and Szmurlo, A., *Arch. Immun. Ther. Exp.*, **26**, 1075 (1978).

90. Cavallo, T., Sade, R., Folkman, J., and Cotran, R. S., *J. Cell Biol.*, **54**, 408 (1972).

91. Knighton, D., Ausprunk, D., Tapper, D., and Folkman, J., *Br. J. Cancer*, **35**, 347 (1977).

92. Kessler, D. A., Langer, R. S., Pless, N. A., and Folkman, J., *Int. J. Cancer*, **18**, 703 (1976).

93. Kumar, P., Kumar, S., Marsden, H. B., Lynch, P. G., and Earnshaw, E., *Cancer Res.*, **40**, 2010 (1980).

94. Selye, H., *The Mast Cells*, Butterworth, Washington, D.C., 1965.

95. Mottaz, J. H., Zelickson, A. S., Thorne, E. G., and Wachs, G., *Acta Dermatol. Venereol.*, **53**, 195 (1973).

96. Smith, S. S., and Basu, P. K., *Can. J. Ophthalmol.*, **5**, 175 (1970).

97. D'Amore, P. A., *Microvasc. Res.*, **15**, 137 (1978).

98. Maca, R. D., Fry, G. L., Hoak, J. C., and Loh, P. T., *Thromb. Res.*, **11**, 715 (1977).

99. Wall, R. T., Harker, L. A., and Striker, G. E., *Lab. Invest.*, **39**, 523 (1978).

100. Jakob, W., Jentzsch, K. D., Mauersberger, B., and Oehme, P., *Exp. Pathol.(Jena)*, **13**, 231 (1977).

101. Gospodarowicz, D., and Thakral, T. K., *Proc. Natl. Acad. Sci. USA*, **75**, 847 (1978).

102. Federman, J. L., Brown, G. C., Felberg, N. T., and Felton, S. M., *Am. J. Ophthalmol.*, **89**, 231 (1980).

103. Nishioka, K., and Ryan, T. J., *J. Invest. Dermatol.*, **58**, 33 (1972).

104. Wolf, J. E., Jr., and Harrison, R. G., *J. Invest. Dermatol.*, **61**, 130 (1973).

105. Koos, R. D., and LeMaire, W. J., in G. S. Greenwald and P. F. Terranova, Eds., *Factors Regulating Ovarian Function*, Raven, New York, in press.

106. Hoffman, H., McAuslan, B., Robertson, D., and Burnett, E., *Exp. Cell Res.*, **102**, 269 (1976).

107. Gimbrone, M. A., Jr., Cotran, R. S., Leapman, S. B., and Folkman, J., *J. Natl. Cancer Inst.*, **52**, 413 (1974).

108. Fournier, G. A., Lutty, G. A., Watt, S. Fenselau, A., and Patz, A., *Invest. Ophthalmol. Vis. Sci.*, **21**, 351 (1981).

109. Langer, R., and Folkman, J., *Nature*, **263**, 797 (1976).

110. Rhine, W. D., Hsieh, D. S. T., and Langer, R., *J. Pharm. Sci.*, **69**, 265 (1980).

111. Hamburger, V., *A Manual of Experimental Embryology*, University of Chicago Press, Chicago, 1960.

112. Auerbach, R., Kubai, L., Knighton, D., and Folkman, J., *Dev. Biol.*, **41**, 391 (1974).

113. Olander, J. V., Marasa, J. C., Kimes, R. C., Johnston, G. M., and Feder, J., *In Vitro*, **18**, 99 (1982).

114. Folkman, J., Merler, E., Abernathy, C., and Williams, G., *J. Exp. Med.*, **133**, 275 (1971).

115. McAuslan, B. R., and Hoffman, H., *Exp. Cell Res.*, **119**, 181 (1979).

116. Phillips, P., and Kumar, S., *Int. J. Cancer*, **23**, 82 (1979).

117. Goodall, C. M., Sanders, A. G., and Shubik, P., *J. Natl. Cancer Inst.*, **35**, 497 (1965).

118. Shubik, P., Feldman, R., Garcia, H., and Warren, B. A., *J. Natl. Cancer Inst.*, **57**, 769 (1976).

119. Greenblatt, M., Choudari, K. V. R., Sanders, A. G., and Shubik, P., *Microvasc. Res.*, **1**, 420 (1969).

120. Sewell, I. A., *J. Anat.*, **100**, 839 (1966).

121. Fenselau, A., and Mello, R. J., *Cancer Res.*, **36**, 3269 (1976).

122. Fenselau, A., and Wallis, K., *Fed. Proc.*, **41**, 737 (1982).

123. Fenselau, A., Kaiser, D., and Wallis, K., *J. Cell. Physiol.*, **108**, 375 (1981).

124. Fenselau, A., Watt, S., and Mello, R. J., *J. Biol. Chem.*, **256**, 9605 (1981).

125. Suddith, R. L., Kelly, P. J., Hutchinson, H. T., Murray, E. A., and Haber, B., *Science*, **190**, 682 (1975).

126. Atherton, A., *Cancer Res.*, **37**, 3619 (1977).

127. Schor, A. M., Schor, S. L., Weiss, J. B., Brown, R. A., Kumar, S., and Phillips, P., *Br. J. Cancer*, **41**, 790 (1980).

128. Keegan, A., Hill, C., Kumar, S., Phillips, P., Schor, A., and Weiss, J., *J. Cell Sci.*, **55**, 261 (1982).

129. Watt, S. L., Kirchmayer, D., and Auerbach, R., in J. Oppenheim and S. Cohen, Eds., *Interleukins, Lymphokines and Cytokines*, Academic, New York, in press.

130. Castellot, J. J., Jr., Karnovsky, M. J., and Spiegelman, B. M., *Proc. Natl. Acad. Sci. USA*, **77**, 6007 (1980).

131. Folkman, J., Haudenschild, C. C., and Zetter, B. R., *Proc. Natl. Acad. Sci. USA*, **76**, 5217 (1979).

132. Mostafa, L. K., Jones, D. B., and Wright, D. H., *J. Pathol.*, **132**, 207 (1980).

133. McAuslan, B. R., and Reilly, W., *Exp. Cell Res.*, **130**, 147 (1980).

134. Zetter, B. R., *Nature*, **285**, 41 (1980).

135. Wall, R. T., Harker, L. A., and Striker, G. E., *Lab. Invest.*, **39**, 523 (1978).

136. Thorgeirsson, G., Robertson, A. L., and Cowan, D. H., *Lab. Invest.*, **41**, 51 (1979).

137. Sholley, M. M., Gimbrone, M. A., Jr., and Cotran, R. S., *Lab. Invest.*, **36**, 18 (1977).

138. Glaser, B. M., D'Amore, P. A., Seppa, H., Seppa, S., and Schiffmann, E., *Nature*, **288**, 483 (1980).

139. Bowersox, J. C., and Sorgente, N., *Cancer Res.*, **42**, 2547 (1982).

140. Albrecht-Buehler, G., *Cell*, **11**, 395 (1977).

141. Rifkin, D. B., Gross, J. L., Moscatelli, D., and Jaffe, E., in H. L. Nossel and H. J. Vogel, Eds., *Pathobiology of the Endothelial Cell*, Academic, New York, 1982.

142. Moscatelli, D., Jaffe, E., and Rifkin, D. B., *Cell*, **20**, 343 (1980).

143. Liotta, L. A., Abe, S., Robey, P. G., and Martin, G. R., *Proc. Natl. Acad. Sci. USA*, **76**, 2268 (1979).

144. Kalebic, T., Garbisa, S., Glaser, B., and Liotta, L. A., *J. Cell Biol.*, **95**, 128a (1982).

145. Russo, R. G., Liotta, L. A., Thorgeirsson, U., Brundage, R., and Schiffmann, E., *J. Cell Biol.*, **91**, 459 (1981).

146. Nicosia, R. F., Tchao, R., and Leighton, J., *In Vitro*, **18**, 538 (1982).

147. Folkman, J., and Haudenschild, C., *Nature*, **288**, 551 (1980).

148. Sholley, M. M., and Cotran, R. S., *Am. J. Pathol.*, **91**, 229 (1978).

149. Thakral, K. K., Goodson, W. H., III, and Hunt, T. K., *J. Surg. Res.*, **26**, 430 (1979).

150. Martin, B. M., Gimbrone, M. A., Jr., Unanue, E. R., and Cotran, R. S., *J. Immunol.*, **126**, 1510 (1981).

151. Greenburg, G. B., and Hunt, T. K., *J. Cell. Physiol.*, **97**, 353 (1978).

152. Banda, M. J., Knighton, D. R., Oredsson, S., Hunt, T. K., and Werb, Z., *Fed. Proc.*, **41**, 456 (1982).

153. Saba, H. I., Hartmann, R. C., and Saba, S. R., *Thromb. Res.*, **12**, 397 (1978).
154. Sholley, M. M., Gimbrone, M. A., Jr., and Cotran, R. S., *Lab. Invest.*, **38**, 32 (1978).
155. Eliason, J. A., *Invest. Ophthalmol. Vis. Sci.*, **17**, 1087 (1978).
156. Auerbach, R., and Sidky, Y. A., *J. Immunol.*, **123**, 751 (1979).
157. Kaminski, M. J., Nowacyk, M., Skopinska-Roazewska, E., Kaminska, G., and Bem, W., *Clin. Exp. Immunol.*, **46**, 327 (1981).
158. Azizkhan, R. G., Azizkhan, J. C., Zetter, B. R., and Folkman, J., *J. Exp. Med.*, **152**, 931 (1980).
159. Leveille, A. S., and Morse, P. H., *Am. J. Ophthalmol.*, **91**, 640 (1981).
160. Thorgeirsson, G., and Robertson, A. L., *Atherosclerosis*, **31**, 231 (1978).
161. Saba, S. R., and Mason, R. G., *Thromb. Res.*, **7**, 807 (1975).
162. Zauberman, H., Michaelson, I. C., and Bergman, E., *Exp. Eye Res.*, **8**, 77 (1969).
163. Buonassisi, V., and Colburn, P., *Adv. Microcirc.*, **9**, 76 (1980).
164. Zetter, B. R., and Antoniades, H. N., *J. Supramol. Struct.*, **11**, 361 (1979).
165. Zetter, B. R., Azizkhan, R. G., Azizkhan, J. C., Brouty-Boye, D., Folkman, J., Haudenschild, C. C., Klagsbrun, M., Potash, R., and Scheiner, C. J., in D. H. Bing and R. A. Rosenbaum, Eds., *Plasma and Cellular Modulatory Proteins*, Center for Blood Research, Inc., Boston, 1981.
166. Huseby, R. A., Currie, C., Lagerborg, V. A., and Garb, S., *Microvasc. Res.*, **10**, 396 (1975).
167. Ryan, T. J., *Br. J. Dermatol.*, **82** (Suppl. 5), 99 (1970).
168. Wolf, J. E., Jr., and Hubler, W. R., Jr., *Br. J. Dermatol.*, **92**, 273 (1975).
169. Wolf, J. E., Jr., and Hubler, W. R., Jr., *Arch. Dermatol.*, **111**, 321 (1975).
170. Hubler, W. R., Jr., and Wolf, J. E., Jr., *Cancer*, **38**, 187 (1976).
171. Jeney, A. V., and Torö, E., *Virchows Arch. Pathol. Anat.*, **296**, 471 (1935).
172. McAuslan, B. R., in L. Jimenez de Asua, Ed., *Control Mechanisms in Animal Cells*, Raven, New York, 1980.
173. Johnson, A. R., Boyden, N. T., and Wilson, C. M., *J. Cell. Physiol.*, **101**, 431 (1979).
174. Henkind, P., *Am. J. Ophthalmol.*, **85**, 287 (1978).
175. Glaser, B. M., D'Amore, P. A., Michels, R. G., Brunson, S. K., Fenselau, A., Rice, T., and Patz, A., *Ophthalmology (Rochester)*, **87**, 440 (1980).
176. D'Amore, P. A., *J. Cell Biol.*, **95**, 192a (1982).
177. Gospodarowicz, D., Bialecki, H., and Greenburg, G., *J. Biol. Chem.*, **253**, 3736 (1978).
178. Maciag, T., Cerundolo, J., Ilsley, S., Kelley, P. R., and Forand, R., *Proc. Natl. Acad. Sci. USA*, **76**, 5674 (1979).
179. Tuan, D., Smith, S., Folkman, J., and Merler, E., *Biochemistry*, **12**, 3159 (1973).
180. Weiss, J. B., Brown, R. A., Kumar, S., and Phillips, P., *Br. J. Cancer*, **40**, 493 (1979).
181. Schor, A. M., Kumar, S., and Phillips, P. J., *Int. J. Cancer*, **25**, 773 (1980).
182. Kissun, R. D., Hill, C. R., Garner, A., Phillips, P., Kumar, S., and Weiss, J. B., *Br. J. Ophthalmol.*, **66**, 165 (1982).
183. Brown, R. A., Weiss, J. B., Tomlinson, I. W., Phillips, P., and Kumar, S., *Lancet*, **i**, 682 (1980).
184. Watt, S. L., Ph.D. Dissertation, Johns Hopkins University, 1981.

185. Schor, A. M., Schor, S. L., and Kumar, S., *Int. J. Cancer*, **24**, 225 (1979).

186. BenEzra, D., *Am. J. Ophthalmol.*, **86**, 455 (1978).

187. BenEzra, D., *Surv. Ophthalmol.*, **24**, 167 (1979).

188. Form, D. M., Sidky, Y. A., Kubai, L., and Auerbach, R., in T. J. Powles, R. S. Bockman, K. V. Honn, and P. Ramwell, Eds., *Prostaglandins and Cancer: First International Conference*, Alan R. Liss, Inc., New York, 1982.

189. Ziche, M., Jones, J., and Gullino, P. M., *J. Natl. Cancer Inst.*, **69**, 475 (1982).

190. Ziche, M., and Gullino, P. M., *J. Natl. Cancer Inst.*, **69**, 483 (1982).

191. McAuslan, B. R., Hannan, G. N., Reilly, W., Whittaker, R. G., and Florence, M., in B. R. McAuslan, Ed., *CSIRO Symposium on the Importance of Copper in Biology and Medicine*, CSIRO, Canberra, 1980.

192. Gospodarowicz, D., Brown, K. D., Birdwell, C. R., and Zetter, B. R., *J. Cell Biol.*, **77**, 774 (1978).

193. Berman, M., Winthrop, S., Ausprunk, D., Rose, J., Langer, R., and Gage, J., *Invest. Ophthalmol. Vis. Sci.*, **22**, 191 (1982).

194. Fenselau, A., and Kaiser, D., *Fed. Proc.*, **37**, 1435 (1978).

195. Gospodarowicz, D., and Ill, C. R., *J. Clin. Invest.*, **65**, 1351 (1980).

196. Gospodarowicz, D., and Lui, G.-M., *J. Cell. Physiol.*, **109**, 69 (1981).

197. Tauber, J.-P., Cheng, J., Massoglia, S., and Gospodarowicz, D., *In Vitro*, **17**, 519 (1981).

198. Kadish, J. L., Butterfield, C. E., and Folkman, J., *Tiss. Cell*, **11**, 99 (1979).

5

PROSTAGLANDINS AND THE PROLIFERATION OF CULTURED ANIMAL CELLS

Christina Smith
Angela M. Otto
Luis Jimenez de Asua

CONTENTS

Abbreviations

MCA	3-Methylcholanthrene
TPA	12-O-Tetradecanoylphorbol-13-acetate
BHK	Baby hamster kidney
EGF	Epidermal growth factor

1. INTRODUCTION: PROSTAGLANDINS AND CELL GROWTH

1.1. Some Physiological Roles of Prostaglandins

Prostaglandins are small molecules that are synthesized from essential fatty acids and found in a wide variety of cell types (1). Although the predominant biosynthetic route begins with a single precursor, arachidonic acid (2), no common physiological function has been described for these cyclopentane derivatives; indeed, many diverse roles have been suggested for the different prostaglandins, with some molecules such as prostaglandin $F_{2\alpha}$ ($PGF_{2\alpha}$) and prostaglandin E_1 (PGE_1) functioning in many seemingly unrelated ways.

The biosynthesis of the prostaglandins has been reviewed by Samuelsson et al. (1, 2). Arachidonic acid is converted by prostaglandin endoperoxide synthase to highly unstable intermediate endoperoxides, which themselves are the precursors of prostaglandins, thromboxanes, other hydroxylated fatty acids, and leukotrienes. These are usually not stored by the cells, but are released and rapidly metabolized. This suggests that the effects of these molecules are local and that they may be involved in carefully balanced control mechanisms.

Prostaglandins may have an important function in mediating hormone action (1). Thyroid-stimulating hormone, for example, activates phospholipase A_2 which, in turn, induces prostaglandin synthesis. Luteinizing hormone stimulates prostaglandin synthesis in isolated Graafian follicles. In nonprimate mammals, $PGF_{2\alpha}$ is released by the uterus and transferred to the ovarian artery, where it causes inhibition of progesterone secretion and regression of the corpus luteum. $PGF_{2\alpha}$ may also mediate the action of prolactin in mouse mammary gland explants.

Kidney functions are also modulated by prostaglandins (3). PGE_2, for example, controls the vasoconstrictor and natriuretic actions of pressor hormones. Renal medullary blood flow may also be controlled by prostaglandins. In addition, some of the renal prostaglandins mediate the effect of bradykinin and may mediate or modulate the actions of other renal kinins as well.

There may be many situations where prostaglandins with opposing effects act in the same process, with the balance between the agents determining the final result. For example, PGI_2 and PGE_2 are able to relax the smooth muscle of airways, and of the vascular, alimentary, and reproductive systems (4). Conversely, $PGF_{2\alpha}$ contracts smooth muscle. A second example is provided by studies of platelet functions. Arachidonic acid and the prostaglandin endoperoxides, PGG_2 and PGH_2, cause aggregation of platelets whereas PGI_2, PGE_2, and PGD_2 inhibit this process (1). The balance between the PGI_2 produced by arterial walls, and the endoperoxides and thromboxanes produced by platelets, controls thrombus formation in blood vessels. In this connection also, endoperoxides and thromboxanes may have a role in the closure of the umbilical artery after birth (1). Prostaglandins are also involved in inflammation (5). PGE_1 and PGE_2 increase blood flow and vascular permeability thus making the entry of other mediators of inflammation possible. Yet again, the balance of different prostaglandins determines the development and regression of inflammation. $PGF_{2\alpha}$, in this respect, is antagonistic to the PGEs.

There is also evidence for the role of prostaglandins in the control of cell proliferation. Psoriasis, an inflammatory proliferative skin disease, may be the result of an imbalance or oversynthesis of prostaglandins, since treatment with glucocorticoids, which decreases the concentration of arachidonic acid, improves the condition (6). Another example is the stimulation of hemopoietic cells. PGE_2, at concentrations as low as 10^{-13} M, stimulates quiescent hemopoietic stem cells to proliferate *in vitro* (7).

This brief description of some of the functions of prostaglandins should suffice to demonstrate the varied roles that prostaglandins play in determining cellular function. It has been suggested that the wide ranging effects of prostaglandins might be elicited by a common mechanism (4). This mechanism might operate by altering intracellular cAMP and/or Ca^{2+} concentrations. Indeed, in many situations a correlation between changes in cAMP and prostaglandin action has been demonstrated (4). The effects of PGI_2 and PGE_2, for example, on smooth muscle are thought to be mediated by increased cAMP levels (4). However, not all the prostaglandins can act in this way; $PGF_{2\alpha}$, for instance, does not affect cAMP levels. Even among those prostaglandins which do substantially alter cAMP concentrations, not all of their functions are necessarily mediated by this mechanism. This is shown by considering the PGE_1 stimulation of hemopoietic cell proliferation, which cannot be prevented by treatment of the cells with imidazole, a compound that increases the destruction of cAMP (7).

One reason for the intense interest in prostaglandin function is their implication in many diseases and abnormal processes. These include asthma, dysmenorrhoea, spontaneous abortion, and premature labor. In particular, increases in prostaglandin levels have been associated with different types of cancer.

1.2. Production of Prostaglandins in Tumor Tissues

The earliest demonstration of a possible connection of prostaglandins with cancerous tissue came from the work of Williams in 1966 (8), who reported high levels of $PGF_{2\alpha}$ and PGE_2 in tumor tissue and plasma of patients with medullary carcinoma of the thyroid. Since then a number of other reports have demonstrated high concentrations of prostaglandins in tumor tissues (see 9). These include some carcinoid tumors, Kaposi's sarcoma, neuroblastomas, and certain kinds of breast cancer. However, no general conclusions can be drawn inasmuch as not all tumors studied contain abnormal levels of prostaglandins.

A condition often occuring in conjunction with carcinomas is the active resorption of bone in the jaw by dental cysts (10, 11). It has been suggested that bone resorption may be connected to the high levels of PGE_2 synthesized and released by the cyst. In support of this, isolated dental cysts continued to synthesize prostaglandins *in vitro*. Moreover, bone resorption by the cysts was also observed in tissue culture. Addition to the cultures of indomethacin or polyphloretin phosphate, compounds which inhibit prostaglandin synthesis, inhibited both processes. Thus prostaglandins, specifically PGE_2, may be associated with bone resorption.

Evidence for the involvement of prostaglandins in the proliferation of cancerous tissue is supported by studies in the induction of tumors in animals with subsequent measurement of prostaglandin concentrations. For example, tumors induced by Moloney sarcoma virus in mouse legs produced a 53-fold increase in PGE_2 and a 7-fold increase in $PGF_{2\alpha}$ compared to untreated leg tissue in the same animal (13). The significance of increased levels of prostaglandins in the growth of tumor cells was studied using inhibitors of prostaglandin synthesis. Aspirin and indomethacin had no effect on patients with medullary carcinoma of the thyroid (14), but another inhibitor of prostaglandin synthesis, nutmeg, did (see 9). Drugs such as aspirin, indomethacin, and flurbiprofen seem to have variable effects in other systems—in some cases tumors decreased and even disappeared; in other systems, for example, mouse B-16 melanomas, these drugs had no effect (for review see 15). Further investigation of the inhibition of prostaglandin synthesis may elucidate the role that prostaglandins play in tumor cell growth.

1.3. Enhancement of Carcinogenesis by Prostaglandins

The understanding of tumor production has been facilitated by thinking of the process as occurring in stages: (i) the initiation and (ii) the promotion of carcinogenesis (see 16). Agents that stimulate initiation may not themselves produce tumors. Promoting factors, alone, sometimes produce tumors at very low rates but, when given after an initiating agent, produce a high incidence of tumors. This model has been especially useful for describing the mechanisms of tumor production in skin, liver, bladder, and mammary gland. The evidence to date favors a role for prostaglandins in the second stage of the process. This is exemplified by the following experiments.

When skin tumors in mice are induced by 3-methylcholanthrene (MCA), the tumors do not begin to appear until, at least, 4 months after the treatment (17). However, when the mice are injected with $PGF_{2\alpha}$ or PGE_2 after MCA treatment, tumors appear in over 90% of the animals after only 2 months (17). Prostaglandins injected into untreated mice do not produce tumors during the experimental period. Thus the prostaglandins have acted as co-carcinogens. In the same study the pattern of DNA synthesis was investigated by injecting the mice with [^{3}H]thymidine. MCA-plus prostaglandin-treated mice showed 15–20-fold greater levels of [^{3}H]thymidine incorporation than control mice. MCA, $PGF_{2\alpha}$, or PGE_2 separately gave only small increases in [^{3}H]thymidine incorporation compared to untreated mice. This suggests that the prostaglandins have stimulated DNA synthesis in MCA-treated cells. This may be related to the shortening of the latency period of carcinogenesis.

In another kind of experiment 12-O-tetradecanoylphorbol-13-acetate (TPA) was used to induce tumors in mouse skin (18–21). Application of TPA is followed by an increase in the synthesis of arachidonic acid, PGE_2, $PGF_{2\alpha}$, and ornithine decarboxylase. When the mice are treated with indomethacin as well as with TPA, these substances are not induced and tumor production is decreased. Tumors reappear, in this situation, when prostaglandins are injected. This suggests a strong connection between prostaglandins and growth of some tumors.

1.4. Production of Prostaglandins in Cultured Cell Lines

The influence of prostaglandins on cell growth has been shown more clearly by looking at the production of prostaglandins by various cells in culture. Untransformed cells such as baby hamster kidney (BHK) or Balb/c 3T3 fibroblasts in culture, excrete low quantities of prostaglandins into the medium ($<$ 1 ng prostaglandin/μg cellular DNA) (22–25). Transformation of the cells with the polyoma virus results in the loss of growth control and also induces up to a 100-fold increase in prostaglandin synthesis and release into the medium (22–25). Both PGE_2 and $PGF_{2\alpha}$ were detected in the medium, although PGE_2 predominated. BHK fibroblasts transformed by a temperature-sensitive mutant of polyoma produced higher prostaglandin levels at the permissive temperature (22). It remains to be investigated whether changes in prostaglandin regulation are causally related to the changes in growth parameters.

Not all virally transformed cells show increased production of prostaglandins. Some host-infectious virus combinations have unaltered prostaglandin synthesis; others do show greater levels of prostaglandin release after infection (26, 27). These latter examples also show increased interferon production. There is some evidence to suggest that prostaglandin formation is a corollary of interferon synthesis (26, 27). The relationship between prostaglandins and interferon, however, is as yet undefined.

Prostaglandins may function in the proliferation of untransformed cells in culture as well. Human embryo lung fibroblasts growing in 10% serum synthesized and released 0.5 ng prostaglandins (combination of PGAs, PGBs, and PGEs) per ml of medium (28). The addition of aspirin, hydrocortisone, and particularly of indomethacin reduced this synthesis to below 0.1 ng/ml. The result of the addition of inhibitors to the cultures was biphasic. Initially, cells growing exponentially were retarded compared to cells growing in medium without inhibitor. However, as cells became more quiescent with increasing cell numbers, the presence of prostaglandin inhibitors stimulated growth. This may reflect the action of different prostaglandins. The effect of adding exogenous prostaglandins separately to cell cultures is considered in the next section.

2.   THE EFFECT OF PROSTAGLANDINS ON ANIMAL CELLS IN CULTURE

2.1.   The Effect of Exogenous Prostaglandins on Tumor Cells in Culture

The role of prostaglandins in the control of tumor cell proliferation has been studied by Karmali et al. (29). They investigated the effect of PGA_1, PGE_1, PGE_2, and $PGF_{2\alpha}$ on the growth of a Raji lymphoid cell line derived from Burkitt lymphoma tissue. Their results show that PGE_1, PGE_2, and $PGF_{2\alpha}$ all stimulated cell growth at concentrations up to 100 pg/ml. Above this concentration, although $PGF_{2\alpha}$ was still stimulatory, PGE_1 and PGE_2 inhibited the growth of Raji cells. PGA_1 had no effect on cellular proliferation at concentrations between 1 pg/ml and 100 ng/ml. The implication that prostaglandins may influence the rate of cell growth was further tested by the addition of indomethacin or chloroquine, drugs known to inhibit the action of prostaglandins (30). Both compounds severely inhibited the growth of Raji cells in culture; in addition, the inhibition of proliferation by chloroquine could be reversed by 1 ng/ml of exogenous PGE_2. This demonstrates that the observed alterations in cell proliferation are, indeed, likely to be a direct effect of prostaglandin action.

2.2.   The Effect of Exogenous Prostaglandins on Untransformed Cells in Culture

The effect of prostaglandins on an untransformed cell line, Swiss 3T3 cells, has been extensively studied by Jimenez de Asua and his colleagues (31–35). In brief, the prostaglandins can be classified into the following groups of compounds:

1.   Those that stimulate cells to initiate DNA synthesis and divide at low, near-physiological concentrations (< 100 ng/ml),
2.   Those that only stimulate cell growth at high concentrations (> 100 ng/ml),
3.   Those that have no effect on cell proliferation at any concentration up to 10 μg/ml.

Of all the prostaglandins studied, only $PGF_{2\alpha}$ can be classified in the first category (Fig. 1). Swiss 3T3 cells respond to $PGF_{1\alpha}$, PGE_1, PGE_2, and PGD_2 but proliferate only at nonphysiological concentrations of these compounds, and the final number of cells that have undergone DNA replication after 28 hours of stimulation is much lower than the number responding to

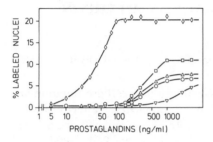

Figure 1. Effect of increasing concentrations of prostaglandins on the initiation of DNA synthesis in Swiss 3T3 cells. O, PGF_{2a}; $\triangle$, PGE_2; ∇, PGE_1; $\square$, PGF_{1a}; and $\diamond$, PGD_{2a}. Data from Jimenez de Asua et al. (35).

$PGF_{2\alpha}$ stimulation (Fig. 1). The PGAs and PGB_2 have no mitogenic effects (Table 1).

2.3. Comparison of the Action of Prostaglandins in Different Cell Cultures

At first sight, some of the results with Raji and Swiss 3T3 cells appear to be contradictory. The effects of $PGF_{2\alpha}$ and the PGAs are the same with both cell types; the former stimulates them to grow at low concentrations and the latter are nonmitogenic in both systems. However, the effects of the PGEs in the two systems are different: PGEs at low concentrations stimulate Raji cells to increase proliferation, but this is not the case with Swiss 3T3 cells.

The effect of a specific prostaglandin alone may not be observed in these culture systems which contain serum factors. Prostaglandins are added to Raji cells grown in 10% fetal calf serum. Quiescent Swiss 3T3 cells are stimulated in "conditioned" medium containing depleted serum. Thus both sets of cells may be responding to a combination of the relevant prostaglandin and unknown serum factors to produce the observed alterations in cell proliferation. The interaction of prostaglandins with other compounds is discussed later.

Can prostaglandins induce quiescent cells to replicate in the absence of serum? $PGF_{2\alpha}$ stimulated initiation of DNA synthesis with a labeling index similar to that observed with Swiss 3T3 cells in conditioned medium (34, 35). The dose response curve to $PGF_{2\alpha}$ was similar in both cell clones (35). Thus the stimulatory effect of $PGF_{2\alpha}$ does not depend on serum factors in these mouse cells. However, for long-term experiments, low levels of serum are required for cell attachment, viability, and division (34). The mitogenic effect of $PGF_{2\alpha}$ is not limited to cloned cells. The response of secondary mouse embryo cells to this prostaglandin is similar to that of Swiss 3T3 and 3T6 cells (35). Furthermore, PGE_1 and PGE_2 had only marginal effects ($< 5\%$ labeling index) on both the cloned and secondary cell cultures.

On the other hand, Balb/c 3T3 cells represent a cell clone that cannot be induced to synthesize DNA by $PGF_{2\alpha}$ alone (35). However, in the presence of 1% serum, which does not significantly stimulate cell proliferation, these cells respond to $PGF_{2\alpha}$ with a labeling index similar to that of Swiss 3T3 cells. It has been suggested that serum may activate a nonoperative prostaglandin receptor or may intervene in a step subsequent to a prostaglandin–receptor interaction (35).

2.4. The Specificity of $PGF_{2\alpha}$ Action on the Induction of DNA Synthesis in Mouse Fibroblastic Cells

Several lines of investigation have indicated that the mitogenic effect of $PGF_{2\alpha}$ is specific among compounds with structural and/or functional sim-

Table 1. Effects of Different Prostaglandins and $PGF_{2\alpha}$ Analogues on the Initiation of DNA Replication in Quiescent Swiss 3T3 Cells[a]

ADDITIONS	LABELED NUCLEI (%)
None	0.5
PGA_1	0.4
PGA_2	0.8
PGB_1	1.1
PGD_2	3.8
$PGF_{1\alpha}$	5.1
$PGF_{2\alpha}*$	14.0
$PGF_{2\alpha}$	20.1
9-epi-$PGF_{2\alpha}$	0.7
11-epi-$PGF_{2\alpha}$	6.4
15-epi-$PGF_{2\alpha}$	6.7
15-keto-$PGF_{2\alpha}$	0.8
$PGF_{2\alpha}$, 15-methylether	20.0
13,14 dihydro $PGF_{2\alpha}*$	5.0
13,14 dihydro $PGF_{2\alpha}$	20.0

[a] The prostaglandins and $PGF_{2\alpha}$ analogues were added at a concentration of 8.5×10^{-7} M except for those marked with * which were 1.6×10^{-7} M. % labeled nuclei was calculated as described (34) after 28 hours of incubation.

ilarities. Neither the prostaglandin precursors, arachidonic and linoleic acids, nor other fatty acids such as myristic, palmitic, and oleic acids had any stimulatory effect on Swiss 3T3 cells. Some stable analogues of prostaglandin endoperoxides were also not mitogenic (31, 35). Eleidosin and acetylcholine, which have effects similar to those of PGF$_{2\alpha}$ on renal and reproductive functions (36), were likewise inactive in stimulating Swiss 3T3 and 3T6 cells. These results suggest that PGF$_{2\alpha}$ may act by means of a prostaglandin receptor.

3. THE STRUCTURAL REQUIREMENT OF PGF$_{2\alpha}$ FOR ELICITING ITS BIOLOGICAL EFFECTS IN SWISS 3T3 CELLS

The structure of PGF$_{2\alpha}$ is shown in Fig. 2. Related prostaglandins which are less active in inducing DNA synthesis in quiescent Swiss 3T3 cells differ in many ways (see also Fig. 2). In order of decreasing mitogenic activity they are: PGF$_{2\alpha}$, PGF$_{1\alpha}$, PGE$_2$, PGD$_2$, and PGE$_1$ (Fig. 1); PGA$_1$, PGA$_2$, and PGB$_1$ show no activity at all (Table 1). PGF$_{1\alpha}$ differs from PGF$_{2\alpha}$ only in a Δ^5 double bond. PGE$_2$ and PGD$_2$ have keto groups replacing hydroxyl groups at C-9 and C-11, respectively. PGE$_1$, which is the least

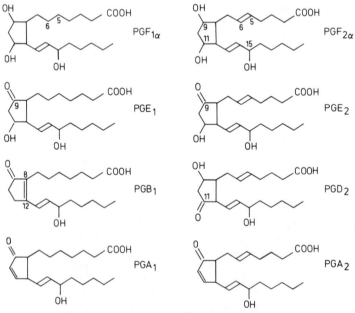

Figure 2. Structures of different prostaglandins.

active, lacks both the Δ^5 double bond and also has a keto group at C-9. Inactive molecules have no hydroxyl (or replacement) groups at all on C-11. PGI$_2$ (not shown), another inactive molecule, lacks the hydroxyl group at C-9. These structures suggest that certain parts of the PGF$_{2\alpha}$ molecule are vitally important for its activity.

The use of structural analogues of PGF$_{2\alpha}$ has further elucidated the specificity of this compound as a mitogenic agent (33). The structures of PGAs, PGB$_1$, and PGI$_2$ suggest that C-9 and C-11 hydroxyl groups are essential for activity. This is supported by epimerisation at both these sites. Whereas PGF$_{2\alpha}$ (at 8.5×10^{-7} M) stimulated 20% of the cell population to undergo DNA synthesis in a 28-hour period, the same concentration of 11-epi-PGF$_{2\alpha}$ induced only 6% of the cells into S phase (Table 1). Epimerisation of the C-9 hydroxyl (PGF$_{2\beta}$) completely abolished mitogenicity under these conditions (37).

It has also been shown that the stereochemistry of the hydroxyl group at C-15 is important for PGF$_{2\alpha}$ activity. Epimerisation at this site reduced the number of cells entering S phase from 20% to 6%. Replacement of this hydroxyl group with a keto group rendered the molecule inactive up to 8.8×10^{-6} M. However, conversion to a methyl ether did not affect the ability of the prostaglandin to induce DNA synthesis (Table 1).

The Δ^{13} double bond appears to be of secondary importance for activity inasmuch as reduction to yield 13,14 dihydro PGF$_{2\alpha}$ gave a less active molecule only at low concentrations (Table 1).

The most important regions for the activity of the PGF$_{2\alpha}$ molecule, then, are the C-9, C-11, and C-15 hydroxyl groups which must be in the correct stereochemical form. The double bonds at Δ^5 and Δ^{13} appear to be of minor importance.

4. INTERACTION OF PGF$_{2\alpha}$ WITH OTHER GROWTH FACTORS AND HORMONES

4.1. Nonsynchronous Additions of PGF$_{2\alpha}$ to Quiescent Swiss 3T3 Cells

When PGF$_{2\alpha}$ is added to cultures of quiescent Swiss 3T3 cells at concentrations ranging between 1 and 1000 ng/ml, the cells respond in a characteristic manner: (i) there is a prereplicative or lag phase, which is always about 15 hours for these cells, before any cell initiates DNA replication, and (ii) after the lag phase has been completed, the cells enter S phase at a rate that can be described by apparent first order kinetics and defined by a rate constant k (Fig. 3). The rate at which cells enter S phase is dependent

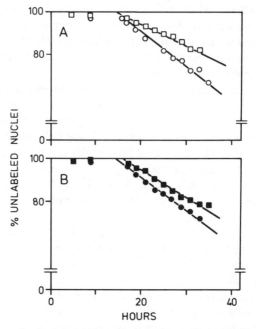

Figure 3. Fraction of cells that remain unlabeled after addition of PGF$_{2\alpha}$ to the medium of quiescent cultures. (A) PGF$_{2\alpha}$ (60 ng/ml) (□) or PGF$_2$ (300 ng/ml) (○) was added at the start. (B) PGF$_{2\alpha}$ (60 ng/ml) was added at the start and then PGF$_{2\alpha}$ (240 ng/ml) after 5 hours. (●) or after 15 hours. (■) Final values of k ($\times$ 10^2/hour) in (A) were 1.1 (□) and 1.8 (○); in (B), 1.7 (●) and 1.6 (■). Data from Jimenez de Asua et al. (34).

on the concentration of PGF$_{2\alpha}$ added, up to a saturation value which is usually about 200 ng/ml.

Nonsynchronous additions of different concentrations of PGF$_{2\alpha}$ have further characterized the differences between the two types of processes (32). When a low concentration of PGF$_{2\alpha}$ (60 ng/ml) is added and a second addition of 240 ng/ml delayed for 5 or 15 hours, the duration of the lag phase was 15 hours from the initial stimulation in all cases (Fig. 3). The final rate, obtained at 15 hours, at which cells entered S phase, was determined by the combined effect of both additions (i.e., k was similar to a single addition of 300 ng/ml). However, when the second addition was delayed for 15 hours, the final rate was not reached until about 24 hours after the first addition (Fig. 3). Thus only low concentrations of PGF$_{2\alpha}$ are necessary to initiate progress through the lag phase. The observation that the final rate of entry into S phase could be altered by additions of PGF$_{2\alpha}$ after the lag phase had commenced further supports the concept that PGF$_{2\alpha}$ acts in at least two different ways to stimulate cell proliferation. Furthermore, k was altered very soon after the second addition at 15 hours; this suggests that the final rate is set toward the end of the lag phase.

4.2. Interaction of PGF$_{2\alpha}$ with Other Prostaglandins

Early experiments in which very high concentrations (50 μg/ml) of PGE$_1$ and PGE$_2$ were added within 8 hours of PGF$_{2\alpha}$ stimulation showed that the PGEs exerted an inhibitory effect on the PGF$_{2\alpha}$ stimulation of Swiss 3T3 cells (31). This is in agreement with previous reports demonstrating an inhibitory effect of PGEs at relatively high concentrations in other cell types (29, 38–40).

More recently, however, it has been shown that PGEs added at concentrations less than 200 ng/ml can enhance cell proliferation (41). These compounds have a synergistic effect on the rate of cells entering S phase after stimulation with PGF$_{2\alpha}$. PGF$_{2\alpha}$ promoted 22% of the cell population to replicate within 28 hours. The PGEs alone, up to 100 ng/ml, did not have any mitogenic effect. However, PGF$_{2\alpha}$ in combination with concentrations of PGE$_1$ as low as 20 ng/ml gave a labeling index of 51%. PGE$_2$ with PGF$_{2\alpha}$ gave a comparable result (Fig. 4). PGE$_1$ and PGE$_2$ appear to be acting synergistically with PGF$_{2\alpha}$ by increasing the rate constant k. The length of the lag phase was not affected by addition of PGEs. A combination of PGF$_{2\alpha}$ with both PGE$_1$ and PGE$_2$ did not further enhance the synergy obtained with PGE$_1$ or PGE$_2$ separately (Fig. 4), suggesting that both compounds may act through a common mechanism. PGE$_1$ and PGE$_2$ can also be added after the beginning of the lag phase but in this case a reduced synergy was observed. Additions at the end of the lag phase also gave a

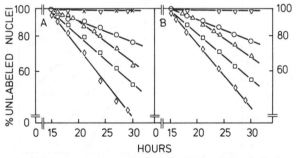

Figure 4. Kinetics of entry in S phase stimulated by PGF$_{2\alpha}$ (300 ng/ml) alone or with PGE$_1$ (100 ng/ml) or PGE$_2$ (100 ng/ml). (*A*) (X), no additions; (∇), PGE$_1$; (O), PGF$_{2\alpha}$. PGF$_{2\alpha}$ with PGE$_1$ added at: ($\diamond$) 0 hours; ($\square$), 9 hours; ($\triangle$), 15 hours. Final values of K ($\times$ 10^{-2}/hour) were (x), 0.05; (∇), 0.06; (O), 1.6; ($\diamond$), 5.5; ($\square$), 3.9; ($\triangle$), 3.3. (*B*) (∇), PGE$_2$; (O), PGF$_{2\alpha}$. PGF$_{2\alpha}$ with PGE$_2$ added at: ($\diamond$), 0 hours; ($\square$), 9 hours; ($\triangle$), 15 hours. Final values of k ($\times$ 10^{-2}/hour) were (∇), 0.06; (O), 1.6; ($\diamond$), 5.1; ($\square$), 3.7; ($\triangle$), 15 hours. Data from Otto et al. (41).

synergistic effect, but there was a delay of 5 hours before an increase in the rate of entry into S phase was detected (Fig. 4). The synergistic effect of PGEs with $PGF_{2\alpha}$ suggests that the PGEs act through a different pathway than $PGF_{2\alpha}$ to increase k.

The synergistic effect of PGE_1 and PGE_2 on $PGF_{2\alpha}$ induction is not general among other prostaglandins (41). Other prostaglandins or precursors of prostaglandins have no effect on $PGF_{2\alpha}$ stimulation. This may indicate that the keto groups on C-9 and the hydroxyl on C-11 (see Fig. 2) may be important for the synergistic action of PGEs inasmuch as these structures are the only ones not shared with the other prostaglandins.

4.3. Interaction of $PGF_{2\alpha}$ with Other Growth Factors

Quiescent Swiss 3T3 cells respond to a variety of growth factors to initiate DNA replication (see 42, 43). Epidermal growth factor (EGF), although structurally unrelated to $PGF_{2\alpha}$, induces similar kinetics for DNA replication (Fig. 5). Each growth factor, alone, stimulated about 15% of the cell population to initiate DNA synthesis. When $PGF_{2\alpha}$ and EGF are added together, 55% of the cells initiate DNA synthesis within 28 hours (Fig. 5). Thus a synergistic effect is observed. When these compounds are added 6 hours apart, a reduced synergy is obtained. However, when EGF is added 15 hours after $PGF_{2\alpha}$ (or vice versa), the synergy is delayed by 15 hours; that is, the duration of another lag phase passes before the combined effects of the two growth factors are seen (Fig. 5). This delay strongly

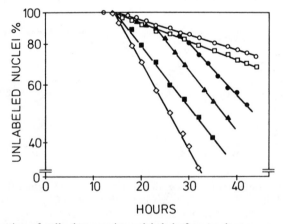

Figure 5. Fraction of cells that remains unlabeled after synchronous or nonsynchronous addition of EGF (20 ng/ml) and $PGF_{2\alpha}$ (300 ng/ml) □, $PGF_{2\alpha}$; 0, EGF. $PGF_{2\alpha}$ with EGF added at: ◇, 0 hours; ■, 6 hours; ▲, 10 hours; □, 15 hours. Data from Jimenez de Asua et al. (43).

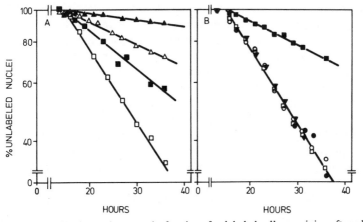

Figure 6.   Effect of hydrocortisone on the fraction of unlabeled cells remaining after addition of PGF$_{2\alpha}$ or of PGF$_{2\alpha}$ and insulin. (*A*) Effect of synchronous addition of PGF$_{2\alpha}$, insulin, and hydrocortisone. △, PGF$_{2\alpha}$ (300 ng/ml); ▲, PGF$_{2\alpha}$ (300 ng/ml) + hydrocortisone (20 ng/ml); □, PGF$_{2\alpha}$ (300 ng/ml) + insulin (50 ng/ml); ■, PGF$_{2\alpha}$ (300 ng/ml) + insulin (50 ng/ml) + hydrocortisone (20 ng/ml). (*B*) Effect of nonsynchronous addition of hydrocortisone to cells stimulated by PGF$_{2\alpha}$ and insulin. □ PGF$_{2\alpha}$ (300 ng/ml) + insulin (50 ng/ml) were added to quiescent cultures at 0 time. Hydrocortisone (40 ng/ml) was added at the start with PGF$_{2\alpha}$ and insulin (■) or at 5 hours, (0); 10 hours, (△); 15 hours, (▼); 27 hours, (□) after addition of PGF$_{2\alpha}$ and insulin. Data from Jimenez de Asua (45).

suggests that some events triggered by the second factor cannot be integrated into the biochemical pathways stimulated by the first factor during the lag phase. However, these two growth factors must trigger some events in common since PGF$_{2\alpha}$ and EGF added before 6 hours produces a synergistic response seen at 15 hours. Furthermore, some processes stimulated by the first growth factor persist to be integrated later into the pathways stimulated by the second growth factor since at 30 hours (for additions 15 hours apart) a synergistic and not additive effect is observed. PGF$_{2\alpha}$ and EGF may, therefore, induce DNA replication by different sequences of events.

4.4. Interaction of PGF$_{2\alpha}$ with Hormones

Insulin is a hormone which can act as a growth-promoting factor under some circumstances (44). However, insulin at near-physiological concentrations (50 ng/ml or less), does not have any mitogenic effect on quiescent Swiss 3T3, Swiss 3T6, or embryonic mouse fibroblasts (31, 32, 35). Despite this, insulin can act synergistically with PGF$_{2\alpha}$ (and other growth factors such as EGF) to increase the rate of initiation of DNA synthesis (Fig. 6). This phenomenon of synergy can occur when insulin is added at any time during or after the lag phase (32). Irrespective of the time of insulin addition, the length of the lag phase remains unaltered, and only the final rate constant k is affected. Insulin is also capable of increasing the rate constant set by $PGF_{2\alpha}$ in combination with EGF, PGE_1, or PGE_2. In these cases, about 80% of the cells have initiated DNA replication by 28 hours.

Glucocorticoids, such as hydrocortisone and dexamethasone (45), inhibit the mitogenic effect of $PGF_{2\alpha}$ by decreasing the final rate of entry into S phase (Fig. 6A). This inhibitory effect, like that of high concentrations of PGE_1 and PGE_2, was observed only when the compounds were present during the first three hours of the lag phase. Hydrocortisone added at 5, 10, or 15 hours after $PGF_{2\alpha}$ failed to exert an inhibitory effect (Fig. 6B).

4.5. Interaction of $PGF_{2\alpha}$ with Microtubule-Disrupting Agents

Recent results (46–48) have demonstrated that microtubule organization plays an important regulatory role in the events leading up to DNA synthesis. Addition of colcemid or colchicine, microtubule-disrupting drugs, to Swiss 3T3 cells produced a synergistic effect with $PGF_{2\alpha}$, alone or with insulin. These drugs do not themselves induce DNA synthesis. However, the synergistic effect is only seen when they are present for the first 5 hours of the lag phase. Addition at 8 or 15 hours after $PGF_{2\alpha}$ gave no increase in the rate constant, even though microtubules were disrupted. Thus the events stimulated by colchicine or colcemid occur early in the lag phase. Furthermore, removal of colcemid, as early as 5 hours after $PGF_{2\alpha}$ stimulation, which allowed cell division, resulted in a loss of the synergistic effect. It appears that microtubules must remain disrupted up to 10 hours of the lag phase for the full synergistic response (48).

A further interesting result with these drugs shows that preincubation of the cells with colchicine or colcemid for 8 hours, and subsequent addition of $PGF_{2\alpha}$ and insulin, shortened the lag phase by about 2 hours (48). When the drug remained in the medium with the growth factor and the hormone, synergy was observed. Removal of colcemid, which is rapidly released from the microtubules, before $PGF_{2\alpha}$ and insulin addition still resulted in a shortened lag phase, but there was no synergistic effect. These results show that disruption of the microtubules affects at least two different processes leading to DNA replication: progression through the lag phase and rate of initiation of DNA synthesis. Furthermore, the results suggest that the regulation of these two processes can be uncoupled.

4.6. A Model for the Interactions of Growth Factors and Hormones

Additions of $PGF_{2\alpha}$ at different times and additions of $PGF_{2\alpha}$ with other growth factors and hormones illuminate the presence of at least two distinctive kinetic phases in the stimulation of cell proliferation. The first, which is the lag phase, is always of a constant duration regardless of the stimulation. The second, the rate of entry into S, can be described by apparent first order kinetics, quantified by a rate constant k, and exhibits a variable rate dependent on the stimulus given. It has been postulated that at least two different signals regulate the two phases (32). Signal 1 initiates progression through the lag phase and is independent of growth factor concentration above a minimal level. Signal 2, which determines the rate of entry of the cells into a replicative phase, may be modulated at times during or even after the lag phase and is dependent on growth factor concentration. The delivery of signal 1 is, experimentally, only seen when signal 2 is also delivered. It can be further postulated that signals 1 and 2 induce different sequences of events resulting in putative products which must interact to promote the cell to enter a replicative phase. This interaction could occur towards the end of the lag phase, at a time when the rate determining step(s) is thought to take place.

The biochemical pathways initiated by a growth factor stimulus, and leading to DNA synthesis and mitosis, are likely to be many with complicated interactions between the pathways. For example, $PGF_{2\alpha}$ and EGF probably stimulate different pathways containing some common events. Modulating agents like insulin, glucocorticoids, PGEs, and microtubule-disrupting drugs, which cannot themselves initiate the proliferative process, but which alter the rate at which cells enter S phase, probably interact with the main pathways using different routes.

5.   BIOCHEMICAL EVENTS STIMULATED BY PROSTAGLANDINS AND INTERACTING HORMONES

5.1.   The Activation of Glucose Transport

One of the events stimulated by addition of $PGF_{2\alpha}$ to Swiss 3T3 cells is an increase in the uptake of 2-deoxyglucose (50). Fig. 7 shows that the stimulation reflects biphasic kinetics. Insulin is only capable of stimulating the first phase, whereas conversely, $PGF_{2\alpha}$ alone stimulates just the second phase two hours later. However, $PGF_{2\alpha}$ and insulin added together give similar kinetics to those of serum (Fig. 7). Experiments with cycloheximide (50) have demonstrated that only the second phase is dependent on protein synthesis. It has been suggested that the late phase requires *de novo* synthesis of new carrier molecules or other membrane components that allow insertion of the carrier into the plasma membrane. The uptake of 2-deoxyglucose probably reflects an increase in a transport process that is not dependent on

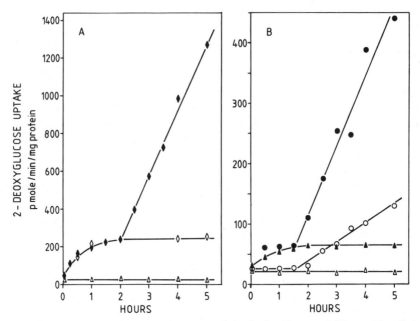

Figure 7. Stimulation of 2-deoxyglucose uptake by fetal calf serum, $PGF_{2\alpha}$, and insulin in quiescent Swiss 3T3 cells. (*A*) △, no addition; ◆, serum (15%); ◇, serum (15%) + cycloheximide (10 μg/ml). (*B*) △, no addition; ▲, insulin (1 μg/ml); 0, $PGF_{2\alpha}$ (400 ng/ml); □, $PGF_{2\alpha}$ (400 ng/ml) + insulin (1 μg/ml). Data from Jimenez de Asua and Rozengurt (50).

phosphorylation since 3-O-methylglucose, a nonphosphorylatable sugar, is also transported in the same way (42).

Table 2 shows the amount of 2-deoxyglucose taken up by Swiss 3T3 cells after various treatments for a 5-hour period during the second, protein-synthesis-dependent phase. The results correlate with the number of cells that have entered S phase after 28 hours. PGE_1 and PGE_2 induced only a very small number of cells to enter S phase and likewise only minimally stimulated 2-deoxyglucose uptake. $PGF_{2\alpha}$ in conjunction with insulin and either PGE_1 or PGE_2 gave over 70% labeled cells and stimulated 2-deoxy-glucose to a high degree. In addition, prostaglandins that are nonmitogenic, such as PGB_1, also do not increase glucose uptake (41). These results suggest that the induction of glucose transport may be one of the events related to the initiation of DNA synthesis. However, it is not yet known whether this event constitutes one of the steps in the pathway leading to DNA replication.

5.2. The Activation of (Na^+-K^+)-ATPase Activity

Ten minutes after $PGF_{2\alpha}$, insulin, or both are added to Swiss 3T3 cells, there is a rapid increase in $^{86}Rb^+$ uptake which has been taken as a measure of the activation of surface membrane $(Na^+\text{-}K^+)$-ATPase enzymes (51). For this biochemical event, insulin gave the same increase in $^{86}Rb^+$ uptake as $PGF_{2\alpha}$ alone or $PGF_{2\alpha}$ and insulin together. Despite this, activation of $(Na^+\text{-}K^+)$-ATPase activity is probably related to the mitogenic effect of $PGF_{2\alpha}$ inasmuch as PGE_1 and PGE_2, at nonmitogenic concentrations, were not able to increase this activity. However, at higher concentrations of PGEs, when some cells did enter S phase, stimulation of $^{86}Rb^+$ uptake was observed (Fig. 8B). The activation of $(Na^+\text{-}K^+)$-ATPase activity, like the first phase of glucose transport, is not dependent on protein synthesis (51).

5.3. The Activation of Phosphate Uptake

Yet another event occurring within minutes of mitogenic stimulation is the activation of phosphate uptake (51). The uptake stimulated by $PGF_{2\alpha}$ or serum shows biphasic kinetics with an early peak observed within 5–10 minutes after stimulation, followed by a more linear increase in uptake up to at least 4 hours after stimulation. The early phase of uptake is independent of protein synthesis, but the second phase is abolished by preincubation of the cells with 10 μg/ml of cycloheximide. The relevance of phosphate uptake stimulation is shown in Fig. 8A. It is demonstrated that the amount of phosphate uptake is dependent on $PGF_{2\alpha}$ concentration. Maximal uptake

Table 2. Changes in 2-Deoxyglucose Uptake and in Number of Nuclei Initiating DNA Synthesis After Addition of Prostaglandins to Quiescent Swiss 3T3 Cells[a]

ADDITIONS	2-DEOXYGLUCOSE UPTAKE (pmol/MINUTE/mg PROTEIN)	LABELED NUCLEI (%)
None	8.8	0.5
Insulin	21.8	0.7
$PGF_{2\alpha}$	39.6	22.0
PGE_1	12.6	1.1
PGE_2	10.5	2.7
$PGF_{2\alpha}$ + insulin	106.2	51.8
$PGF_{2\alpha}$ + PGE_1	95.8	52.0
$PGF_{2\alpha}$ + PGE_2	85.0	49.7
$PGF_{2\alpha}$ + PGE_1 + PGE_2	96.0	54.1
Serum	312.0	95.0

[a] Additions to cells were: insulin, 60 ng/ml; $PGF_{2\alpha}$, 300 ng/ml; PGE_1, 100 ng/ml; PGE_2, 100 ng/ml; fetal calf serum, 10%. Determinations of 2-deoxyglucose uptake and % labeled nuclei were as described in Otto et al. (41). Data from Otto et al. (41).

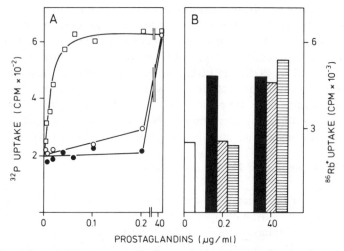

Figure 8.   Effect of different prostaglandins on the early increase in phosphate uptake (A) and $^{86}Rb^+$ uptake (B) in quiescent 3T3 cells. (A) Cells were incubated for 15 minutes with addition of (□) PGF$_{2\alpha}$, (○) PGE$_2$, or (●) PGE$_1$, and then pulsed for 5 minutes with $^{32}P_i$. (B) For $^{86}Rb^+$ uptake determinations the cells were incubated for 15 minutes with □ no additions ■ PGF$_{2\alpha}$, ▨ PGE$_1$, ▤ PGE$_2$, and then labeled for 10 minutes. Reprinted from Lever et al. (51).

is observed at 0.1 μg/ml PGF$_{2\alpha}$, a concentration saturating for the stimulation of DNA synthesis. When PGE$_1$ or PGE$_2$ was added to the cells, phosphate uptake was only stimulated at high (40 μg/ml) concentrations. This parallels the results obtained with $^{86}Rb^+$ uptake (Fig. 8B). Indeed, the early kinetic phase of phosphate uptake may be partially coupled to $^{86}Rb^+$ uptake. Preincubation of the cells with 1.2 mM ouabain, a concentration that completely inhibits $^{86}Rb^+$ uptake, also inhibits phosphate uptake by 50% after PGF$_{2\alpha}$ and 30% after serum stimulation.

5.4.   Changes in Cyclic Nucleotide Levels

When PGF$_{2\alpha}$ was first shown to induce quiescent Swiss 3T3 cells to proliferate, it was suggested that the initial action of the prostaglandin might be mediated by changes in cyclic nucleotide levels (31). Serum has been reported to cause a 14-fold increase in cGMP levels and a 30% decrease in cAMP levels. Only part of this response was obtained with PGF$_{2\alpha}$ or insulin alone, but the two compounds together produced changes comparable to those induced by serum. PGE$_1$, in contrast, increased cAMP levels. These results, taken together, suggested a role for cyclic nucleotides in regulating cell proliferation stimulated by prostaglandins.

Increasing cAMP levels by preincubation of the cells with an inhibitor of phosphodiesterase, SQ 20006, did not affect $PGF_{2\alpha}$ stimulated phosphate or $^{86}Rb^+$ uptake (51). In addition, PGE_1, at 40 μg/ml, greatly increased cAMP concentrations, but at the same time also increased $^{86}Rb^+$ uptake and stimulated the late phase of phosphate uptake. Thus it seems unlikely that changes in cAMP mediate at least those biochemical events stimulated by $PGF_{2\alpha}$. More recently, a study of the early changes in cAMP levels during the first hour after various treatments of Swiss 3T3 cells, has also cast doubt on the role of cAMP as an initial mediator of the stimulus to proliferate in this system. Table 3 depicts these results, which show no correlation between cAMP concentrations and the rate of initiation of DNA synthesis. To date, then, there is no agreement as to the role of cyclic nucleotides in cell proliferation (52, 53).

5.5. Phosphorylation of Membrane Proteins

Mastro and Rozengurt have investigated the phosphorylation of membrane proteins in different cellular states (54). They found a net increase in the incorporation of phosphate into membrane proteins in growing and SV40-

Table 3. Changes in Intracellular cAMP Levels and Number of Nuclei Initiating DNA Synthesis After Addition of Prostaglandins to Quiescent Swiss 3T3 Cells[a]

| | cAMP | | |
| | (pmol/mg PROTEIN) | | LABELED NUCLEI |
ADDITIONS	30 MINUTES	60 MINUTES	(%)
None	17	17	0.5
Insulin	19	17	0.7
$PGF_{2\alpha}$	17	12	22.0
PGE_1	92	30	1.1
PGE_2	23	16	2.7
$PGF_{2\alpha}$ + insulin	20	14	51.8
$PGF_{2\alpha}$ + PGE_1	96	51	52.0
$PGF_{2\alpha}$ + PGE_2	9	17	49.7
Serum	5	14	95.0

[a] Additions to cells were: insulin, 60 ng/ml; $PGF_{2\alpha}$, 300 ng/ml; PGE_1, 100 ng/ml; PGE_2, 100 ng/ml; fetal calf serum, 10%. Determinations of cAMP and % labeled nuclei were as described in Otto et al. (41). Data from Otto et al. (41).

transformed cells as compared to quiescent cells. The same effect was observed when quiescent cells were stimulated with serum (54). This suggested that an increase in protein kinase activity and the phosphorylation of membrane proteins might be part of the sequence of events following growth factor stimulation of resting cells. Mastro (44) further investigated the kinetics of membrane protein phosphorylation after serum stimulation and found that mitogenic concentrations of $PGF_{2\alpha}$ and PGE_1 also increased phosphorylation activity (Fig. 9). Insulin at low concentrations (50 ng/ml) did not stimulate this activity (44), but at mitogenic concentrations (5 μg/ml) increased phosphorylation was observed (Fig. 9). At least two sets of membrane proteins controlled by different mechanisms exist. The basal level of quiescent cell phosphorylation is unaffected by cycloheximide, but the stimulated activity, after growth factor addition, is dependent on protein synthesis. Theophylline, which causes increases in cAMP in 3T3 cells, does not affect the $PGF_{2\alpha}$ or PGE_1-stimulated phosphorylation. This is further evidence to suggest that the initiation of biochemical events leading to DNA replication may not be affected by cAMP levels.

5.6. Phosphorylation of S6 Protein

One of the noticeable differences between quiescent and proliferating cells is the phosphorylation state of the 40 S ribosomal protein S6 (55, 56). In quiescent cells, most of the S6 protein is unphosphorylated. Serum-stimulated cells contain highly phosphorylated S6 derivatives. The degree

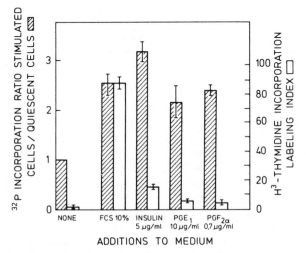

Figure 9. The effects of insulin, PGE_1, or PGF_2 on phosphorylation of quiescent 3T3 cells. Reprinted from Mastro (53).

of phosphorylation and the pattern of S6 derivatives is dependent on the concentration of serum used to stimulate the cells. Low concentrations up to 2.5% yield all phosphorylated S6 derivatives (designated a–e and characterized by a progressively higher state of phosphorylation). Saturating concentrations of 7.5% serum or greater produce a shift to highly phosphorylated derivatives d and e only. $PGF_{2\alpha}$, at saturating concentrations, gives a pattern that is similar to low concentrations of serum. This correlates with the number of cells induced to replicate (Table 4). Combinations of growth-promoting factors such as $PGF_{2\alpha}$ and EGF, or $PGF_{2\alpha}$ and insulin, which increase the rate of cell proliferation compared to a single growth factor, also stimulate more S6 phosphorylation and the derivatives are shifted to the higher phosphorylated form (towards the e derivative). $PGF_{2\alpha}$, EGF, and insulin, all together, give a phosphorylation pattern similar to 10% serum. The correlation between S6 phosphorylation and labeling index suggests a function for this protein in cell proliferation. However, activation of S6 phosphorylation is not sufficient to induce DNA synthesis inasmuch as insulin alone, at a concentration that is not mitogenic, stimulates S6 phosphorylation to the same extent as $PGF_{2\alpha}$ or EGF alone.

5.7. Stimulation of Protein Synthesis

It has long been known that protein synthesis is essential for the progression through the lag phase (57). Cells incubated with growth-promoting factors and cycloheximide will not proliferate. Serum stimulation of quiescent cells induces a 2–3-fold increase in the rate of protein synthesis which is reflected by a large shift of inactive 80S ribosomes and stored nonpolysomal mRNA into actively translating polysomes (55). The withdrawal of serum is followed by a decrease in protein synthesis and a net dephosphorylation of the S6 protein (55). The rate of protein synthesis can be inferred by investigating the percentage of ribosomes found in polysomes on sucrose gradients. This technique has shown that $PGF_{2\alpha}$, EGF, or insulin increases the number of ribosomes in polysomes by 12% (56). Combinations of these factors, which give a synergistic effect on the number of cells entering S phase in a given time, also give a synergistic effect on the percentage of ribosomes in polysomes (Table 4). As with the results of S6 phosphorylation, insulin alone also induces some polysome formation. There is evidence, however, that insulin cannot maintain the increased level of protein synthesis in the same way that serum does (58). This may partly explain why insulin alone does not induce DNA synthesis.

5.8. Changes in the Pattern of Nuclear Nonhistone Proteins

Two-dimensional gel electrophoretic analysis of nuclear proteins of Swiss 3T3 cells treated with $PGF_{2\alpha}$, insulin, or hydrocortisone (42) is shown in

Table 4. Changes in the Degree of Ribosomal Protein S6 Phosphorylation, % Ribosomes in Polysomes, and % Nuclei Initiating DNA Replication After Growth Factor Stimulation of Quiescent Swiss 3T3 Cells[a]

Additions	Relative Degree of S6 Derivative Phosphorylation						Ribosomes in Polysomes (%)	Labeled Nuclei (%)
	NP[b]	a	b	c	d	e		
None	+++	++					36	0.5
Insulin	+	+	+	+	+	+	49	0.8
PGF$_{2\alpha}$	+	+	+	+	+	++	48	15.0
PGF$_{2\alpha}$ + EGF				+	++	+++	68	55.0
PGF$_{2\alpha}$ + insulin				+	++	+++	66	48.0
PGF$_{2\alpha}$ + EGF + insulin				+	+++	++++	72	79.0
Serum				+	+++	++++	74	98.0

[a] Additions to cells were: insulin, 50 ng/ml; PGF$_{2\alpha}$, 300 ng/ml; EGF, 20 ng/ml; fetal calf serum, 10%. Determination of S6 phosphorylation, % polysomes, and % labeled nuclei were as described in Thomas et al. (55). Data from Thomas et al. (55).
[b] NP: nonphosphorylated.

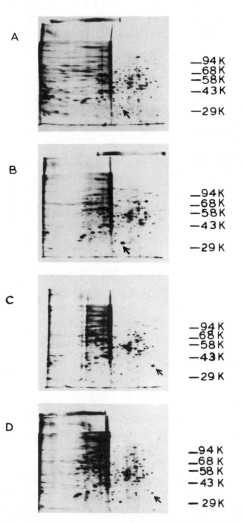

Figure 10. Two-dimensional separation of nuclear proteins labeled with [^{35}S]methionine. (*A*) Quiescent 3T3 cells labeled for 5 hours (arrow indicates polypeptide P$_1$). (*B*) 3T3 cells labeled 0–5 hours after the addition of PGF$_{2\alpha}$ and insulin (arrow polypeptide P$_1$). (*C*) 3T3 cells labeled 25–30 hours after the addition of PGF$_{2\alpha}$ and insulin (arrow, polypeptide P$_2$). (*D*) 3T3 cells labeled from 25–30 hours after the addition of PGF$_{2\alpha}$ and insulin together with hydrocortisone (arrow, polypeptide P$_2$). The figures on the horizontal axis indicate the pH in the isoelectric focusing dimension and those on the vertical axis, the molecular weights of standard proteins included in the SDS gel electrophoresis dimension. Reprinted from Jimenez de Asua et al. (42).

Fig. 10. The conclusions from this work can be summarized as follows: (a) some proteins present in quiescent cells (Fig. 10 A) are greatly reduced after the growth factors are added, and (b) some polypeptides are synthesized at specific times after stimulation. Polypeptide P_1 increases in production and peaks between 2.5 and 7.5 hours after the beginning of the lag phase. The appearance of a second polypeptide, P_2, is temporally correlated with the time when cells begin to enter S phase. The kinetics of the appearance of P_2 is slightly slower under these conditions than when the cells are stimulated with serum (42). This matches the rate of cellular exit from G_1 under the two proliferating conditions. $PGF_{2\alpha}$ and insulin-stimulated cells have a lower rate of exit than serum-stimulated cells. Hydrocortisone added with $PGF_{2\alpha}$ and insulin decreases the rate of entry into S phase and also reduces the amount of P_2 synthesized. P_1 may be related to progression through the lag phase since its production is constant irrespective of the stimuli given to the cells and the rate at which they enter S phase. Further work of this kind may provide a correlation between the particular proteins synthesized at specific points in the lag phase and the effects of different prostaglandins and modifying agents such as insulin, hydrocortisone, and microtubule-disrupting drugs.

6. CONCLUSIONS

It is clear that prostaglandins play a major role in the proliferation of various cells. In mouse fibroblastic cells, $PGF_{2\alpha}$ is the main growth stimulating prostaglandin. PGE_2 stimulates hemopoietic stem cell proliferation. PGE_1 and $PGF_{2\alpha}$ also stimulate Raji tumor cells. It is not known whether these and other prostaglandins stimulate other cell types. It is unlikely that in most situations, a single prostaglandin is responsible for the control of the growth of a cell population. Thus combinations of growth factors and other agents such as hormones must be considered. Stimulation of Swiss 3T3 cells has proved a useful model system to investigate how prostaglandins can control cell proliferation. $PGF_{2\alpha}$ stimulates cell proliferation by inducing two kinetic phases: progression through a lag phase and, subsequently, the initiation of DNA synthesis. Nonmitogenic agents such as insulin, gluco-corticoids, PGEs, and microtubule-disrupting drugs were shown to act by modulating the rate at which cells entered S phase. $PGF_{2\alpha}$ stimulates a number of biochemical events, some of which are also induced by the nonmitogenic agents. It remains to be seen whether these events are causally related to the progression through the lag phase and/or the initiation of DNA synthesis.

The function of PGEs is, at present, unclear although low concentrations stimulate the growth of some cells, high concentrations in many systems inhibit cell proliferation. Whether PGEs can function in both ways in one situation, or preferentially stimulate or inhibit specific cell types, or whether the inhibitory effect is not physiologically significant is as yet unknown.

Another indication that prostaglandins are involved in cell proliferation comes from studies adding inhibitors of prostaglandin action to cell cultures. In Raji cells, SV40-transformed mouse fibroblasts, and untransformed human lung fibroblasts, addition of such inhibitors decreased the rate of cell growth. With the latter system, a biphasic response of the cells to prostaglandin inhibitors indicates the complexity of the effects of prostaglandins on cells. Inhibiting prostaglandin synthesis decreased cell growth in a population that was logarithmically growing; however, the same inhibitors stimulated cell growth in density-inhibited cells (13). These results may reflect the importance of ratios of prostaglandins, perhaps a balance between $PGF_{2\alpha}$ and PGEs, in the maintenance and control of proliferative and quiescent cell states.

An oversynthesis or imbalance of prostaglandins may contribute to the abnormal control of tumor cell growth. Indeed, virally transformed cells, cultured tumor cells, and tissues, in some cases, produce high levels of prostaglandins, especially PGEs. Inasmuch as high concentrations of PGEs can be inhibitory, this would seem to be a contradictory response. Hammerström (22, 23) has suggested that the PGE production by transformed fibroblasts may inhibit the proliferation of cells involved in host-defense mechanisms against cancer cells. It is possible that production of PGEs is a normal cell response to high rates of proliferation and is designed to control cell growth by inhibiting the rate of DNA replication. It may be that tumor cells have lost the ability to respond to PGEs in this way, and that high levels of PGEs continue to be produced because of a fault in a feedback machanism. On the other hand, tumor cells may have altered responses to PGEs; thus these agents may now stimulate cell proliferation at high concentrations. In the future, further research may resolve these problems, and define the complicated interactions of prostaglandins and other compounds and their effects on the proliferation of both normal and cancerous cells.

ACKNOWLEDGMENTS

We thank Drs. Margret Eschenbruch, Ilse Hofer, and Dieter Wächter for careful reading of the manuscript. One of the authors (C. S.) is a recipient of a European fellowship from the Royal Society (London). A. M. O. is a Special Fellow of the Leukemia Society of America, Inc.

REFERENCES

1. Samuelsson, B., Goldyne, M., Granström, E., Hamberg, M., Hammarström, S., and Malmsten, C., *Annu. Rev. Biochem.*, **47**, 997 (1978).

2. Samuelsson, B., *Prostaglandins and Cancer: First International Conference*, Alan R. Liss, Inc., New York, 1982.

3. Terragno, N. A., Malik, K. U., Nasjletti, A., Terragno, D. A., and McGriff, J. C., *Advances in Prostaglandin and Thromboxane Research*, Raven, New York, Vol. 2, 1976.

4. Ramwell, P. W., Karanian, J. W., and Foegh, M. L., *Prostaglandins and Cancer: First International Conference*, Alan R. Liss, Inc., New York, 1982.

5. Greaves, M. W., *Prostaglandins: Physiological and Pathological Aspects*, MTP Press, Lancaster, PA, 1976.

6. Hammarström, S., Hamberg, M., Duell, E. A., Stawiski, M. A., Anderson, T. F., and Voorhees, J. J., *Science*, **197**, 994 (1977).

7. Feher, I., and Gidali, J., *Nature*, **247**, 550 (1974).

8. Williams, E. D., *Proc. Roy. Soc. Med.*, **59**, 602 (1966).

9. Karim, S. M. M., and Rao, B., *Prostaglandins: Physiological and Pathological Aspects*, MTP Press, Lancaster, PA, 1976.

10. Mundy, G. R., *Prostaglandins and Cancer: First International Conference*, Alan R. Liss, Inc., New York, 1982.

11. Tashjian, A. H., Jr., Voelkel, E. F., and Levine, L., *Prostaglandins and Cancer: First International Conference*, Alan R. Liss, New York, 1982.

12. Martin, T. J., and Partridge, N. C., *Prostaglandins and Cancer: First International Conference*, Alan R. Liss, Inc., New York, 1982.

13. Humes, J. L., and Strausser, H. R., *Prostaglandins*, **5**, 183 (1974).

14. Isaacs, P., Whittaker, S. M., and Turnberg, L. A., *Gastroenterology*, **67**, 521 (1974).

15. Bennet, A., *Prostaglandins and Cancer: First International Conference*, Alan R. Liss, Inc., New York, 1982.

16. Slaga, T. J., Fischer, S. H., Nelson, K., and Gleason, G. L., *Proc. Natl. Acad. Sci. USA*, **77**, 3659 (1980).

17. Lupulescu, A., *Nature*, **272**, 634 (1978).

18. Verma, A. K., Rice, W. M., and Boutwell, R. K., *Biochem. Biophys. Res. Commun.*, **79**, 1160 (1977).

19. Ashendel, C. L., and Boutwell, R. K., *Biochem. Biophys. Res. Commun.*, **90**, 623 (1979).

20. Bresnick, E., Meunier, P., and Lamden, M., *Cancer Lett.*, **7**, 121 (1979).

21. Furstenberger, G., and Marks, F., *Biochem. Biophys. Res. Commun.*, **92**, 749 (1980).

22. Hammarström, S., Samuelsson, B., and Bjursell, G., *Nature New Biol.*, **243**, 50 (1973).

23. Hammarström, S., *Eur. J. Biochem.*, **74**, 7 (1977).

24. Goldyne, M. E., Lindgen, J. A., Claesson, H. E., and Hammarström, S., *Prostaglandins*, **19**, 155 (1980).

25. Roos, P., Lindgen, J. A., and Hammerström, S., *Eur. J. Biochem.*, **108**, 279 (1980).

26. Fitzpatrick, F. A., and Stringfellow, D. A., *J. Immunol.*, **125**, 431 (1980).

27. Fitzpatrick, F. A., and Stringfellow, D. A., *Prostaglandins and Cancer: First International Conference*, Alan R. Liss, Inc., New York, 1982.

28. Taylor, L., and Polgar, P., *FEBS Lett.*, **79**, 69 (1977).

29. Karmali, R. A., Horrobin, D. F., Menezes, J., and Patel, P., *Pharmacol. Res. Commun.*, **11**, 69 (1979).

30. Manku, M. S., Mtabaji, J. P., and Horrobin, D. F., *Prostaglandins*, **13**, 701 (1976).

31. Jimenez de Asua, L., Clingan, D., and Rudland, P., *Proc. Natl. Acad. Sci. USA*, **72**, 2724 (1975).

32. Jimenez de Asua, L., O'Farrell, M. K., Clingan, D., and Rudland, P., *Proc. Natl. Acad. Sci. USA*, **74**, 3845 (1977).

33. Jimenez de Asua, L., Otto, A. M., Ulrich, M.-O., Martin-Perez, J., and Thomas, G., *Prostaglandins and Cancer: First International Conference*, Alan R. Liss, Inc., New York, 1982.

34. Rudland, P. S., Durbin, H., Clingan, D., and Jimenez de Asua, L., *Biochem. Biophys. Res. Commun.*, **75**, 556 (1977).

35. O'Farrell, M. K., Clingan, D., Rudland, P. S., and Jimenez de Asua, L., *Exp. Cell Res.*, **118**, 311 (1979).

36. Karino, S. M. M., *The Prostaglandins. Progress in Research*, Medical and Technical Publishing Ltd., Oxford and Lancaster, 1972.

37. Jimenez de Asua, L., Otto, A. M., Lindgren, J. A., and Hammarström, S., *J. Biol. Chem.*, **258**, 8774 (1983).

38. Johnston, G. S., and Pastan, I., *J. Natl. Cancer Inst.*, **47**, 1357 (1971).

39. Honn, K. V., Romic, M., and Skoff, A., *Proc. Soc. Exptl. Biol. Med.*, **166**, 562 (1982).

40. Santoro, M. G., Philpott, G. W., and Jaffe, B. M., *Nature*, **263**, 777 (1976).

41. Otto, A. M., Nilsen-Hamilton, M., Boss, B. D., Ulrich, M. O., and Jimenez de Asua, L., *Proc. Natl. Acad. Sci. USA*, **79**, 4992 (1982).

42. Jimenez de Asua, L., Richmond, K. M. V., Otto, A. M., Kubler, A. M., O'Farrell, M. K., and Rudland, P. S., *Hormones and Cell Culture*. Cold Spring Harbor Conferences on Cell Proliferation, Cold Spring Harbor Laboratory, New York, Vol. 6, 1979.

43. Jimenez de Asua, L., Richmond, K. M. V., and Otto, A. M., *Proc. Nat. Acad. Sci. USA*, **78**, 1004 (1981).

44. Mastro, A., *J. Cell. Physiol.*, **99**, 349 (1979).

45. Jimenez de Asua, L., O'Farrell, M. K., Bennett, D., Clingan, D., and Rudland, P. S., *Nature*, **265**, 450 (1977).

46. Otto, A. M., Zumbé, A., Gibson, L., Kubler, A. M., and Jimenez de Asua, L., *Proc. Natl. Acad. Sci. USA*, **77** 2748 (1979).

47. Otto, A. M., Ulrich, M.-O., and Jimenez de Asua, L., *Cell Biol. Int. Rep.*, **5**, 717 (1981).

48. Otto, A. M., *Prostaglandins and Cancer: First International Conference*, Alan R. Liss, Inc., New York, 1982.

49. Otto, A. M., Smith, C., and Jimenez de Asua, L., *Cell Biol. Int. Rep.*, **6**, 791 (1982).

50. Jimenez de Asua, L., and Rozengurt, E., *Nature*, **251**, 624 (1974).

51. Lever, J. E., Clingan, D., and Jimenez de Asua, L., *Biochem. Biophys. Res. Commun.*, **71**, 136 (1976).

52. Rudland, P. S., and Jimenez de Asua, L., *Biochim. Biophys. Acta*, **560**, 91 (1979).

53. Rozengurt, E., Legg, A., Strong, G., and Courtenay-Luck, N., *Proc. Natl. Acad. Sci. USA*, **78**, 4392 (1981).

54. Mastro, A., and Rozengurt, E., *J. Biol. Chem.*, **251**, 7899 (1976).

55. Thomas, G., Siegmann, M., Gordon, J., Jimenez de Asua, L., Martin-Perez, J., and Nielsen, P., *Cold Spring Harbor Conferences on Cell Proliferation, Vol. 8: Protein Phosphorylation*, Cold Spring Harbor Laboratory, New York, 1981.

56. Thomas, G., Martin-Perez, J., Siegmann, M., and Otto, A., *Cell*, **30**, 235 (1982).

57. Brooks, R. F., *Cell*, **12**, 311 (1977).

58. Hershko, A., Mamont, P., Shields, R., and Tomkins, G. M., *Nature New Biol.*, **232**, 206 (1971).

6

GROWTH-PROMOTING
FACTORS IN HUMAN
AND BOVINE MILK
Michael Klagsbrun
Yuen Shing

CONTENTS

Abbreviations

EGF	Epidermal growth factor
mEGF	Mouse epidermal growth factor
hEGF	Human epidermal growth factor
HMGF	Human milk growth factor
HPLC	High performance liquid chromatography
DTT	Dithiothreitol
PDGF	Platelet-derived growth factor
DMEM	Dulbecco's modified Eagle's medium
MDCK	Mardin–Darby canine kidney

1. INTRODUCTION

Milk is a biological fluid produced by lactating mammals. The physiological function of milk is to provide substances that are important for the nutrition, development, and growth of the mammalian newborn. The composition of milk has been well documented (1). Among the constituents of milk are lipids, proteins, carbohydrates, salts, and trace elements. The composition of milk is strongly affected by variables such as the stage of lactation and the diet of the mother. Ingestion of milk is associated with the growth of the newborn. Aside from contributing nutrients required for

DNA SYNTHESIS

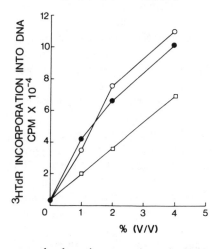

Figure 1. Stimulation of DNA synthesis in Balb/c 3T3 cells by human milk. Milk was collected from three volunteers and added along with [³H]thymidine to confluent monolayers of quiescent Balb/c 3T3 cells at various concentrations. DNA synthesis was assayed after a 48-hour incubation period by measuring tricholoroacetic acid-precipitate radioactive DNA in a scintillation counter.

growth, there is a question of whether milk also contributes macromolecular factors that are capable of stimulating cell division in the various tissues and organs of the newborn.

There is evidence that milk is a source of growth factors, that is, of mitogenic substances capable of stimulating cellular proliferation *in vitro*. In 1978, Klagsbrun developed an assay for the measurement of growth factor activity in human milk (2). The assay was based on the ability of milk samples to stimulate both DNA synthesis and cell division in confluent monolayers of quiescent fibroblasts. Fig. 1 shows the dose-dependent stim-

CELL DIVISION

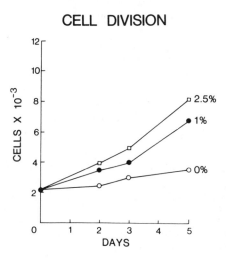

Figure 2. Stimulation of cell division by human milk. Confluent monolayers of quiescent 3T3 cells were incubated with 0% (○), 1% (●), or 2.5% (■) milk. After 2, 3, and 5 days, the cells were detached with trypsin and counted.

ulation of DNA synthesis in cultured cells by milk samples obtained from three lactating women. Fig. 2 shows a dose-dependent time course of stimulation of cell division by one of the milk samples. Serum is a well-known source of growth factor activity and will stimulate DNA synthesis in confluent monolayers of quiescent cells (3). A given volume of milk is more active than the same volume of serum in stimulating DNA synthesis (Fig. 3). For example, human milk at 1% (vol/vol) is as active in stimulating DNA synthesis as is 5% (vol/vol) human serum obtained from the same donor. Human milk at a concentration of 0.5% (vol/vol) is as active as 6% (vol/vol) calf serum. The protein concentrations of human milk and human serum are approximately 9.80 and 70 mg/ml, respectively. Therefore, the specific activity of human milk in stimulating DNA synthesis in confluent quiescent 3T3 cells is 50–100 greater than that of serum. The growth factor activity of human milk is dependent on the stage of lactation (Fig. 4). In general, growth factor activity declines as the lactation period progresses, but never totally disappears.

Another line of evidence for the existence of growth factors in milk was the demonstration of the presence of epidermal growth factor (EGF). EGF is a polypeptide with a molecular weight of 6100 and an isoelectric point of 4.6 (4). EGF was first discovered in the submaxillary gland of the mature male mouse (5). An homologous species of EGF (originally named urogastrone) is found in human urine (6) and has also been detected in the human salivary gland and in the gland of Brunner in the gastrointestinal tract (7). Antibodies to both mouse (mEGF) and human EGF (hEGF) have

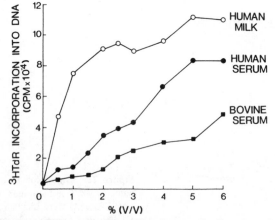

Figure 3.   Stimulation of DNA synthesis by milk and serum. Confluent monolayers of quiescent 3T3 cells were incubated with various concentrations of human milk (O), human serum from the same donor (●), and calf serum (□). DNA synthesis was measured.

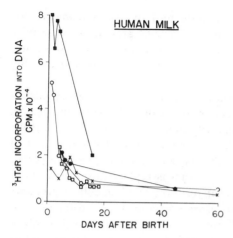

Figure 4. Growth factor activity in human milk as a function of the lactation period. Milk was collected from 5 donors (O, ●, X, ■, □) at various intervals after giving birth. The ability to stimulate DNA synthesis in 3T3 cells was measured at a final milk concentration of 0.25% (vol/vol).

been prepared. Using the antibodies to hEGF, it has been demonstrated that immunologically reactive EGF is found in human milk at a level of 80 ng/ml (8). More important, Carpenter has shown that antibodies to human urine-derived EGF neutralize about 67% of the mitogenic activity of milk for 3T3 cells in culture (9). Thus the conclusion from the studies of Klagsbrun, Carpenter, and colleagues is that human milk contains growth factors, a substantial part of which can be accounted for by EGF.

Table 1. Stimulation of DNA Synthesis by Milk After Protease Digestion[a]

	[³H]THYMIDINE INCORPORATION INTO DNA, cpm	
SAMPLE ADDED TO CELLS	EXP. 1	EXP. 2
No addition	1,869	2,421
Human milk + buffer	66,500	64,000
Human milk + trypsin and α-chymotrypsin	10,900	5,200
Human milk + heat-inactivated trypsin and α-chymotrypsin	65,300	51,400

[a] Samples of human milk were incubated for 4 hours at 37°C with a mixture of trypsin and α-chymotrypsin (each at 500 μg/ml); a mixture of trypsin and α-chymotrypsin (each at 500 μg/ml) that had been inactivated by heating at 100°C for 20 minutes; or a buffer of 0.01 M Tris-HCl, pH 7.8. In Exp. 1, incubation was terminated after 4 hours by the addition of soybean trypsin inhibitor at 2 mg/ml. In Exp. 2, the 4-hour incubation was terminated by heating samples for 20 minutes at 100°C.

Growth factor activity is also found in the milk of cows and sheep (10). In these animals there is a dramatic dependence of growth factor activity on the stage of lactation. The growth factor activity is very high in colostrum, which is the milk obtained right after birth, but is virtually undetectable within 4 days after birth.

Both human and bovine colostrum contain viable cells, mostly macrophages and lymphocytes (11, 12). The presence of viable cells and growth factors in colostrum raises the possibility that colostrum will support the growth of cells in culture. In fact, it has been demonstrated that many cell types including epithelial cells, fibroblasts, and smooth muscle cells will proliferate readily in a medium where serum is replaced by colostrum or milk (13–16). The ability of milk to support the growth of cells is probably due to the presence of a number of macromolecules required for growth. These include hormones, growth factors, attachment factors such as fibronectin, and transport proteins such as transferrin (17). All of these factors can be found in milk. Thus milk can be considered to be a biological fluid rich in factors necessary to support cellular proliferation.

The growth factors found in human milk are polypeptides (Table 1) that are not inactivated by exposure to pH 1 (Table 2). The presence of trypsin

Table 2.   Characterization of Human Milk Growth Factors[a]

	Growth Factors		
	I	II	III
Percent of total activity	5	20	75
Molecular weight in:			
phosphate buffer, pH 7.0	100–120,000	30–34,000	5–6,000
guanidine-HCl, pH 6.5	34–38,000	12–16,000	5–6,000
Isoelectric point	4.2–5.2	3.2–4.8	4.4–4.7
		7.4–8.5	
Inactivation by 6 M guanidine-HCl	No	No	No
Inactivation by 5 mM DTT	Yes	Yes	No
Inactivation 1 M HCl, pH 1	No	No	No

[a] HMGF I, II, and III were prepared by gel filtration chromatography on Sephadex G-100. Molecular weights were determined on HPLC TSK 2000-size exclusion columns under nondenaturing conditions (0.1 M ammonium sulfate, 0.05 M potassium phosphate, pH 7.0), and on HPLC TSK 3000-size exclusion columns under denaturing conditions (6 M guanidine hydrochloride, 0.02 M MES, pH 6.5). Isoelectric points were determined by preparative isoelectric focusing. Sensitivity to inactivation by 6 M guanidine-HCl, 5 mM DTT, and pH 1 was also tested.

inhibitors in milk (18) along with the resistance of milk-derived growth factors to inactivation by pH 1 makes it plausible that these macromolecules could survive passage through the gastrointestinal tract. The targets for milk-derived growth factors *in vivo* have not been ascertained. The presence of EGF in human milk suggests a possible epithelial cell target. EGF has been shown to stimulate epithelial proliferation in mice *in vivo* and in cultured epithelial cells *in vitro* (4, 19). The types of epithelial cells stimulated by EGF include mammary epithelial cells (20–22), keratinocytes (23–25), corneal cells (26), and granulosa cells (27). It is possible that milk-derived growth factors stimulate the growth of certain epithelial cells of the newborn. On the other hand, it is also possible that milk-derived growth factors stimulate the growth of mammary epithelial cells and are secreted into milk by the developing mammary gland.

The rest of the chapter is devoted primarily to a biochemical analysis of milk-derived growth factors. The use of these factors in promoting the growth of cells in culture is also described.

2. CHARACTERIZATION OF GROWTH FACTOR ACTIVITY IN HUMAN MILK

2.1. Measurement of Growth Factor Activity

Growth factor activity is assayed by measuring DNA synthesis in confluent monolayers of quiescent cells (28). About 200 μl containing 10^4 Balb/c 3T3 cells are plated into 0.3 cm^2 microtiter plate wells. The cells become confluent within 3 days. After 5 days the cells are quiescent and very little [^{3}H]thymidine is incorporated into their DNA (about 1000 cpm). Test samples of up to 50 μl are added to the cells along with [^{3}H]thymidine. After a 30–40 hour incubation period, the amount of [^{3}H]thymidine incorporated into DNA is measured. In this assay, about 100,000–120,000 cpm represents maximal incorporation. A unit of growth factor activity is defined as the amount of growth factor required to elicit half-maximal DNA synthesis. Alternatively, after stimulation with growth factor, it is possible to trypsinize the cells and count them in a Coulter counter to assess the increase in cell number. Increases in DNA synthesis correlate directly with increases in cell number. Because of the ease of the measurement, DNA synthesis is the preferred method for assaying growth factor activity. The dose-dependent growth factor activity of a sample of human milk is shown in Fig. 5. In this experiment human milk was obtained from a donor and fats and cells were removed by centrifugation at 13,000 g for 30 minutes at 4°C. The defatted, acellular milk was added at various concentrations to 3T3 cells. The stim-

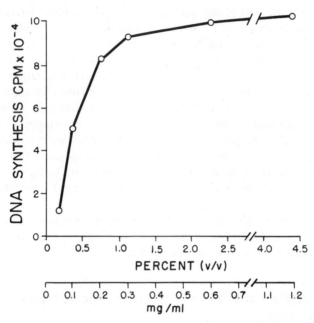

Figure 5. Growth factor activity in defatted, acellular human milk. Human milk obtained about 1 month postpartum was centrifuged to remove fat and cells. Growth factor activity was measured by testing the ability of varying concentrations of human milk to stimulate DNA synthesis in 3T3 cells.

ulation of DNA synthesis by milk is found to be dose-dependent. Half-maximal stimulation is obtained with 0.4% (vol/vol) milk (about 0.1 mg/ml) and maximal stimulation is obtained with 1.2% milk (about 0.3 mg/ml). Human defatted, acellular milk contains about 220 units/ml.

2.2.   Acid Precipitation of Milk

After removal of fats and cells by centrifugation, concentrated HCl is added to the milk to obtain a pH of 4.3. The acidified milk is incubated at 37°C for 60 minutes and is subsequently centrifuged for 60 minutes to remove the precipitate, mostly casein. Of the 220 units/ml present in the original defatted milk, 187 units/ml or 85% of the growth factor activity is found in the clear, soluble supernatant fraction of acidified milk.

2.3.   Gel Filtration and Size Exclusion Chromatography

A supernatant fraction is prepared by the acidification of defatted, acellular human milk. Approximately 1 gram of the sample which represents about

100 ml of the starting whole milk is analyzed by chromatography on Sephadex G-100 equilibrated at pH 4.3 (Fig. 6). Three peaks of growth factor activity with different molecular weights are found and designated as human milk growth factors (HMGF) I, II, and III (29). The relative activities of HMGF I (molecular weight greater than 100,000), HMGF II (molecular weight between 30,000 and 40,000), and HMGF III (molecular weight less than 6,200) vary from batch to batch but in general account for about 5, 20, and 75%, respectively, of the total growth factor activity found in the acid supernatant fraction.

The molecular weights of human milk growth factors I, II, and III can be characterized further by size exclusion chromatography on TSK-size exclusion columns using high performance liquid chromatography (HPLC). Chromatography is carried out both under nondenaturing conditions using phosphate buffer and under denaturing conditions using 6 M guanidine hydrochloride either in the presence or absence of the sulfhydryl reducing agent, dithiothreitol (DTT). The molecular weight distributions of growth

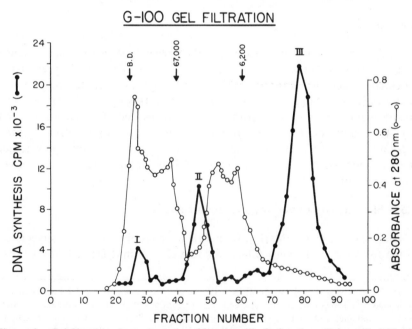

Figure 6. Gel filtration chromatography of human milk. Defatted, acellular milk (100 ml) was acidified to pH 4.3 and the precipitate formed was removed by centrifugation and discarded. The supernatant fraction (1.5 g in 20 ml) was applied to a Sephadex G-100 column (5 × 90 cm) equilibrated with 0.1 M NaCl and 0.01 M sodium acetate, pH 4.3. Fractions (18 ml) were collected, measured for absorbance at 280 nm, and tested for the ability to stimulate DNA synthesis in 3T3 cells.

factor I under nondenaturing and denaturing conditions and the effects of DTT on growth factor activity are shown in Fig. 7. HMGF I has a molecular weight of about 100,000–120,000 under nondenaturing conditions (Fig. 7A) and of about 34,000–38,000 in the presence of guanidine-HCl (Fig. 7B). Thus this growth factor either forms aggregates or is bound to a large molecular weight carrier. The addition of 5 mM DTT to the guanidine results in total loss of growth factor activity (Fig. 7C).

A similar pattern is found with HMGF II (Fig. 8). Under nondenaturing conditions, HMGF II has a molecular weight of about 30,000–34,000 (Fig. 8A), but in the presence of guanidine, the molecular weight is about 12,000–16,000 (Fig. 8B). HMGF II is also inactivated by 5 mM DTT (Fig. 8C).

HMGF III appears to be of a different class than HMGFs I and II (Fig. 9). HMGF III has the same molecular weight of between 5000 and 6000 whether analyzed under nondenaturing conditions (Fig. 9A) or under denaturing conditions (Fig. 9B). Thus this growth factor does not appear to aggregate or bind to carrier. In addition, 5 mM DTT does not adversely affect the biological activity of HMGF III (Fig. 9C).

2.4.   Isoelectric Focusing

To determine their isoelectric points, the three growth factor peaks obtained by gel filtration chromatography, shown in Fig. 6, are analyzed by preparative isoelectric focusing (Fig. 10). HMGF I and III are anionic polypeptides with isoelectric points between 4 and 5. HMGF II is resolved by isoelectric focusing into an anionic fraction with isoelectric points between 3.2 and 4.8 and a more cationic fraction with isoelectric points between 7.4 and 8.5. Whether HMGF II contains two distinct growth factors or whether there is one growth factor, some of which is bound to a carrier, has not yet been determined.

2.5.   Stability of Human Milk Growth Factors

Aliquots of human HMGF I, II, and III were lyophilized and resuspended in the following solutions: 6 M guanidine HCl, 5 mM DTT, 1 M HCl (pH

Figure 7.   Analysis of peak I using HPLC TSK size exclusion columns. HMGF I was prepared by Sephadex G-100 gel filtration as shown in Fig. 6. Samples of about 8 mg were resuspended in 100 μl and analyzed on TSK-size exclusion columns at a flow rate of 1 ml/min. Fractions (0.85 ml) were collected, dialyzed against distilled H_2O, and tested for their ability to stimulate DNA synthesis in 3T3 cells. (A) Analysis on TSK 2000 equilibrated with 0.1 M ammonium sulfate and 0.05 M potassium phosphate, pH 7.0. (B) Analysis on TSK 3000 equilibrated with 6 M guanidine hydrochloride and 0.02 M MES, pH 6.5. (C) Analysis on TSK 3000 equilibrated with 6 M guanidine hydrochloride, 0.02 M MES, pH 6.5, and 5 mM DTT. The thick lines represent stimulation of DNA synthesis and the thin lines represent absorbance at 280 nm.

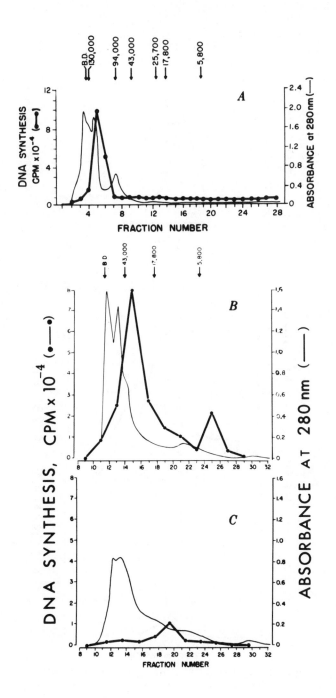

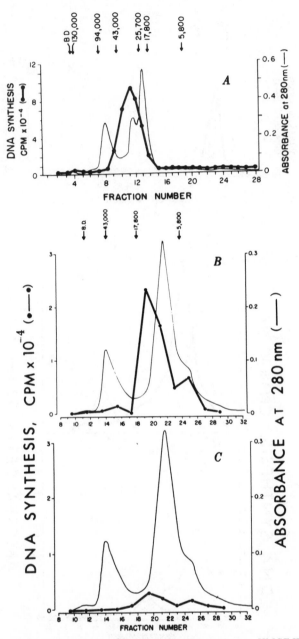

Figure 8. Analysis of peak II using HPLC-size exclusion columns. HMGF II was prepared by Sephadex G-100 gel filtration as shown in Fig. 6. Samples of about 4 mg were resuspended in 100 μl and analyzed on TSK-size exclusion columns at a flow rate of 1 ml/min. HPLC conditions are described in legend of Fig. 7.

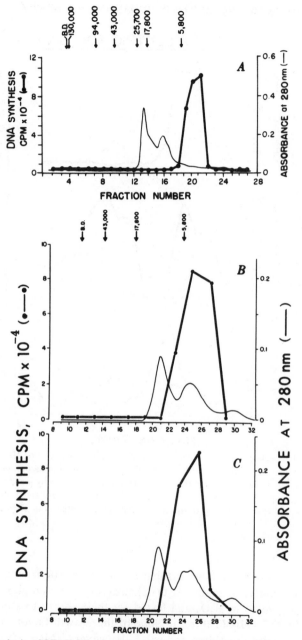

Figure 9. Analysis of PEAK III using HPLC TSK-size exclusion columns, HMGF III was prepared by Sephadex G-100 gel filtration as shown in Fig. 6. Samples of about 2 mg were resuspended in 100 μl and analyzed on TSK-size exclusion columns at a flow rate of 1 ml/min. HPLC conditions are described in legend of Fig. 7.

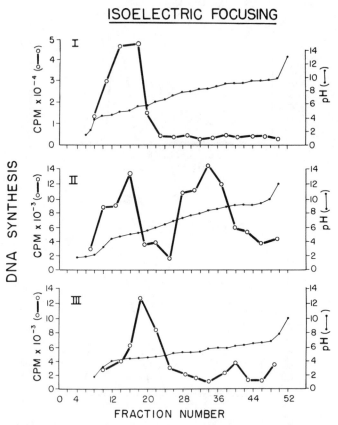

Figure 10.   Isoelectric focusing of human milk growth factors I, II, and III. The three biologically active peaks obtained after Sephadex G-100 filtration chromatography as shown in
Fig. 6 were dialyzed against distilled H_2O, concentrated, and analyzed by preparative isoelectric
focusing using ampholytes in the 3.5–10 pH range. Fractions were collected, dialyzed against
distilled H_2O, and tested for their ability to stimulate DNA synthesis in 3T3 cells.

1), and H_2O. After a 2-hour incubation period at room temperature, all
samples were dialyzed against H_2O exhaustively. The samples were lyophilized, resuspended in H_2O, and tested for their ability to stimulate DNA
synthesis in 3T3 cells (Table 2). None of the growth factors are sensitive
to treatments with guanidine and pH 1. However, HMGF III differs from
HMGFs I and II by being resistant to inactivation by DTT. The stabilities
of the three growth factors along with their molecular weights and isoelectric
points are summarized in Table 2.

2.6. Conclusions

There appear to be at least three growth factors in human milk. HMGF III is the major growth factor species and represents about 75% of the total growth factor activity in human milk. HMGF III is structurally similar to human epidermal growth factor (hEGF). hEGF, also known as urogastrone, is a polypeptide with a molecular weight of 6200 and an isoelectric point of 4.5. HMGF III has a molecular weight between 5000 and 6000 and an isoelectric point between 4.4 and 4.7. Further evidence that HMGF III is related to hEGF is Carpenter's observation that antibodies to hEGF neutralize 67% of the mitogenic activity of human milk for 3T3 cells (9). The purification of an EGF-like growth factor from human milk is outlined in the next section.

3. PURIFICATION OF A HUMAN MILK-DERIVED EGF-LIKE GROWTH FACTOR

3.1. Preliminary Fractionation of Human Milk Growth Factor Activity

HMGF III is the major growth factor species in human milk (75%) and has been purified to homogeneity (29). A flow chart for the purification of milk-derived growth factor is shown in Fig. 11. About 100 ml of whole

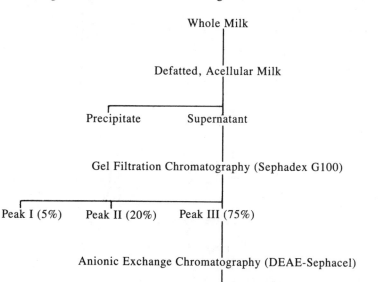

Figure 11. Purification of a human milk-derived growth factor.

milk is centrifuged at 12,000 g for 30 minutes. Fat floating at the top of the centrifuge tube and the cells and debris sedimenting at the bottom of the centrifuge tube are discarded. The defatted, acellular fraction is adjusted to pH 4.3 by addition of 6 N HCl. After 1 hour at room temperature, the precipitate that is formed is removed by centrifugation at 30,000 g for 50 minutes.

The supernatant fraction of acidified milk is analyzed by gel filtration chromatography on Sephadex G-100 (Fig. 6). Three peaks of growth factor activity are detected. Of the three peaks, the one designated as human milk growth factor (HMGF) III contains approximately 75% of the growth factor activity recovered from the column. Size exclusion chromatography on HPLC TSK 2000 columns indicates that the molecular weight of this peak is approximately 5000–6000 (Fig. 9).

3.2. Anion Exchange Chromatography

The major growth factor species in human milk, HMGF III, is further purified by DEAE-Sephacel anion exchange chromatography (Fig. 12).

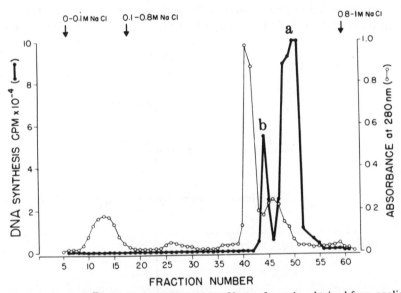

Figure 12. Ion exchange chromatography. About 50 mg of protein, obtained from pooling fractions in peak III shown in Fig. 6, were applied to a DEAE-Sephacel anionic exchange column (2.5 × 32 cm) equilibrated with 0.01 M sodium acetate, pH 5.6. Three successive gradients of NaCl (0.0–0.1 M, 0.1–0.8 M, 0.08–1.0 M) in 0.01 M sodium acetate, pH 5.6, were applied to the column. Fractions (8 ml) were collected, dialyzed against distilled H_2O, measured for absorbance at 280 nm, and tested for their ability to stimulate DNA synthesis in 3T3 cells.

HPLC GEL FILTRATION

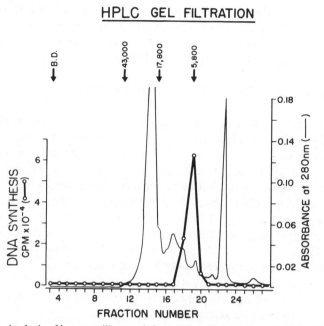

Figure 13. Analysis of human milk growth factor III on HPLC size exclusion columns. The major active peak (a-fraction 49–51), prepared by ion exchange chromatography as shown in Fig. 12, was pooled and analyzed on HPLC TSK 2000-size exclusion columns equilibrated with 0.1 M ammonium sulfate and 0.05 M potassium phosphate, pH 7.0. Fractions were collected, dialyzed against distilled H_2O and tested for their ability to stimulate DNA synthesis in 3T3 cells.

Virtually all of the growth factor activity adheres to the anion exchanger. When a gradient of NaCl (0.1–0.8 M) is applied to the column, two peaks of growth factor activity (a and b) are eluted. The major species a is eluted second at about 0.7 M NaCl and contains about 80% of the activity. Species b, which elutes several tubes earlier, contains about 20% of the activity.

3.3. Size Exclusion Chromatography

HMGF III (Fig. 12, peak a) was further analyzed by HPLC using TSK 2000-size exclusion columns (Fig. 13). HMGF III migrates as a sharp peak of growth factor activity on the TSK 2000 column and has a molecular weight of about 5000–6000 (fraction 19).

3.4. SDS-Polyacrylamide Gel Electrophoresis

HMGF III purified by ion exchange chromatography as shown in Fig. 12, followed by chromatography on size exclusion columns as shown in

Fig. 13, was analyzed by SDS-polyacrylamide gel electrophoresis (Fig. 14). A single sharp band with a molecular weight of about 6000 was found after visualization with the highly sensitive silver stain (slot 1). HMGF III migrates slightly slower than mouse EGF (slot 2).

3.5.   Specific Activity and Recovery of HMGF III

Purified HMGF III (Fig. 14, slot 1) shows a dose-dependent stimulation of DNA synthesis in 3T3 cells (Fig. 15). Half-maximal stimulation (1 unit of activity) occurs at a concentration of about 25 ng/ml. The purification scheme for HMGF III is summarized in Table 3. Starting with defatted, acellular milk, acid precipitation followed by Sephadex G-100 gel filtration chromatography, DEAE-Sephacel anion exchange chromatography, and TSK 2000 HPLC results in a 9200-fold purification. From 100 ml of defatted, acellular milk, which contains about 1400 mg of protein, 1.2 μg of purified HMGF III is obtained. The recovery is about 0.8%. Based on the yield and percent of activity recovered, and taking into account that HMGFs I and II account for 25% of the activity recovered from the Sephadex G-100 column, it can be estimated that the concentration of biologically active HMGF III in human milk may be as high as 1 μg/ml.

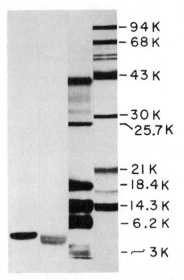

Figure 14.   SDS polyacrylamide gel electrophoresis of growth factors. HMGF III (Fig. 13, fraction 19) was analyzed by SDS polyacrylamide gel electrophoresis. The polyacrylamide gels were developed with a silver stain. Slot 1: human milk growth factor III; slot 2: mEGF purified on HPLC TSK 3000 columns; slot 3: Bethesda Research Labs molecular weight standards, 400 ng/protein; slot 4: Bio-Rad molecular weight standards, 200 ng/protein.

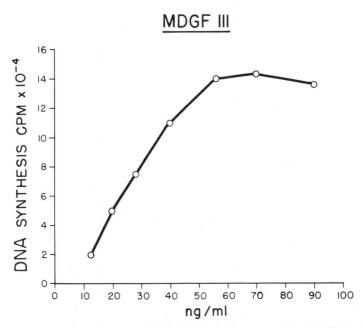

Figure 15. Dose-dependent stimulation of DNA synthesis by purified HMGF III. Various concentrations of a homogeneous preparation of human milk growth factor III (Fig. 14, slot 1) were tested for the ability to stimulate DNA synthesis in 3T3 cells. In this assay maximal incorporation, corresponding to 100% labeled nuclei, was about 150,000 cpm.

3.6.   Is HMGF III Human Epidermal Growth Factor?

HMGF III has a molecular weight of about 5000–6000 (Fig. 13), migrates close to mEGF on SDS-polyacrylamide gels (Fig. 14), and has an isoelectric point between 4.4 and 4.7 (Fig. 10). Thus this growth factor bears structural similarities to mEGF (molecular weight 6100, pI 4.6) and hEGF (molecular weight 6200, pI 4.5). The three polypeptide factors were further compared by HPLC on TSK-size exclusion columns both in nondenaturing buffer and in the presence of 6 M guanidine-HCl and 5 mM DTT. Under nondenaturing conditions HMGF III comigrates with a highly purified sample of hEGF (Fig. 16, *top*). The hEGF peak is broader than the HMGF III peak. mEGF activity elutes from this column several fractions after HMGF III and in a region well below its known molecular weight of 6100. mEGF is apparently interacting with the TSK 2000 column and is being retarded to a great extent. However, when the HPLC TSK columns are equilibrated with 6 M guanidine-HCl in order to suppress column-polypeptide interactions, HMGF III and mouse EGF comigrate suggesting that they actually have the same molecular weight (Fig. 16, *bottom*).

Table 3. Purification of Human Milk Growth Factor III

	TOTAL PROTEIN (mg)	TOTAL ACTIVITY (UNITS[a])	SPECIFIC ACTIVITY (UNITS/mg)	RECOVERY OF ACTIVITY (%)	FOLD PURIFICATION
Defatted human milk, 100 ml	1400	21,800	15.6	100	1.0
Acid precipitation, pH 4.3	1100	18,000	16.4	83	1.1
Sephadex G-100, Peak III	52	3,750[b]	72	17	4.6
DEAE-Sephacel	3.4	960	282	4.4	18.1
HPLC, TSK-2000	0.0012 (1.2 µg)	172	143,000	0.8	9200

[a] A unit of growth factor activity is defined as the amount of factor needed to stimulate half-maximal incorporation of [methyl-^{3}H]thymidine into trichloroacetic acid-insoluble DNA. Under standard conditions of the bioassay, a microtiter well contains 20,000 confluent quiescent Balb/c 3T3 cells in a volume of 250 µl. Background incorporation is about 2,000 cpm and maximal incorporation is 100,000-120,000 cpm.
[b] An additional 800 units of activity are found associated with milk growth factors I and II.

HPLC GEL FILTRATION

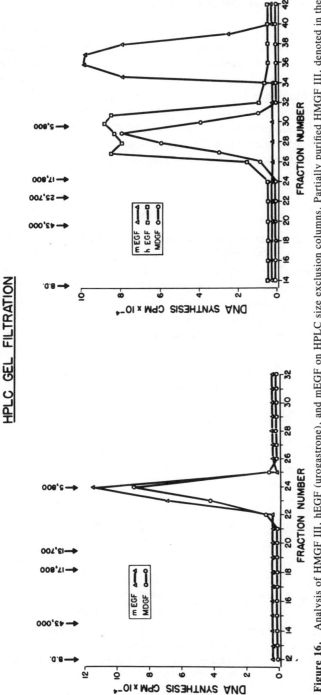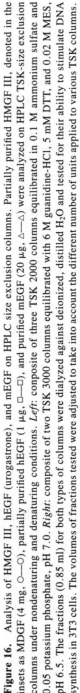

Figure 16. Analysis of HMGF III, hEGF (urogastrone), and mEGF on HPLC size exclusion columns. Partially purified HMGF III, denoted in the insets as MDGF (4 mg, ○—○), partially purified hEGF (1 μg, □—□), and purified mEGF (20 μg, △—△) were analyzed on HPLC TSK-size exclusion columns under nondenaturing and denaturing conditions. *Left:* composite of three TSK 2000 columns equilibrated in 0.1 M ammonium sulfate and 0.05 potassium phosphate, pH 7.0. *Right:* composite of two TSK 3000 columns equilibrated with 6 M guanidine-HCl, 5 mM DTT, and 0.02 M MES, pH 6.5. The fractions (0.85 ml) for both types of columns were dialyzed against deionized, distilled H₂O and tested for their ability to stimulate DNA synthesis in 3T3 cells. The volumes of fractions tested were adjusted to take into account the different number of units applied to various TSK columns.

181

In addition, HMGF III can be resolved into two peaks of growth factor activity by anion exchange chromatography (Fig. 12). Both hEGF-urogastrone (30) and mEGF (31) can be isolated in two forms. In the case of hEGF-urogastrone the two forms, β and γ have 53 and 52 amino acids, respectively. The difference in the two polypeptides is that γ-urogastrone is missing the C-terminal arginine present in β-urogastrone. The variant form of mEGF is a 51 amino acid polypeptide missing a C-terminal leucine–arginine dipeptide; the fractionation of HMGF III by anion exchange chromatography into two closely related peaks is, therefore, further evidence for a structural relationship to EGF.

3.7. Conclusions

To summarize, purification and structural analysis of the major growth factor in human milk, HMGF III, indicates that this polypeptide is very similar if not identical to hEGF. In addition, Carpenter (9) has found that antibodies produced against hEGF neutralize 67% of the mitogenic activity of human milk for 3T3 cells. Thus there is immunological evidence for the presence of EGF as a major component of the growth factor activity of human milk. However, the antibodies used to detect EGF in milk were

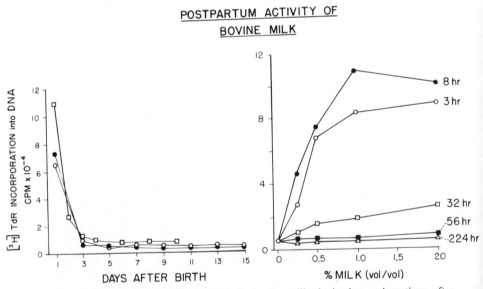

Figure 17.   Stimulation of DNA synthesis by bovine milk obtained at various times after birth of a calf. Milk samples were added to confluent monolayers of 3T3 cells and DNA synthesis was measured. (*Left*) Milk obtained from three different cows. (*Right*) Milk collected from one cow at 3, 8, 32, 56, and 224 hours after birth.

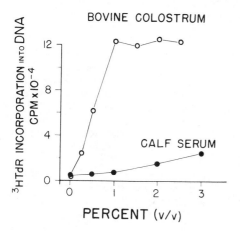

Figure 18. Stimulation of DNA synthesis by bovine colostrum and by calf serum. Confluent monolayers of Balb/c 3T3 cells were incubated with various concentrations of bovine colostrum obtained on the day of the birth of a calf (O—O) and with various concentrations of calf serum (●—●), and DNA synthesis was measured.

prepared against EGF found in urine. It should be stressed, therefore, that although the available evidence points to a similarity between HMGF found in milk and hEGF found in urine, identity of the two polypeptides can be ascertained only by sequencing studies.

4. CHARACTERIZATION OF GROWTH FACTOR ACTIVITY IN BOVINE MILK

4.1. Stage of Lactation

Bovine milk is also a source of growth factor activity. However, unlike human milk, the growth factor activity of bovine milk shows a marked dependence on the stage of lactation. Growth factor activity is highest in colostrum, which is the milk produced in the first few days after birth of a calf (Fig. 17, *left*). Samples of milk obtained 32 and 60 hours after birth are 20% and 1% as active, respectively, as a sample obtained from the same cow 8 hours after birth (Fig. 17, *right*). No growth factor activity is detectable 4 days after birth and thereafter. Bovine colostrum is more active than bovine serum when equivalent volumes are compared (Fig. 18). Bovine colostrum at a concentration of 0.25% (vol/vol) is as active as bovine serum at a concentration of 2.5% (vol/vol). Bovine colostrum can also be shown to stimulate cell division as well as DNA synthesis (Fig. 19). Bovine colostrum obtained on the day of birth stimulates cell division in a dose-dependent manner, whereas bovine milk obtained 10 days after birth is inactive in stimulating cell division.

CELL DIVISION

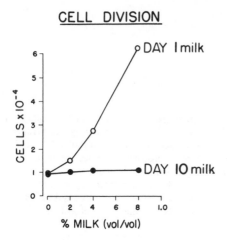

Figure 19. Stimulation of cell division by bovine milk. Confluent monolayers of quiescent Balb/c 3T3 cells were incubated for 6 days with various concentrations of colostrum obtained on the day of the birth of a calf (O—O) and milk obtained 10 days after birth of a calf (●—●). The final concentrations of milk used were 0, 0.2, 0.4, and 0.8% (vol/vol). The cells were refed on day 3 of the experiment. On day 6 of the experiment, the cells were detached from the microtiter wells by incubation with 0.1% (w/v) trypsin and counted in a Coulter counter.

4.2.   Biochemical Characterization

The growth factor activity of bovine colostrum can be partially purified by acid precipitation. Colostrum which has been stored at $-20°C$ is thawed and centrifuged at 12,000 g for 30 minutes at 4°C. The fat which floats to the top and the insoluble cellular debris which is found at the bottom of the

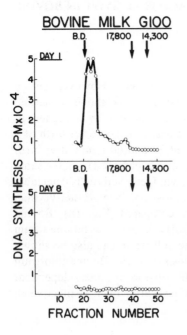

Figure 20. Gel filtration chromatography of bovine milk. Bovine milk obtained on the day of birth (colostrum—day 1) and 8 days after birth were analyzed by chromatography on Sephadex G100 equilibrated with 0.05 M NaCl and 0.001 M sodium phosphate, pH 7.0. Fractions were tested for their ability to stimulate DNA synthesis in 3T3 cells.

HPLC GEL FILTRATION (BOVINE COLOSTRUM)

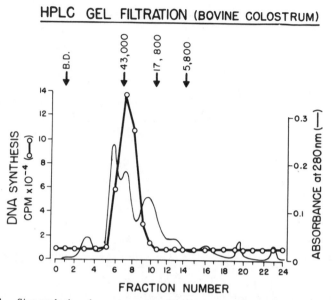

Figure 21. Size exclusion chromatography of bovine colostrum. Defatted bovine colostrum was adjusted to pH 4.3. The precipitate that formed was removed by centrifugation. The supernatant was analyzed on an HPLC TSK 2000 column equilibrated with 0.05 M phosphate, pH 7, and 0.1 M ammonium sulfate. Fractions were tested for their ability to stimulate DNA synthesis in 3T3 cells.

centrifuge tube are removed. The defatted milk is adjusted to pH 4.3 with concentrated HCl and allowed to stand at room temperature for an hour. A precipitate forms which is removed by centrifugation at 12,000 g for 30 minutes at 4°C. The supernatant fraction is a green-clear yellowish liquid that contains 85% of the growth factor activity, but only 40% of the milk protein.

Gel filtration chromatography of bovine colostrum obtained on day 1 and bovine milk obtained on day 8 after birth are shown in Fig. 20. A peak of relatively large molecular weight is found in colostrum. No activity peak is found in day-8 milk. The molecular weight of colostrum-derived growth factor activity was ascertained by size exclusion chromatography on a HPLC TSK 2000 column (Fig. 21). One major peak of activity is found with molecular weight between 30,000 and 45,000. Upon isoelectric focusing this peak of activity is resolved into two peaks, one with a pI of about 6.5 and the other with a pI of about 9 (Fig. 22). It is not clear whether there are two growth factors in this preparation or whether one of the peaks of activity represents growth factor bound to carrier. Preliminary evidence indicates that all of the bovine colostrum growth factor activity adheres to a cation exchange resin.

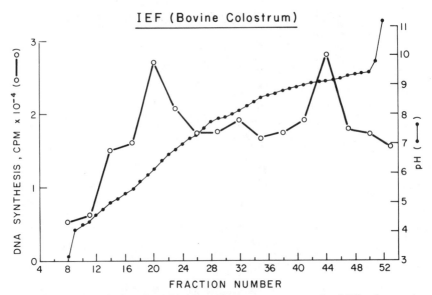

Figure 22.   Isoelectric focusing of bovine colostrum on a preparative LKB column using ampholytes in the pH 3.5–10 range. Fractions were dialyzed against distilled H_2O and assayed for their ability to stimulate DNA synthesis in 3T3 cells.

4.3.   Conclusions

The growth factor activity of bovine milk appears to differ from the growth factor activity of human milk. First of all, bovine milk growth factor activity shows a strong temporal dependence on the stage of lactation and is undetectable within 4 days after birth of a calf. On the other hand, although HMGF activity appears to decline as lactation progresses, it never totally disappears and in some cases can be detected 6 months after birth. Second, the growth factors found in bovine milk appear to be different biochemically than those found in human milk. There is no evidence in bovine colostrum of a low molecular weight anionic EGF-like growth factor, the major growth factor species found in human milk. Instead, the growth factors in bovine milk appear to be relatively large molecular weight, cationic polypeptides.

5.   GROWTH OF CULTURED CELLS IN HUMAN AND BOVINE MILK

5.1.   Introduction

Conventionally, cells in culture are grown in nutrient media supplemented with serum. The importance of serum in cell culture can be partially ascribed to the presence of growth factors, primarily the platelet-derived growth factor (PDGF) which is released from platelets during clotting (32, 33). As we have shown, both human and bovine milk are sources of growth factors. The presence of growth factors suggests that milk, like serum, can be used as a supplement to media used for the growth of cells in culture. Indeed, milk can be used to replace serum and will support the growth of a wide variety of cell types (13–16).

5.2. Methodology for the Growth of Cells in Culture

Frozen samples of bovine colostrum or human milk are thawed and centrifuged at 12,000 g for 30 minutes. The fat floating at the top of the centrifuge tube is removed and discarded. Cellular debris and other sediment at the bottom of the centrifuge tube are also discarded. The milk is sterilized by filtration through 0.45 micron Nalgene filter units. In order to filter the milk, it must be diluted to a concentration no greater than 10% (vol/vol). Sterile milk can be kept frozen at −20°C for at least 3 months without apparent loss of activity. The culture medium is prepared by adding milk at a final concentration of 5% or less (vol/vol) to Dulbecco's modified Eagle's medium (DMEM) containing glucose (4.5 g/liter), penicillin (50 units/ml), and streptomycin (50 μg/ml).

The following protocol is used to measure cellular proliferation. Cells are resuspended in unsupplemented DMEM at a concentration of 10^4 cells/

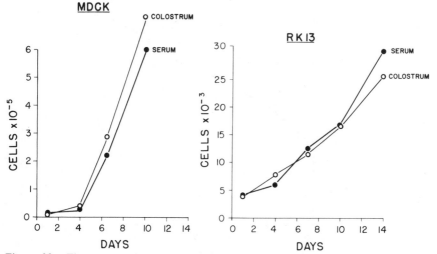

Figure 23.   Time course of growth of epithelial cells in DMEM supplemented with 2.5% bovine colostrum or 5% serum. Cells were originally plated at a density of 10^4 cells/2 cm^2 well. (*Left*) MDCK cells. (*Right*) RK13 cells.

ml and 1 ml of cell suspension is plated into each well of a 24-well microtiter plate (Costar, 16 mm diameter well). The plating density is 5×10^3 cells/cm^2). Between 2 and 6 hours after plating, the DMEM containing unattached cells is replaced with DMEM supplemented with milk. Cells are refed every second day with fresh medium. To obtain cell number, cells are detached with 0.1% trypsin and counted in a Coulter counter.

The first cells chosen to test a milk-supplemented medium were Mardin–Darby canine kidney (MDCK) epithelial cells. It was speculated that milk might support the growth of epithelial cells inasmuch as cells of this type come into contact with milk after ingestion. MDCK is an established cell line that preserves the structure and function of kidney epithelium (34). The other cells chosen were RK13, a rabbit kidney epithelial cell line. MDCK and RK13 cells grow in media supplemented with bovine colostrum at the same rate as in media supplemented with serum (Fig. 23). MDCK cells also grow in media supplemented with human milk (Fig. 24). Bovine colostrum can be used to support the growth of other cells as well. Cell lines of epithelial cell origin will proliferate directly in bovine colostrum-supplemented media but fibroblasts require precoating of the culture dish with fibronectin to allow proliferation in a bovine colostrum-supplemented

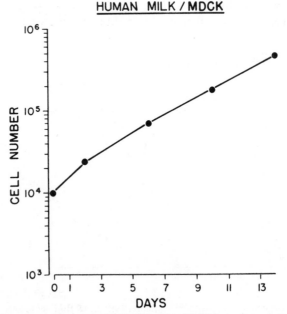

Figure 24. Time course of growth of MDCK cells in DMEM supplemented with 1% human milk (1 month postpartum) and 5 μg/ml transferrin.

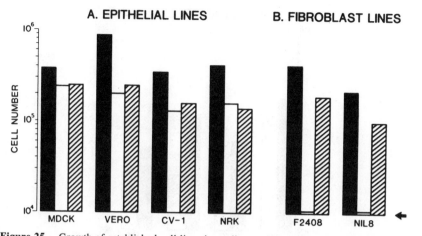

Figure 25. Growth of established cell lines in media supplemented with bovine colostrum. Each cell line was cultured in DMEM supplemented with 10% calf serum and DMEM supplemented with bovine colostrum at concentrations ranging from 0 to 20% in the presence and absence of fibronectin. The colostrum concentration yielding maximal growth for each cell line was: Vero, CV-1, and F2408, 2% colostrum; MDCK, 2.5% colostrum; NRK, 5% colostrum; NIL8, 2% colostrum with insulin (10 μg/ml). MDCK, vero, and CV-1 cells were counted on day 11; NRK, F2408, and NIL8 were counted on day 7. The results reported are the average of duplicate cell counts. The arrow indicates the initial plating density (1 $\times$ 10^4 cells/well/2 cm^2). Solid bars, 10% calf serum; open bars, colostrum; hatched bars, colostrum in wells precoated with fibronectin.

medium (15; Fig. 25). In the presence of fibronectin and other supplements such as transferrin and insulin, it is possible to grow early passage cell strains such as chondrocytes, smooth muscle cells, and fibroblasts even in post-colostral milk (Fig. 26).

5.3. Conclusions

Both bovine milk, in particular colostrum, and human milk can replace serum as the supplement for the proliferation in culture of sparse cells. The cells will grow until they reach confluence. The growth of cells in milk *in vitro* might yield clues as to which cells respond to milk growth factors *in vivo*.

6. SUMMARY AND PERSPECTIVES

6.1. Summary

Human and bovine milk contain growth factors. The predominant growth factor species in human milk is a polypeptide with a molecular weight of

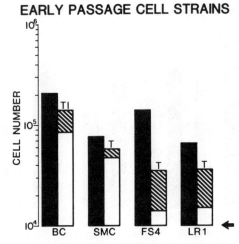

Figure 26.   Growth of early passage cell strains in bovine milk and plasma fibronectin. See Fig. 25 legend. Cells were counted on day 10. Bovine chondrocytes (BC), smooth muscle cells (SMC), fibroblasts (FS4, LR1). Arrow indicates initial plating density (1 × 10⁴ cell/well/2 cm²). Solid bars, 10% calf serum; open bars, 10% milk plus fibronectin; hatched bars, 10% milk plus fibronectin plus factors when applicable (T = 10 μg/ml transferrin, I = 10 μg/ml insulin).

about 6000 and a pI of between 4.4 and 4.7. This growth factor species can be purified by a combination of acid precipitation, gel filtration chromatography, anion exchange chromatography, and size exclusion chromatography on HPLC. This milk-derived growth factor is in all probability hEGF or at least a polypeptide that is structurally very similar to hEGF. Two other growth factor species can be found in human milk. They differ from the EGF-like growth factor in that they have larger molecular weights and are inactivated irreversibly by treatment with DTT. Thus these two species have disulfide bonds that are necessary for biological activity whereas the EGF-like polypeptide does not.

The growth factor activity in bovine milk appears to be different than that found in human milk. The predominant species in bovine milk is a 30,000–45,000 molecular weight species that appears to be cationic. In addition, the bovine milk growth factor is inactivated by DTT. Bovine milk growth factor activity shows a marked dependence on the stage of lactation. Growth factor activity is high in colostrum but is undetectable 4 days after birth of a calf and thereafter. On the other hand, although HMGF activity appears to decline as the lactation period progresses, it can be detected even 6 months after birth. The differences between human and bovine milk growth factor activity in terms of both biochemical composition and dependence on lactation stage are intriguing. They may be a reflection of the different patterns involved in the nursing of the human infant and other mammalian newborns. The presence of growth factors and other macromolecular factors make milk a replacement for serum in media used to support cellular proliferation. Virtually all types, including early passage strains and cell lines, proliferate in milk-supplemented media.

6.2. Future Perspectives

Milk-derived growth factors may play a role in the development of tissues in the newborn or perhaps in the development of the mammary gland of the mother. A major goal in this area of research would be to purify all of the human and bovine milk-derived growth factors and to prepare antibodies against them. With these probes it may be possible to answer a number of important questions: Where are milk-derived growth factors synthesized? What happens to these growth factors after milk is ingested? Are there any specific cells whose proliferation is stimulated *in vivo*? Since EGF and urogastrone are the same polypeptide, there appears to be a hormone in milk that can inhibit gastric acid secretion in the stomach. Thus there is a question of whether milk-derived growth factors play a role in regulating the pH of the gastrointestinal tract. Most milk proteins are synthesized by the mammary glands. It would be of interest to know if milk-derived growth factors are involved in the growth of mammary epithelium and whether their presence in milk reflects an end product of that process. At present, very little is known about the physiological role of growth factors in general. The answers to these questions about milk-derived growth factors may provide clues to their possible involvement in the growth process.

REFERENCES

1. Jenness, R., in B. L. Larson and V. R. Smith, Eds., *Lactation, A Comprehensive Treatise*, Academic, New York, Vol. III, 1978.
2. Klagsbrun, M., *Proc. Natl. Acad. Sci. USA*, **75**, 5057 (1978).
3. Todaro, G. J., Lazar, G. K., and Green, H., *J. Cell. Physiol.*, **66**, 325 (1965).
4. Carpenter, G., and Cohen, S., *Ann. Rev. Biochem.*, **48**, 193 (1979).
5. Cohen, S., *J. Biol. Chem.*, **237**, 1555 (1962).
6. Gregory, H., *Nature*, **257**, 325 (1975).
7. Elder, J. B., Williams, G., Lacey, E., and Gregory, H., *Nature*, **271**, 466 (1978).
8. Starkey, R. H., and Orth, D. N., *J. Clin. Endocrin. Metab.*, **45**, 1144 (1977).
9. Carpenter, G., *Science*, **210**, 198 (1980).
10. Klagsbrun, M., and Neuman, J., *J. Supramol. Struct.*, **11**, 349 (1979).

11. Ogra, S. S., and Ogra, P. L., *J. Pediatr.*, **92**, 550 (1978).

12. Head, J. R., and Beer, A. E., in B. L. Larsen and V. R. Smith, Eds., *Lactation, A Comprehensive Treatise*, Academic, New York, Vol. IV, 1978.

13. Klagsbrun, M., *J. Cell Biol.*, **84**, 808 (1980).

14. Steimer, K. S., and Klagsbrun, M., *J. Cell Biol.*, **88**, 294 (1981).

15. Steimer, K. S., Packard, R., Holden, D., and Klagsbrun, M., *J. Cell. Physiol.*, **109**, 223 (1981).

16. Sereni, A., and Baserga, R., *Cell Biol. Int. Rept.*, **5**, 339 (1981).

17. Barnes, D., and Sato, G., *Cell*, **22**, 649 (1980).

18. Lindberg, T., *Pediat. Res.*, **13**, 969 (1979).

19. Hollenberg, M. D., in *Vitamins and Hormones*, Academic, New York, Vol. 37, 1979.

20. Stoker, M. G. F., Pigott, D., and Taylor-Papadimitrious, J., *Nature*, **264**, 764 (1976).

21. Osborne, C. K., Hamilton, B., Titus, G., and Livingston, R. B., *Cancer Res.*, **40**, 2361 (1980).

22. Yang, J., Guzman, R., Richards, J., Imagawa, W., McCormick, K., and Nandi, S., *Proc. Natl. Acad. Sci. USA*, **107**, 35 (1980).

23. Rheinewald, J. G., and Green, H., *Nature*, **265**, 421 (1977).

24. Sun, T. T., and Green, H., *Cell*, **9**, 511 (1976).

25. Sun, T. T., and Green, H., *Nature*, **268**, 489 (1977).

26. Savage, C. R., and Cohen, S., *Exp. Eye Res.*, **15**, 361 (1973).

27. Gospodarowicz, D., Ill, C. R., and Birdwell, C. R., *Endocrinology*, **100**, 1108 (1977).

28. Klagsbrun, M., Langer, R., Levenson, R., Smith, S., and Lillehei, C., *Exp. Cell Res.*, **105**, 99 (1977).

29. Shing, Y., and Klagsbrun, M., submitted.

30. Savage, C. R., and Harper, R., *Anal. Biochem.*, **111**, 195 (1981).

31. Savage, C. R., Jr., and Cohen, S., *J. Biol. Chem.*, **247**, 7609 (1972).

32. Ross, R., and Vogel, A., *Cell*, **14**, 203 (1978).

33. Antoniades, H. N., Scher, C. D., and Stiles, C. D., *Proc. Natl. Acad. Sci. USA*, **76**, 1809 (1979).

34. Misfeldt, D. S., Hamamoto, S., and Pitelka, D. R., *Proc. Natl. Acad. Sci. USA*, **73**, 1212 (1976).

7

AFFINITY LABELING
OF RECEPTORS
Catherine L. Oppenheimer
Michael P. Czech

CONTENTS

Abbreviations

DSS	Disuccinimidyl suberate
DSP	Dithiobis-(succinimidyl proprionate)
HSAB	Hydroxysuccinimidyl azidobenzoate
MBTA	4-(*N*-maleimido) benzyltrimethylammonium iodide
DAP	1, 10-Decane bis(3-azidopyridinium) diiodide
NAP	4-Azido-2-nitrophenyl
ANB-A1	Ethyl N-5-azido-2-nitrobenzoylaminoacetimidate
NHNP-NBE	*N*-[2-hydroxy-3-(1-naphthoxy)-propyl]-N′ bromoacetylethylenediamine
pABC	p-Azidobenzylcarazolol
pAMBC	p-Aminobenzylcarazolol
SANAH	*N*-succinimidyl-6-(4′-azido 2′-nitrophenylamino) hexanoate
EGF	Epidermal growth factor
PAPDIP	Methyl 3-[(p-azidophenyl) dithio] proprionimidate
IGF	Insulinlike growth factor
NGF	Nerve growth factor
PDGF	Platelet-derived growth factor
EGS	Ethylene glycol bis(succinimidyl succinate)
TGF	Transforming growth factor
SGF	Sarcoma growth factor
NRK	Normal rat kidney

1.   GENERAL AFFINITY LABELING TECHNIQUES

1.1.   Criteria for Affinity Labeling

The study of the mechanism of receptor action is one of the most rapidly advancing areas of modern biochemistry. A great deal of valuable data about the ligand specificity of a receptor can be obtained by bioassays and binding studies employing ligands and analogues (1, 2), but such information is descriptive in nature and does not address questions of receptor structure and molecular mechanism. Such studies require the physical identification of the receptor. One approach is by detergent solubilization of membrane-bound receptors followed by purification of the receptor by classical and affinity chromatography methods (3–7). Such studies, however, are often quite difficult technically because the majority of receptors are present in extremely low abundance and represent only minor components of the membrane. Hence very large amounts of starting material, or identification of a mutation causing receptor overproduction, is required to obtain sufficient quantities of receptor for biochemical studies. In addition, many recently discovered growth factors are available in only limited quantities, so that purification of their receptor by ligand affinity chromatography is not feasible. Alternatively, antibodies directed against the receptor of interest can be employed to investigate receptor biosynthesis and structure using immunoprecipitation. Receptor distribution in the cell may also be studied using such antibodies (8–10). Because of the very low abundance of most receptors, however, it is often difficult to obtain sufficient quantities of purified receptor for use as antigen in preparing antibodies in the laboratory. In some cases, therefore, the technique has been limited to the availability of patients with naturally occurring anti-receptor antibodies such as have been reported for the insulin receptor (11).

Affinity labeling is another technique for the identification of receptors which has come into increasing use in recent years. This method, which was originally developed to study mechanisms of enzyme catalysis (12, 13), circumvents the necessity for purification or antibody availability and hence is often the method of choice for receptor studies *in vivo* and *in vitro*. In this technique, the natural high affinity of the ligand for its receptor is used to aim it at its binding site, where it reacts covalently through an added or attached highly reactive chemical group. The covalently "tagged" receptor can then be identified by electrophoresis or other techniques (13).

The ideal affinity labeling reagent should have very high affinity for the receptor of interest to ensure high specificity of labeling in crude systems such as membranes where only small amounts of receptor are present. It should contain a reactive group that can attack both nucleophilic and hydrophobic regions, and that has a relatively short half-life so that its reactivity is confined to residues near the binding site. The reaction of the affinity label with the receptor is expected to block receptor binding of other ligands irreversibly and noncompetitively. Such irreversible blockade should be prevented by preincubation of the receptor with an excess of unmodified ligand. These characteristics are useful for the demonstration that successful affinity labeling has been achieved. The ligand should be easy to synthesize and relatively stable to aqueous solution. Finally, it should be possible to synthesize it with high specific radioactivity, preferably with [^{125}I]iodine, so that identification of the labeled receptor in complex solutions by electrophoresis and autoradiography is feasible.

Two general approaches to affinity labeling have been most successful in receptor studies to date. In photoaffinity labeling (14–17) a reactive group attached to the ligand is activated by ultraviolet light to generate an extremely reactive intermediate such as a nitrene or a carbene, which reacts indiscriminately and with a short half-life to covalently label binding site residues. Alternatively, the necessity for chemical modification of peptide ligands can be circumvented by the use of bifunctional reagents such as disuccinimidyl suberate (18, 19), which covalently cross-link the radio-actively labeled ligand to the receptor. These techniques are discussed in more detail in the following sections. This is followed by an historical overview of affinity labeling studies on the acetylcholine, β-adrenergic, and insulin receptors, which have been most extensively investigated by these methods. Finally, more recent work on the growth factor receptors is discussed.

1.2.   Photoaffinity Labeling

Photoaffinity labeling offers the advantages of (i) a modifying group stable in aqueous solutions which can be "unmasked" at a time precisely determined by the experimenter, (ii) a very highly reactive intermediate which is capable of reaction with hydrophobic C–H bonds and aromatic bonds as well as with nucleophilic centers, (iii) a short half-life of light-activated reactive groups, and (iv) a relatively high efficiency of covalent labeling.

The principal disadvantage is the necessity to modify the ligand with an often bulky substituent group. In some cases such modification seriously compromises the biological activity of the ligand (20). Synthesis, isolation, and characterization of the photoactive derivative may be difficult if only very small quantities of ligand are available, as with some recently discovered growth factors.

The first photoaffinity labeling reagents developed for use with enzymes made use of diazo groups (21), which generate carbenes on photolysis.

$$R_2CN_2 \overset{h\gamma}{\to} R_2\overset{..}{C} + N_2 \tag{1}$$

Carbenes are extremely reactive in either the singlet (zwitterionic) state or the triplet (diradical) state. They are capable of insertion into a C–H bond, insertion into a C=C bond (including an aromatic ring), or attachment to the sulfur atom of a sulfide bond through attack on nonbonded electrons.

The carbon adjacent to the diazo group must not bear a hydrogen, or the generation of the carbene will result in olefin formation:

$$R\text{---}CH_2\text{---}\overset{..}{C}H \to R\text{---}CH{=}CH_2 \tag{2}$$

Thus the first photoaffinity ligand, used to modify chymotrypsin, contained a diazoacetyl group (21). Unfortunately, diazoacetyl compounds are not very stable, especially at acid pH. Moreover, the α-keto carbene formed on photolysis is very prone to rearrangement by means of the Wolff reaction (22):

$$R-\overset{\overset{\displaystyle O}{\|}}{C}-\ddot{C}H \rightarrow R-CH{=}C{=}O \qquad (3)$$

The resulting ketene is much less reactive than the carbene and attacks nucleophilic groups exclusively. Electron-withdrawing substituents on the α-keto carbene diminish the tendency to rearrangement; thus diazomalonyl esters came into use (23). However, such substituents increase the electrophilic nature of the carbene and hence its tendency to react with O–H bonds in water. The principal absorption of diazo groups is generally in the range of 250 nm. Therefore, photolysis times must be minimized to avoid damage to the receptor being studied.

Diazoacetylation is generally accomplished by attachment of radiolabeled glycine to an amino or hydroxyl group on the ligand. This is followed by diazotization with nitrous acid. Diazomalonyl groups can be added to the ligand by the reaction of hydroxyl or amino groups with ethyl 2-diazomalonylchloride, or with the N-hydroxysuccinimide ester of ethyl diazomalonate.

A second category of photogenerated reactive intermediates are nitrenes, generated from azide groups (17, 24).

$$RNN_2 \overset{h\gamma}{\rightarrow} R\ddot{\ddot{N}} + N_2 \qquad (4)$$

Nitrenes are generally much less reactive than carbenes, but undergo similar reactions in singlet or triplet states. They are somewhat more electrophilic than carbenes preferring insertion into O—H or N—H bonds over insertion into C—H bonds.

As with carbenes, the carbon adjacent to the nitrene group should not bear a hydrogen, or rearrangement to an imine will occur:

$$R-CH_2-\ddot{\ddot{N}} \rightarrow R-CH{=}NH \qquad (5)$$

Thus alkyl azides are not useful. Similarly, acyl azides are ruled out, as α-keto nitrenes undergo the Curtius reaction (analogous to the Wolff reaction for carbenes) to form the isocyanate.

Nitrenes are most commonly generated from aryl azides, whose use was introduced by Knowles' group in 1969 (25). The major advantage of aryl azides over diazo esters is their much greater stability in aqueous solution over a wide range of pH. Also, they often absorb light at longer wavelengths, with strong absorption maxima above 300 nm, thus minimizing damage to photolabile biological systems.

The presence of an electron-withdrawing substituent, such as a nitro group, on the aromatic ring will increase the reactivity of the generated aryl nitrene and increase the wavelength of maximal activation. As with carbenes, however, such derivatives are more electrophilic and hence react more readily with water. Substituents ortho to the azide group should be avoided as the nitrene will insert into the neighboring group (26). Also, the presence of a ring nitrogen ortho to the azide group will lead through rearrangement to a much less reactive tetrazole (27):

$$\text{(6)}$$

This limits the usefulness of azidopurines and pyrimidines as photoaffinity reagents.

Aryl azides are generally synthesized by diazotization of the aryl amine with nitrous acid, followed by treatment with azide:

$$ArNH_3^{\oplus} \xrightarrow{HNO_2} ArN_2^{\oplus} \xrightarrow{HN_3} ArN_3 \qquad (7)$$

Conjugation to the ligand is most readily accomplished by reaction of ligand amino groups with the N-hydroxysuccinimide ester of the aryl azide.

If the ligand of interest contains a conjugated ring system, it may be possible to use it directly as a natural photoaffinity label, eliminating the necessity for introduction of a photolabile group. For example, [^{3}H]N^6-butyryl cAMP has been used with no chemical modification as a specific photoaffinity probe for cAMP binding protein in human erythrocyte ghosts (28) and in rat liver cytoplasm (29).

Before investing a great deal of effort in the synthesis of a photoaffinity labeling reagent, it is wise to determine the effect of ultraviolet light on the biological system being examined. Fat cells, for instance, rapidly lose viability on exposure to short wavelength ultraviolet light. It is recommended that "black glass" or other short wavelength ultraviolet filters be used to avoid extensive biological damage (30). The time course of receptor labeling by the photoactive ligand should be determined in order to use a minimum photolysis time.

An important control for photoaffinity reagents is the demonstration that no labeling occurs in the absence of photolysis, as "dark reactions" may have little specificity for the receptor binding site. Similarly, affinity ligands prephotolyzed in the absence of protein before addition to the receptor should not label the receptor. Of course, labeling should also be blocked by the presence of excess unlabeled ligand.

1.3. Bifunctional Cross-Linking Reagents

This technique employs hetero or homobifunctional cross-linking reagents having specificity for a particular chemical group, such as amino groups, but no particular specificity for a given biological function. Specific affinity labeling is achieved by covalent cross-linking of the highly specific natural ligand, usually labeled with ^{125}I, to the receptor-binding site. The labeled hormone then acts as a covalent tag to permit identification of the receptor, usually by sodium dodecyl sulfate gel electrophoresis and autoradiography (18, 19).

The principal advantage of this technique is that no chemical modification of the ligand is required, avoiding the necessity for time-consuming synthesis, purification, and characterization of a derivatized molecule. This is especially important in the case of growth factors which may be available only in small amounts. The most commonly used cross-linking reagents, such as disuccinimidyl suberate (DSS), are available commercially at modest cost. The method generally is most useful for peptide ligands which contain functional groups such as the amino group of lysine which are susceptible to chemical modification. Reaction conditions are usually quite mild (reaction in less than 15 minutes at 0°C is commonly achieved). Thus damage to the receptor, such as may occur with short wavelength ultraviolet light, is not a problem.

A disadvantage of the technique is that no covalent cross-linking will be observed if the receptor and/or the ligand do not possess the required functional groups located at an appropriate distance. Thus it may be necessary to employ a range of cross-linking reagents of differing lengths and chemical specificities. Fig. 1 lists some of the cross-linking reagents most commonly used for this purpose.

Another disadvantage is that cross-linking reagents will react nonspecifically with all proteins in the membrane, so that it cannot be assumed that other biological functions of a viable cell will be unperturbed. Generally, therefore, the method is not suitable for following the movements of a "tagged" receptor in a living cell, as is possible with a photoaffinity-labeled receptor (31, 32).

The efficiency of covalent labeling achieved with chemical cross-linking reagents is generally found to be somewhat less than that achieved with

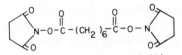

DISUCCINIMIDYL SUBERATE (DSS)

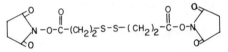

DITHIOBIS (SUCCINIMIDYL PROPRIONATE) (DSP)

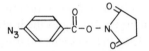

HYDROXYSUCCINIMIDYL AZIDOBENZOATE (HSAB)

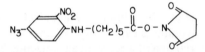

N- SUCCINIMIDYL-6-(4'- AZIDO -2'- NITROPHENYLAMINO) HEXANOATE
(SANAH)

ETHYLENE GLYCOL BIS (SUCCINIMIDYL SUCCINATE) (EGS)

FIGURE 1. Structures of cross-linking reagents which have been used to affinity-label receptors.

photoaffinity labeling, probably because cross-linking agents are less specific and indiscriminately reactive. However, the efficiency of labeling is highly dependent on the receptor and the ligand being studied, and in some cases has been found to be equal to that achieved with photolabile derivatives. For instance, covalent labeling efficiency of the insulin receptor in adipocytes using [^{125}I]insulin and DSS was found to reach 10–20% (33), which is comparable to the best results obtained with photolabile insulins (31, 34).

Cross-linking reagents were originally developed as "molecular rulers" for establishing spatial relationships in proteins (35) and determining quaternary structures of soluble oligomeric proteins (36), using alkylimidates such as dimethyl suberimidate (37). The cleavable cross-linker dithiobis-(succinimidyl proprionate) (DSP; Fig. 1) was introduced by Lomant and

Fairbanks (38). This reagent, which contains an N-hydroxysuccinimide leaving group at each end of the molecule, acylates free primary and secondary aliphatic amino groups:

$$RNH_2 \; + \; \left\langle \text{NO}\overset{\text{O}}{\overset{\|}{\text{C}}}(CH_2)_2\text{—SS—}(CH_2)_2\overset{\text{O}}{\overset{\|}{\text{C}}}\text{ON} \right\rangle \; + \; H_2NR' \tag{8}$$

$$\rightarrow RNH\,\overset{\text{O}}{\overset{\|}{\text{C}}}(CH_2)_2\text{—SS—}(CH_2)_2\overset{\text{O}}{\overset{\|}{\text{C}}}NHR' \; + \; 2 \,\left\langle \text{NOH} \right\rangle$$

Here R represents the receptor and the R' the ligand. The disulfide group shown in structure (8) is readily cleaved under mild reducing conditions (38). DSP offers a number of advantages over the imidates, including no introduction of charge, improved stability and reactivity at neutral pH and low temperatures, formation of a stable amide bond, and membrane solubility. This permits the use of very mild reaction conditions (typically 0°C for 15 minutes) using low concentrations (generally, 0.1–2 mM) of cross-linking reagents.

Although the cleavable nature of this cross-linker is useful for some experiments, it represents a drawback for affinity labeling experiments in which dodecyl sulfate electrophoresis in the presence of reductant is employed to locate the labeled receptor. Therefore, Pilch and Czech (18, 33) introduced a noncleavable analogue of DSP, disuccinimidyl suberate (DSS; Fig. 1). This compound has been used to identify receptors for insulin (18, 19, 33), insulinlike growth factors (39, 40), platelet-derived growth factor (41), and transforming growth factor (42).

The requirement for appropriately spaced functional groups on both ligand and receptor can be partially circumvented by the use of heterobifunctional reagents which combine a functional group modifying agent with a photoreactive group. A prominent example of this is hydroxysuccinimidyl azidobenzoate (HSAB; 43), which combines an amino-reactive group with a photoreactive aryl azide. It has been successfully used to affinity label receptors for glucagon (43) and nerve growth factor (7, 44) for which affinity cross-linking with DSS was unsuccessful.

2.   RECEPTOR STUDIES USING AFFINITY LABELING

2.1.   Acetylcholine Receptor

Because the acetylcholine receptor can be readily purified in large quantities from the electric organ of electric eels, this receptor is perhaps the most extensively studied of all receptors. Ligands used as affinity labels for this receptor are shown in Fig. 2. It was first successfully affinity labeled using alkylating reagents structurally related to agonists and antagonists (45–48), notably 4-(N-maleimido) benzyltrimethylammonium iodide (MBTA), a cholinergic antagonist (46, 49), and bromoacetylcholine bromide, a cholinergic agonist (47, 50). Both are reversible inhibitors of acetylcholine binding to the native receptor. If, however, the receptor is reduced with dithiothreitol, an exposed sulfide is specifically alkylated by the affinity ligand. MBTA fixes the receptor in the inactive state (46), whereas bromoacetylcholine irreversibly activates the receptor (47, 51). These reagents were used to quantitate acetylcholine receptors (50) and to identify the

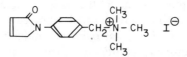

4 - N-MALEIMIDOBENZYLTRIMETHYLAMMONIUM   IODIDE (MBTA)

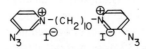

BROMOACETYLCHOLINE

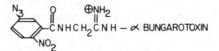

1,10 DECANE BIS (3 - AZIDOPYRIDINIUM) DIIODIDE (DAP)

N-5-AZIDO-2-NITROBENZOYLAMINOACETIMIDATE-
α BUNGAROTOXIN (ANB - Al - α BUTX)

FIGURE 2.   Structures of ligands used to affinity label the acetylcholine receptor.

subunit of the receptor bearing the acetylcholine binding site. Both MBTA and bromoacetylcholine label a single polypeptide of molecular weight 40,000, designated the α subunit, in acetylcholine receptors from a variety of sources including electric eel *Electrophorus electricus* (52, 53), marine ray *Torpedo californicus* (50, 51, 54, 55), and cat denervated muscle (45).

Purified acetylcholine receptors from many sources are known to have subunits of molecular weights 50,000, 60,000, and 65,000, designated β, γ, and δ, respectively, in addition to the 40,000 molecular weight α subunit (56–58). Inasmuch as a purified preparation of receptors containing only α subunits appeared to be fully functional, it seemed reasonable to ask whether the additional subunits constituted a functional part of the receptor (59). To investigate this problem various photoaffinity reagents were employed, most of them acetylcholine agonists modified by the addition of an aryl azide group. The first of these to be reported was the photolabile cholinergic agonist 1,10 decane [^{3}H]bis (3-azidopyridinium) diiodide (DAP; Fig. 2; 60). Binding of this ligand to *Torpedo* acetylcholine receptor in membranes followed by photolysis resulted in the labeling of the α and β subunits. If, however, the purified, Triton-solubilized receptor was used, the α and γ subunits predominantly were labeled. These findings suggested that (i) DAP binds to a site on the α subunit in close proximity to the β and γ subunits, or (ii) DAP binds to all three subunits, possibly at homologous sites. The results support the view that the additional subunits are an integral part of the functional receptor (60).

Subsequent investigators focused on the synthesis of photolabile derivatives of snake venom toxins, such as α-bungarotoxin, which are classic antagonists of acetylcholine. In 1978, Witzemann and Raftery (61) reported the successful photoaffinity labeling of the *Torpedo* acetylcholine receptor using α-bungarotoxin covalently cross-linked to an aryl azide group. The investigators took advantage of the fact that all long neurotoxins contain an exposed disulfide bridge between cysteines 30 and 34 which can be selectively reduced and alkylated without the loss of binding or toxicity (62). Acetylcholine receptors were reduced with NaBH$_4$, then treated with a cross-linking reagent 2-[(4-azido-2-nitrophenyl)amino]ethyl-3-carboxy-4-nitrophenyl disulfide, which can be represented as RSSR'N$_3$. Covalent attachment of the azido group by disulfide exchange was monitored by the release of RS$^-$, thionitrobenzoic acid. Binding of the radiolabeled, photolabile α-bungarotoxin derivative to membrane-bound *Torpedo* acetylcholine receptor followed by photolysis resulted in covalent attachment of the ligand to the α and δ subunits. Again, these results indicate that subunits other than α are in close proximity to the toxin-binding site in the acetylcholine receptor in the membrane. These findings were extended (63) by increasing the length of the photolabile side chain from 14 Å to 33 Å. Using this longer cross-linking agent, only the δ subunit was labeled. Similar results were obtained by Hucho (64) using a 4-azido-2-nitrophenyl (NAP) derivative of α-bungarotoxin, which labeled the α and the δ subunits.

A third photolabile derivative of α-bungarotoxin was prepared by Nathanson and Hall (65). They incubated [^{125}I]α-bungarotoxin with ethyl N-5-azido-2-nitrobenzoylaminoacetimidate (ANB-A1), which resulted in the covalent attachment of a photolabile side chain to lysine (Fig. 2). When ANB-α-bungarotoxin was bound to *Torpedo* receptors or to rat diaphragm muscle receptors *in situ*, all 4 chains —α, β, γ, and δ—were labeled.

Thus the photoaffinity labeling results, taken as a whole, demonstrate that all four subunits are integral parts of the functional receptor. This was unequivocally confirmed by the partial microsequencing of all four subunits from the membrane-bound and Triton-solubilized, purified receptor, which showed the receptor to be a complex of homologous subunits in the ratio of $\alpha_2\beta\gamma\delta$ (66).

2.2. β-Adrenergic Receptor

Atlas and Levitzki (67–69) reported the synthesis of the first successful affinity label for the β-adrenergic receptor. The compound, N-[2-hydroxy-3-(1-naphthoxy)-propyl]-N' bromoacetylethylenediamine (NHNP-NBE; Fig. 3) was a bromoacetyl derivative of propranolol, a potent β antagonist. The precursor amine compound, not bromoacetylated, reversibly inhibited epinephrine-induced adenylate cyclase activation in turkey erythrocytes with a relatively low affinity (K_d = 250 nM) (68). The bromoacetyl derivative, NHNP-NBE, irreversibly inhibited epinephrine stimulation of the adenylate cyclase, but not fluoride-stimulated activation, indicating that only the β-adrenergic receptor was affected. Treatment with NHNP-NBE eliminated [^{3}H]propranolol binding to turkey erythrocytes (67, 68), whereas pretreatment with unlabeled propranolol or epinephrine gave partial protection.

This affinity label was used by Tolkovsky and Levitzki (70) and Ventner (71) to analyze the coupling of the hormone receptor to the cyclase. NHNP-NBE was used at increasing concentrations to blockade irreversibly β-adrenergic receptors of the turkey erythrocyte (70) and cardiac muscle (71). It was found that increasing inhibition of the β-adrenergic receptor delayed the time course of adenyl cyclase activation, but had no effect on the maximal level of cyclase activation achieved. This finding was interpreted as evidence against a "precoupled" receptor–cyclase complex and in favor of a collision-coupling model (70).

In order to identify the protein to which the affinity label was covalently bound, [^{3}H]NHNP-NBE was prepared (72) and incubated with turkey erythrocytes and with rat skeletal myoblasts. Membranes were subjected to elec-

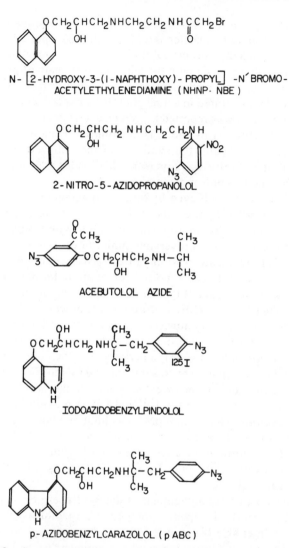

N-[2-HYDROXY-3-(1-NAPHTHOXY)-PROPYL]-N′BROMO-
ACETYLETHYLENEDIAMINE (NHNP- NBE)

2-NITRO-5-AZIDOPROPANOLOL

ACEBUTOLOL AZIDE

IODOAZIDOBENZYLPINDOLOL

p-AZIDOBENZYLCARAZOLOL (pABC)

FIGURE 3. Structures of ligands used to affinity-label the β-adrenergic receptor.

trophoresis and autoradiography. Two bands at M_r = 37,000 and 41,000 were identified as candidates for the β-adrenergic receptor; the relationship between the two bands was unknown. Labeling was partially blocked by the β-blocker hydroxybenzylpindolol. In general, however, the low affinity (K_d = 250 nM) and low specific radioactivity of NHNP-NBE (due to the [³H] label) limited its usefulness as an affinity label in identifying receptors present in small quantities.

The first attempts at the synthesis of photoaffinity labeling reagents also met with limited success. Darfler and Marinetti (73) reported the synthesis of 2-nitro-5-azidophenyl propranolol (Fig. 3); they reacted the reagent 5-fluoro-4-nitro phenylazide with the ethylene side chain of propranolol. It was not radioactive, however, and was of low affinity (K_d = 100 nM), and its use was not demonstrated in actual photolysis experiments. Another aryl azide labeling reagent was reported by Wrenn and Homcy (74) who prepared acebutolol azide (Fig. 3) by the diazotization of acebutol amine, a β-adrenergic antagonist. Again, the synthesis of the radioactive material was not described, the affinity was low (400 nM), and it was not conclusively shown to label the receptor molecule.

Greater success was achieved by turning to antagonists of much higher affinity. Pitha et al. (75) prepared a derivative of the potent antagonist alprenolol by replacing its isopropylamine residue with 1,8 diamino-p-menthane. This compound was a reversible inhibitor of β-adrenergic receptors in the frog erythrocyte with an affinity of 210 pM, three orders of magnitude stronger than that previously reported for propranolol derivatives. When bromoacetylated, it irreversibly bound to the receptor, and was 60-fold more potent than NHNP-NBE. Unfortunately, however, the efficiency of covalent coupling was very low, so that attempts to identify the labeled receptor were not very successful (75, 76). A more useful reagent was iodoazidobenzylpindolol (Fig. 3), a derivative of the potent antagonist hydroxybenzylpindolol reported by Rashidbaidi and Ruoho (77). This compound could be prepared with ^{125}I, thus yielding a much higher specific radioactivity than had been obtained with the tritiated labels previously described. In addition, the affinity (K_d = 220 pM) was high enough to permit labeling and identification of the receptor in crude membranes. In duck erythrocytes, photolysis at long ultraviolet wavelengths for 3 seconds resulted in an 8% efficiency of covalent labeling. Two bands at M_r = 45,000 and 48,500 were specifically labeled.

One of the most potent antagonists of the β-adrenergic receptor reported to date is the recently discovered compound carazolol which has a K_d = 5–15 pM. Lavin et al. (78) reported the synthesis of a photoactive, radiolabeled derivative, [3H]p-azidobenzylcarazolol (pABC). This derivative was chosen in order to combine the carbazole moiety of carazolol and the benzyl moiety of hydroxybenzylpindolol or hydroxybenzylisoproterenol and to maximize the binding affinity for the β-adrenergic receptor. The affinity of pABC for the β-adrenergic receptor is high (K_d = 100 pM). Photoactivation of pABC irreversibly abolished 60% of dihydroalprenolol binding sites in frog erythrocyte membranes, and this could be completely prevented by incubation with excess unlabeled carazolol. Sodium dodecyl sulfate electrophoresis of pABC-labeled preparations of β-adrenergic receptors from frog erythrocytes showed a labeled band at $M_r = 58,000$. Because of the low specific activity obtainable with tritium labeling, however, the peak was very small (less than 100 cpm above background) and the resolution was relatively poor. Partial purification of the receptor by detergent solubilization followed by chromatography on alprenolol-Sepharose was necessary to obtain better labeling; again a single broad band of radioactivity was seen at $M_r = 58,000$.

To identify the receptor conclusively with this affinity labeling reagent, it was necessary to increase the specific radioactivity of the reagent by introducing a [^{125}I] label. This was initially approached by iodination of the amino derivative, p-aminobenzylcarazolol (pAMBC), prepared in the synthesis of pABC (79). The presence of an aryl amine in this carazolol derivative permitted its covalent incorporation using the photoactivatable bifunctional cross-linker N-succinimidyl-6-(4'-azido 2'-nitrophenylamino) hexanoate (SANAH, Fig. 1). The very high affinity of pAMBC ($K_d = 4$ pM) and its high specific radioactivity (2200 Ci/mMol) permitted the labeling of the receptor in crude frog erythrocyte membranes as well as in a highly purified preparation; in each case a single band of $M_r = 58,000$ was labeled, in agreement with the results obtained by purification (6) or by the use of [^{3}H]pABC (78). The efficiency of covalent incorporation was rather low due to the use of the cross-linking reagent—0.5–1.5% of radioactivity bound by crude membranes and up to 2.5% by purified preparations.

An improved efficiency of labeling was achieved by direct iodination of p-azidobenzylcarazolol (80, 81). Using [^{125}I]pABC it was possible to label the β-adrenergic receptor in membranes directly, permitting a rapid screening of receptor structures in a variety of tissues including frog and turkey erythrocytes, rat reticulocytes, rat lung, and rabbit lung. The ability to rapidly label small quantities of receptors in crude membranes made possible further studies of receptor function such as the recent report by Stadel et al. (82) on isoproterenol desensitization of the β-adrenergic receptor in turkey erythrocytes. In control cells, photolysis of [^{125}I]pABC covalently labeled two receptor bands at $M_r = 38,000$ and $M_r = 50,000$. After preincubation of intact cells with isoproterenol, however, the apparent molecular weight of both bands was increased to $M_r = 42,000$ and $M_r = 53,000$ concurrently with receptor desensitization. The antagonist propranolol prevented both the desensitization and the change in band mobility. These results were interpreted as evidence for structural alteration, possibly phosphorylation, of the receptor at a location other than the ligand binding site (inasmuch as the degree of pABC labeling and antagonist binding were not affected by isoproterenol treatment). Detection of this small structural alteration probably would have been impossible without the use of a rapid, high-specificity photoaffinity label.

2.3.   Insulin Receptor

The synthesis of potential photoaffinity ligands for the insulin receptor was first reported by Levy (83). He described the preparation of insulins derivatized with 4-fluoro-3-nitrophenylazide under mild conditions (incubation in dimethylformamide for 5 hours at room temperature) and showed that photoactive groups were incorporated on the amino terminals of the A chain (glycine) and B chain (phenylalanine) as well as on lysine B29. B1 and B29 derivatives had unchanged biological activity in the fat-pad glucose oxidation assay whereas the A1 derivative had only 60% of its original activity. The derivatives could be prepared in iodinated form. However, actual photolysis experiments were not described in this report.

The first covalent receptor labeling with a photoactive insulin was reported by Yip et al. (34) in 1978. The N-hydroxysuccinimide ester of 4-azidobenzoic acid was added to $[^{125}I]$insulin under the same mild conditions reported by Levy (83). The product, precipitated with acetone, contained a mixture of unlabeled, monoazidobenzoyl, and diazidobenzoyl insulins. The mixture was used, without further purification, to label the insulin receptor in membranes with an estimated efficiency of 7–10%. Electrophoresis and autoradiography of the membranes revealed a multitude of $[^{125}I]$labeled bands, only one of which was specific (i.e., was blocked by the addition of unlabeled insulin). It was postulated that this band, at 130,000 daltons, was a subunit of the insulin receptor.

Similar results were reported by Jacobs et al. (84) using the 4-azido-2-nitrophenyl insulin described by Levy to label the insulin receptor in rat liver and in human placental membranes, as well as in a purified insulin receptor, prepared by use of immobilized insulin agarose, containing subunits of 135,000, 90,000, and 45,000. The 135,000 molecular weight band present in the purified receptor preparation was specifically labeled with 3% incorporation. However, the 45,000 and 90,000 molecular weight bands were not labeled under these conditions, suggesting that they may not be directly involved in insulin binding. In the absence of reductant, a band of molecular weight greater than 300,000 was observed, indicating that the native receptor was present as a large disulfide-linked complex.

The results of photoaffinity labeling of insulin receptors were dramatically improved with improved ligand preparation and characterization. The high degree of nonspecific labeling seen in crude mixtures of photoactive ligands (34) was eliminated by careful purification of the labeled insulins. Thus Yip et al. (20, 85, 86), using a highly purified and well-characterized azidobenzoyl insulin derivative, demonstrated improved resolution and specificity of labeling. With this affinity ligand, receptor subunits at 130,000 and 90,000 daltons were seen in membranes from liver and adipocyte, with the $M_r = 130,000$ band exhibiting much greater labeling. Manipulation of amino-blocking agents such as trifluoroacetyl, t-butyloxycarbonyl, and methylsulfonylethyloxycarbonyl groups, removable under mild conditions, permitted the synthesis of insulins labeled on any of the three reactive amino groups reported by Levy—A1 glycine, B1 phenylalanine, or B29 lysine (87, 88). Characterization of these labeled insulins showed that A1 derivatives and disubstituted insulins generally exhibited impaired biological activity (20, 83, 89).

Fig. 4 lists the photoactive aryl azides that have been used to prepare photolabile derivatives of insulin (20, 30, 83, 87). The 4-azidophenylacetyl group suffers from the disadvantage of a short wavelength of maximum activation (252 nM). This was overcome by the use of nitro substituents which increased the maximum to more than 300 nM. However, these bulky, uncharged hydrophobic substituents may render the ligand insoluble, particularly when multiple substitution occurs. In such cases, the charged 4-azidobenzimidyl group can be employed. All of these photoactive groups are stable to commonly used iodination techniques, such as the chloramine T reaction, if performed in the dark (30).

Other groups have investigated the structure of the insulin receptor using bifunctional cross-linking agents. Sahyoun et al. (90) used glutaraldehyde followed by reduction with sodium borohydride to covalently link [^{125}I]insulin to its receptors in rat liver membranes. Labeled bands were separated by

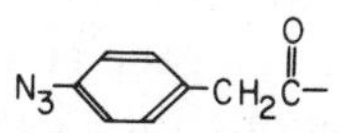

4-AZIDOPHENYLACETYL (APA) λmax = 252nm

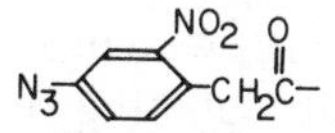

2-NITRO, 4-AZIDOPHENYLACETYL (NAPA)
λmax = 247, 329 nm

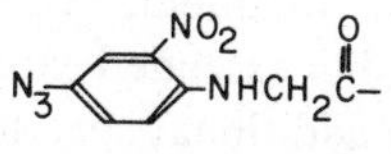

2-NITRO, 4-AZIDOPHENYLGLYCYL (NAP-GLY)
λmax = 250, 460 nm

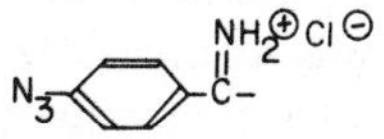

4-AZIDOBENZIMIDYL (ABI) λmax = 275nm

Figure 4. Structures of aryl azide groups used to prepare photolabile insulin derivatives (30).

gel filtration. Five peaks of radioactivity were observed for insulin, only one of which was clearly inhibited by preincubation of the membranes with excess unlabeled insulin. Because gel filtration rather than dodecyl sulfate electrophoresis was used for the separation of these bands, an accurate estimate of their molecular weight was not obtained. The multiplicity of bands observed probably resulted from the relatively harsh reaction conditions employed, which severely limited the usefulness of this technique.

Greater success in achieving highly specific affinity labeling under very mild conditions was reported by Pilch and Czech (18, 33) using disuccinimidyl suberate (DSS, Fig. 1). Treatment of intact adipocytes with DSS (15°C for 15 minutes) was shown to inhibit insulin stimulation of glucose transport completely at concentrations of 1–2 mM, whereas basal rates were unaffected; the monofunctional analog succinimidyl butyrate had no effect. If, however, cells were pretreated with insulin before the addition of DSS, glucose transport was irreversibly stimulated even after prolonged washing to remove non-covalently bound hormone. Scatchard analysis of insulin binding showed that high affinity receptor binding of insulin (K_d = 3 nM) was abolished by pretreatment with DSS, and dilution studies showed that dissociation of the hormone from the receptor was drastically inhibited by DSS treatment. These findings established that covalent linkage of insulin to its receptor was achieved with this cross-linking agent. [^{125}I]Insulin (1.7 nM) was then cross-linked to the receptor in adipocyte membranes using 1.0 mM DSS (18, 33). Unreacted DSS was quenched with excess Tris buffer, unbound hormone was washed away, and the membranes were subjected to electro-phoresis and autoradiography. In the absence of reductant, a band at M_r = 300,000 was observed, whereas in the presence of dithiothreitol a band at 125,000 was labeled. Nonspecific background was very low, and labeling was completely abolished in the presence of excess unlabeled insulin.

These observations were extended by Massague et al. (19) who proposed a model of insulin receptor structure based on the affinity labeling results shown in Fig. 5. The use of highly porous polyacrylamide gels resolved the M_r = 300,000 band observed in the absence of reductant into three distinct bands at M_r = 350,000, 320,000, and 290,000. These bands were excised from the gel and subjected to dithiothreitol treatment. All three forms generated a band at M_r = 125,000 designated α, but extended exposure of the autoradiographs permitted identification of two additional specifically labeled bands at M_r = 90,000 (designated β) and M_r = 45,000 (designated $β_1$). The 350,000 band generated α and β subunits upon reduction, the 320,000 band generated α, β, and $β_1$ subunits, and the 290,000 band generated α and $β_1$ subunits. Mild treatment with elastase or lysosomal enzymes (91) converted the β subunit to the $β_1$ form, apparently at a site uniquely sensitive to protease action. It was therefore proposed, as shown in Fig. 5, that the

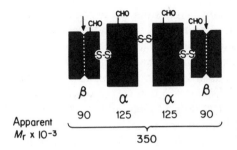

$$Apparent$$
$$M_r \times 10^{-3}$$

Figure 5.   Model of insulin receptor structure proposed by Massague et al. (19).

insulin receptor is a disulfide-linked tetramer with an immunoglobulinlike structure. The 350,000 form had the composition $(\alpha\beta)_2$, the 320,000 form represented $\alpha_2\beta\beta_1$, and the 290,000 form was composed of $(\alpha\beta_1)_2$. This was supported by the treatment of all three forms with very low concentrations of dithiotreitol, which resulted in the generation of intermediate forms: from the 350,000 form, a band at 210,000 $(\alpha\beta)$; from the 290,000 form, a band at 160,000 $(\alpha\beta_1)$; from the 320,000 form, a mixture of $\alpha\beta$ and $\alpha\beta_1$. Subsequent studies using DSS affinity labeling in the presence of different dithiothreitol concentrations (92) demonstrated that disulfide bonds linking the $(\alpha\beta)$ receptor halves were readily reduced, with no effect on insulin binding or receptor function in intact cells, whereas bonds between α and β subunits require solubilization with dodecyl sulfate as well as high concentrations of dithiothreitol to effect complete reduction. This model of insulin receptor structure is consistent with results from photolabeling (34, 84–86, 88), immunoprecipitation with anti-receptor antibody (10), and receptor purification (93).

A somewhat different model of insulin receptor structure based on generally similar data has been proposed by Yip et al. (94). Photolabeling of intact rat adipocytes using insulin labeled with an azidobenzoyl group on lysine B29 showed three specifically labeled bands at M_r = 130,000, 90,000, and 40,000; when the azidobenzoyl group was attached to B_1 phenylalanine, only the 130,000 and the 90,000 bands were labeled. Importantly, however, the 40,000 band was observed only in intact cells, but not in isolated membranes (94), in contrast to the finding of Massague et al. (91). The appearance of the M_r = 40,000 band in intact cells was reported to be unaffected by time, temperature of incubation, or protease inhibitors. Treatment of M_r = 130,000 and 90,000 bands with trypsin or chymotrypsin did not generate a band at M_r = 40,000. However, the effect of treatment with elastase or lysosomal proteases, used by Massague et al. (91) for this purpose, was not tested. The M_r = 40,000 band labeled by the B29 azidobenzoyl insulin appeared different in its protease digestion pattern than the M_r = 40,000 band labeled by B1 azidobenzoyl insulin, suggesting the existence of two different M_r = 40,000 subunits. Based on these results and especially on the presence of the M_r = 40,000 subunit(s) in intact cells but not in isolated membranes, Yip et al. (94) concluded that this subunit is not a proteolytic fragment of the M_r = 90,000 subunit as proposed by Massague et al. (91). In the absence of reductant, a band at M_r = 300,000 was observed which, when reduced, generated subunits of 130,000, 90,000, and 40,000. It was proposed, therefore, that the intact insulin receptor consists of one 130,000, one 90,000, and two possibly nonidentical 40,000 subunits, all disulfide linked in a complex of M_r = 300,000. The organization of these subunits within the complex was not addressed. The strongest evidence against this model is its lack of consistency with immunoprecipitation results (10). Antibodies obtained from an insulin-resistant patient immunoprecipitate subunits of M_r = 135,000 and 95,000 from human IM-9 lymphocytes, in agreement with photolabeling and affinity cross-linking data. However, no M_r = 45,000 subunit was precipitated by these antibodies, even if the intact cells were subjected to biosynthetic labeling or surface iodination before solubilization and immunoprecipitation. These results suggest that the M_r = 45,000 subunit observed by Yip et al. (94) is not an integral part of the native receptor, but may instead be a proteolytic fragment as proposed by Massague et al. (19, 91).

In more recent studies, photoreactive derivatives of insulin have been used to attach a covalent radioactive tag to the insulin receptor without perturbing other cell functions, so that the fate of the insulin receptor after hormone binding can be directly monitored in the intact cell (31, 32, 95). Previous studies following the fate of [^{125}I]insulin bound to cells could not monitor the receptor after dissociation of ligand from the binding site. Studies using covalently labeled receptor–ligand complexes in rat hepatocytes and adipocytes have shown that, at 37°C, the receptor is rapidly internalized to the lysosomal compartment, then recycled to the cell surface over approximately 4 hours. This process is temperature-dependent, being totally blocked at 16°C.

2.4. Growth Factor Receptors

2.4.1. Epidermal Growth Factor Receptor

The receptor for epidermal growth factor (EGF) was first successfully identified by Das et al. (96) using the photoactive cross-linking agent methyl 3-[(p-azidophenyl)dithio]proprionimidate (PAPDIP). [^{125}I]EGF was preincubated with PAPDIP (1 hour, 23°C, in the dark) to allow reaction of its only lysine group to form [^{125}I]EGF-PAPDIP. This compound was then incubated with Swiss mouse 3T3 fibroblasts and photolyzed. A covalently labeled band incorporating 1.5–2% of bound radioactivity was identified by dodecyl sulfate electrophoresis at M_r = 190,000. This photoaffinity label was later used to demonstrate EGF-induced internalization and degradation of the cross-linked complex in 3T3 cells (97).

Another photoactive cross-linking agent, SANAH (Fig. 1), was used by Hock et al. (98, 99) to label the EGF receptor in human placenta membranes using a protocol very similar to that of Das et al. (96, 97). Specific, covalently labeled bands at 180,000 and 160,000 daltons were identified, in good agreement with the earlier results.

A simpler method of covalently labeling the EGF receptor was reported by Baker et al. (100) and Linsley et al. (101) who discovered that the incubation of [^{125}I]EGF alone (in the absence of additional cross-linking agents or photolysis) with human fibroblasts or 3T3 cells resulted in the incorporation of 2–9% of the radioactivity into bands at M_r = 190,000 and 170,000. Similar results were reported by Wrann and Fox (102) using A431 cells, which are overproducers of the EGF receptor. The linkage was evidently covalent, inasmuch as it was stable to boiling in 3% dodecyl sulfate, 0.1 M β-mercaptoethanol, and 6 M guanidine HCl. It was originally thought that such covalent incorporation might be of physiological importance in receptor function. Later studies (103) demonstrated, however, that such cross-linking is an artifact of the chloramine T oxidation used during the preparation of iodinated EGF.

All of the preceding results are consistent with the structure reported for the EGF receptor purified from human A431 carcinoma cells, which has a molecular weight of 170,000 (5). A lower molecular weight band at 150,000 seen in earlier purified preparations (104) and in some affinity labeling procedures (98–101) appears to be a proteolytic breakdown product (5).

The finding that the EGF receptor is clearly associated with a tyrosine kinase activity and that this activity copurifies with the receptor (5, 104–107) led to the use of another affinity labeling procedure using a ligand specific for kinases, 5-p-fluorosulfonylbenzoyl adenosine, which labels the ATP/ADP binding site (108). In membrane vesicles prepared from A431 cells, bands at 170,000 and 150,000 molecular weight were labeled (along with many other bands). The labeling was blocked by the nonhydrolyzable analogue AMP-PNP, and treatment with N-ethylmaleimide or heat, which inactivates kinase activity, also drastically inhibited labeling. The finding that the kinase activity comigrates with the EGF receptor strongly supports the conclusion that both activities reside in the same protein, apparently in different domains (109).

The EGF receptor has also been affinity labeled with [^{125}I]sarcoma growth factor, demonstrating a direct interaction between transforming growth factors and this receptor (42; see Section 2.4.5).

2.4.2. Insulinlike Growth Factors I and II

The receptor for insulinlike growth factor I (IGF-I) in human placenta was identified by Bhaumick et al. (110) using the photoreactive cross-linking reagent SANAH (Fig. 1) and [^{125}I]IGF-I. A specifically labeled band at $M_r = 140,000$ was seen, similar to that of the most intensely labeled subunit of the insulin receptor. However, this photolabeled receptor was shown to be distinct from the insulin receptor, as it was not precipitated by anti-insulin receptor antibody and could be differentially solubilized from membranes using Triton X-100.

Kasuga et al. (111) examined receptors for both IGF-I and IGF-II in rat liver plasma membranes and in a cultured line of rat liver cells (BRL-3A) using the DSS technique. Two distinct receptors were identified. [^{125}I]IGF-I appeared to be cross-linked to two bands of $M_r > 300,000$ in the absence of reductant, or with a single band of $M_r = 130,000$ following reduction—again very similar to the pattern seen with the insulin receptor. [^{125}I]IGF-II, in contrast, labeled a single band of $M_r = 220,000$ (nonreduced) or 260,000 (reduced), apparently a single polypeptide chain containing internal disulfide bonds. Very similar findings on IGF-II receptor structure using the DSS technique were reported by Massague et al. (39). Based on competition studies with unlabeled IGF-I and II and insulin, it was concluded that the two receptors are distinct from one another and from the insulin receptor. Cross-linking of labeled hormone to the IGF-I receptor, but not the IGF-II receptor, was inhibited by insulin.

The structural similarity between the IGF-I receptor and the insulin receptor was further investigated by Massague and Czech (40). DSS cross-linking with [^{125}I]IGF-I to membranes from rat adipocytes and from liver and to human placenta and skin fibroblasts under nonreducing conditions showed covalently labeled bands at 350,000, 320,000, and 290,000. Under reducing conditions, subunits of 130,000 (α) and 98,000 (β) were seen. Partial reduction of the IGF receptor into half-fragments resulted in the generation of bands at 155,000 (predicted to consist of $\alpha\beta_1$ half-fragments, where β_1 is a proteolytic fragment of β), and 205,000 (corresponding to $\alpha\beta$ half-fragments). Thus it has been proposed that the intact receptor is a disulfide-linked tetramer $(\alpha\beta)_2$, where the β subunit contains a protease-sensitive site, leading to the generation of $(\alpha\beta)(\alpha\beta_1)$ and $(\alpha\beta_1)_2$ forms. Competition studies in which the affinity labeling of the IGF-I receptor was inhibited by the addition of unlabeled insulin, IGF-I, or IGF-II showed some variability in relative ligand affinities in various tissues, but generally indicated that this receptor possesses the highest affinity for IGF-I, a moderate affinity for IGF-II, and a very low affinity for insulin. Thus it is distinct from the insulin receptor, though it may be very homologous to it.

In contrast, competition studies with the IGF-II receptor monitoring inhibition of [^{125}I]IGF-II affinity labeling by insulin and by IGF-I and II indicated that the IGF-II receptor has the highest affinity for IGF-II, a moderate affinity for IGF-I, and no affinity at all for insulin. DSS crosslinking has also been used to demonstrate that preincubation of intact rat adipocytes with insulin dramatically increases the binding of [^{125}I]IGF-II to the IGF-II receptor (112).

2.4.3. Nerve Growth Factor Receptor

The receptor for nerve growth factor (NGF) was identified by Massague et al. (44) using [^{125}I]NGF and the photoreactive cross-linking agent hydroxysuccinimidyl azidobenzoate (HSAB, Fig. 1). In membranes from adult rabbit superior cervical ganglia, two major components were seen at M_r = 130,000 and M_r = 100,000 (assuming one molecule of NGF bound per subunit). Attempts to affinity label the receptor using DSS were unsuccessful, presumably because either ligand or receptor lacked appropriately positioned amino groups. Affinity labeling was inhibited by unlabeled NGF, but not by insulin, IGF-I, IGF-II, or EGF, and no labeling was seen in membranes from non-neuronal tissues. Peptide mapping experiments using chymotrypsin suggested that the 100,000 band may be a proteolytic fragment of the 130,000 band; the latter was thought to be the native receptor (44).

More recently, the NGF receptor has been identified by HSAB affinity labeling and extensively purified by affinity chromatography from A875 melanoma cells, which overproduce the receptor (7). Affinity labeling with [^{125}I]NGF in intact cells, membranes, and solubilized, purified receptor showed two subunits of 220,000 and 93,000 molecular weight. Assuming one NGF molecule (M_r = 13,000) bound per subunit, this finding was in excellent agreement with the apparent structure of the purified receptor, which displayed subunits of 200,000 and 85,000 molecular weight. No band was seen at 130,000 in the purified preparation. Because of the finding of the M_r = 85,000 subunit in intact cells, membranes, and in the purified receptor, Puma et al. (7) thought it was unlikely to be a proteolytic fragment of a larger band. The explanation for the differences in apparent molecular weight observed in these two studies is not clear.

2.4.4. Platelet-Derived Growth Factor

The receptor for platelet-derived growth factor (PDGF) has been affinity labeled by Glenn et al. (41) in a variety of PDGF-responsive tissues using the cross-linking agents DSS and ethylene glycol bis (succinimidyl succinate) (EGS; Fig. 1). A single band at M_r = 164,000 is labeled (assuming one molecule of [^{125}I]PDGF bound per complex). The labeling pattern was not significantly altered by the presence of reductant. Labeling was completely blocked by the presence of excess unlabeled PDGF, but was unaffected by large excesses of other hormones including EGF, insulin, or fibroblast growth factor. This receptor was identified in Swiss 3T3 fibroblasts, human fibroblasts, and monkey arterial smooth muscle cells, all of which are responsive to PDGF. Labeling of the M_r = 164,000 band was eliminated by trypsin treatment of 3T3 cells indicating that the receptor was present at the cell surface. Incubation of the cells at 37°C for 1–2 hours after trypsin treatment was necessary before intact receptor was detectable by this technique, and full restoration of labeling required 24 hours of post-trypsin incubation.

The identification of the band at M_r = 164,000 as the PDGF receptor is especially intriguing in light of reports (113, 114) that a protein of similar molecular weight is phosphorylated on tyrosine residues in response to PDGF treatment. By analogy to the EGF receptor, it has been speculated that PDGF receptor is a tyrosine kinase capable of autophosphorylation.

2.4.5. Transforming Growth Factors

Transforming growth factors (TGFs) have been isolated from a variety of transformed and nontransformed tissues, and are able to induce a transformed phenotype when continuously present in the media of untransformed cells (115, 116). Many TGFs interact strongly with the EGF receptor, and some require the presence of EGF in order to generate the transformed phenotype. However, the findings that (i) EGF itself is totally unable to support transformation, and (ii) some TGFs do not bind to EGF receptors, suggest that a TGF receptor distinct from the EGF receptor may mediate the transformation events. This possibility was investigated by Massague et al. (42) using sarcoma growth factor (SGF) as well as a TGF isolated from the conditioned media of murine sarcoma virus-transformed mouse 3T3 fibroblasts (116). [^{125}I]EGF and [^{125}I]SGF were cross-linked to membranes of human A431 carcinoma cells, overproducers of the EGF receptor, and to normal rat kidney (NRK) fibroblasts using DSS or HSAB (Fig. 1). In A431 cells, both [^{125}I]EGF and [^{125}I]SGF covalently labeled two bands at M_r = 160,000 and 140,000, which were identified as the EGF receptor (Section 2.4.1). Affinity labeling of these bands was eliminated by the presence of excess unlabeled EGF or SGF. Thus both growth factors bind to the EGF receptor on A431 cells; such cells are not affected by the addition of SGFs. NRK cells, in contrast, are highly sensitive to the transforming effects of SGF (116). These cells contain only small amounts of the EGF receptor. When [^{125}I]EGF is cross-linked to NRK membranes with DSS, a band at M_r = 150,000–170,000 corresponding to the EGF receptor is labeled;

this labeling is decreased by the addition of an excess of either SGF or EGF. In contrast, the cross-linking of [^{125}I]SGF to NRK membranes with DSS or HSAB resulted in the labeling of a major band at $M_r = 60,000$ as well as a minor species at $M_r = 170,000$ (presumably the EGF receptor). The affinity labeling of both bands was blocked by the addition of excess unlabeled SGF, or by the addition of another TGF purified from Abelson murine leukemia virus-transformed rat embryo cells. The addition of an excess of unlabeled EGF eliminated the labeling of the $M_r = 170,000$ band, but was unable to compete with [^{125}I]SGF for affinity labeling of the $M_r = 60,000$ component. It was, therefore, concluded that the $M_r = 60,000$ band may represent a TGF receptor, distinct from the EGF receptor, which is believed to mediate the generation of the transformed phenotype. Thus SGF and other TGFs are capable of binding to the EGF receptor, and in some cases require its stimulation of cell growth to effect the transformation event, but the latter appears to be mediated by a distinct TGF receptor.

3. CONCLUSION

The preceding examples illustrate the versatility of the affinity labeling methodology in a variety of receptor systems. This technique is often the method of choice for specific identification of receptors present in minute quantities, for which purification would represent a formidable task. It also permits rapid and precise monitoring of receptor movement or modification in the intact cell in response to hormones or other agents, providing information not readily available by other means. The receptor labeling methods described here are currently being used in a number of laboratories to gain new insight into the molecular mechanisms by which receptors mediate hormone and growth factor action.

REFERENCES

1. Kahn, C. R., *Methods Memb. Biol.*, **3**, 81 (1975).
2. Cuatrecasas, P., and Hollenberg, M. D., *Adv. Prot. Chem.*, **30**, 251 (1976).
3. Conti-Tronconi, B. M., and Raftery, M. A., *Annu. Rev. Biochem.*, **51**, 491 (1982).
4. Cuatrecasas, P., *Proc. Natl. Acad. Sci. USA*, **69**, 1277 (1972).
5. Cohen, S., Ushiro, H., Stoscheck, C., and Chinkers, M., *J. Biol. Chem.*, **257**, 1523 (1982).
6. Shorr, R. G. L., Lefkowitz, R. J., and Caron, M. G., *J. Biol. Chem.*, **256**, 5820 (1981).
7. Puma, P., Buxser, S. E., Watson, L., Kelleher, D. J., and Johnson, G. L., *J. Biol. Chem.*, **258**, 3370 (1983).

8. Lindstrom, J., Walter, B., and Ernarson, B., *Biochemistry*, **18**, 4470 (1979).

9. Jacobs, S., Hazum, E., Schechter, Y., and Cuatrecasas, P., *Proc. Natl. Acad. Sci. USA*, **76**, 4918 (1979).

10. Kasuga, M., Hedo, J. A., Yamada, K. M., and Kahn, C. R., *J. Biol. Chem.*, **257**, 10392 (1982).

11. Flier, J. S., Kahn, C. R., Roth, J., and Bar, R. S., *Science*, **190**, 63 (1975).

12. Singer, S. J., *Adv. Prot. Chem.*, **22**, 1 (1967).

13. Wold, F., *Methods Enzymol.*, **46**, 1 (1977).

14. Bayley, H., and Knowles, J. R., *Methods Enzymol.*, **46**, 69 (1977).

15. Zisapel, N., and Sokolovsky, M., *Methods Enzymol.*, **46**, 572 (1977).

16. Chowdry, V., and Westheimer, F. H., *Annu. Rev. Biochem.*, **48**, 293 (1979).

17. Turro, N. J., *Ann. N.Y. Acad. Sci.*, **346**, 1 (1980).

18. Pilch, P., and Czech, M. P., *J. Biol. Chem.*, **254**, 3375 (1979).

19. Massague, J., Pilch, P., and Czech, M. P., *Proc. Natl. Acad. Sci. USA*, **77**, 7127 (1981).

20. Yip, C. C., Yeung, C. W. T., and Moule, M. L., in D. Brandenburg and A. Wollman, Eds., *Insulin: Chemistry, Structure and Function of Insulin and Related Hormones*, Walter de Gruyter, New York, 1980.

21. Singh, A., Thornton, E. R., and Westheimer, F. H., *J. Biol. Chem.*, **237**, 3006 (1962).

22. Chaimovich, H., Vaughan, R., and Westheimer, F. H., *J. Am. Chem. Soc.*, **90**, 4088 (1968).

23. Hexter, C. S., and Westheimer, F. H., *J. Biol. Chem.*, **246**, 3934 (1971).

24. Lwowski, W., *Ann. N.Y. Acad. Sci.*, **346**, 491 (1980).

25. Fleet, G. W. J., Porter, R. R., and Knowles, J. R., *Nature*, **224**, 511 (1969).

26. Smith, P. A. S., and Brown, B. B., *J. Am. Chem. Soc.*, **73**, 2435 (1951).

27. Hyatt, J. A., and Swenton, J. S., *J. Heterocycl. Chem.*, **9**, 409 (1972).

28. Guthrow, C. E., Rasmussen, H., Brunswick, D. J., and Cooperman, B. S., *Proc. Natl. Acad. Sci. USA*, **70**, 3344 (1973).

29. Kallos, J., *Nature*, **265**, 705 (1977).

30. Saunders, D., Thamm, P., and Brandenburg, D., in D. Brandenburg and A. Wollmer, Eds., *Insulin: Chemistry, Structure and Function of Insulin and Related Hormones*, Walter de Gruyter, New York, 1980.

31. Berhanu, P., Olefsky, J. M., Tsai, P., Thamm, P., Saunders, D., and Brandenburg, D., *Proc. Natl. Acad. Sci. USA*, **79**, 4069 (1982).

32. Fehlmann, M., Carpentier, J. L., Van Obberghen, E., Freychet, P., Thamm, P., Saunders, D., Brandenburg, D., and Orci, L., *Proc. Natl. Acad. Sci. USA*, **79**, 5921 (1982).

33. Pilch, P. F., and Czech, M. P., *J. Biol. Chem.*, **255**, 1722 (1980).

34. Yip, C. C., Yeung, C. W. T., and Moule, M. L., *J. Biol. Chem.* **253**, 1743 (1978).

35. Peters, K., and Richards, F. M., *Annu. Rev. Biochem.*, **46**, 523 (1977).

36. Davies, G. E., and Stark, G. R., *Proc. Natl. Acad. Sci. USA*, **66**, 651 (1970).

37. Hartman, F. C., and Wold, F., *J. Am. Chem. Soc.*, **88** 3890 (1966).

38. Lomant, A. J., and Fairbanks, G. J., *J. Mol. Biol.*, **104**, 243 (1976).

39. Massague, J., Guillette, B. J., and Czech, M. P., *J. Biol. Chem.*, **256**, 2122 (1981).

40. Massague, J., and Czech, M. P., *J. Biol. Chem.*, **257** 5038 (1982).

41. Glenn, K., Bowen-Pope, D. F., and Ross, R., *J. Biol. Chem.*, **257**, 5172 (1982).

42. Massague, J., Czech, M. P., Iwata, K., DeLarco, J. E., and Todaro, G. J., *Proc. Natl. Acad. Sci. USA*, **79**, 6822 (1982).

43. Johnson, G. L., MacAndrew, V. I., and Pilch, P. F., *Proc. Natl. Acad. Sci. USA*, **78**, 875 (1981).

44. Massague, J., Guillette, B. J., Czech, M. P., Morgan, C. J., and Bradshaw, R. A., *J. Biol. Chem.*, **256**, 9419 (1981).

45. Changeux, J. P., Podleski, T. R., and Wofst, L., *Proc. Natl. Acad. Sci. USA*, **58**, 2063 (1967).

46. Karlin, A., and Winnik, M., *Proc. Natl. Acad. Sci. USA*, **60**, 668 (1968).

47. Silman, I., and Karlin, A., *Science*, **164**, 1420 (1969).

48. Chao, Y., Vandlen, R. L., and Raftery, M. A., *Biochem. Biophys. Res. Commun.*, **63**, 300 (1975).

49. Karlin, A., *Methods Enzymol.*, **46**, 582 (1977).

50. Damle, V. N., McLaughlin, M., and Karlin, A., *Biochem. Biophys. Res. Commun.*, **84**, 845 (1978).

51. Moore, H. H., and Raftery, M. A., *Biochemistry*, **18**, 1862 (1979).

52. Cowburn, D., and Karlin, A., *Proc. Natl. Acad. Sci. USA*, **70**, 3636 (1973).

53. Reiter, M. J., Cowburn, D. A., Prives, J. M., and Karlin, A., *Proc. Natl. Acad. Sci. USA*, **69**, 1168 (1972).

54. Weill, C. L., McNamee, M. G., and Karlin, A., *Biochem. Biophys. Res. Commun.*, **61**, 997 (1974).

55. Damle, V. N., and Karlin, A., *Biochemistry*, **17**, 2039 (1978).

56. Lydiatt, A., Sumikawa, K., Wolosin, J. M., Dolly, J. O., and Barnard, E. A., *FEBS Lett.*, **108**, 20 (1979).

57. Hidmann, T., and Changeux, J. P., *Annu. Rev. Biochem.* **47**, 317 (1978).

58. Reynolds, J. A., and Karlin, A., *Biochemistry*, **17**, 2035 (1978).

59. Sobel, A., Heidmann, T., Hofler, J., and Changeux, J. P., *Proc. Natl. Acad. Sci. USA*, **75**, 510 (1978).

60. Witzemann, V., and Raftery, M. A., *Biochemistry*, **16**, 5862 (1977).

61. Witzemann, V., and Raftery, M. A., *Biochem. Biophys. Res. Commun.*, **85**, 623 (1978).

62. Chicheportiche, R., Vincent, J. P., Kopeyan, C., Schwertz, H., and Lazdunski, M., *Biochemistry*, **14**, 2081 (1975).

63. Witzemann, V., Muchmore, D., and Raftery, M. A., *Biochemistry*, **18**, 5511 (1979).

64. Hucho, F., *FEBS Lett.*, **103**, 27 (1979).

65. Nathanson, N. M., and Hall, Z. W., *J. Biol. Chem.*, **255**, 1698 (1980).

66. Raftery, M. A., Hunkapiller, M. W., Strader, C. D., and Hood, L. E., *Science*, **208**, 1454 (1980).

67. Atlas, D., and Levitzki, A., *Biochem. Biophys. Res. Commun.*, **69**, 397 (1976).

68. Atlas, D., Steer, M. L., and Levitzki, A., *Proc. Natl. Acad. Sci. USA*, **73**, 1921 (1976).

69. Atlas, D., *Methods Enzymol.*, **46**, 591 (1977).

70. Tolkovsky, A. M., and Levitzki, A., *Biochemistry*, **17**, 3795 (1978).

71. Ventner, J. C., *Mol. Pharmacol.*, **16**, 429 (1979).

72. Atlas, D., and Levitzki, A., *Nature*, **272**, 370 (1978).

73. Darfler, F. J., and Marinetti, G. V., *Biochem. Biophys. Res. Commun.*, **79**, 1 (1977).
74. Wrenn, S. M., and Homcy, C. J., *Proc. Natl. Acad. Sci. USA*, **77**, 4449 (1980).
75. Pitha, J., Zjawiony, J., Nasrun, N., Lefkowitz, R. J., and Caron, M. G., *Life Sci.*, **27**, 1791 (1980).
76. Caron, M. G., Shorr, R. G. L., Lefkowitz, R. J., Heald, S. L., Jeffs, P. W., Zjawiony, J., and Pitha, J., *Adv. Cyclic Nucleotide Res.*, **14**, 127 (1981).
77. Rashidbaidi, A., and Ruoho, A. E., *Proc. Natl. Acad. Sci. USA*, **78**, 1609 (1981).
78. Lavin, T. N., Heald, S. L., Jeffs, P. W., Shorr, R. G. L., Lefkowitz, R. J., and Caron, M. G., *J. Biol. Chem.*, **256**, 11944 (1981).
79. Shorr, R. G. L., Heald, S. J., Jeffs, P. W., Lavin, T. N., Strohsacker, M. W., Lefkowitz, R. J., and Caron, M. G., *Proc. Natl. Acad. Sci. USA*, **79**, 2778 (1982).
80. Lavin, T. N., Nambi, P., Heald, S. L., Jeffs, P. W., Lefkowitz, R. J., and Caron, M. G., *J. Biol. Chem.*, **257**, 12332 (1982).
81. Shorr, R. G. L., Strohsacher, M. W., Labin, T. N., Lefkowitz, R. J., and Caron, M. G., *J. Biol. Chem.*, **257**, 12341 (1982).
82. Stadel, J. M., Nambi, P., Lavin, T. N., Heald, S. L., Caron, M. G., and Lefkowitz, R. J., *J. Biol. Chem.*, **257**, 9242 (1982).
83. Levy, D., *Biochim. Biophys. Acta*, **322**, 329 (1973).
84. Jacobs, S., Hazum, E., Schechter, Y., and Cuatrecasas, P., *Proc. Natl. Acad. Sci. USA*, **76**, 4918 (1978).
85. Yip, C. C., Yeung, C. W. T., and Moule, M. L., *Biochemistry*, **19**, 70 (1980).
86. Yeung, C. W. T., Moule, M. L., and Yip, C. C., *Biochemistry*, **19**, 2196 (1980).
87. Thamm, P., Saunders, D., and Brandenburg, D., in D. Brandenburg and A. Wollmer, Eds., *Insulin: Chemistry, Structure and Function of Insulin and Related Hormones*, Walter de Gruyter, New York, 1980.
88. Wisher, M. H., Brown, M. D., Jones, R. H., Sonksen, P. H., Saunders, D. J., Thamm, P., and Brandenburg, D., *Biochem. Biophys. Res. Commun.*, **92**, 492 (1980).
89. Rees, A. R., and Whittle, M. R., in D. Brandenburg and A. Wollmer, Eds., *Insulin: Chemistry, Structure and Function of Insulin and Related Hormones*, Walter de Gruyter, New York, 1980.
90. Sahyoun, N., Hock, R. A., and Hollenberg, M. D., *Proc. Natl. Acad. Sci. USA*, **75**, 1675 (1978).
91. Massague, J., Pilch, P. F., and Czech, M. P., *J. Biol. Chem.*, **256**, 3181 (1981).
92. Massague, J., and Czech, M. P., *J. Biol. Chem.*, **257**, 6729 (1982).
93. Jacobs, S., Hazum, E., and Cuatrecasas, P., *J. Biol. Chem.*, **255**, 6937 (1980).
94. Yip, C. C., Moule, M. L., and Yeung, C. W. T., *Biochemistry*, **21**, 2940 (1982).
95. Fehlmann, M., Carpentier, J. L., LeCam, A., Thamm, P., Saunders, D., Brandenburg, D., Orci, L., and Freychet, P., *J. Cell Biol.*, **93**, 82 (1982).
96. Das, M., Miyakawa, T., Fox, C. F., Pruss, R. M., Aharonov, A., and Herschman, H. R., *Proc. Natl. Acad. Sci. USA*, **74**, 2790 (1977).
97. Das, M., and Fox., C. F., *Proc. Natl. Acad. Sci. USA*, **75**, 2644 (1978).
98. Hock, R. A., Nexo, E., and Hollenberg, M. D., *Nature*, **277**, 403 (1979).
99. Hock, R. A., Nexo, E., and Hollenberg, M. D., *J. Biol. Chem.*, **255**, 10737, (1980).
100. Baker, J. B., Simmer, R. L., Glenn, K. C., and Cunningham, D. D., *Nature*, **278**, 743 (1979).

101. Linsley, P. S., Blifeld, C., Wrann, M., and Fox, C. F., *Nature*, **278**, 745 (1979).
102. Wrann, M. M., and Fox, C. F., *J. Biol. Chem.*, **254**, 8083 (1979).
103. Comens, P. G., Simmer, R. L., and Baker, J. B., *J. Biol. Chem.*, **257**, 42 (1982).
104. Cohen, S., Carpenter, G., and King, L., Jr., *J. Biol. Chem.*, **255**, 4384 (1980).
105. Hunter, T., and Cooper, J. A., *Cell*, **24**, 741 (1981).
106. Ushiro, H., and Cohen, S., *J. Biol. Chem.*, **255**, 8363 (1980).
107. Gill, G. N., and Lazar, C. S., *Nature*, **293**, 305 (1981).
108. Buhrow, S. A., Cohen, S., and Staros, J. V., *J. Biol. Chem.*, **257**, 4019 (1982).
109. Carpenter, G., King, L., Jr., and Cohen, S., *J. Biol. Chem.*, **254**, 4884 (1979).
110. Bhaumick, B., Bala, R. M., and Hollenberg, M. D., *Proc. Natl. Acad. Sci. USA*, **78**, 4279 (1981).
111. Kasuga, M., Van Obberghen, E., Nissley, S. P., and Rechler, M. M., *J. Biol. Chem.*, **256**, 5305 (1981).
112. Oppenheimer, C. L., Pessin, J. E., Massague, J., Gitomer, W., and Czech, M. P., *J. Biol. Chem.*, **258**, 4824 (1983).
113. Ek, B., Westermark, B., Wateson, A., and Heldin, C. H., *Nature*, **295**, 419 (1982).
114. Nishimura, J., Huang, J. S., and Deuel, T. F., *Proc. Natl. Acad. Sci. USA*, **79**, 4303 (1982).
115. Todaro, G. J., DeLarco, J. E., Fryling, C., Johnson, P. A., and Sporn, M. B., *J. Supramol. Struct.*, **15**, 187 (1981).
116. DeLarco, J. E., and Todaro, G. J., *Proc. Natl. Acad. Sci. USA*, **75**, 4001 (1978).

8

THE GROWTH-PROMOTING
EFFECTS OF INSULIN

George L. King
C. Ronald Kahn

CONTENTS

Abbreviations

IGF	Insulinlike growth factor
MSA	Multiplication-stimulating activity
DAA	Desalanine-desasparagine
DOP	Desoctapeptide
PDGF	Platelet-derived growth factor
EGF	Epidermal growth factor
NSILA	Nonsuppressible insulinlike activity
AIB	α-Aminoisobutyric acid

1. INTRODUCTION

Insulin is a polypeptide hormone of 51 amino acids which has been shown to possess a variety of biological activities that are essential for the maintenance of life in higher animals (1–3). This myriad of biological actions described in the intact animal can be reproduced with isolated cell systems, indicating the direct involvement of insulin in initiating each of these effects (1–5). Although the spectrum of the actions of insulin is continuous, these activities are often arbitrarily separated into two categories: acute metabolic effects and chronic growth-promoting activities (Table I). The criteria for the separation of these biological effects are based largely on studies in isolated cell systems and include the concentration of insulin required to produce the effect and the length of time that is necessary before the initiation of biological effect is observed. In general, the metabolic effects of insulin, such as its ability to stimulate glucose transport, glycogen synthesis, and glucose oxidation, are observed at low insulin concentrations (0.1–1 nM) and the time of onset for these actions is very rapid, usually within minutes after exposure of cells to insulin (6–9). In contrast the growth-promoting effects of insulin, such as the stimulation of DNA synthesis and of cell proliferation, are usually observed at concentrations of 0.1–1 μM, and the incubation time required before the effect can be observed is usually measured in hours to days (1–10).

In the past, most of the research and reviews on the mechanism of insulin action have concentrated on the metabolic effects of insulin, and the growth-promoting effect of insulin has been treated primarily as a laboratory and pharmacological phenomenon. However, recent studies from our laboratory and others have begun to explore the growth-promoting action of insulin in detail using cells in tissue culture (6, 7, 10–17). These studies have revealed very interesting information which is increasing our understanding

Table 1. Partial List of the Actions of Insulin

METABOLIC	GROWTH-PROMOTING
Hexose transport and glycogen synthesis	RNA and DNA synthesis
Anti-lipolysis	Cellular proliferation
Amino acid transport	
Protein synthesis	

of how insulin influences the growth of cells. Inasmuch as this area has not been summarized in detail, the present review first surveys the early literature on the establishment of the growth effects of insulin. The main portion of this article is concerned with the recent progress made on the mechanisms of the growth-promoting actions of insulin using cells grown in culture. And finally, in the last part of the article, the data supporting a physiological role for the growth effects of insulin is discussed.

2. THE GROWTH-PROMOTING EFFECT OF INSULIN ON CELLS IN CULTURE

The growth-promoting effect of insulin on cells grown in tissue culture was first reported in 1924 by Gey and Thalhimer, who observed that insulin increased the growth of fibroblasts harvested from chick embryos (18). Subsequently, Latta and Bucholz (19) confirmed and extended this observation using fibroblasts from embryonic chick heart cultured with high concentrations of insulin (1 to 2 IU/ml, approximately 10^{-6}M). In 1940, Von Haam and Cappel, using fibroblasts derived from mouse embryonic heart showed the first dose response curve of insulin for the stimulation of cell growth (20). A clear effect of insulin was observed at 1 mIU/ml (1×10^{-8} M). This still must be regarded as a pharmacologic effect, inasmuch as plasma insulin concentrations are between 10 and 100 μIU/ml (1×10^{-9} M). Since that time, the requirement for pharmacological doses of insulin for demonstration of a growth effect has been confirmed repeatedly. A probable explanation for the gross disparity of the concentration requirement between the metabolic and the growth effects of insulin is presented later. Another interesting observation made by these investigators was that the addition of insulin to the mouse fibroblast caused "differentiation" of the cells in that they enlarge and incorporate fat granules after 10 days of exposure (20). This is one of the earliest findings of insulin as a maturation or differentiation factor and is supported by the recent work on the conversion of 3T3-L1 cells to adipocytelike cells (21, 22). These investigators also observed that the effect of insulin varied in different cell types and in different media. Thus insulin could stimulate DNA synthesis in human fibroblasts grown in minimal media, whereas no effect was seen if insulin was added to media fortified by embryonic extracts and 20% serum (20). However, in Hela cells, insulin did not have any effect on cell growth either alone or in medium containing 20% serum. These data are significant since they point out that the responsiveness of cells to growth effect of insulin varies greatly, and that transformed cells behave differently from nontransformed diploid cells in their responses to hormones and growth factors.

The inconsistent effect of insulin in stimulating DNA synthesis or cell replication was clarified by a series of subsequent studies by others (23–26) using both Hela cells and mouse L cells. These studies revealed that the addition of insulin, even at high concentration, would not result in a stimulation of DNA synthesis unless the cells had been incubated in either a serum-free medium or a medium containing low concentrations of serum. The serum-sparing nature of insulin was further put in perspective by studies of Temin (27) and Griffiths (28, 29), who showed that insulin alone (i.e., in serum-free media) has a rather weak growth-promoting effect when compared to serum. However, the addition of small amounts of serum will greatly enhance the effectiveness of insulin. This suggests that serum contains

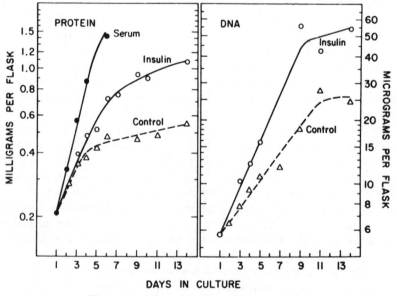

Figure 1.   Effect of insulin on DNA synthesis.

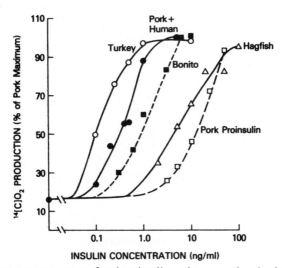

Figure 2. Dose-response curves of various insulin analogues on the stimulation of glucose oxidation in rat adipocytes.

other growth factors which are more potent than insulin and may enhance its action. In addition, Temin showed that some transformed cells will respond to insulin in serum-free media, whereas the same cells in a non-transformed state require some serum component in addition to insulin before significant cellular replication will occur (27). Thus the process of transformation appears to reduce the cellular requirement for growth factors, as well as the growth-promoting effect of insulin itself.

Since the early, classical studies of the growth-promoting effects of insulin, there have been a large number of publications which have centered on this topic showing that there are many types of cells in which insulin can either stimulate DNA synthesis or cellular replication. Because of its importance as a tool for the study of disease, one of the most extensively characterized cells has been the human fibroblast. Using these cells, Rechler et al. have shown that insulin can stimulate DNA synthesis, that is, [^{3}H]thymidine incorporation, (Fig. 1; 10). The characteristics of the insulin effect are similar to those seen in most other deploid cells. The effect of insulin is much weaker than that of serum, and the concentrations of insulin required (10^{-8} to 10^{-6} M) are high as compared to the concentrations required for metabolic effects (Figs. 2 and 3). In addition to the difference in the concentration required, the dose-response curves for the growth and for the metabolic effects also exhibit very different slopes. This is apparent in Figs. 2 and 3 in which we have shown the effect of insulin on glucose oxidation

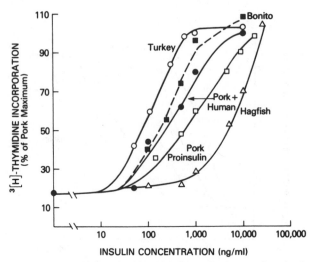

Figure 3.   Dose-response curves of various insulin analogues on the stimulation of DNA synthesis in human fibroblasts.

in adipocytes and its effect on thymidine incorporation into the DNA of human fibroblasts (7). Clearly 100 to 1000 times more hormone is required for the growth effect, and the shape of the dose-response curve for metabolic effects is rather sharp, whereas for the growth responses the dose-response curve is broad and extends over several logs of concentration. The time course for the onset of the insulin effect on DNA synthesis in the human fibroblast also demonstrates the characteristic 8–12-hour lag. (Fig. 4; 10). This delay of onset for the DNA synthesis appears to hold true for all cells and for other growth factors as well (30–32). Using autoradiographic techniques, the effect of insulin on DNA synthesis can be shown to be due to its ability to induce a higher percentage of cells to move into the S phase of the cell cycle (10).

Insulin alone does not produce a stimulation of DNA synthesis in all cell types. In some cells, such as mouse 3T3-L1 cells or mammary epithelial cells, insulin alone is unable to stimulate DNA synthesis (33). However, in this cell, when insulin is added along with other hormones such as dexamethasone, there is a synergistic effect on DNA synthesis or cell replication. In Cloudman S91 melanoma cells, insulin at low concentrations is a potent inhibitor of growth (34). The exact reason for these differences in insulin effect remains unknown.

Recently, in a few cell types, insulin has been shown to stimulate cellular growth at low concentrations (10^{-10} to 10^{-9} M) similar to those required for its metabolic effects. This has been observed in a rat hepatoma cell line

(35, 36), and in diploid pericytes isolated from bovine retinal capillaries (17). Thus the effect of insulin on cell growth in tissue culture depends upon the cell type. In general, very high concentrations of insulin are required but there are a few interesting exceptions.

The requirement for pharmacological concentrations of insulin for its growth effects has puzzled many investigators and, not surprisingly, many hypotheses have been offered to explain this observation. One possible reason is that significant amounts of insulin might be degraded over the 16 to 20 hours of preincubation required for the growth activity bioassays (37). The degradation could be due to the high cysteine content of the media which may disrupt the disulfide bonds in the insulin molecule, and/or degradative proteases present in the cultured cells which could modify the insulin structure and decrease its biological potency. However, assays of culture media from these experiments indicate that if the medium contains

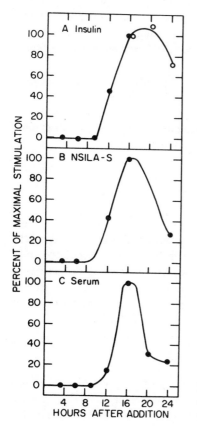

Figure 4. Time requirement for preincubation with insulin, NSILA (= IGF), and serum on the stimulation of DNA synthesis in human fibroblasts.

high concentrations of insulin (i.e., 10^{-8} M), incubation with human fibroblasts for 24 hours at 37°C does not produce more than 5% degradation of the insulin as measured by either radioimmunoassay or bioassay (7, 38).

Another plausible explanation for the need for pharmacological levels of insulin is that insulin itself is not the actual growth factor, but that a small contaminant of the insulin preparation is responsible. Inasmuch as very large amounts of insulin are used for these experiments (1 × 10^{-6} M), even an impurity of 0.1% would result in a concentration of 1 × 10^{-9} M, a concentration at which many other growth factors have been shown to be active in the stimulation of DNA synthesis (30–32). This seems unlikely for several reasons. Various studies have shown that all of the known impurities in insulin preparations, such proinsulin, glucagon, or C-peptide, have either no or very little effect on growth. Also, increasingly purified insulin preparations exhibit increasing potency for growth. Finally, the strongest evidence that has clearly established the growth-promoting effect of insulin itself has come from studies using insulin preparations that had been chemically synthesized directly from amino acids (16, 8). We and others showed that synthetic human insulin was equally potent with monocomponent insulin purified from the pancreas in both metabolic effects, assayed by the stimulation of glucose oxidation in rat adipocytes, and growth effects, indicated by its ability to stimulate thymidine incorporation into the DNA of human fibroblasts (Figs. 2 and 3). These data conclusively demonstrate that the insulin molecule itself can stimulate DNA synthesis, inasmuch as any contaminants occurring during the chemical synthesis cannot be the same as those in insulin purified from the pancreas.

3.   MECHANISM OF THE GROWTH-PROMOTING ACTION OF INSULIN

Although the exact mechanisms involved in insulin action remain unknown, certain aspects of the growth effect of insulin have been elucidated over the past several years. To understand these, however, it is necessary to introduce a family of related polypeptide hormones, the insulinlike growth factors (IGFs), inasmuch as the discussion of the growth effects of insulin cannot be fully grasped without a familiarity with the IGFs.

3.1.   Insulinlike Growth Factor (IGF)

The insulinlike growth factors are a family of polypeptide hormones which are defined by their ability to mimic the biological effects of insulin while at the same time being of sufficiently different structure that, for example, they are not recognized by specific anti-insulin antibodies (30, 39, 40). The IGFs were first described by Salmon and Daughaday in 1957 (41). Since then, through the careful work of many groups, the IGFs have been structurally characterized and their biological activities studied both *in vivo* and *in vitro* (30, 39, 40, 42).

Structurally, two IGFs have been defined, and these have been termed IGF-I and IGF-II. IGF-I and II are polypeptides of 70 and 67 amino acid residues, respectively, and are 62% identical in their primary amino acid sequence (43, 44). The structure of IGF-I is shown in Fig. 5. It is identical to insulin at 49% of the amino acid residues. Physiologically, the IGFs appear to be controlled more by the level of growth hormone than by the level of glucose. This finding, coupled with the results of animal infusion studies, suggests that IGFs are at least one of the mediators for the effect of growth hormone on bone growth. In plasma, the IGFs circulate bound to specific binding proteins (30, 39, 40, 42, 45).

Although structural data is not yet complete, the IGFs appear to be identical to two other classes of polypeptide hormones. The somatomedins, isolated from human or rodent plasma, have exactly the same spectrum of biological properties (30, 39, 40, 42), and recent data suggest that somatomedin C is immunologically indistinguishable from IGF-I. A similar group of growth factors have also been isolated from a cultured line of liver cells derived from the Buffalo rat which are capable of growing in serum-free media (46). These have been referred to as multiplication-stimulating activity (MSA; 11, 46, 4). One of the peptides of this group has been purified and

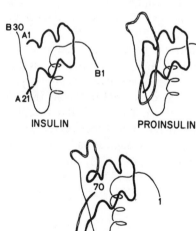

Figure 5. Postulated structures of insulin, proinsulin, and IGF-I.

sequenced, and differs from IGF-II by only five amino acids in the sequence (47).

In a series of classical and elegant studies, Froesch and his colleagues have shown that the IGFs are capable of simulating all of the biological activities of insulin on metabolism and growth in a variety of cells (30). However, the IGFs differ from insulin in the dose-response curves for various activities. Thus the IGFs stimulate DNA synthesis at the very low concentration of 1×10^{-9} M, whereas the concentrations required for metabolic responses are 400 to 1000-fold higher (6, 7, 30).

3.2.   Receptors for Insulin and the Insulinlike Growth Factors

Polypeptide hormones initiate their biological effects by binding to specific receptors on the cellular membrane (48, 49). Over the past 10 years, it has been possible to study this interaction directly using ^{125}I-labeled hormones and a variety of cell membrane preparations (48, 49). Insulin binds to its receptor with high affinity (K_D about 1×10^{-9} M or less). In addition, using various analogues of insulin, it was shown that the relative affinity of each of these analogues for binding to the receptor correlated very tightly with the potency of that analogue for stimulating the metabolic effects of insulin, such as glucose oxidation in fat cells (48–50).

In 1974, Megyesi et al., using [125I]insulin and an ^{125}I-labeled preparation of partially purified IGF showed that specific and different receptors existed on a variety of cells to which each hormone can bind with high affinity (Fig. 6; 51, 52). Not surprisingly, inasmuch as these peptides are similar in structure, insulin and the IGFs were also capable of binding to each others' receptors, although with a much lower affinity. These data have been confirmed and extended by others (11, 13, 30, 39, 46, 53). It is now clear that at least two types of IGF receptors can be distinguished based on their relative reactivity with IGF-I and IGF-II and their ability to interact with insulin (11, 13, 30, 39, 46, 53–55). The type I IGF receptor reacts preferentially with IGF-I (somatomedin C) as compared to IGF-II (MSA) and also reacts with insulin at high concentrations. The type II IGF receptor reacts preferentially with IGF-II as compared to IGF-I, and does not recognize insulin even at very high concentration. Some cells, such as cultured human lymphocytes, possess only IGF-I and insulin receptors (55), some, such as liver cells, possess only IGF-II and insulin receptors (52), and some cells, such as human fibroblasts, possess all three types: IGF-I, IGF-II, and insulin receptors (46).

Using affinity labeling techniques, Massague et al. (56), Kasuga et al. (57), and Hollenberg et al. (58) have begun to elucidate the structure of

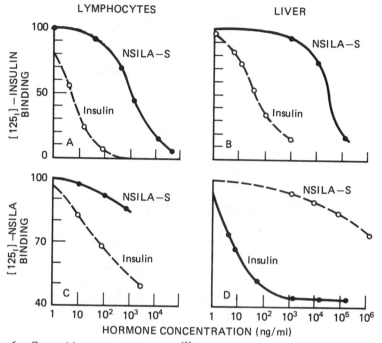

Figure 6. Competition curves (*top*) using [^{125}I]insulin, and (*bottom*) [^{125}]NSILA (IGFs) in lymphocytes and liver membranes.

these three different receptor types (Fig. 7). The insulin receptor is the best characterized and consists of two types of subunits linked by disulfide bonds. The α subunit has a molecular weight of about 135,000 and contains the insulin-binding site (59). The β subunit has a molecular weight of about 95,000 and appears to possess a tyrosine-specific protein kinase activity (60, 61). In the native receptor, these are linked by means of disulfide bridges to form what is thought to be a $\alpha_2-\alpha_2$ structure of molecular weight 350,000. This structure has been confirmed by gel electrophoresis of immunoprecipitates of the labeled receptor (62) and by purification (61). The IGF-I receptor appears to be very similar to the insulin receptor in structure, with a $M_r = 130,000$ binding subunit and an $M_r = 90,000$ β subunit (57). Gel electrophoresis under nonreducing conditions suggests that these are joined in the native receptor to form a complex of $M_r > 300,000$. Lectin chromatography also suggests that both the insulin and IGF-I receptor are glycoproteins and both possess similar lectin specificities. Despite their similar structure, the IGF-I and insulin receptors can be distinguished by

IGF RECEPTORS

TYPE I: NOT INHIBITED BY INSULIN

TYPE II : INHIBITED BY INSULIN

MODEL I

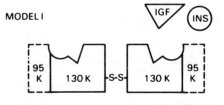

MODEL II

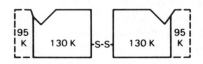

INSULIN RECEPTORS

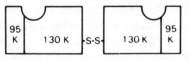

Figure 7. Schematic drawings of the postulated structures of the receptors for insulin, IGF-I, and IGF-II.

the relative abilities of insulin and IGFs to inhibit the binding of the labeled ligands (57). The IGF-II receptor, on the other hand, appears on nonreduced gel electrophoresis to be a single polypeptide of $M_r = 220,000$. Upon reduction, there is actually a slight increase in apparent molecular weight ($M_r = 260,000$), suggesting that there are intra-chain disulfide bonds (56, 57). Interestingly, when examined by the technique of radiation inactivation (63), this molecule appears to have a functional molecular weight of 110,000, very similar to that of the binding subunits of the insulin and IGF-I receptors.

3.3. Anti-Receptor Antibodies as Probes of Receptor Function

From the foregoing discussion, it is clear that insulin and the IGFs could produce their metabolic and growth effects through the insulin receptor or the IGF receptors or both. Therefore, another reagent is needed at the receptor level that will interact specifically with insulin or IGF receptors and will either mimic or block the effect of the hormones on metabolism or growth (Fig. 8). Such a specific reagent could be, for example, an antibody to one or the other type of receptors. In 1975, Flier et al. (64, 65) reported that the sera of some patients with a severe form of insulin resistance associated with Acanthosis nigricans contained autoantibodies to the insulin receptor. These autoantibodies are mostly of the IgG class and are capable of binding to the insulin receptor with a very high affinity (Fig. 9; 64, 67). In addition to being potent inhibitors of insulin binding to its receptors on all cell types,

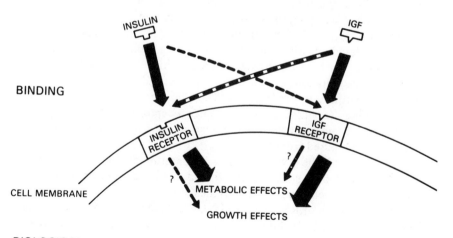

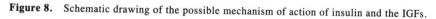

Figure 8. Schematic drawing of the possible mechanism of action of insulin and the IGFs.

THE ROLE OF VALENCE IN THE ACTION OF ANTIBODIES TO THE INSULIN RECEPTOR

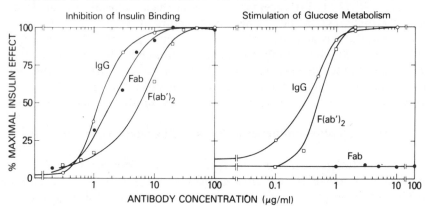

Figure 9.   Effect of anti-insulin receptor antibodies (IgG, $(F_{ab})_2$, and F_{ab}) on insulin binding (*left*) and metabolic effect (*right*).

these antibodies can immunoprecipitate the solubilized insulin receptor (62) and can also mimic the biological actions of insulin (Table 2; 64, 65). This biological activity requires bivalence. When the IgGs are treated with papain and cysteine, monovalent F_{ab} fragments are generated, which will still bind to the insulin receptors and inhibit insulin binding, but are incapable of stimulating biological effects (Fig. 9; 6, 66). Both the intact IgG and the monovalent F_{ab} fragment appear relatively specific for the insulin receptor (6, 13). Neither will inhibit MSA (IGF-II) binding except at very high concentration (Fig. 10). Not surprisingly, when the F_{ab} anti-receptor antibody is added to isolated rat adipocytes, insulin binding is inhibited and the dose-response curves for both insulin and MSA are shifted to the right (6). This suggests that the metabolic effects of both insulin and the IGFs are mediated through the insulin receptor (Fig. 11). Thus the autoantibody to the insulin receptor provides a specific probe for insulin receptor function with agonist activity when intact, and with antagonist activity when monovalent F_{ab} fragments are prepared from the IgG.

As already noted, the bivalent anti-receptor antibody mimics most of the biological effects of insulin. These include acute effects on membrane transport processes, changes in the activities of a variety of cellular enzymes, and even stimulation of RNA synthesis. On the other hand, in our studies, the anti-receptor antibody did not stimulate DNA synthesis in human fibroblasts in culture, suggesting that this effect was not mediated by means of the insulin receptor (6). Likewise, the addition of the monovalent F_{ab} fragments to human fibroblasts did not have any effect on the dose-response curves of either insulin or MSA (rat IGF-II) for stimulation of DNA synthesis, suggesting that the growth effects of insulin or of the IGFs are not mediated by the receptor for insulin (Fig. 12). These data support the hypothesis that the difference observed in the insulin requirement for metabolic effects and that for growth effects is likely due to the fact that these effects of insulin are mediated through different receptors. The metabolic effects are mediated through the insulin receptor whereas the growth effects are mediated through one of the growth factor receptors which binds insulin with low affinity (6).

Table 2.   Insulinlike Effects of Anti-Insulin Receptor Antibody

BIOLOGICAL EFFECTS	CELL TYPES STUDIED
Stimulation of Transport Processes	
2-Deoxyglucose	Adipocytes, 3T3-L1 cells, muscle, human fibroblasts
Amino acid (A1B)	Adipocytes
Stimulation of Enzymatic Processes	
Insulin receptor phosphorylation	3T3-L1 cells
Cytoplasmic protein phosphorylation	Adipocytes, 3T3-L1 cells
Glycogen synthase	Adipocytes, hepatocytes, muscle
Tyrosine aminotransferase	Hepatoma cells
Pyruvate dehydrogenase	Adipocytes
Acetyl CoA carboxylase	Adipocytes
Lipoprotein lipase	3T3-L1 cells
Stimulation of Glucose Metabolism	
Glucose incorporation into glycogen	Adipocytes, 3T3-L1 cells, muscle
Glucose incorporation into lipids	Adipocytes
Glucose oxidation to CO_2	Adipocytes
Stimulation of Macromolecular Synthesis	
Leucine incorporation into protein	Adipocytes, human fibroblasts
Uridine incorporation into RNA	Hepatoma cells
Thymidine incorporation into DNA	Hepatoma cells, melanoma cells, retinal pericytes
Miscellaneous Effects	
Inhibition of lipolysis	Adipocytes
Stimulation of glucosaminoglycan secretion	Chondrosarcoma cells

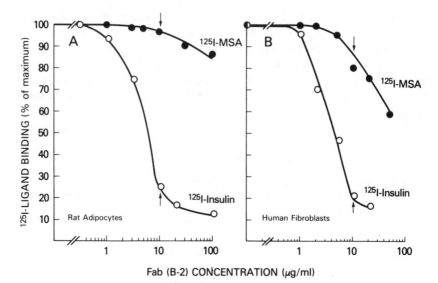

Figure 10.   Effect of F_{ab}, monovalent fragment of anti-insulin receptor antibody, on [^{125}I]MSA binding.

A few caveats and exceptions to the preceding concept deserve further comment. First, recent studies suggest that many anti-insulin receptor antibodies, including the antibodies used in the foregoing studies cross-react with IGF-I receptors, even though they are without effect on IGF-II receptors (Kasuga et al., personal communication). Thus the failure of the monovalent F_{ab} to block the growth effect of insulin and MSA in human fibroblasts

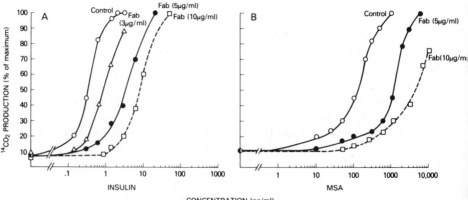

Figure 11.   Effect of F_{ab} on the dose-response curves for insulin (*left*) and MSA (*right*) on the stimulation of glucose oxidation in rat adipocytes.

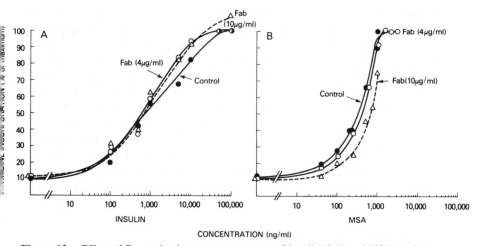

Figure 12.   Effect of F$_{ab}$ on the dose-response curves of insulin (*left*) and MSA (*right*) on DNA synthesis in human fibroblasts.

suggests that, in this cell, DNA synthesis requires neither the insulin nor the IGF-I receptors, or that very high concentrations of IgG are needed before growth effects can be observed.

Secondly, in some cells, insulin appears to initiate its growth effect by means of the insulin receptor. Recently, we have studied the pericyte isolated from bovine retinal capillaries. These cells are thought to provide structural

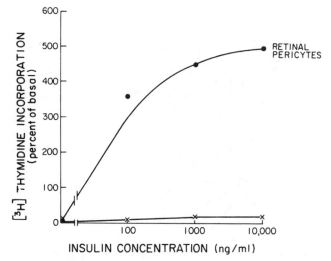

Figure 13.   Effect of insulin on DNA synthesis in bovine retinal pericytes of capillary.

support to the capillary endothelial cells, and loss of these cells is one of the earliest lesions present in diabetic retinopathy. Unlike most other non-transformed cells, the pericyte has the unique property of being able to respond to insulin at very low concentrations (1×10^{-9} M) for growth (Fig. 13). The dose-response curve, however, is still very broad extending from 10^{-9} to 10^{-7} M. Direct binding studies suggest that these cells have insulin receptors as well as receptors for both IGF-I and II. Interestingly, autoantibodies to the insulin receptor which previously have been shown to be unable to stimulate DNA synthesis in fibroblasts are capable of stimulating DNA synthesis in the pericyte, supporting the idea that in this cell the growth effects of insulin can be mediated through its own receptor. Koontz et al. have presented similar data for a cultured hepatoma cell line (35).

3.4.   Mapping the Bioactive Sites of Insulin

Although the insulin molecule is usually depicted as a simple linear two-chain structure, elegant studies by Hodgkin and co-workers (67), using x-ray crystallography, have revealed a more complex three-dimensional structure (Fig. 14). Using both naturally occurring and chemically derived analogues of insulin, Blundell et al. (9) have defined on this structure the specific regions of the insulin molecule which appear to be involved in binding to the insulin receptor and producing metabolic effects, the major areas of immunogenicity, and the areas involved in dimer formation. The insulin receptor binding site is a small portion of the molecule which includes

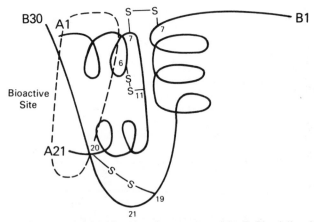

Figure 14.   Insulin structure with bioactive site as proposed by T. Blundell and G. Dodson (9).

the N and C-terminal portions of the A-chain (A1 and A21) and most of the C-terminal part of the B-chain (B22 and B34). These regions come together on one surface of the molecule in its three-dimensional structure (Fig. 14). This region accounts for the metabolic activity of the molecule, and thus the relative binding affinity of an insulin analogue for the insulin receptor is closely correlated with its biological potency in stimulating metabolic activities. Because our previously cited study had suggested that the growth effect of insulin may be mediated through another receptor, it was important to determine if the site responsible for the growth-promoting activity might be different from the metabolic activity site on the insulin molecule. To this end, we have analyzed over 20 different analogues of insulin and 3 different IGFs (Table 3) and compared their relative potency for metabolic and for growth-promoting effects (7).

An example of the dose-response curves for metabolic and growth activities are shown in Fig. 15. It is obvious that the relative potencies of these insulin analogues are different for these two different effects. For example, in the stimulation of glucose oxidation, the order of relative potency for these analogues was Turkey > Pork > Bonito > Proinsulin > DOP, whereas for stimulation of DNA synthesis the order was Turkey > Bonito > Pork > Proinsulin $\approx$ DOP. The maximal level of stimulation for each of these insulin analogues was the same, indicating that these insulins differ from each other only in terms of relative affinity for binding to their respective receptors.

The data from these studies (Table 3) revealed several interesting trends. First, there is a striking divergence between metabolic and growth effects of various insulins. With the exception of hagfish insulin, all insulins tested were more potent for growth than for metabolic activity. This was true for both naturally occurring and chemically synthesized analogues. The most extreme divergence occurs with the IGFs (IGF-I, IGF-II, and MSA; Fig. 16). All IGFs have less than 1% of the metabolic effects of pork insulin, but are four to eightfold more potent than pork insulin for growth effect. Another way of measuring the divergence between these two effects is to compare the ratios of growth to metabolic potencies of the insulin (Table 3, column B/A) using pork insulin as a standard. If the metabolic and growth effects of an insulin analogue are equally altered as compared to pork insulin, then the B/A ration would be 1. However, if the growth effect of an analogue is less affected by structural changes than its metabolic effect, the B/A ratio would be greater than 1. Note that this is particularly true for the IGFs, proinsulin, desalanine-desasparagine (DAA) insulin, and desoctapeptide (DOP) insulin.

The second interesting finding in this study is that the insulin from one family of mammals, namely, the hystricomorphs (guinea pig, porcupine,

Table 3. Comparison of Insulins and IGFs in Metabolic and Growth Assays

| | $(ED_{50}$ PORK/ED_{50} ANALOGUE) $\times$ 100 | | |
	STIMULATION OF GLUCOSE OXIDATION A	STIMULATION OF THYMIDINE INCORPORATION B	B/A
Pork (monocomponent)	100	100	1.0
Beef	100	98	1.0
Human (synthetic)	94	120	1.3
Mouse	82	130	1.6
Sheep	75	100	1.3
Horse	87	112	1.3
Proinsulin (pork)	2	51	26
Proinsulin (beef)	3	63	21
Turkey	240	350	1.5
Bonito (fish)	42	160	3.8
Hagfish	7	8	1.1
Guinea pig[a]	3	12	4
Porcupine[a]	3	110	37
Coypu[a]	1	190	190
Casiragua[a]	2	43	22
Desoctapeptide (DOP) insulin	0.4	30	75
Des-Ala des-Asp insulin	5	10	2
Des-Gly A1 des-Phe B1 insulin	0.8	14	18
Butoxycarbonyl A1 insulin	50	80	1.6
A1-B29 adipoyl insulin	6	98	16
Insulinlike growth factor I (IGF-I)	0.2	860	4300
Insulinlike growth factor II (IGF-II)	1.0	430	430
Multiplication-stimulating activity (MSA)	0.2	120	600

[a] ED_{50} values for the hystricomorphs were derived by taking the concentration of insulin needed to stimulate thymidine incorporation that corresponds to the half-maximum of pork insulin's dose-response curve.

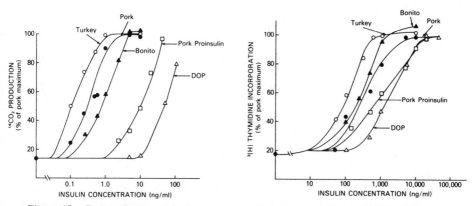

Figure 15.   Dose-response curves for various insulin analogues on the stimulation of glucose oxidation in rat adipocytes (*left*) and DNA synthesis in human fibroblasts (*right*).

coypu, and casiragua), are very different from all the other insulins or IGFs tested (Fig. 17). The hystricomorph insulins are relatively weak in terms of metabolic effect, usually less than 5% of the activity of pork insulin. However, dose-response curves for their growth-promoting response are very interesting in two ways. First, at low concentrations, the hystricomorph insulins have retained more growth-promoting activity than metabolic activity.

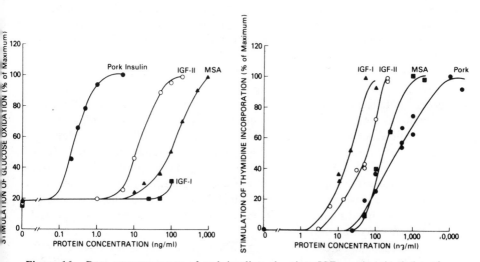

Figure 16.   Dose-response curves of pork insulin and various IGFs on the stimulation of glucose oxidation in rat adipocytes (*left*) and DNA synthesis in human fibroblasts (*right*).

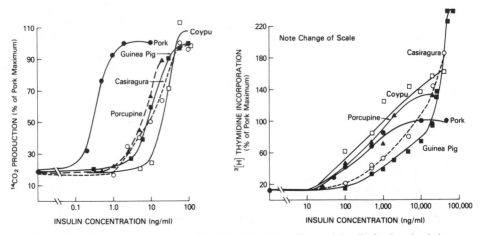

Figure 17. Dose-response curves of pork insulin and hystricomorph insulin for the stimulation of glucose oxidation in rat adipocytes (*left*) and DNA synthesis in human fibroblasts (*right*).

Secondly, however, at higher concentrations, these insulins actually stimulate DNA synthesis to a greater maximum than all the other insulins or IGFs.

From these studies, several conclusions can be drawn. First, the growth-promoting actions of insulin can tolerate a greater change in the structure than the metabolic effect. Second, there is nonparallel evolution between these two functions of insulin. Third, the insulins of the hystricomorphs are unique in their growth effects as compared to other insulins and IGFs. Fourth, the sites on the insulin molecule responsible for its metabolic and its growth effects are different, and thus the two activities behave differently in response to structural changes.

Inasmuch as the amino acid sequences for all the insulins and IGFs are known, it is possible to correlate these data with the bioactivity data in order to determine some features of the insulin molecule important for growth. In general, the sites for metabolic and growth-promoting effects on the insulin molecule are probably very close together or overlapping because all of the structural changes that decreased the metabolic effects of insulin also lessen its growth properties. Even changes outside the major area of bioactivity influenced both effects in parallel for some cases. For example, a substitution of the histidine residue at A8 (A chain, residue 8) as in turkey insulin enhanced the metabolic effect of insulin and increased its growth effect as well.

However, there are some striking differences between the two bioactivity sites. The B22–B30 region of insulin has been shown to be crucial for metabolic activity (9) inasmuch as in DOP insulin where it was removed, metabolic effects are reduced by 200-fold but growth effect was not greatly altered. Other areas on the insulin molecule which might be important for growth are those in which there are similarities between the IGFs and the insulin analogues with highest growth effects. These areas are B10 residues (asparagine, glutamine, and glutamic acid in IGFs and hystricomorphs; histidine in other insulins), B13 (aspartic acid in IGF and hystricomorphs, glutamic acid in others), B25 (tyrosine in coypu insulin, casiragua insulin, and IGFs, phenylalanine in others), and A4 (aspartic acid in hystricomorph insulin, glutamic acid in others).

Another area in which the IGFs and hystricomorph insulins differed from other insulins is the region of B20-21 (aspartate in hystricomorph insulins and IGF, glutamate in other insulins).

3.5. Bioactivity of Insulin-IGF Hybrid Molecules

In an effort to define better the structural features important for the growth-promoting effect of insulin, we have studied a molecular hybrid molecule which contains part of the IGF molecule linked to an insulin backbone. The IGFs are single chain polypeptide hormones which may be divided into four regions, termed A, B, C, and D (Fig. 18). Regions A and B correspond to the A and B chains of insulin and are 50% homologous in amino acid sequence. The C region corresponds to the C peptide of proinsulin. In

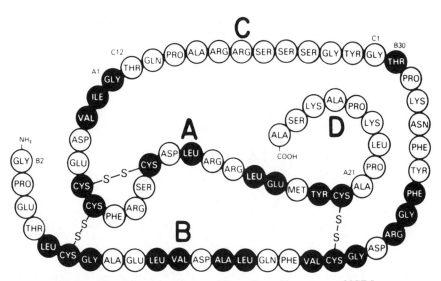

Figure 18. Schematic drawing of the amino acid sequence of IGF-I.

contrast to the proinsulin C peptide, however, the C region is shorter (8 versus 33 amino acids) and does not contain basic amino acids. The D region consists of eight and five amino acids, respectively, in IGF-I and IGF-II and are unique to the IGFs (43, 44). The D region is located at the carboxy terminal of the A chain and in the three-dimensional structure is presumed to be in close proximity to the B21–B22 region.

We have chemically synthesized an insulin-IGF-I hybrid molecule by fusing the octapeptide sequence of the IGF-I D region to the carboxy terminal of the A chain of a human insulin molecule (15). The resultant hybrid molecule is a human insulin with the IGF-I D region connected to the A21. This insulin-IGF-I hybrid has only 28% and 20% of the potency of pork insulin in insulin receptor assay and metabolic effects, respectively. Likewise, in radioimmunoassay with guinea pig anti-pork insulin antibodies, the hybrid had only 11% the potency of pork insulin. By contrast, in a growth-promoting assay measuring [³H]thymidine incorporation into the DNA of human fibroblasts, the insulin-IGF-hybrid was actually more potent than pork insulin by two to fivefold. These data suggest that the D region octapeptide is important for the IGFs in two ways. First, blocking the A21 residue of insulin lowers its metabolic activity. Second, the extension also increases growth-promoting activity. Because the D region of IGF-I and IGF-II have little similarity, this may also play a role in determining their relative affinity for the IGF-I and IGF-II receptors.

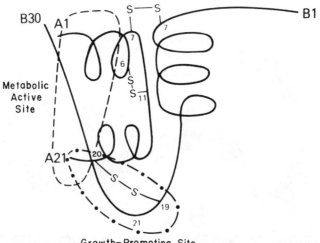

Figure 19.   Schematic drawing of the three-dimensional structure of insulin with postulated metabolic and growth-promoting sites.

From the studies of the various analogues of insulin and the IGFs and this insulin-IGF-I hybrid, we can begin to speculate as to the location of the growth-promoting site on the insulin molecule. We believe the site is probably a region centered around the B20–B22 area of the molecule. In this region, the D peptide as well as primary C peptide amino acid differences are maximally concentrated. Both the D peptide and C peptide also block regions of the insulin molecule important for its metabolic activity. This region is schematically illustrated in Fig. 19.

3.6. A Relationship between Hystricomorph Insulin and Platelet-Derived Growth Factor

From the study of insulin analogues, it became apparent that the hystricomorph insulins differed from other insulins and IGFs in their effect on DNA synthesis in human fibroblasts. As noted previously, the hystricomorph insulins were able to stimulate DNA synthesis in human fibroblasts to a greater maximum than other insulins and IGFs (Fig. 17; 7, 16). In fact, at a concentration of 50 μg/ml, guinea pig insulin was able to stimulate DNA synthesis two to threefold more than was pork insulin. These data were confirmed using autoradiography as a measure of the effect of the hormones in increasing the number of cells which incorporate [^{3}H]thymidine into nuclear DNA as the cells progress into the S phase of the cell cycle (Fig. 20). Again, guinea pig insulin alone is more potent than pork insulin or the IGFs. Further, the maximal effect reached by the addition of pork insulin and IGFs is no different than the effect of a maximal concentration of each of these growth peptides alone. Interestingly, when guinea pig and pork insulins are incubated together with the fibroblasts, an additive effect was observed. Similar increases in DNA synthesis were observed when guinea pig insulin and MSA are added together. Inasmuch as the guinea pig insulin effect is additive with other insulins and IGFs, the effects of these peptides are probably mediated through different mechanisms. These observations lead us to explore the growth-promoting actions of hystricomorph insulins further, and to compare them to those of other growth factors (7, 16).

When pork insulin or MSA are added to fibroblasts in the presence of 5% platelet-poor plasma, no synergistic effects are observed. This result is similar to those of previous studies of the insulinlike growth factors and indicates that their action is independent from that of other plasma components on stimulation of DNA synthesis. When guinea pig insulin is added to platelet-poor plasma, a large synergistic effect is seen. This effect of plasma in enhancing the action of guinea pig insulin is very similar to the effect of plasma on a growth factor of different origin, namely, platelet-derived growth factor (PDGF; 7, 16, 31).

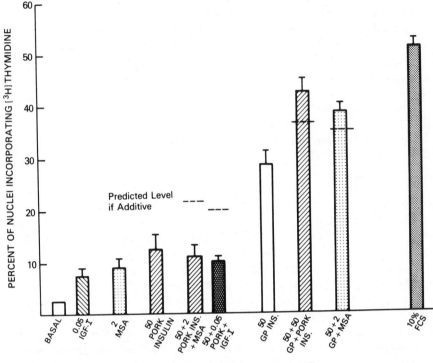

Figure 20. Effect of various insulins and IGFs on the stimulation of human fibroblasts from G_0 to S phase of the cell cycle.

If the growth effects of guinea pig insulin are mediated through a different mechanism than that of the IGFs and other insulins, it seems likely that it is binding to a different receptor on the surface of the cell. In recent studies, we have looked for and found such a specific guinea pig insulin receptor on human fibroblasts (Fig. 21). Incubating [^{125}I]guinea pig insulin with 10^6 human fibroblasts leads to the binding of 3% of the tracer. This binding is inhibited by unlabeled guinea pig insulin and 50% displacement occurs at a concentration of 0.8 μg/ml (140 nM). Casiragua insulin, another hystricomorph insulin, was two to threefold more potent than guinea pig insulin in inhibiting the binding of labeled guinea pig insulin, whereas pork insulin and MSA (rat IGF-II) did not show any competition, even at very high concentration.

Inasmuch as the binding studies suggested that the receptor under study has high specificity, but low affinity for guinea pig insulin, it seemed likely that the receptor involved could be a receptor for another growth factor. A variety of known growth factors was tested and only PDGF was found to bind to this receptor. Four preparations of PDGF that varied in purity and potency for stimulation of growth competed with guinea pig insulin in concordance with their biological effect (Fig. 22). PDGF was able to displace 50% of the [^{125}I]guinea pig insulin at 8 ng/ml, indicating that PDGF is binding to this receptor with high affinity. Likewise, serum competed for guinea pig insulin binding in concentrations similar to those which produce growth effects, whereas platelet-poor plasma was very weak in this regard.

These data suggest that the unusual growth effects of hystricomorph insulins are due to their ability to bind to the PDGF receptor. Although PDGF is known to alter the binding of other growth factors to their receptors by noncompetitive mechanisms (60–70), PDGF was able to compete for guinea pig insulin binding even at 4°C, suggesting that PDGF and guinea pig are interacting at the receptor level in a process which does not require metabolic activity of the cell. The exact mechanism by which polypeptides of 32,000 and 6,000 molecular weights could share a receptor is unknown (71–74). However, it is possible that when the three-dimensional structure of PDGF is known, some homology between these two polypeptides will be found. Certainly, the bioactivity data suggest a common evolutionary source for the hystricomorph insulins and PDGF.

3.7. Interaction between IGF and Insulin Receptors

In addition to stimulating DNA synthesis in cells through the IGF receptors, insulin is also capable of influencing the binding of the IGFs to their receptors.

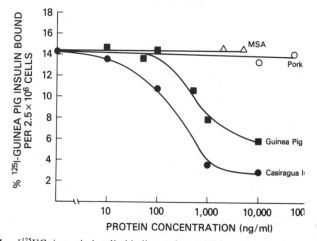

Figure 21.   [^{125}I]Guinea pig insulin binding and competition curves on human fibroblasts.

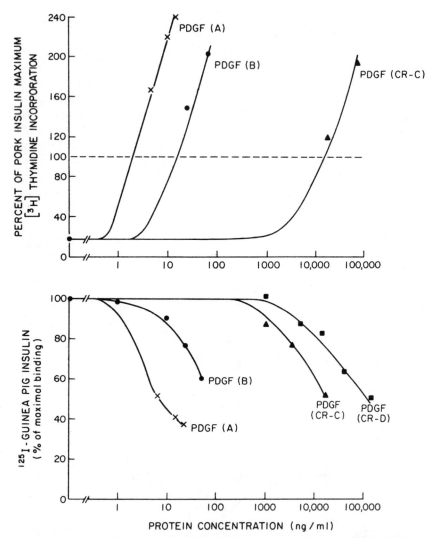

Figure 22. Comparison growth-promoting effect of various preparations of PDGF (*top*) with their potency for competing with [^{125}]guinea pig insulin for binding to human fibroblasts (*bottom*).

This was first observed in studies using rat adipocytes (14, 75, 76). In these cells, competition experiments revealed that insulin did not inhibit the binding of [^{125}I]IGF-I, [^{125}I]IGF-II, or [^{125}I]MSA to their receptors, but actually produced a modest increase in tracer binding (14, 75, 76). This insulin effect occurs at physiologic concentrations, that is, between 10^{-10} and 10^{-9} M (Fig. 23). Competition curves and Scatchard analysis of the binding data indicate that the effect of insulin is to increase the affinity of the insulinlike growth factors for their receptors. No change in receptor number can be detected. Kinetic experiments using various concentrations of labeled MSA (IGF-II) suggest that the affinity increase is due to a decrease in dissociation rate. Although the exact mechanism of this effect is unknown, some metabolic events appear to be involved inasmuch as the effect is not observed in broken cell preparations.

The effect of insulin occurs at low hormone concentrations and this suggests that this effect of insulin is mediated through the insulin receptor. This observation is supported by studies using insulin analogues and specific antibodies to the insulin receptor. Proinsulin, which is only 5% as potent as pork insulin in binding to the insulin receptor and in metabolic effects,

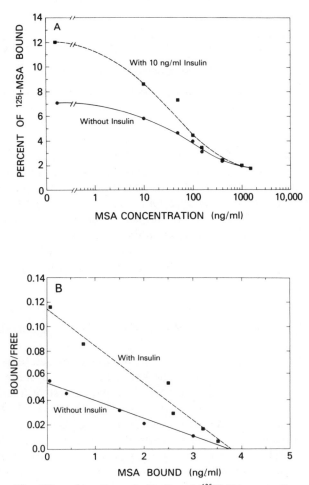

Figure 23.   Effect of insulin on the binding of $[^{125}I]MSA$ to rat adipocytes.

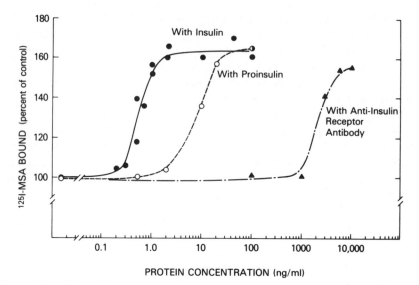

Figure 24.   Effect of insulin, proinsulin, and anti-insulin receptor antibody on [^{125}I]MSA binding to rat adipocytes.

can also increase [^{125}I]MSA binding to adipocytes, but at concentrations 20-fold higher than those required for pork insulin. Autoantibodies to the insulin receptor which can bind only to insulin receptors and mimic the metabolic effect of insulin can also mimic this insulin effect (Fig. 24). In addition, the monovalent F_{ab} fragment made from the anti-insulin receptor antibody that acts as a competitive inhibitor of insulin action also inhibits the effect of insulin in increasing MSA binding. These studies strongly suggest that insulin is increasing MSA binding by acting through the insulin receptor (14).

4.   POST-RECEPTOR STEPS OF THE GROWTH EFFECT OF INSULIN

The various steps which occur after the binding of insulin to its receptor or to the IGF receptor and before the beginning of the S phase of a cell cycle are not yet understood. The only clear and consistent finding in the action of insulin and most growth factors is a delay of 12–18 hours between the addition of hormone and the finding of increased DNA synthesis (10). Further, insulin must be present for most of the time if a maximal effect is to be observed. This suggests an ongoing signal event, rather than a "triggering event" upon initial hormone binding. Several recent observations must be also be considered when discussing the growth-promoting actions of insulin.

4.1. Hormone Internalization

Recent studies on the fate of hormones and growth factors have revealed that most polypeptide hormones, including growth hormone (77), epidermal growth factor (EGF) (78), and insulin (79) will initiate the aggregation of hormone–receptor complexes and are internalized by specific receptor-mediated endocytosis after binding to a specific receptor (77–80). This process is schematically illustrated in Fig. 25. The process of internalization is rapid and can take place in a few minutes at 37°C (77–81). Once inside the cells, the hormone–receptor complexes fuse with lysosomelike structures and are either degraded or recycled (77–81). However, some authors have postulated that this involved process is linked to the chronic or growth effects of insulin (80).

In our opinion, several lines of reasoning seem to be against this hypothesis. First, the time of onset of the growth effect of insulin is not consistent with this picture. As noted previously this effect of insulin requires the continued

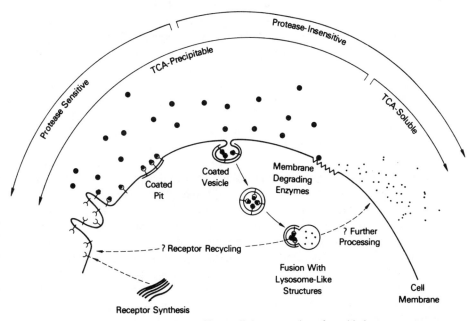

Figure 25. Postulated mechanisms of intracellular processing of peptide hormone–receptor complex.

presence of the hormone for at least 6 hours (10). The process of internalization, on the other hand, can occur over several minutes and is largely complete by 1 hour (77–81). Second, Carpentier et al. have shown that the anti-insulin receptor antibodies and their monovalent F_{ab} fragments are also internalized by this receptor-mediated mechanism and are processed in a manner very similar to that of insulin itself (82). However, neither the bivalent IgG anti-insulin receptor antibody nor its monovalent F_{ab} fragments can mimic the growth-promoting effects of insulin in most cells (6, 7). Lastly, in an experiment in collaboration with Dr. Hayden Coon (National Institutes of Health), porcine insulin or diluent was microinjected directly into the perinuclear area of 400–500 human fibroblasts in monolayer culture. The amount of insulin injected into the cell was equal to the amount internalized when the cells are exposed to 10^{-6} M insulin, that is, the concentration at which insulin can produce a maximal effect on the stimulation of DNA synthesis in human fibroblasts. After the cells were microinjected with insulin or diluent, they were incubated for 24 hours in a medium supplemented with [^{3}H]thymidine. The culture dishes were then covered with emulsion and developed several days later. The number of cells that incorporated [^{3}H]thymidine is an indication of how many have moved from the G_0 phase into the S phase. No difference in the percent of cells in S phase was observed between cells injected with insulin or with diluent. In addition, no significant difference in cell viability in injected and noninjected cells was found. Although these studies provide only negative data, they suggest that the internalization of insulin is not a major factor in the production of its growth effect.

4.2.   Receptor Phosphorylation

Over the past few years, a possible clue to the mechanisms of action of insulin (85), EGF (83), and PDGF has been uncovered (86, 87). This is that each of these receptors possesses a protein kinase activity and undergoes autophosphorylation upon ligand binding. Insulin receptor phosphorylation has been demonstrated in both intact and broken cell systems (85, 88).

In the experiments with intact cells, the ATP pool is first labeled by preincubation of cells with [^{32}P]orthophosphate for 2 hours. Insulin receptor can then be isolated before or after insulin treatment using lectin chromatography and immunoprecipitation, and the receptor subunits identified by sodium dodecyl sulfate polyacrylamide gel electrophoresis (85, 89). Using this technique, Kasuga et al. (85, 89) observed that the subunits of the insulin receptor appeared to undergo posttranslational covalent modification by phosphorylation. Evidence that this was indeed the subunit of the insulin receptor included the findings that: (1) its migration in gel electrophoresis under reducing conditions was identical to that of the β subunit of the receptor; (2) on nonreducing gels, the radioactivity was associated with proteins of $M_r = 350,000$ and $520,000$; (3) the protein was precipitated by four different sera containing antibodies to the insulin receptor; (4) insulin stimulated the phosphorylation three to fivefold. Phosphoamino acid analysis in the basal state revealed predominately phosphoserine and a small amount of phosphothreonine (89). After insulin stimulation, there was an increase in the level of phosphoserine and appearance of phosphotyrosine (89).

The tyrosine phosphorylation of the insulin receptor appears to be catalyzed by a protein kinase activity present in the receptor itself (90, 91). This autophosphorylation can be observed *in vitro* when [γ-^{32}P] ATP and insulin are incubated with solubilized crude receptor preparations from hepatoma cells (85, 89), cultured lymphocytes (85), 3T3-L1 cells (61), freshly isolated hepatocytes (92) or adipocytes (93), or with normal rat liver membranes (94), as well as with partially purified and highly purified preparations of insulin receptors from human placenta (90, 61). This phosphorylation reaction is sensitive to insulin added *in vitro*, and shows a 3 to 10-fold increase in the amount of ^{32}P incorporated into the receptor. In all cases, the phosphorylation occurs exclusively on the tyrosine residues and predominately on the β subunit of the receptor. This reaction is quite rapid, reaching a maximum within a few minutes in the presence of insulin. [γ-^{32}P]ATP, but not [γ-^{32}P]GTP, will act as a phosphate donor for the reaction, and Mn^{2+} is required as a co-factor (89, 94).

Evidence that the receptor itself is the tyrosine kinase involved in the phosphorylation is threefold. First, receptor kinase activity and binding activity co-purify and both are retained in a preparation of receptor purified to near homogeneity (61, 90, 91). Second, if the partially purified receptor is immunoprecipitated using the anti-receptor antibody, the kinase activity is in the immunoprecipitate rather than in the supernatant (Kasuga, personal communication). Finally, Roth and Cassell have recently succeeded in labeling the β subunit of the receptor with a photo-affinity analogue of ATP, further confirming the kinase nature of the 95,000 M_r subunit (91).

Although receptor phosphorylation has been recognized for only a relatively short period of time, at least seven different receptor proteins have been shown to undergo this type of covalent modification. The most interesting of the receptor-mediated phosphorylations are those which occur at tyrosine residues and are stimulated upon ligand binding. Such reactions have been observed to occur for the receptors for EGF (83), a protein presumed to be the receptor for PDGF (86, 87), and the insulin receptor (89, 90). In contrast to the insulin receptor-kinase, the EGF receptor-kinase is a single peptide chain of $M_r = 160,000$ which possesses both the hormone-binding site and the kinase-active site (83). The gene products of several avian and mammalian

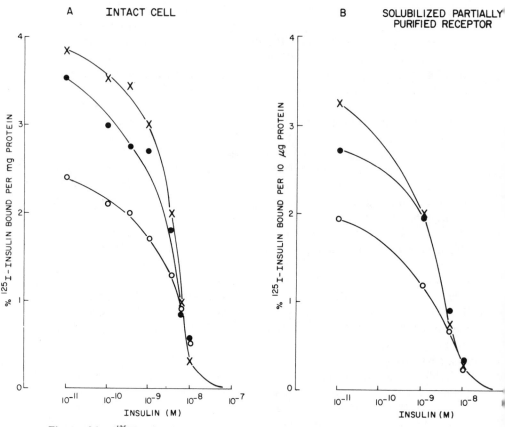

Figure 26. [^{125}I]Insulin binding to Cloudman S91 melanoma cells (O——O) (III), (X——X) (46), and (●——●) (IA).

retroviruses have also been shown to be associated with tyrosine protein kinase activity. In an effort to determine the functional significance of receptor phosphorylation action of insulin, Haring et al. have performed studies of insulin binding and receptor phosphorylation in cell lines on which the action of insulin has been altered by mutagenesis (84). The lines studied are the Cloudman S91 melanoma and two of its variants initially isolated by John Pawelek et al. (95). Inasmuch as insulin inhibits cell replication in the wild type Cloudman melanoma (1A), it has been possible to select two types of variants with respect to insulin response by treatment of the cells with a mutagen (EMS) and culture in medium containing insulin. One type is a variant in which insulin stimulates growth (type 46) and the other variant (type III) is termed insulin-resistant, inasmuch as insulin neither stimulates nor inhibits growth (95).

[^{125}I]Insulin binding is similar for the wild type (1A) and the insulin-stimulated variant (46). The insulin-resistant variant (III), on the other hand, exhibits approximately a 30% decrease in insulin binding. This is due to a decrease in receptor affinity with no change in receptor concentration (Fig. 26; 84).

Insulin stimulates phosphorylation of the 95,000 M_r subunit of its receptor in all three cell types with similar kinetics. The amount of ^{32}P incorporated into the 95,000 Mr band of the insulin-resistant cell line (III), however, is approximately 50% of the amount present in the receptors of the two other cell lines (Fig. 27). The difference in the (III) line was reflected throughout the entire dose-response curve and throughout the entire time course of phosphorylation (84).

These data suggest that the insulin-resistant melanoma (III) possesses a defect in the insulin receptor which alters both its binding and autophosphorylation properties and also the effect of insulin on growth. This suggests a possible role of receptor autophosphorylation in both the binding and signaling function of the insulin receptor.

4.3. Relationship between the Early Effects and the Growth Effects of Insulin

Although stimulation of DNA synthesis and cellular replication by serum or insulin usually requires 8 to 12 hours for onset, many studies have reported

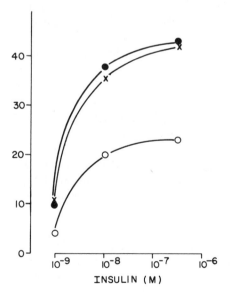

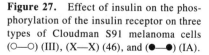

Figure 27. Effect of insulin on the phosphorylation of the insulin receptor on three types of Cloudman S91 melanoma cells (O—O) (III), (X—X) (46), and (●—●) (IA).

that within minutes after the addition of these growth factors to quiescent cells, a variety of activities can be observed. These include an increased uptake of hexose (97), uridine (98), Mg^{2+} (99), Ca^{2+} (100), K^+ (101), $^{86}Rb^+$ (101), Na^+ (Li^+) (102), and amino acids (103). Similarly, protein synthesis is also stimulated before cellular replication can occur (104). Studies by many authors have shown that these early biological effects of growth factors and sera appear to be very important for the ultimate stimulation of DNA synthesis and cellular replication. However, it is also clear that the stimulation of these cellular activities does not automatically start a chain of events that necessarily leads to DNA synthesis and cellular growth. In fact, the effect of insulin on the metabolism and growth of cells provides excellent support for the conclusion that these early events are not the key steps in signalling cells onto an irreversible path of replication.

Insulin is similar to other growth factors with respect to these biological effects in cultured cells (1–5). At concentrations less than 10^{-9} M, a concentration at which insulin binds only to its own receptor on the cells, insulin has been shown to be able to stimulate glucose transport in many types of cells including adipocytes, muscle cells, and fibroblasts (1–5). In isolated hepatocytes and other cells, insulin also increases Na^+ influx by stimulating (Na^+-K^+)-ATPase (105). This effect of insulin is rapid and reaches a maximum at concentrations less than 5 nM. Fehlmann and Freychet found a close concordance between this biological effect of insulin and the occupancy of insulin receptors. Inasmuch as an increase in Na^+ influx appears to be important in the initiation of cellular proliferation in many types of cells such as rat hepatocytes and cultured mouse fibroblasts, this effect of insulin has been suggested to be a crucial early step in the action of insulin on growth (105).

However, the exact relationship between the effect of insulin on intracellular levels of Na^+ and K^+ and its other biological actions is unknown. Some studies have reported that the inhibition of (Na^+-K^+)-ATPase will result in an inhibition of hexose transport, suggesting that the effect of insulin on Na^+ and K^+ levels is related to its metabolic activity (2, 106). Arguments have also been made for a role for ion flux in the effect of insulin on uridine uptake and phosphorylation, amino acid transport, protein synthesis, and RNA synthesis. On the other hand, Fehlmann and Freychet have shown that the inhibition of (Na^+-K^+)-ATPase by insulin does not inhibit the effect of insulin on aminoisobutyric acid (AIB) transport in hepatocytes (105).

The association between these early biological effects and the stimulation of cell growth remains unclear for several reasons. In most cells, including fibroblasts, muscle cells, chondrosarcoma cells, and hepatocytes, insulin can stimulate both fast metabolic events, such as Na^+ influx, and chronic growth effects, such as DNA synthesis. However, unlike other growth factors, two distinct ranges of insulin concentrations are required, as discussed previously. We have also provided some evidence that the growth effects and the metabolic events are mediated through different receptors (6). Therefore, the observations made on the earlier effect of insulin with only low concentrations of the hormone may only be relevant to its metabolic effects. This hypothesis would explain the findings that insulin can stimulate many of these rapid events at low concentration, yet it cannot stimulate DNA synthesis in most cell types except at high concentration. This postulation does not rule out the possibility that early effects of insulin on Na^+ influx may play a crucial role leading to cellular replication, because it is possible that insulin could stimulate Na^+ influx and initiate its growth effects by binding at low affinity to a receptor of an insulinlike growth factor. Obviously, further data in regard to the role of Na^+ influx on cellular proliferation are needed.

5. GROWTH EFFECTS OF INSULIN *IN VIVO*

All of the data presented thus far deal with the growth-promoting effects of insulin in tissue culture. Evidence for the growth-promoting effects of insulin *in vivo* is primarily surmised from studies of various diseases which are associated with hyperinsulinemia. The best-known example of a possible growth effect of insulin *in vivo* is the finding of macrosomia and organomegaly in infants of poorly controlled diabetic mothers (107), and infants suffering from the Beckwith–Wiedeman syndrome, β-cell hyperplasia, and nesideoblastosis (108). The associated finding of hyperinsulinemia in each of these has been postulated to be responsible for the macrosomia and organomegaly. From pathological studies, the effect of insulin on somatic growth appears to start after the twenty-ninth to thirtieth week of gestation. Fetuses with pancreatic agenesis have both weight and length within the normal range up to that time of pregnancy whereas, after that time, they gradually diverge from curves of normal embryonic development (108). The mechanism by which insulin acts on growth in the third trimester in not clear.

Pedersen formulated the "hyperglycemia–hyperinsulinemia" hypothesis in 1954 to explain the macrosomia of offspring from diabetic mothers (107). With some modifications, this hypothesis still appears to be a plausible explanation. This hypothesis states that hyperglycemia in the diabetic mother leads to fetal hyperglycemia because glucose, unlike insulin, will cross the placental membrane. The fetal hyperglycemia stimulates the hypertrophy of fetal islets, resulting in hyperinsulinemia. Originally, it was thought that the hyperinsulinemia would stimulate an increase in the uptake and utilization of glucose and amino acids which would ultimately enhance fetal growth (107). However, recent evidence suggests that insulin may be able to stimulate growth directly by increasing DNA synthesis and cellular proliferation (109).

Animal models of diabetes, including the rhesus monkey treated with streptozotocin, also exhibit macrosomia and selective organomegaly similar to human infants (109). Using this model, Susa et al. asked whether the macrosomia was due to the availability of excessive substrates or to a direct effect of insulin on growth (109). To study this question, mini-pumps were implanted into pregnant rhesus monkeys; these mini-pumps infused insulin into the fetus and thus produced a hyperinsulinemic but euglycemic state. The insulin-treated fetuses had a 34% increase in body weight, and enlargement of the liver, placenta, heart, and spleen was observed (109). Analysis of the liver indicated that its enlargement was due primarily to hyperplasia and not hypertrophy of cells, although liver glycogen content was mildly elevated (109). These findings closely resemble what is found in the offspring of diabetic mothers. From these data, the authors concluded that insulin can induce cellular growth directly *in vivo* and is responsible for the findings of macrosomia and organomegaly in diabetes (109). However, these pathological findings can still be due to a relative increase in the utilization of substrate that is facilitated by insulin rather than a direct effect on growth inasmuch as these studies only measured glucose levels and not its turnover rate.

The finding of hepatomegaly in the offspring of diabetic mothers has led to the postulate that insulin is an important growth factor *in vivo* for the liver. In primary cultures of hepatocytes and in hepatoma cell lines, insulin has been shown to be able to stimulate DNA synthesis and cellular proliferation at both pharmacological and physiological ranges (109). Several authors have tested the growth effect of insulin *in vivo* by measuring its ability to stimulate DNA synthesis and to increase regeneration of the liver after hepatectomy in dogs (111, 112). Starzle et al. showed that high levels of insulin help to perserve hepatic ultrastructure and cellular proliferation when pancreatic blood flow has been directed from the liver (112). Other studies have suggested that a combination of glucagon and insulin is required (111). Nevertheless, together, these studies support strongly the notion that insulin has an important role in the maintenance of hepatic integrity and regeneration after injury.

Another potent role for the growth effects of insulin *in vivo* which has been suggested to be pathophysiologically important is in the proliferation of aortic smooth muscle cells observed in atherosclerosis. Stout has postulated that the slightly elevated insulin levels observed in the treatment of diabetes or naturally occurring in Type I and II diabetics might be responsible for the accelerated rate of atherosclerosis observed in this disease (113). Considering other recent data on the effects of insulin on endothelial cells and pericytes (17), it is quite likely that insulin plays a role in vascular maintenance in a variety of ways. Even the islet itself may require insulin for growth (114). Transplanted pancreatic cells exhibit improved survival with insulin treatment and control of glucose (114). Whether this is due to the metabolic or the growth effect of insulin is not clear.

In summary, the growth effect of insulin *in vivo* is probably important physiologically both during fetal and the normal development. As shown in tissue culture, insulin *in vivo* can affect growth by providing substrates, stimulating growth itself, and influencing the levels of somatomedins or other growth factors.

6. SUMMARY

From this brief review, it is clear that although much has been learned about the growth-promoting actions of insulin, more remains to be studied. The growth effects of insulin, like those of other growth factors, have been studied mainly in tissue culture. In this setting, insulin can induce many biological effects, but its growth effects require long incubation times and relatively high hormone concentrations. At least three receptors may be involved in these actions, and in addition there are interactions between one receptor type and another.

Although many other growth factors have been characterized, insulin is the only peptide hormone for which detailed information on its production, secretion, and physiological metabolism are known. Physiologically, insulin is the only one among the known growth factors shown to be crucial for survival. Furthermore, virtually every cell type which can be grown in a defined medium requires insulin. However, it likely that the *in vivo* growth effects of insulin are even more important than previously believed. The complications of diabetes have provided a glimpse of the potential importance of the growth-promoting actions of insulin.

The study of insulin action is entering a very exciting era. For the first time, detailed biochemical and biological analysis on hormone receptors and post-receptor events can be studied using very sophisticated techniques. These studies should provide information both on the mechanisms of action of insulin and its role in physiological states.

ACKNOWLEDGMENTS

George L. King is a recipient of an American Diabetes Association Career and Development Award. Some of the work has been supported by an award from the Juvenile Diabetes Foundation.

REFERENCES

1. Cahill, G. F., Jr., *Diabetes*, **20**, 785 (1971).
2. Czech, M. P., *Annu. Rev. Biochem*, **46**, 359 (1977).
3. Kahn, C. R., *Trends Biochem. Sci*, **263**, 4 (1979).
4. Fajans, S. S., in L. J. DeGroot, Ed., *Endocrinology*, Grune and Stratton, New York, Vol. 2, 1979.
5. Steiner, D. F., Rubenstein, A. H., and Melani, F., in R. V. Greep and E. B. Astwood, Eds., *Handbook of Physiology*, Waverly Press, Baltimore, Vol. 1, 1972.
6. King, G. L., Kahn, C. R., Rechler, M. M., and Nissley, S. P., *J. Clin. Invest.*, **66**, 130 (1980).
7. King, G. L., and Kahn, C. R., *Nature*, **292**, 644 (1981).
8. Petrides, P. E., and Bohler, P., *Biochem. Biophys. Res. Commun.*, **95**, 1138 (1980).
9. Blundell, T. L., Dodson, G. C., Hodgkins, D. C., and Marcola, R. A., *Adv. Protein Chem.*, **26**, 229 (1972).
10. Rechler, M. M., Goldfine, I. D., Podskalny, J., and Wells, C. A., *J. Clin. Ednocrinol. Metab.*, **39**, 512 (1974).
11. Rechler, M. M., Nissley, S. P., King, G. L., Moses, A., Schilling, E. E., Romonus, J., Short, P. A., and White, R. M., *J. Supramol. Struct.*, **292**, 644 (1981).
12. Danho, W., Bullesbach, E. E., Gattner, H. G., King, G. L., and Kahn, C. R., in D. H. Rich and E. Gross, Eds., *Peptides: Synthesis, Structure and Function*, Pierce Co., Rockford, IL, 1981.
13. Foley, T. P., Nissley, S. P., Stevens, R. L., King, G. L., Hascall, V. C., Humbel, R. E., Short, P. A., and Rechler, M. M., *J. Biol. Chem.*, **257**, 663 (1982).
14. King, G. L., Kahn, C. R., and Rechler, M. M., *J. Biol. Chem.*, **257**, 10001 (1982).
15. King, G. L., Kahn, C. R., and Samuels, B., *J. Biol. Chem.*, **257**, 10869 (1982).
16. King, G. L., Kahn, C. R., and Heldin, C. H., *Proc. Natl. Acad. Sci. USA*, **80**, 1308 (1983).
17. King, G. L., Buzney, S. M., Kahn, C. R., Hetos, N., Buchwald, S., and Rand, L., *J. Clin. Invest.*, **71**, 974 (1983).
18. Gey, G. O., and Thalhimer, W., *J. Amer. Med. Assoc.*, **82**, 1609 (1924).
19. Latta, J. S., and Bucholz, D. J., *Arch. Exp. Zellforsch.*, **23**, 146 (1939).
20. Von Haam, E., and Cappel, L., *Am. J. Cancer*, **39**, 350 (1940).
21. Karlson, F. A., Van Obberghen, E., Grunfeld, C., and Kahn, C. R., *Proc. Natl. Acad. Sci. USA*, **76**, 809 (1979).
22. Van Obberghen, E., Spooner, P. M., Kahn, C. R., Chernick, S. S., Garrison, M. M., Karlsson, F. A., and Grunfeld, C., *Nature*, **280**, 500 (1979).
23. Leslie, I., and Davidson, J. N., *Biochem. J.*, **49** (1952).
24. Leslie, I., and Paul, J., *J. Endocrinol.*, **11**, 110 (1954).
25. Leslie, I., Fulton, W. C., and Sinclair, R., *Biochim. Biophys. Acta*, **24**, 365 (1957).
26. Paul, J., and Pearson, E. S., *J. Endocrinol.*, **21**, 287 (1960).
27. Temin, H. M., *J. Cell. Physiol.*, **69**, 377 (1967).
28. Griffiths, J. B., *J. Cell. Sci.*, **8**, 143 (1971).
29. Griffiths, J. B., *Exp. Cell Res.*, **78**, 4 (1922).
30. Zapf, J., Rinderknecht, R. E., and Froesch, E. R., *Metab. Clin. Exp.*, **27**, 1803 (1978).

31. Pledger, W. J., Stiles, C. D., Antoniades, H. N., and Scher, C. D., *Proc. Natl. Acad. Sci. USA*, **74**, 4481 (1979).

32. Gospodarowicz, D., and Moran, J. S., *Annu. Rev. Biochem.*, **45**, 531 (1976).

33. Rozengurt, E., in G. H. Sato and R. Ross, Eds., *Hormones and Cell Culture*, Cold Spring Harbor Conference, Cold Spring Harbor, New York, 1978.

34. Kahn, R., Murray, M., and Pawelek, J., *J. Cell. Physiol.*, **103**, 109 (1980).

35. Koontz, J. W., *J. Supramol. Struct.*, **4**, 171 (1980).

36. Koontz, J. W., and Iwahashi, M., *Science*, **211**, 947 (1981).

37. Hayashi, I., Larner, J., and Sato, G., *In Vitro*, **14**, 23 (1978).

38. Mott, D. M., Howard, B. V., and Bennett, P. H., *J. Biol. Chem.*, **254**, 8762 (1979).

39. Van Wyk, J. J., and Underwood, L. E., in G. Litwack, Ed., *Biochemical Actions of Hormones* Academic, New York, Vol 5, 1974.

40. Rinderknecht, E., and Humbel, R., *Proc. Natl. Acad. Sci. USA*, **73**, 2365 (1976).

41. Salmon, W. D., and Daughaday, W. H., *J. Lab. Clin. Med.*, **49**, 825 (1956).

42. Phillips, L. and Vassilopoulous-Sellin, R., *N. Engl. J. Med.*, **302**, 371 (1980).

43. Rinderknecht, E., and Humbel, R. E., *J. Biol. Chem.*, **253**, 2769 (1978).

44. Rinderknecht, E., and Humbel, R. E.', *FEBS Lett.*, **89**, 283 (1978).

45. White, R. M., Nissley, S. P., Moses, A. C., Rechler, M. M., and Johnsonbaugh, R. E., *J. Clin. Endocrinol.*, **53**, 49 (1981).

46. Nissley, S. P., and Rechler, M. M., *Natl. Cancer Inst. Monogr.*, **48**, 167 (1978).

47. Marquardt, H., Todaro, G. J., Henderson, L. E., and Oroszlan, S., *J. Biol. Chem.*, **256**, 6859 (1981).

48. Kahn, C. R., in E. D. Kahn, Ed., *Methods in Membrane Biology*, Plenum, New York, Vol. 3, 1975.

49. Roth, J., in L. DeGroot, Ed., *Endocrinology*, Grune and Stratton, New York, 1979.

50. DeMeyts, P., Van Obberghen, E., Roth, J., Wollmer, A., and Brandenburg, D., *Nature*, **273**, 504 (1978).

51. Megyesi, K., Kahn, C. R., Roth, J., Froesch, E. R., Humbel, R. E., Zapf, J., and Neville, D. M., Jr., *Biochem. Biophys. Res. Commun.*, **57**, 307 (1974).

52. Megyesi, K., Kahn, C. R., Roth, J., Neville, D. M., Jr., Nissley, S. P., Humbel, R. E., and Froesch, E. R., *J. Biol. Chem.*, **250**, 8990 (1975).

53. Zapf, J. E., Schoenle, E., and Froesch, E. R., *Eur. J. Biochem.*, **87**, 285 (1978).

54. Rechler, M. M., Zapf, J., Nissley, S. P., Froesch, E. R., Moses, A. C., Podskalny, J. M., Schillings, E. E., and Humbel, R. E., *Endocrinology*, **107**, 1451 (1980).

55. Rosenfeld, R. G., Thorsson, A. V., and Hintz, R. L., *Endocrinology*, **107**, 1841 (1980).

56. Massague, J., Guillette, B. J., and Czech, M. P., *J. Biol. Chem.*, **256**, 2122 (1981).

57. Kasuga, M., Van Obberghen, E., Nissley, S. P., and Rechler, M. M., *J. Biol. Chem.*, **256**, 5305 (1981).

58. Bhavmick, B., Bala, R. M., and Hollenberg, M. D., *Proc. Natl. Acad. Sci. USA*, **78**, 4779 (1981).

59. Pilch, P. F., and Czech, M. P., *J. Biol. Chem.*, **255**, 1722 (1980).

60. Kasuga, M., Zick, Y., Blithe, D. L., Karlsson, F. A., Haring, H. U., and Kahn, C. R., *J. Biol. Chem.*, **257**, 9891 (1982).

61. Petruzzelli, L. M., Ganguly, S., Smith, C. J., Cobb, M. H., Rubin, C. S., and Rosen, O. M., *Proc. Natl. Acad. Sci. USA*, **79**, 6792 (1982).

62. Van Obberghen, E., Kasuga, M., Le Cam, A., Hedo, J. A., Itin, A., and Harrison, L. C., *Proc. Natl. Acad. Sci. USA*, **78**, 1052 (1981).

63. Harmon, J. T., Kahn, C. R., Kempner, E. S., and Schlegel, W., *J. Biol. Chem.*, **255**, 3412 (1980).

64. Kahn, C. R., Baird, K., Flier, J. S., and Jarrett, D. B., *J. Clin. Invest.*, **60**, 1094 (1977).

65. Kahn, C. R., Baird, K., and Flier, J. S., *Rec. Prog. Horm. Res.*, **37**, 477 (1981).

66. Kahn, C. R., Baird, K. L., Jarrett, D. B., and Flier, J. S., *Proc. Natl. Acad. Sci. USA*, **75**, 4209 (1978).

67. Hodgkins, D. C., and Mercola, D., in R. O. Greep and E. B. Astwood, Eds., *Handbook of Physiology*, American Physiological Society, Waverly Press, Baltimore, 1972.

68. Wrann, M., Fox, C. F., and Ross, R., *Science*, **210**, 1363 (1980).

69. Heldin, C. H., Wasteson, A., and Westermark, B., *J. Biol. Chem.*, **257**, 4216 (1982).

70. Clemmons, D. R., Van Wyke, J. J., and Pledger, W. J., *Proc. Natl. Acad. Sci. USA*, **77**, 6644 (1980).

71. Heldin, C. H., Westermark, B., and Wasteson, A., *Proc. Natl. Acad. Sci. USA*, **76**, 3722 (1979).

72. Deuel, T. F., Huang, J. S., Proffitt, R. T., Baenziger, J. U., Chang, D., and Kennedy, B. B., *J. Biol. Chem.*, **256**, 8896 (1981).

73. Antoniades, H. A., *Proc. Natl. Acad. Sci. USA*, **78**, 7314 (1981).

74. Raines, E. W., and Ross, R., *J. Biol. Chem.*, **257**, 5154 (1982).

75. Schoenle, E., Zapf, J., and Froesch, E. R., *Diabetabologia*, **13**, 243 (1977).

76. Zapf, J., Schoenle, E., and Froesch, E. R., *Eur. J. Biochem.*, **87**, 85 (1978).

77. Gorden, P., Carpentier, J. L., Freychet, P., and Orci, L., *Diabetologia*, **18**, 263 (1980).

78. Gorden, P., Carpentier, J. L., Cohen, S., and Orci, L., *Proc. Natl. Acad. Sci. USA*, **75**, 5025 (1978).

79. Schlessinger, J., Schecter, Y., Willingham, M. C., and Pastan, I., *Proc. Natl. Acad. Sci. USA*, **75**, 2659 (1978).

80. Haigler, H. T., Ash, J. F., Singer, S. J., and Cohen, S., *Proc. Natl. Acad. Sci. USA*, **75**, 3317 (1978).

81. Posner, B. I., Bergeron, J. J. M., Josefsbery, Z., Khan, M. N., Khan, R. J., Patel, B., Sikstroth, R. A., and Verma, A. K., *Rec. Prog. Horm. Res.*, **37**, 539 (1981).

82. Carpentier, J. L., Van Obberghen, E., Gorden, P., and Orci, L., *Diabetes*, **28**, 354 (1979).

83. Cohen, S., Chinker, M., and Ushiro, in O. M. Rosen and E. S. Krebs, Eds., *Protein Phosphorylation*, Cold Spring Harbor Laboratory, Cold Spring Harbor, New York, Book 2, 1981.

84. Haring, H., Kasuga, M., Pawelek, J., and Kahn, C. R., *Clin. Res.*, 502A (1983).

85. Kasuga, M., Karlsson, F. A., and Kahn, C. R., *Science*, **215**, 185 (1982).

86. Ek, B., Westermark, B., Wasteson, A., and Heldin, C. H., *Nature*, **295**, 419 (1982).

87. Nishimura, J., Huang, J. S., and Deuel, T. F., *Proc. Natl. Acad. Sci. USA*, **79**, 4303 (1982).

88. Kasuga, M., Zick, Y., Blithe, D. L., Crettaz, M., and Kahn, C. R., *Nature*, **298**, 667 (1982).

89. Kasuga, M., Zick, Y., Blithe, D. L., Karlsson, F. A., Haring, H. U., and Kahn, C. R., *J. Biol. Chem.*, **257**, 9891 (1982).

90. Kasuga, M., Fujita-Yamaguchi, Y., Blithe, D. L., and Kahn, C. R., *Proc. Natl. Acad. Sci. USA*, in press.

91. Roth, R. A., and Cassell, D. J., *Science*, **219**, 299 (1983).

92. Van Obberghen, E., and Kowalski, A., *FEBS Lett.*, **143**, 179 (1982).

93. Haring, H. U., Kasuga, M., and Kahn, C. R., *Biochem. Biophys. Res. Commun.*, **108**, 1538 (1982).

94. Zick, Y., Kasuga, M., Kahn, C. R., and Roth, J., *J. Biol. Chem.*, **258**, 75 (1983).

95. Pawelek, J., Murray, M. and Fleischmann, R., in *Cold Spring Harbor Conferences on Cell Proliferation*, Cold Spring Harbor Laboratory, Cold Spring Harbor, New York, Vol. 9, 1982.

96. Kahn, C. R., Murray, M., and Pawelek, J., *J. Cell. Phys.*, **103**, 109 (1980).

97. Sefton, B., and Rubin, H., *Proc. Natl. Acad. Sci. USA*, **68**, 3154 (1971).

98. Rozengurt, E., and Stein, W. D., *Biochim. Biophys. Acta*, **464**, 417 (1977).

99. Sanui, H., and Rubin, H., *J. Cell. Physiol.*, **92**, 23 (1977).

100. Clausen, T., *FEBS Symp. on Biochemistry of Membrane Transport*, **42**, 481 (1977).

101. Rozengurt, E., and Heppel, L. A., *Proc. Natl. Acad. Sci. USA*, **72**, 4492 (1975).

102. Schuldiner, S., and Rozengurt, E., *Proc. Natl. Acad. Sci. USA*, **79**, 7778 (1982).

103. Fehlman, M., LeCam, A., and Freychet, P., *J. Biol. Chem.*, **254**, 10431 (1979).

104. Liberman, I., Abrams, R., and Ove, P., *J. Biol. Chem.*, **238**, 2141 (1963).

105. Fehlmann, M., and Freychet, P., *J. Biol. Chem.*, **256**, 7449 (1981).

106. Blatt, L. M., McVerry, P. N., and Kim, K. H., *J. Biol. Chem.*, **247**, 6551 (1972).

107. Pedersen, J., in *The Pregnant Diabetic and Her Newborn*, Williams and Wilkins, Baltimore, 1977.

108. Hill, P. E., *Semin. Perinatal.*, **2**, 319 (1978).

109. Susa, J. B., McCormick, K. L., Widness, J. A., Singer, D. B., Oh, W., Adamsons, K., and Schwartz, R., *Diabetes*, **28**, 1058 (1979).

110. Leffert, H. L., *J. Cell Biol.*, **62**, 792 (1974).

111. Price, J. B., Jr., *Metabolism*, **25** (Suppl. 1), 1427 (1976).

112. Starzl, T. E., Porter, K. A., Watanabe, K., and Putnam, C. N., *Lancet*, **1**, 821 (1976).

113. Stout, R. W., *Diabetologia*, **16**, 141 (1979).

114. McEvoy, R. C., and Hegre, O. D., *Diabetes*, **27**, 988 (1978).

9

T-CELL GROWTH FACTOR

Marjorie Robert-Guroff
M. G. Sarngadharan
Robert C. Gallo

CONTENTS

Abbreviations

IL-2	Interleukin 2
PHA	Phytohemagglutinin
TCGF	T-cell growth factor
Con A	Concanavalin A
IgG	Immunoglobulin G
PMA	Phorbol myristic acetate
LAF	Lymphocyte-activating factor
IL-1	Interleukin 1
HTLV	Human T-cell leukemia/lymphoma virus
MHC	Major histocompatibility complex
PMSF	Phenylmethylsulfonyl fluoride
TMAC	Trimethylmethylammonium chloride
TFA	Trifluoroacetic acid
PEG	Polyethylene glycol
PBS	Phosphate-buffered saline

IFNγ   Immune interferon
IFNα   α-Interferon
TRF   T-cell replacing factor
CSF   Colony-stimulating factor

1. INTRODUCTION

The ability to grow pure populations of hematopoietic cells for extended periods in culture has been a goal of many laboratories for a long time. The development of hematopoietic cell clones would be invaluable for use in elucidating critical interactions in the regulation of normal hematopoiesis and in understanding breakdowns in such regulations resulting from modifications in certain cellular compartments. Although some humoral factors for the growth and differentiation of granulocytic, monocytoid, erythroid, megakaryocytic, and T and B-lymphoid cells in semisolid media have been identified and characterized (1), obviously the ability to grow these cells in liquid suspension cultures would provide major advantages for biochemical, immunological, and virological studies. Until recently, long-term growth of human leukocytes was achieved only with B-lymphocytes stimulated with Epstein–Barr virus (2) and with some myeloid (3) and lymphoid (4, 5) leukemic cells. In 1976, Morgan et al. (6) discovered that normal T-cells could be grown for extended periods using the conditioned media from phytohemagglutinin (PHA)-stimulated human peripheral blood lymphocyte cultures. Inasmuch as these conditioned media contained a large number of other mitogenic factors (7, 8) and inasmuch as almost every group used a different assay system for identification of these biological activities, a confusing array of empirical designations (9) arose. The factor responsible for the long-term growth of human T-cells, T-cell growth factor (TCGF), has now been purified and its properties analyzed in detail, alleviating much of the initial confusion. It is appropriate here to state our preference for the terminology "T-cell growth factor." In 1979, participants in the Second International Lymphokine Workshop attempted to simplify the then-current nomenclature and termed the murine factor which supported continuous proliferation of cytotoxic T-lymphocytes interleukin-2 (Il-2; 10). Although it was a reasonable approach, the eventual outcome in the intervening years has been the erroneous attribution of several biologic activities present in lymphocyte-conditioned media to Il-2, a factor which thus apparently possessed multiple functions. To avoid this unfortunate grouping of activities and the implication that they might be attributed to a single molecular species, we feel the most accurate designation for the factor in question remains TCGF. This terminology is used extensively throughout this review, even frequently when original works on Il-2 are described.

Since the initial description of human TCGF (6), studies have proceeded in parallel with TCGF from other species. Although there are some species restrictions, for the most part these factors appear to be analogous to the human TCGF. In this chapter, we discuss some of the relevant features of TCGF, including its production, purification, and biological and biochemical properties, with emphasis on the human factor wherever possible. The role of TCGF in the establishment of some human neoplastic T-cell lines that have resulted in the isolation of a unique human retrovirus with a specific disease correlation is discussed, as is a possible interaction of TCGF and the human retrovirus in leukemogenesis. Potential therapeutic uses of the factor are also outlined. We have not attempted to cover all the available literature on TCGF simply because of its voluminous nature. Instead we have drawn only on those examples necessary to illustrate particular points.

2.   PRODUCTION OF TCGF

2.1.   Conditioned Media as a Source

TCGF was initially detected in conditioned medium obtained from PHA-stimulated human lymphocytes (6). The peripheral blood leukocytes which proliferated in response to periodic addition of this factor were clearly shown to be T-cells based on both morphologic and functional criteria (6, 11). The significance of this growth factor lay in its potential use in elucidating the biology of normal T-cells, as well as neoplastic ones. Until this time the only T-cell culture systems available relied on repeated allogeneic stimulations or else were derived from malignant T-cells. The methodology of producing conditioned medium containing active factor was soon adapted to murine T-cells as well (12) and our understanding of the factor and the cells it supports has been advanced in both areas. Much more rapid progress in the TCGF field could have occurred if sufficiently large quantities of factor were available for detailed biologic and biochemical studies.

Much of the early work was concerned with defining optimal conditions for TCGF production following lectin or antigen stimulation. The literature even now abounds with these reports reflecting the failure of investigators to identify a reliable source which will repeatedly yield high levels of TCGF. Although conditioned media produce amounts of TCGF insufficient for detailed chemical analysis, they do produce sufficient growth factor for T-cell culture. As discussed in the following, partially purified TCGF from conditioned media is particularly useful in culture systems. Therefore, it is worthwhile to summarize some of the variables involved in preparing good quality conditioned media. Five parameters may be considered and have also been reviewed previously (13, 14).

2.1.1. Cell Source

Species and tissue type will dictate in some cases the method of conditioned-media production and will influence the quantity of factor produced and its subsequent uses. TCGF produced by human cells has so far been shown to support the growth of T-cells from subhuman primates and other mammals including rodents (13). On the other hand, conditioned media obtained from rodent sources do not support the growth of T-cells from higher mammals. Thus human TCGF is often prescribed. Spleen cells are perhaps the best choice for factor production, both because of the ease of obtaining large numbers of cells and the fact that spleen cell cultures may be restimulated to give a second batch of conditioned media of equally high titer (14). As human spleens in particular are not always available, other cell types may be used; these include peripheral blood leukocytes, bone marrow, tonsils, and lymph nodes.

2.1.2. Stimulation of Cells

Antigen or lectin stimulation is necessary for factor production. A variety of choices exists including PHA, concanavalin A (Con A), pokeweed mitogen, and staphylococcus protein A (13–15). The choice is influenced mostly by the response of the particular cell source to the mitogenic stimulus. It is not known why some cultures respond better to particular mitogens. The use of protein A to stimulate human peripheral blood leukocytes has been reported to be particularly advantageous due to the ease with which the mitogen subsequently can be removed from the conditioned medium based on its high affinity for immunoglobulin G (IgG; 15). Con A might be the mitogen of choice for many systems due to its easy removal by adsorption onto Sepharose or its neutralization by the addition of α-methyl mannoside. Unfortunately, human cells in general do not respond well to Con A; much better TCGF production is obtained with PHA (16).

2.1.3. Multiple Donors

The choice of single or multiple donors is important when peripheral blood leukocytes are used for TCGF production. Some allogeneic stimulation is necessary for adequate factor production in this system, although this is not the case with either rodent (14) or human (17) spleen cell cultures. Multiple peripheral blood donors have, therefore, generally been used to meet this requirement. It is also possible, however, to provide allogeneic stimulation by adding B-lymphoblastoid cell lines to the culture system (18). These B-cell lines do not produce TCGF themselves, as Daudi cell membranes can provide equally effective stimulation (19). Moreover, actual cell contact seems to be necessary, as supernatants of Daudi cell cultures are ineffective stimulators. The Ia antigens present on Daudi cells may explain their effectiveness in stimulating TCGF production. Ia antigens are known to play a role in antigen recognition by T-lymphocytes prior to subsequent T-cell proliferation (20, 21).

2.1.4.   Kinetics of TCGF Production

TCGF production is both time and cell-concentration dependent. This is due to two opposing phenomena. On one hand, sufficient time must be allowed for TCGF production by the producer cells. At the same time responder cells begin to actively bind TCGF and proliferate, thereby removing it from the medium (22, 23). Thus the kinetics of factor production must be carefully monitored in order to harvest conditioned media containing maximal factor concentrations. Other parameters to be considered include the induction of inhibitory substances and the release of degradative enzymes, both of which result in lessened TCGF yield. In general, these phenomena occur at relatively late time periods. A possible early regulatory control has been suggested from observations of mouse spleen cell cultures. Rather than a feedback control mechanism, the induction of suppressor cells by lectin has been postulated to occur as early as 24 hours following the establishment of cultures (24). The nature of these cells has not been determined, but the suggestion is that they actively arrest *de novo* TCGF production.

2.1.5.   Additional Stimulatory Treatments

Finally, a variety of stimulatory substances or treatments have sometimes been used effectively to enhance TCGF production. Among these are the addition of phorbol ester tumor promoters or of indomethacin, and irradiation. Indomethacin is a prostaglandin synthetase inhibitor (25). The rationale for its use in stimulating the production of TCGF has been based on observations in several systems that monocytes suppress lymphokine production due to their synthesis and release of prostaglandins (26, 27). The addition of indomethacin to PHA-stimulated human lymphocyte cultures has indeed been shown to augment TCGF production (16, 28, 29), particularly after 72 to 96 hours of culture. However, inhibitory effects of prostaglandins are perhaps more easily removed from cultures if peripheral blood leukocytes are simply incubated overnight at 37°C prior to lectin stimulation, or if the majority of monocytes are first removed by adherence to nylon fiber columns (16). Irradiation of the lymphocytes to be cultured has also been shown to stimulate TCGF production (28, 29). In fact, the effects of the removal of monocytes and the irradiation of the nonadherent cell population are additive (29). The suggestion is that in an optimally irradiated culture, T-cell proliferation will cease, thereby allowing accumulation of TCGF rather than its removal from the culture by continual generation of T-cells with specific TCGF receptors. It has been shown by the use of inhibitors of macromolecular synthesis that although TCGF production requires protein synthesis, it continues in the absence of DNA synthesis (19). Phorbol myristic acetate (PMA), one of a series of phorbol ester tumor promoters, has recently been shown to enhance the production of TCGF in Con A-stimulated mouse spleen cells and in human peripheral blood lymphocytes (30–32). Although effective in this regard, it seems more likely that PMA and similar substances will play a greater role in the elucidation of the mechanism of action of the activating and growth-promoting factors, rather than merely serving as stimulatory agents. PMA, for example, seems to be able to substitute for macrophages in the activation of T-cells by mitogens (33), suggesting that it may act in a similar fashion as lymphocyte-activating factor (LAF; IL-1). More recently, it has been shown that human peripheral blood lymphocytes bind phorbol esters by means of specific receptors which may, therefore, mediate the enhanced TCGF production by these human T-cells (34). Use of such synthetic substances, available in large quantities, may greatly facilitate biochemical studies on the induction and action of TCGF.

Considering all these variables, it is impossible to prescribe procedures here which will provide optimal factor yield in any system. Listed in Table 1, however, is a standard method used in our laboratory for TCGF production

Table 1.   Production of PHA-Stimulated Human Lymphocyte-Conditioned Media

1. Mononuclear cells are obtained from buffy coats of samples from 3–20 human donors.
2. The cells are passed through nylon wool columns.
3. 10^6 cells/ml are incubated in RPMI 1640 medium containing 10 μg/ml PHA-P (Difco Laboratories); 0.25% bovine serum albumin (no serum) for 72 hours at 37°C.
4. Cells are removed by centrifugation and the medium is frozen at −20°C until use.

by human peripheral blood lymphocytes. We have found that this method gives reliable TCGF production in amounts satisfactory for subsequent purification.

2.2. Activation of T-Cells and Production of TCGF

In order for TCGF to be elaborated and subsequently stimulate T-cells to proliferate, a complex series of interactions must take place. Basically, three events are involved. First, in order for T-cells to become responsive to TCGF they must be activated and acquire TCGF receptors. This occurs upon the presentation of antigen or lectin. Second, a different subset of T-cells interacts with the antigen or lectin and the macrophages and initiates TCGF production. The precise role of macrophages in this process is not yet known, although they are involved with the presentation of the antigen to the T-cells (35) and they also produce IL-1, a factor apparently involved in the TCGF production process (36, 37). Finally, the activated T-cells possessing specific TCGF receptors bind the newly produced factor and begin proliferating. This sequence of events is pictured in Fig. 1. The

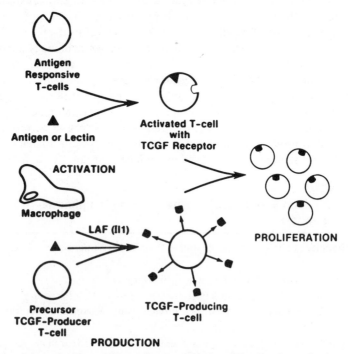

Figure 1. Schematic diagram illustrating the activation of T-cells, the production of TCGF, and the proliferation of activated T-cells possessing TCGF receptors.

particular subsets of T-cells which produce and respond to TCGF are discussed in Section 2.4.

One can appreciate that in addition to these interactions involved with TCGF production and T-cell proliferation, a number of other complex interactions take place in mitogen-stimulated cell cultures leading to the elaboration of additional factors and the response of different cell types. Conditioned medium containing TCGF is also known to contain interferon (38), colony-stimulating factors (39), T-cell replacing factors (40), LAF (41), as well as lymphokines which regulate the growth of B-cells (42) and mast cells (43). Along with both the ability to culture cloned T-cells using TCGF to sustain cell growth and the creation of T-cell hybridomas, have come the findings that T-cells produce several additional regulatory substances which may also be present in conditioned media. These include migration inhibition factor (44), a multipotential hemopoietic stem cell factor distinct from granulocyte-macrophage colony-stimulating factor (45), and macrophage activating factor (46). Because the routine assay for TCGF production and the growth of T-cells is a bioassay involving thymidine incorporation (see Section 3.8), any inhibition or stimulation of cell growth either of T-cells or of other cells in the culture may be reflected in the assay results. Thus when a conditioned medium is used, the results must be interpreted with caution, both with regard to the measurement of TCGF levels and to the attribution of particular functions or reponses of cells cultured in its presence to T-cells. It is equally clear that most biologic and biochemical studies of TCGF and the cells which respond to it must utilize purified or at least partially purified TCGF rather than crude conditioned medium.

2.3. Alternate Sources of TCGF

Although conditioned media have been useful in growing cells, the amount of factor produced in a typical culture has been small and insufficient for large-scale biochemical procedures or the growth of large quantities of cells. As a result, new sources of TCGF have been actively pursued. Two approaches have been used with some success and are reviewed here. Most recently the TCGF gene has been cloned (47, 48; see Section 9). As the cloned DNA apparently is able to direct the synthesis of biologically active factor (48), large quantities of TCGF should soon be available for both basic studies and clinical uses.

2.3.1. Established Cell Lines

Some established cell lines, following mitogen stimulation, have been found to produce substantially greater amounts of TCGF than mitogen-activated peripheral blood lymphocyte cultures or spleen cell cultures (49, 50). These lines include the mouse LBRM-33 line derived from a radiation-induced splenic lymphoma and the human JURKAT line, originally designated JM (51), derived from a patient with acute lymphocytic leukemia of T-cells. Other cell lines, such as HSB-2 (52), have been shown to produce TCGF following lectin stimulation also, but not in significantly greater amounts than those obtained routinely in peripheral blood lymphocyte-conditioned media. While TCGF is produced by a subset of mature T-cells, the control mechanisms regulating the levels of TCGF production are not known. Until such mechanisms are elaborated, the empirical observation that some clones of TCGF-producing lines produce even greater amounts of factor than the parent culture while other clones produce none (49) suggests an explanation for the variation in results obtained by various investigators with particular lines. More important, cloning may be one of the better methods for obtaining greater factor production by selecting appropriate clones that produce high levels of TCGF.

Cell lines of the type described have produced conditioned media yielding quantities of TCGF sufficient for a number of biochemical studies following fairly rigorous purification procedures. Yet for biologic experiments one major drawback to the use of these conditioned media has been the presence of T-cell mitogens that are not easily or completely removed even with extensive purification. Any contaminating lectin or mitogen obscures the biologic functions of TCGF itself. Thus a better source of TCGF would be cell lines which produce the factor constitutively. With this in mind, established T-cell lines as well as T-cell hybridoma lines have been examined for constitutive TCGF production. Limited success has been achieved using this approach. A gibbon ape T-cell leukemia line, MLA144, has been found to be a constitutive producer of TCGF, capable of supporting the growth of primate T-cells, including human, as well as T-cells of mice and rabbits (53). Conditioned media obtained from this cell line should be used cautiously, however, with the full understanding that these gibbon cells release the horizontally transmitted type-C RNA tumor virus, gibbon ape leukemia virus (GaLV) (54), which can infect human cells and influence their growth (55, 56). The media are thus both a potential hazard to humans, and a virus source possibly leading to transmission of GALV to any cells with which they come in contact. With regard to this constitutive release of TCGF in conjunction with release of a retrovirus, constitutive production of TCGF by cell lines established from humans with adult T-cell malignancies has been described (57). Isolates of a human T-cell leukemia/lymphoma virus (HTLV) have also been obtained from these cells and cells of other patients with this disease (58–64). These findings suggest that prudence is in order when using conditioned media from any constitutive TCGF producer. The findings also form the basis of an hypothesis for viral leukemogenesis involving a possible interaction of TCGF and retroviruses (see Section 7).

2.3.2. T-Cell Hybridomas

Perhaps better sources than tumor cell lines for constitutive TCGF production are T-cell hybridomas created by fusing cells capable of TCGF production with immortal T-cell lines. Such an approach has been successful in murine (65) and human systems (66). The TCGF production of the human hybridoma is not remarkably high, whereas the murine hybridoma line secretes approximately 10-fold more TCGF than a standard mitogen-stimulated lymphocyte preparation. On the other hand, the parental TCGF-producing murine line used for fusion, LBRM-33, is still capable of secreting up to 1,000 to 10,000-fold more TCGF in comparison. Both the hybrid cell lines can be stimulated with lectin to yield higher levels of factor; however, this negates the advantage of having a constitutive producer. Conditioned media from hybridoma cell lines may, therefore, still be inadequate in supplying the amounts of factor necessary for extensive biochemical characterization. In addition, the possible secretion of other mitogenic factors by these T-cell hybridomas has not yet been adequately explored. Several investigators have, in fact, reported on cloned murine T-cell lines which secrete multiple activities (67–70).

2.4. The TCGF-Producing Cell

The precise nature of the TCGF-producing cell and the manner in which TCGF production is regulated are not known. It is also not known whether all TCGF produced by normal cells is the same, and whether all responsive T-cells respond to the same TCGF by means of a common receptor. TCGF with altered biochemical properties has, in fact, been described in neoplastic cell populations (71; see Section 7). Whether this biochemical difference reflects a consequence of the malignancy resulting in an altered protein, or whether the variant TCGF produced by malignant cell lines is a product of a clonal expansion of a T-cell producing one type among a spectrum of possible TCGF molecules is not yet known either. In general, it has been shown that TCGF is produced by thymic-derived mature T-cells. This was in fact inferred from the first studies on TCGF, since media from nylon–column purified T-cells, activated by PHA, were used as the TCGF source (6). Evidence was also acquired from the murine system where it had been shown that spleen cells of congenitally athymic (nu/nu) mice were incapable of producing TCGF (72, 73). Although this finding has recently been contradicted in part, the basic tenet has held true. Spleen cells of *aged* mice have been shown to produce TCGF; however, production occurred concomitantly with the development of cells with T-cell surface markers. The producer cells were in fact shown to be Thy-1$^+$, Lyt-2$^-$ (74). This result suggests that the thymus may play more of a quantitative rather than a qualitative role in the development of functional T-cells.

Until recently a second basic tenet concerning TCGF production held that helper T-cells, in the murine system those cells possessing the Lyt-1$^+$, 2$^-$ phenotype (75; see Table 2), are responsible for TCGF production. Two major classes of mature T-cells have been described based on both functional and phenotypic criteria (Table 2). With the development of specific monoclonal antibodies against surface antigens of these cell populations it has become possible to differentiate more easily the responses of the two subsets by means of cell sorting techniques. Recently, it was demonstrated that both helper and cytotoxic human T-cells (OKT-4$^+$ and OKT-8$^+$) were capable of producing TCGF (76). Of most importance, however, was the observation that the nature of the antigenic stimulus determined which cell type became capable of producing the factor. Both subsets of T-cells were capable of responding to a mitogenic stimulus, but only the OKT-4$^+$ subset produced TCGF in response to an allogeneic stimulus (76). Likewise, in the mouse system, recent results show that either Lyt-1$^+$ or Lyt-2$^+$ T-cells produce TCGF depending on the nature of the difference between major histocompatibility complex (MHC) antigens of the stimulator and responder cells in mixed lymphocyte culture (77). Evidence further suggests that human helper and suppressor T-cells are activated in response to different MHC antigens (78). Thus identification of a phenotypic subset of T-cells capable of producing TCGF may be irrelevant. A functional subset will be more relevant, and depending on the antigen presented, may include most T-cells. It is clear that surface phenotype as defined here by monoclonal antibodies does not always correlate with biologic function. Perhaps the T4/T8 phenotypic markers merely distinguish cells that can respond to different antigenic stimuli to be either activated or induced to produce TCGF in the "helper" mode. So far as we know at present, TCGF is a nonspecific effector molecule in that, once it is produced, any activated T-cell is capable of responding to it. Perhaps every T-cell, if appropriately stimulated, is capable of also producing it. Thus the important considerations become the elucidation of the regulatory mechanisms involved in antigenic stimulation, induction of TCGF receptors, and activation of the TCGF gene.

3. PURIFICATION OF TCGF

Several procedures have been published for the purification of TCGF (79–83). In all instances, the first step involves a substantial concentration

Table 2. Correlation of Surface Phenotype of Murine and Human Mature T-Cells With Presumed Function

Phenotype

Mature T-Cells
Cortisone Resistent
Terminal Deoxyribonucleotidyl Transferase ($-$)
20-α Hydroxysteroid Dehydrogenase ($+$)
Pan T-Antibody ($+$)

Murine Pan-T:
Thy-1$^+$
(2 alloantigenic determinants: Thy-1.1, Thy-1.2)

Human Pan-T:
OKT-1$^+$,
Leu-1$^+$

"Helper/Inducer" T-Cells

Murine	*Human*
Lyt-1$^+$	OKT-4$^+$, Leu 3A$^+$
(2 alleles, i.e., Lyt-1.1, Lyt-1.2)	

Pre-"Suppressor/Cytotoxic" T-Cells
Lyt-2,3$^+$

"Suppressor/Cytotoxic" T-Cells

Murine	*Human*
Lyt-2$^+$	OKT-8$^+$, OKT-5$^+$, Leu-2A$^+$
(2 alleles, i.e., Lyt-2.1,Lyt-2.2)	

Functions

Help in differentiation and/or expansion of cytotoxic T-cells
Help T cell–dependent B-cell response
Help T-cell–macrophage interactions
Produce lymphokines

Cell mediated cytotoxicity
Suppress immune response in antigen-specific manner
Produce lymphokines (?)

279

of the conditioned medium because of the low levels of TCGF present in these media and the consequent necessity to process large volumes of the starting material. Since TCGF is often produced by lectin stimulation of T-cells in culture media containing serum proteins, the latter often accounting for nearly 90% of the total protein content of the conditioned media, the purification protocols should also include steps that remove lectins such as PHA and the extraneous protein additives.

3.1. Concentration of TCGF in Conditioned Media

Various procedures have been described in the literature for concentration of TCGF in crude conditioned media. The size of the sample may have some bearing on the choice of the procedure. Ammonium sulfate precipitation may be the most convenient procedure for small volumes (79). An added advantage of this procedure is that proteins precipitable at 50% saturation do not include TCGF. Proteins precipitating between 50–75% saturation contain all the TCGF activity and are collected and dissolved in a small volume (usually a 40-fold concentration). This procedure is highly impractical when handling large volumes (5 liters or more) of culture media. A convenient alternative, extensively used in concentrating interferon fractions (84), is to use Millipore Pellicon Cassette (Millipore Corporation) filtration. This procedure has been used successfully to concentrate TCGF in large-scale production lots of tissue culture media (85; R. Montagna, personal communication). The polysulfone filter, PTGC with a molecular weight cut-off limit of 10,000 (Millipore), is recommended for this purpose. Using this system one can concentrate 5 liters of clarified TCGF medium to 300–400 ml in less than 30 minutes. The concentrated sample can be further fractionated by ammonium sulfate precipitation as noted previously. A batch procedure using hydroxyapatite also has been described which, in addition to concentrating murine TCGF from culture media, provides a modest degree of purification (82).

3.2. Removal of Lectins

The major demand for TCGF is for initiation and maintenance of T-cell cultures. Such uses do not require high levels of purification. However, crude conditioned media contain a number of other proteins secreted by the cells in addition to the lectins used to induce TCGF production. Residual lectins such as PHA in the media, although stimulatory for normal peripheral blood lymphocytes, often inhibit growth of some TCGF-dependent normal and neoplastic T-cells. The continued presence of PHA in TCGF preparations further complicates analyses of the direct effects of TCGF, such as selective growth of antigen-primed T-cells. Therefore, the effective removal of PHA is of great practical value. A combination of $(NH_4)_2SO_4$ fractionation and an affinity adsorption on columns of Sepharose-bound anti-PHA has been shown to remove more than 99% of the PHA from lymphocyte-conditioned media while retaining most of the TCGF activity (86). Thyroglobulin-Sepharose has been used as another affinity-matrix with which to remove PHA (87), but since two to three successive chromatographic adsorptions are required (86) to remove PHA effectively, this method is less practical and considerably more expensive for handling large TCGF preparations. Ion exchange chromatography on DEAE-Sepharose (79) is probably the least expensive and the most convenient procedure for the removal of PHA from lymphocyte-conditioned media and it has the capability for large-scale operations involving up to tens of liters of starting material.

3.3. Removal of TCGF Inhibitors

Assays of serial dilutions of PHA-stimulated human lymphocyte-conditioned media for TCGF activity usually show an increase in activity with several initial dilutions indicating the presence of a dissociable inhibitor(s). Much of this inhibitory substance(s) can be removed by acidifying the conditioned media (for instance, by dialysis against 1 M acetic acid) and removing the precipitate that forms by centrifugation (M. G. Sarngadharan, unpublished results). The supernatant usually shows an increase in TCGF activity over that of the crude conditioned media and exhibits a more normal dilution curve. The nature of the inhibitor removed by this procedure is not known. One of the components of the crude conditioned media from PHA-stimulated lymphocyte cultures is immune interferon (88) which may have an antiproliferative effect on T-cells and, therefore, may act as a growth inhibitor. Acidification is known to inactivate immune interferon (89) and, therefore, the observed increase in TCGF activity after acidification of the conditioned medium may reflect, in part, the abolition of the antiproliferative effect of immune interferon.

3.4 Anion-Exchange Chromatography

TCGF in human lymphocyte-conditioned media was found to bind to the anion exchanger DEAE-Sepharose under low ionic strength conditions (79). This step has been found to be extremely useful in the purification of TCGF. The affinity of TCGF for the ion-exchanger is not very strong. The factor elutes at about 0.07 M NaCl, clearly ahead of the major protein component in the conditioned media, namely, bovine serum albumin (79, 85). The following procedure has been quite satisfactory for routine purifications.

Twenty-fold concentrated conditioned medium (100 ml) is dialyzed against 10 mM Tris-HCl (pH 7.8) containing 0.1 mM phenylmethylsulfonyl fluoride (PMSF) and 0.1% polyethylene glycol (PEG 6000) and applied to a 100-ml column of DEAE-Sepharose (Pharmacia) equilibrated with the same buffer. After washing with 2–3 bed volumes of the buffer to remove the unadsorbed proteins, the column is developed with a 500 ml 0–0.15 M NaCl gradient in the equilibration buffer. Fractions of 5 ml are collected and aliquots assayed for TCGF activity (85). A typical elution profile is given in Fig. 2. A major part of the TCGF activity elutes between 0.05 and 0.07 M NaCl. The bulk of the protein is eluted only upon continued washing of the column with 0.15 M NaCl.

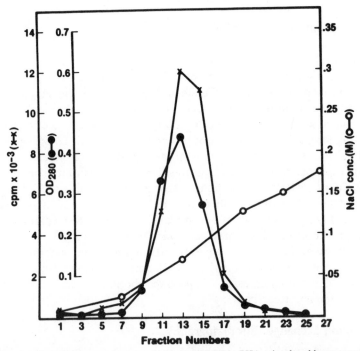

Figure 2.   DEAE-Sepharose chromatography of TCGF in PHA-stimulated human peripheral blood lymphocyte-conditioned media. Ammonium sulfate precipitate was dialyzed against Tris-HCl (pH 7.9) containing 0.1% polyethylene glycol and 0.1 mM phenylmethylsulfonyl fluoride and applied to a 100-ml column of DEAE-Sepharose equilibrated with the same buffer. After extensive washing to remove unadsorbed proteins, the column was developed with a 0–0.15 M NaCl gradient in the buffer. At the end of the gradient (arrow) the column was further washed with 0.15 M NaCl. Fractions of 5 ml were collected and assayed for TCGF activity (x——x), absorbance at 280 nm (●——●), and NaCl concentration (by conductance) (O——O).

In addition to separating TCGF from most of the albumin in the medium, the DEAE-Sepharose step removes all remaining PHA from the preparation. The removal of this lectin, as discussed, may be the most important practical step in the purification of TCGF. As indicated earlier, in most biological experiments the absolute purity of TCGF is less important than the absence of PHA and other proteins which, if present, may influence subsequent analyses of TCGF effects and complicate analyses of biologic functions.

3.5 Gel Filtration

Most purification schemes for TCGF incorporate a step in which proteins are separated on the basis of their molecular size. Active fractions from DEAE-Sepharose chromatography may be pooled and concentrated by ultrafiltration through an Amicon UM-05 membrane and applied to an LKB Ultrogel AcA-54 column (2.5 × 170 cm) previously equilibrated with 10 mM Tris-HCl buffer, pH 7.8, containing 0.5 mM NaCl, 0.05% PEG, and 0.1 mM PMSF. The column is developed with the equilibration buffer and 10-ml fractions are collected. TCGF activity elutes from the column with an apparent molecular weight of approximately 20,000–25,000 following a large peak composed of the majority of contaminating proteins. Active fractions of TCGF can be pooled, concentrated, and rechromatographed on the same column. Several preparations can be combined for this rechromatography. It is not unusual to achieve about a 10-fold purification in each of these gel filtration steps, but the yield of the recovered TCGF activity is low, especially during the second gel filtration.

An alternative procedure that combines separation on the basis of molecular weight and also hydrophobic affinity has been developed in our laboratory (M. G. Sarngadharan et al., to be published). The basis of the procedure is the finding that TCGF binds to glass. By using porous glass beads of the proper pore size one can selectively exclude molecules larger than a given size from entering the pores. Inasmuch as an overwhelming excess of the surface area of these porous beads is inside the pores, large molecules do not bind to the beads to any substantial extent even though they might have an affinity for glass. The DEAE-Sepharose fractions are allowed to equilibrate with the glass beads overnight with gentle mixing. The unbound proteins are washed off with phosphate-buffered saline, and the slurry of glass is packed into a column. TCGF is then eluted with 2 bed volumes of 1M tetramethylammonium chloride (TMAC). The eluate is exhaustively dialyzed against Tris-HCl buffer, pH 7.8, to remove the TMAC before assaying for TCGF activity. A purification of up to 100-fold is obtained by this procedure, with a recovery of greater than 80% of the TCGF activity. Analysis of the fractions from the glass column by polyacrylamide gel electrophoresis confirms that the large molecular weight contaminants are almost entirely removed by this step.

3.6. High Performance Liquid Chromatography

Purification of TCGF to apparent homogeneity can be subsequently achieved by high performance liquid chromatography. TCGF fractions from the gel filtration step or the glass affinity step are acidified to pH~2 with 0.1% trifluoroacetic acid (TFA) and filtered through a 0.5 μ filter. The sample is injected onto a reverse phase liquid chromatography column (Waters, μBondapak C_{18}, 0.38 × 30 cm) equilibrated with 0.1% TFA in glass-distilled water. The column is sequentially eluted with 10% and 50% aqueous acetonitrile acidified to 0.1% TFA and the proteins in the column

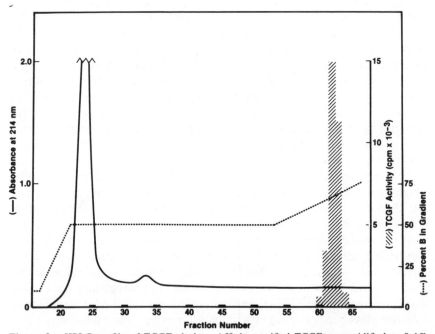

Figure 3. HPLC profile of TCGF elution. Affinity-purified TCGF was acidified to 0.1% trifluoroacetic acid (TFA) and applied to a 0.38 × 30 cm HPLC column (μ Bondapak C-18 Waters) and eluted successively with 10% and 50% aqueous acetonitrile containing 0.1% TFA. When a stable absorbance (214 nm) baseline was established, the column was developed with a 30 minute 50–75% acetonitrile gradient at a flow rate of 1 ml/1 minute. Fractions (2 ml) were individually lyophilized and reconstituted in 100 μl PBS and assayed for TCGF activity. The dotted line represents the percentage of acetonitrile (B) in the aqueous-acetonitrile gradient.

effluent are monitored by absorbance at 214 nm. When no more protein elutes at 50% acetonitrile, the column is eluted with a 30-minute gradient between 50 and 75% acetonitrile at a flow rate of 1 ml per minute. Fractions of 2 ml are collected, 100 μl of 0.1% PEG are added to each, and the solvents are removed by lyophilization. The fractions are reconstituted in 100 μl of PBS each and aliquots are assayed for TCGF activity. Fig. 3 shows the profile of a representative experiment.

The procedure has been scaled up using up to 40 liters of conditioned media per batch. These peripheral blood lymphocyte cultures were induced to produce TCGF with PHA and PMA in the absence of protein additives (Cellular Products, Inc., Buffalo, N.Y.). A 20-fold concentrate (Pellicon Cassette) of the starting material (2 liters) was chromatographed on a 400 ml column of DEAE-Sepharose. The active fractions were pooled and adsorbed to approximately 200 ml of controlled pore glass (pore size, 75 Å). The bound proteins were eluted with 4 bed volumes of 1 M TMAC, dialyzed, and used for the HPLC step. Repeated chromatography on the reverse phase C-18 column yielded a homogeneous peak of TCGF eluting at about 60% acetonitrile (M. G. Sarngadharan et al., in preparation).

Results of amino acid sequence analysis of TCGF from peripheral blood lymphocytes and JURKAT cells (the latter purified by immunoaffinity chromatography as described below) show no difference between the two in the NH_2-terminal 16 amino acid residues. Since the recently cloned TCGF gene from human peripheral blood lymphocytes (48) and JURKAT cells (47) have the same nucleotide sequence, one does not expect to find differences in the primary sequence of the amino acids. However, TCGFs from the two sources may have differences in their post-translational modifications as indicated by the differences in their isoelectric points (Table 3).

3.7. Immunoaffinity Chromatography

A monoclonal antibody has been produced against TCGF (90) purified from the human cell line, JURKAT. This antibody was used in developing an immunoaffinity procedure for isolating pure TCGF from a culture medium in a single adsorption and elution step (90). The usefulness of this antibody in the purification of TCGF from other cellular sources is not known, but development of similar antibodies to TCGF from other sources will certainly be of advantage in several studies as well as in TCGF purification itself. Although reports of monoclonal antibodies to rat TCGF (91) and TCGF produced by lectin-stimulated human peripheral blood lymphocytes (92) have appeared in the literature, they apparently have lacked either appropriate specificity or affinity, as no subsequent reports on affinity-purified TCGF obtained using these reagents have been forthcoming. Unfortunately,

Table 3. Comparison of TCGF Obtained from Normal PHA-stimulated Lymphocytes, Leukemic T-Cells, and JURKAT Cells

Property	Normal TCGF	Leukemic TCGF	JURKAT TCGF
Elution from DEAE-Sepharose	~0.07 M NaCl	>0.2M NaCl	~0.07 M NaCl
Molecular Weight			
By gel filtration on Biogel P60	24,000	27,000	
By amino acid analysis	15,000		15,000
Isoelectric Point:			
Untreated	4 peaks (pH 6.5; 6.8; 7.5; 8.0)	1 peak (pH 4.5)	1 peak (pH 8.2)
Neuraminidase-treated	2 peaks (pH 7; 7.8)	1 peak (pH 4.5)	1 peak (pH 8.2)

most of these antibodies have not been made widely available. These antibodies have been utilized in studies on translation of the mRNA for TCGF (see Section 9).

3.8. Properties of Purified TCGF

A summary of the properties of highly purified TCGF from both murine and human sources is presented in Table 4. Substantial similarities are evident, but the factors possess some distinct differences, notably in isoelectric point and their related chromatographic behavior. The higher molecular weight of the murine factor apparently reflects dimerization. The differences in species specificity for biologic activity have been mentioned in Section 2.1.1.

3.9. Assays of TCGF Activity

Certainly the success in obtaining pure TCGF preparations was made possible in large part by the development of simple and rapid assays for

Table 4. Properties of Human and Murine TCGF

Property	Human TCGF	Murine TCGF
Molecular Weight	15,420[a]	25,000
Elution from DEAE-Sepharose	0.05M NaCl	0.185M NaCl
Elution from CM-Sepharose	0.225M NaCl	0.05M NaCl
Isoelectric point(s)	6.5, 7.2	4.5, 5.4
Sensitivity to degradative enzymes:		
Proteases	Yes	Yes
DNAse, RNAse	No	No
Neuraminidase	No	No
Stability:		
pH	2–10	2–10
SDS	0.1%	0.1%
Urea	6M	6M
Target cell for biological activity	Activated T-cells of all mammalian species tested	Activated murine T-cells
Receptor specificity	No species restriction	Only activated murine cells

[a] By amino acid sequence.

TCGF activity. Although the ultimate test of TCGF integrity rests on its ability to support the growth of factor-dependent T-cells, assays of cell growth are much too tedious for biochemical investigations. The development of a microassay based on [^{3}H]thymidine incorporation by murine cytotoxic T-cells (93) and the adaptation of this assay for use in the human T-cell system (19) made the subsequent biochemical approaches possible. The microassays are simple and reliable, but will give false results if factors other than TCGF which stimulate thymidine uptake and cell growth are also present. Thus, as noted previously, results must be interpreted cautiously. Table 5 briefly outlines micro-thymidine incorporation assays using both murine and human TCGF-dependent indicator cells.

3.10.   Quantitation of TCGF Activity

Although thymidine incorporation assays provide a reliable indication of TCGF activity, the quantitation of this activity has been difficult and contentious. The reasons for this are the number of variables which together result in thymidine incorporation. Put more simply, as yet no easily measured unique action of TCGF has been identified which could accurately reflect

Table 5. Microassays for TCGF Activity

Murine System

1. Washed TCGF-dependent mouse cytotoxic T-lymphocytes, CTLL (93) (4 × 10^3 cells in 50 μl) are added to a microtiter well.
2. Dilutions (50 μl) of TCGF-containing material are added to each well.
3. Cells are incubated 24–48 hours at 37°C.
4. [^{3}H]Thymidine (20 μl, 20 μCi/ml) is added to each well and incubated 4 hours.
5. Cells are harvested onto filter paper strips, washed, and counted in a scintillation counter.

Human System

1. Washed human peripheral blood lymphocytes (2 × 10^5 in 50 μl) previously stimulated with PHA for 7 days and subsequently cultured for 7 days with TCGF are added to a microtiter well.
2. Dilutions (50 μl) of TCGF-containing material are added to each well.
3. Cells are incubated 72 hours at 37°C.
4. [^{3}H]Thymidine (20 μl, 20 μCi/ml) is added to each well.
5. Cells are harvested onto filter paper strips, washed, and counted in a scintillation counter.

the amount of TCGF present. The quantitative methods in current use are all relative ones in which thymidine incorporation by various factor preparations is compared with that elicited by a "standard" laboratory preparation. Thymidine incorporation by serial dilutions of the preparations is determined and dose-response curves are generated. These titrations may be graphically analyzed in several ways, for example by probit analysis (93) or by logarithmic representation (85). Whatever the method, "units" of TCGF activity have always been defined in terms of a more active standard. Although meaningful for each laboratory, it has been and will continue to be impossible to compare accurately TCGF preparations from different groups based on the published units of activity determined in this way.

4. FUNCTIONS OF TCGF

4.1. Growth of T-Cells

Obviously, the prime function of TCGF is the stimulation and maintenance of the proliferation of responsive T-cells. When proliferative T-cells are deprived of TCGF for a period of hours, proliferation stops and the cells eventually die unless TCGF is resupplied (11). It seems apparent that among normal cells, the T-cells which respond to TCGF are different from those which produce TCGF. This conclusion is based on the observation that TCGF-dependent lines do not produce TCGF, at least in sufficient quantity; the cells die unless exogenous TCGF is continually resupplied. It is not clear, however, that responder cells are incapable of TCGF production. They may merely be under the influence of a regulatory mechanism which allows only brief periods or low levels of productivity. It is also not clear whether TCGF producer cells are normally capable of responding to the factor. This situation could lead to uncontrolled cell proliferation if regulatory mechanisms were not present to control production. A T-cell capable of both producing and responding to TCGF was, in fact, one of the early models proposed to explain some forms of malignant T-cell proliferation (94; see Section 7).

4.2. Induction of Cytotoxic T-Lymphocytes

A second function of TCGF is its role in the differentiation of cytotoxic T-lymphocytes. Earlier reports showed that a soluble mediator(s) was necessary for this occurrence based on the lack of cytotoxic T-lymphocyte differentiation if metabolically inactive stimulator cells were used in a mixed lymphocyte reaction. Exogenously added "helper" factor present in cell-free supernatants from mixed lymphocyte cultures or mitogen-stimulated lymphocytes was shown to be capable of replacing the necessity for met- abolically active stimulator cells in this system in order to obtain a cytotoxic response (77, 95, 96). Purified TCGF preparations have been shown to mediate the generation of cytotoxic T-cells from thymocyte cells and re- sponder cells of spleens of nude mice (97, 98). Recently, a monoclonal antibody prepared against murine TCGF (91) was used to confirm even further the involvement of the factor in the differentiation of cytotoxic T- cells. Precipitation with the monoclonal antibody removed the ability of supernatants from mixed lymphocyte cultures of Con A-stimulated spleen cells to maintain the growth of TCGF-dependent cell lines and to help in the generation of cytotoxic T-cells (99). Absorption of the active supernatants with TCGF-dependent T-cell lines was similarly shown to remove both functions. Rigorously purified TCGF also was capable of supporting cytotoxic T-lymphocyte generation (99). Thus the role of TCGF in cytotoxic T-lym- phocyte generation seems quite probable, but rests heavily on the reported specificity of the murine monoclonal antibody for TCGF. It is also apparent that TCGF is not the only lymphokine involved in induction of cytotoxic T-cell function (100).

4.3.   Regulation of Immune Interferon Production

As previously discussed, the generation of cytotoxic T-lymphocytes re- quires TCGF. In addition, immune interferon (IFNγ) is apparently required for this process. The evidence in support of this is twofold. First, in the murine system, it has been shown that antibody to immune interferon blocks the induction of cytotoxic T-cells by TCGF (101). This same antibody did not diminish the ability of TCGF to support the growth of T-lymphocytes, however. Second, multiple factors secreted by a human helper T-cell clone were partially purified from conditioned media and fractions with immune interferon activity and TCGF activity were separated by gel filtration (70). A fraction with molecular weight of 45,000–50,000 possessed interferon activity and also helped in the induction of cytotoxic T-cells. Both these activities were heat and acid-labile. The anti-viral activity was not due to α-interferon (IFNα) as shown by lack of absoprtion with a monoclonal anti-IFNα. In contrast, a second fraction with a molecular weight of 15,000– 20,000 possessed TCGF activity as well as helper activity for cytotoxic T- cell induction. The ability of this fraction to induce cytotoxic T-cells was heat stable. Thus these experiments suggest that more than one molecular species helps in cytotoxic T-cell differentiation and that the factor involved in addition to TCGF is IFNγ.

Recent evidence suggests that IFNγ and TCGF may not merely function together in the differentiation of cytotoxic T-cells, but that the production of IFNγ may, in fact, be regulated by TCGF. First, both the induction of IFNγ and the differentiation of cytotoxic T-lymphocytes follow a similar TCGF dose-response curve (101). Second, both a Lyt-1$^+$ helper cell and Lyt-2$^+$ lymphocyte are necessary for IFNγ production in mitogen-stimulated spleen cell cultures, as shown by experiments in which the particular cell populations were depleted using monoclonal antibodies plus complement (102). TCGF could substitute for the Lyt-1$^+$ helper cells in the induction of IFNγ, suggesting that it was the factor responsible for the help given by Lyt-1$^+$ cells. It was concluded that Lyt-2$^+$ cells were the IFNγ producer cells that functioned in response to the influence of TCGF. Further regulation of these events was suggested by the participation of suppressor cells capable of absorbing TCGF from the media, and thus inhibiting IFNγ production. The nature and function of these suppressor cells is not completely understood, however. They may be activated T-cells possessing TCGF receptors and thus capable of absorbing TCGF and thereby preventing its action. This suggestion has also been made by others (103), although this mechanism has yet to be proven. Nevertheless, an attractive hypothesis for the interaction of macrophages, T-cells, and regulatory molecules in the induction of cytotoxic T-cells has now been presented and may be rigorously tested. The events involved would include the following:

1. Production of IL-1 by antigen-activated macrophages.
2. Induction of TCGF production by T-cells under the stimulus of IL-1.
3. Production of IFNγ by precytotoxic T-cells and their differentiation to cytotoxic T-cells under the stimulus of TCGF.
4. Abrogation of IFNγ production and cytotoxic T-cell generation by suppressor cells possibly functioning by the removal of TCGF from the medium.

4.4 Role in B-Lymphocyte Differentiation

It has been suggested in the past that TCGF plays a role in the activation or differentiation of B-lymphocytes to immunoglobulin-producing cells (104–106). Helper T-cells are involved in this process, and function through soluble products, yet the identity of these lymphokines has not been elucidated. As has been mentioned, conditioned media from lectin-activated peripheral blood lymphocyte cultures contain a number of lymphokine activities. Ascribing functions to particular biochemical entities has been difficult. It is known that helper T-cells or helper factor(s), in particular one called T-cell replacing factor(s) (TRF), are involved in the generation of immunoglobulin-secreting B-cells (107). The nature of the factor(s) possessing this activity has not been determined and even very recent literature contains contradictions. According to recent studies in the rat system, TCGF provides helper activity for differentiation of rat B-cells (108). However, the TCGF used in these experiments was purified only by gel filtration and was not examined for other factor activities which could have explained the observations. Colony-stimulating factor (CSF) which is present in lymphocyte-conditioned media was separated by phenyl-Sepharose chromatography from TCGF (109). Studies of these two factors in the murine system concluded clearly that CSF did not possess helper activity for B-cells, and thus attributed this activity to the TCGF fraction. In this case also, the TCGF was not further purified. A more definitive study was recently published indicating that human factors responsible for differentiation of cytotoxic T-cells and immunoglobulin-secreting B-cells reside on different molecules (70). The basis of this conclusion was differential absorption of the activities from supernatants of a helper T-cell clone possessing both activities with either a TCGF-dependent cytotoxic T-cell line or a B-cell line capable of differentiation to an IgG-producing state. The recent studies of Pure et al. (110) also lead to the conclusion that TCGF is not responsible for the induction of differentiation of B-cells. These latter studies are the most conclusive and correlate with reports of a distinct factor with B-cell growth activity (111). The studies of Nakanishi et al. (112) point out in addition that while B-cell growth factor is necessary for B-cell proliferation, two TRFs are required for differentiation to immunoglobulin-secreting cells. While TCGF does not seem to play a role in this latter anti-IgM stimulating system, its role in all B-cell responses has not been ruled out. It still would be worthwhile to see the results of studies carried out with TCGF purified to homogeneity and T-cell depleted B-cells.

5.   REGULATION OF TCGF

Because of the multiplicity of interactions which occur during the induction of TCGF production and its subsequent function in T-cell proliferation and effector cell differentiation, there are many steps at which its actions could effectively be controlled. A number of possible regulatory phenomena has been observed *in vitro*; it is not yet known which, if any, or if an as yet undiscovered mechanism, functions *in vivo*. As shown in Fig. 1, regulatory mechanisms could occur at any step in the pathway. Regulatory controls already have been identified which could possibly affect TCGF actions in all three categories: activation, production, and proliferation. TCGF is hormonelike in that it functions through a receptor mechanism (71, 113, 114; see Section 8). Substances that prevent the formation of receptors prevent the development of TCGF-responsive cells. Thus for any TCGF effect to be expressed, specific receptors must be induced. The mechanism(s) by which this induction occurs is not known, but clearly this step in the process involving antigen recognition and cellular response is influenced by immune response gene products. The interaction of antigen, macrophages, and TCGF producer-precursor cells leading to TCGF production is also a prime area for control. This process too is controlled in part by the immune response gene products. In addition, a monokine (LAF,IL-1) is produced as a result of this interaction which functions in inducing the "second signal," TCGF. Here some known agents which may function physiologically have been identified. Prostaglandins, for example, which are secreted by monocytes, are known to inhibit the synthesis of lymphokines (26, 27). Thus the monocyte-macrophage may play an even greater regulatory role by elaborating both a TCGF inducer, LAF, and an inhibitor of TCGF production, prostaglandin. Clearly, the control of these synthetic events must be finely tuned.

TCGF production is affected by controls on T-cell activation and IL-1 production, but in addition it is also apparently regulated directly by physiologic effectors. Glucocorticoids have been shown to abrogate the production of TCGF directly (115). These agents also suppress LAF production and activity but also suppress TCGF production directly as shown by the inability of exogenously added LAF to restore TCGF production in glucocorticoid-treated cultures (116). Whether glucocorticoid hormones play a role in regulating *in vivo* TCGF production normally is not known, although they are known to be potent immunosuppressive agents.

Finally, once TCGF is synthesized and T-cells are proliferating in response, control mechanisms must operate to turn off production, diminish available TCGF pools, or limit the number of TCGF-responsive receptor-bearing T-cells. One of the simplest regulatory devices to control the continued proliferation of specific T-cell clones would be competition among various activated T-cells for available factor. The induction of specific suppressor cells to either absorb out available TCGF (103) or turn off TCGF production (24) has been suggested. A true feedback regulatory mechanism, characteristic of other hormones, has not yet been identified in this system (93).

6.   THERAPEUTIC USES OF TCGF

An important potential use for TCGF may be in the therapy of various immune deficiency diseases. In this regard a number of experiments have been carried out using athymic (nu/nu) mice which fail to produce TCGF, at least when they are young (64–66), but can respond to TCGF (64). When such nude mice are treated with TCGF they become capable of generating cytotoxic effector cells in response to antigens (97, 117).

An additional use of TCGF lies in the ability to generate cytotoxic T-cell lines and maintain their long-term growth *in vitro*. Cytotoxic T-cells with tumor cell specificity can be generated *in vitro* and inoculated back into a patient in order to decrease tumor load. This has been attempted in the murine system with limited success (14). Some inhibition of tumor growth was observed, but the effect was not long lasting. One explanation for the brief response might be that there was insufficient TCGF *in vivo* to sustain the growth of the cytotoxic T-cells. Indeed, the administration of TCGF together with cytotoxic cells has been shown to augment the therapeutic effect of the cells (118). Recently, studies have been initiated to determine methods for maintaining adequate serum levels of TCGF following *in vivo* administration in mice (119). These techniques will be important for any clinical applications of TCGF in humans.

A number of immune deficiency diseases of humans are potential targets for therapeutic uses of TCGF. Such treatment might be effective if the T-cell deficiency resulted from the lack of synthesis of TCGF with the retention of the ability to respond to exogenous TCGF. A recent study on two patients with Nezelof's syndrome showed that T-cells of one patient were, in fact, able to respond to TCGF *in vitro* with improved proliferative responses to antigenic stimulation and generation of cytotoxic effector cells in mixed lymphocyte culture (120). A brief *in vivo* trial similarly suggested that T-cells could respond to TCGF and that the immune defect was therefore in the synthesis of the lymphokine. The cells of the second patient were less responsive to exogenous TCGF and a TCGF deficiency was less apparent. Presumably factors other than impaired TCGF synthesis contributed to the immune deficiency in this patient. In the same report, the cells of three children with severe combined immunodeficiency syndrome failed to respond to TCGF *in vitro* indicating impaired responsiveness. Studies on the therapeutic effectiveness of TCGF in other T-cell deficiencies are contemplated, notably in the acquired immunodeficiency syndrome.

7.   TCGF AND LEUKEMOGENESIS

Although TCGF may well have very important therapeutic uses, it is also clear that the factor has the potential to support unrestrained proliferation of T-cells if regulatory controls are disrupted. A mechanism whereby growth controls could be circumvented would involve, in this case, T-cells capable of both producing and responding to TCGF. In the case of malignant T-cells, constitutive TCGF production has been observed in some cell lines established from cells of patients with malignancies of mature T-cells (57). In these cases, the cells were also capable of responding to TCGF as shown by their ability to absorb TCGF as well as by their enhanced growth when exogenous TCGF was added to the culture medium. The TCGF produced by these leukemic T-cells was shown to be biochemically distinct from the TCGF produced by normal PHA-stimulated peripheral blood T-cells or other T-cell lines (71; see Table 3). Differences in the biologic activity of, or the responses to, this leukemic TCGF are currently under investigation. It seems likely that the production of a variant form of TCGF by leukemic cells arises from a clonal expansion of one of a spectrum of "normal" TCGF molecules as a result of an *in vitro* growth advantage. There is not necessarily any relevance to the process of malignant transformation.

The malignant T-cell lines described previously which were shown to produce TCGF constitutively also release a human retrovirus (RNA tumor virus) called the human T-cell leukemia/lymphoma virus (HTLV; 58–64). Molecular biologic studies have shown that the virus is not an endogenous (i.e., germ-line transmitted) retrovirus (60, 121). In addition, the ability of the virus to be horizontally transmitted naturally has been suggested by several sero-epidemiologic studies (122–126). Indeed, direct infection of human adult or cord blood T-cells by cell-free virus or virus-infected cells has also been demonstrated (61, 127–129). Other studies have shown that although normal lymphocytes require activation by mitogens or antigens in order to respond to TCGF, cells from patients with these mature T-cell malignancies are capable of responding with no prior lectin activation as if they were already activated (130). In earlier experiments we have shown that following antigen or mitogen stimulation, T-cells acquire an activation antigen on the surface, detected with a monoclonal antibody, termed HAA (131). We have also obtained preliminary evidence that retroviruses can also induce the expression of the same HAA (131). It is interesting to speculate that HAA might be involved in some step in T-cell proliferation. A second monoclonal antibody, anti-Tac (132, 133) is believed to be directed against the TCGF receptor (134), although some contradictory evidence exists on this point (see Section 8.3). The Tac antigen is expressed on activated T-cells and is found in high amounts on all cells so far examined which are infected with HTLV (61). An hypothesis for leukemogenesis by a virus such as HTLV might then encompass HTLV infection of T-cells with subsequent provirus integration into the cellular genome at a location leading to derepression of the TCGF receptor gene. Could this in itself be sufficient cause for malignancy? The infected cell might not be regulated by normal control mechanisms and continue to respond to TCGF produced *in vivo* as a consequence of natural environmental stimuli. If, as has been reported (57), some HTLV-infected cells also produce TCGF, these cells might have even more of a growth advantage and certainly would be easily observed upon *in vitro* culturing. Recent experiments have made clear, however, that contrary to a model proposed earlier (94), T-cell leukemogenesis does not in general result from induction of cells which both produce and respond to TCGF. The majority of cord blood T-cells transformed by HTLV were found not to produce TCGF, although they were anti-Tac positive (129). The technology is now available for testing the above hypothesis. Cloned probes of HTLV have been obtained (135) and preliminary experiments have shown that leukemic cells from HTLV-infected patients are monoclonal with regard to the site of provirus integration (136). Monoclonality is essential for hypotheses explaining transformation as a result of activation of specific genes involved in certain aspects of cell growth. It is also of interest that a specific cellular gene has been found to have increased expression following HTLV infection (137). Experiments to determine the nature of the gene product and whether it is involved in any way with regulation and/or growth of T-cells are underway. The availability of cloned probes for TCGF (see Section 9) enables this question of a possible interaction of HTLV and TCGF in leukemogenesis to be investigated more directly.

8. TCGF RECEPTORS

The realization that, whereas antigens and lectins can stimulate T-cells, T-cell growth is dependent on TCGF, brings into focus two obligatory steps in a sustained T-cell proliferative response: the production of TCGF and the acquisition of a state of responsiveness to TCGF by antigen-activated T-cells. Such a concept envisions a signaling apparatus that converts an exogenous antigenic stimulus into an endogenous hormonelike control system involving lymphokines (73, 116). In many ways TCGF functions like a polypeptide hormone. Its effect on the clonal expansion of T-cell populations is strictly concentration-dependent. It only acts on antigen or lectin-activated T-cells and has no mitogenic activity on unstimulated lymphocytes, activated B-cells, or cells of other lineages (13, 22, 73, 116). Further, TCGF activity is absorbed only by activated T-cells (22, 57) and such absorption is time, temperature, and cell-concentration dependent. Also, viable cells and glutaraldehyde-fixed cells are equally effective in absorbing TCGF activity. These findings strongly suggest a mechanism for the interaction of TCGF with T-cells involving specific cell-surface binding sites (22, 57).

8.1 Direct Demonstration of TCGF Receptors

Direct evidence for TCGF receptors was obtained by binding studies using metabolically radiolabeled human TCGF (113). Serial dilutions of [^{35}S]methionine or [^{3}H]leucine, [^{3}H]lysine-labeled TCGF were incubated at 37°C with $0.5 - 2 \times 10^6$ cells in a total volume of 200 μl of RPMI1640 medium supplemented with 25 mM HEPES buffer, pH 7.2, and 10 mg/ml of bovine serum albumin in 1.5 ml Eppendorf centrifuge tubes. After various time intervals, the reaction mixtures were analyzed for free radioactive TCGF in the medium and bound radioactivity on the cell. Such experiments

Table 6. Presence of Cell Surface Receptors for TCGF on Murine and Primate Cells[a]

Cell Type	Stimulant	Binding of [^{35}S]TCGF
Mouse Cells		
Splenocytes	None	−
Thymocytes	None	−
Splenocytes	Con A	+
Splenocytes	Alloantigen	+
Thymocytes	Con A	+
Splenocytes	LPS	−
CTLL-2, subclone 15H	None	+
CTLL-2, subclone 15H (glutaraldehyde-fixed)	None	+
Human Cells		
Peripheral blood mononuclear	None	±
Peripheral blood mononuclear	PHA	+
	Alloantigen	+
HUT102, clone B2	None	+
Molt 4	None	−
CCRF-CEM	None	−
JURKAT	−	−[b]
Gibbon Cells		
MLA144	None	+

[a] From Robb et al., (113).

[b] JURKAT cells were shown to bind a monoclonal antibody against a cell surface antigen (TAC) believed to be the TCGF receptor (134).

clearly showed a saturable binding of TCGF to activated T-cells (113). At 37°C, the binding reached a maximum at about 15 minutes. The same maximum was also reached at 4°C, but only after 60 minutes of incubation. The kinetics of binding were similar for a TCGF-dependent cytotoxic murine T-cell clone, CTLL, and for PHA-stimulated human peripheral blood lymphocytes. In both cases the binding of radiolabeled TCGF was blocked by the presence of unlabeled TCGF. In addition, the binding of TCGF was shown to be reversible.

The binding of TCGF followed a very strict specificity pattern. Only TCGF-dependent or responsive cells (activated human peripheral blood lymphocytes, Con A or alloantigen-stimulated mouse splenocytes, cloned murine cytotoxic and helper T-cells, etc.) showed binding of TCGF (Table 6). Several established T-cell lines that grow independently of TCGF had no TCGF receptors. Some neoplastic T-cell lines that constitutively produce TCGF (HUT102, clone B2, and MLA144) and have no TCGF requirement for growth, nonetheless expressed TCGF receptors. On the other hand, the JURKAT cell line which produces TCGF does not bind the factor. The binding of TCGF is not blocked by a large number of other growth factors, including epidermal growth factor, nerve growth factor, fibroblast growth factor, lymphocyte activating factor, colony-stimulating factor, erythropoietin, insulin, interferon type 1 and type 2, multiplication-stimulating activity, PHA, and Con A (113). TCGFs with varying levels of sialylation all show the same high degree of competition. The species specificity observed in T-cell proliferative responses was also reflected in the receptor studies. Although unlabeled TCGF from JURKAT cells competed equally for the binding of [^{35}S]methionine-TCGF to both PHA-stimulated human peripheral blood lymphoblasts and murine CTLL cells, TCGF produced by Con A-activated rat spleen cells was only able to block the binding of the labeled human TCGF to murine CTLL cells.

8.2. Correlation Between TCGF Binding and Proliferative Response

Is there a significant correlation between binding of TCGF molecules and the proliferative response of the cell? This question was analyzed by Robb et al. (113) by comparing the receptor binding and the observed thymidine incorporation by the same cells as a function of TCGF concentration. The results showed a significant degree of correlation between the two events. The TCGF concentration that stimulated a given fraction of the maximum proliferation was similar to the concentration of TCGF that resulted in the same fraction of receptor site occupancy. The maximum biological response was obtained at a TCGF concentration that corresponded to approximately 90% saturation of the binding sites.

Like most peptide hormones (138, 139), TCGF appears to be internalized after being bound to the receptor (113). The evidence for this is somewhat indirect, but convincing. Thus cell-bound TCGF becomes degraded in a time and temperature-dependent fashion. The process is blocked by agents such as NH_4Cl and chloroquine which have been shown to prevent lysosomal degradation of internalized hormones (138–140). Further, degradation of labeled TCGF can be prevented if the binding is performed in the presence of 25 mM unlabeled TCGF, a concentration that nearly completely inhibits the specific binding of the labeled TCGF.

8.3. Affinity and Abundance of TCGF Receptors

Direct binding measurements using labeled TCGF showed a single class of receptors on the TCGF-responsive murine and human cells. The affinity of binding was quite high, the Kd being on the order of 20 pM for murine cells and 5–8 pM for PHA-stimulated peripheral blood lymphocytes, a human (HUT102, clone B2), and a gibbon (MLA144) cell line (113). The number of receptors per cell was found to be 10,000–15,000 from Scatchard plots (141) of the binding data (113).

A monoclonal antibody (anti-TAC) raised against a human cultured T-cell line derived from the peripheral blood of a patient with a malignant variant of a cutaneous T-cell lymphoma (the same patient whose lymph node was the source of the HUT102 cells described elsewhere in this chapter; 132) appears to bind to the receptor for TCGF. The monoclonal antibody reacts with activated functionally mature T-cells (134), can block the binding of radiolabeled TCGF to a cloned human continuous T-cell line, and also can suppress TCGF-induced proliferation of T-cells (134). Immune precipitation of lysates of cells metabolically labeled with either [^{35}S]methionine or [^{3}H]glucosamine, or labeled *in vitro* with [^{125}I] identified a 47,000–53,000 molecular weight glycoprotein as the antigen reacting with monoclonal anti-Tac (134).

Although the data obtained with the monoclonal anti-Tac suggest that the Tac antigen might be the receptor for TCGF, some observations are difficult to explain on that basis. First, the number of TCGF binding sites per cell has been estimated at about 10,000–15,000, whereas similar T-cells appear to bind approximately 100,000 anti-Tac molecules. The authors attribute this difference to differences in the experimental binding conditions and somewhat different derivations of the cell lines (134). The dissociation constant for the antibody binding is 100-fold higher than for TCGF binding. This, however, may merely indicate a low-affinity antibody. Second, perhaps the most conspicuous discordance between the results of these two sets of studies is that, by direct TCGF binding, no receptors were detected on HSB-

2 or JURKAT cells whereas 20–25% of these cells reacted with anti-Tac upon induction. Induced JURKAT cells possessed approximately 80,000 antibody binding sites per Tac(+) cell (142). This crucial difference seen on cells which produce TCGF bears further careful investigation. Conversely, MLA144 cells which also produce TCGF also bound labeled TCGF but did not react with anti-Tac. This difference might be explained by a type-specific determinant recognized by anti-Tac in the human TCGF receptor, but not in the receptor of the MLA144 gibbon line. Based on these differences, it is difficult at this time to conclude that Tac antigen and TCGF receptor are one and the same. If not the same, both the observed blocking of TCGF binding and the inhibition of T-cell proliferation by anti-Tac may be caused by possible overlap of Tac antigen and TCGF receptor, or by some steric hindrance. Binding of the antibody could, therefore, block the access of TCGF to its receptor and, in turn, inhibit all the cellular events that normally follow TCGF activation.

9. CLONING OF THE TCGF GENE

As referred to before, a major advance in the area of T-cell biology would arise from the successful cloning of the gene encoding TCGF. Not only would this allow molecular biologic studies concerning regulation of TCGF activity in both normal and neoplastic T-cells, but it would also provide a rapid and inexpensive means of generating large amounts of TCGF for biologic and therapeutic uses. The approach to cloning the TCGF gene has been by means of translation of mRNA isolated from good TCGF producer cells with the aim of identifying specific message for cDNA production and eventual cloning. Two groups have used the *Xenopus laevis* oocyte system for translation of mRNA. Bleackley et al. translated poly(A)-containing mRNA isolated from the murine EL4 thymoma line which produces high levels of TCGF following stimulation with phorbol myristate acetate (143). A biologically active product was obtained which allowed the growth of a cytotoxic T-cell line and which possessed an appropriate molecular weight on gel filtration of 31,000. Lin et al. also used the oocyte system to translate poly(A)-containing mRNA from the gibbon TCGF producer line, MLA144 (144). A product was obtained that stimulated thymidine incorporation by TCGF-dependent T-cells. Cell proliferation could not be demonstrated, however, apparently due to the use of insufficient quantities of oocyte fluid. Although inhibition of thymidine incorporation stimulated by the oocyte translation product was observed following treatment with monoclonal antibodies to human TCGF, the specificity of the monoclonal antibodies used (92) has not been rigorously tested. The concentrations of the monoclonal antibodies necessary to inhibit TCGF activity are very high (100 μg/ml) relative to the amount of TCGF present in [³H]thymidine incorporation microassays. This suggests some lack of specificity or else very low affinity antibody binding to determinants removed from the active site of the molecule. Although these antibodies have been reported to bind TCGF by immunoaffinity chromatography (92), the material bound has not been characterized.

A third approach at translating TCGF mRNA has made use of the rabbit reticulocyte system and poly(A)-containing mRNA from the human JURKAT TCGF producer cells (145). This study has been the most complete, showing the production of a biologically active product as well as immunoprecipitation using a monoclonal antibody to rat TCGF (91). Analysis of the immuno-precipitates showed proteins of 16,000, 27,000, and 48,000 daltons which are reasonable candidates for monomeric and multimeric TCGF. The biological activity of these resultant proteins has not yet been demonstrated.

Successful cloning of the gene for human TCGF has been achieved by two laboratories, one of them our own. In one approach (47), cDNA molecules of >600 base pairs, prepared using fractionated mRNA from con A-induced JURKAT cells that were capable of programming the synthesis of biologically active TCGF in *Xenopus* oocytes, were introduced into the plasmid PBR322 using the standard G-C tailing method (146). The resulting hybrid plasmid was used to transform *Escherichia coli* K-12 and to prepare a cDNA library. This library was screened by an mRNA hybridization procedure as follows. Hybrid plasmids were prepared from groups of 24 bacterial clones and aliquots of each plasmid group were cleaved, denatured, and bound to nitrocellulose filters. These filters were then hybridized to poly(A)-RNA from induced JURKAT cells. Hybridized RNA was then recovered, purified, and injected into *Xenopus* oocytes to identify the group that hybridized to TCGF mRNA. By this procedure 1 out of 18 groups, each consisting of 24 clones, gave a positive result. The procedure was repeated using the plasmid DNAs prepared from the individual clones of the positive group to identify the cDNA clone coding for TCGF gene. These experiments of Taniguchi et al. (47) gave them a cDNA clone consisting of 650 base pairs which was apparently shorter than the corresponding mRNA (11-12S). However, screening a second cDNA library by in situ hybridization using a ³²P-labeled cDNA insert from the initial clone yielded a second clone containing a plasmid whose cDNA insert consisted of about 880 base pairs (47).

Using a different approach, our laboratory, in collaboration with two other groups, has also succeeded in obtaining cDNA clones coding for human TCGF (48). We purified human TCGF to homogeneity and determined its partial amino acid sequence. The amino acid sequence data were used to synthesize oligonucleotide hybridization probes for screening a cDNA library prepared from lectin-stimulated normal peripheral blood lymphocytes.

From the amino acid sequence, we selected the pentapeptide Lys-Phe-Tyr-Met-Pro which can be represented by a relatively small pool of oligonucleotides. Based on this pentapeptide, we synthesized the pool of 8 tetradecapeptides which contain all of the oligonucleotides that are complementary to the first 14 nucleotides of the codons for these amino acids in the TCGF gene. Also, from the recently published sequence of JURKAT cDNA clone (47) we synthesized 2 more unique oligonucleotide probes to facilitate our cloning effort. Using these oligonucleotides directly as hybridization probes, we identified 6 cDNA clones from among 40,000 clones screened that hybridized to all 3 probes. Five of these clones had inserts ranging in size between 800 and 900 base pairs while the insert from the sixth clone was approximately 1100 base pairs. All 6 clones contained the recognition sequences for the restriction enzymes Xba I and Stu I, suggesting, along with the hybridization data, that they were all derived from the same mRNA. We subsequently determined the nucleotide sequence of all or part of these clones confirming that they encoded the protein that we had sequenced. That the cDNA clones that were isolated encoded biologically active TCGF was demonstrated by TCGF production by mammalian cells after the introduction of appropriately engineered expression plasmids containing the TCGF coding region by DNA transfection methods.

Analysis of cellular DNA by Southern blot hybridization using the cloned cDNA probes has revealed that TCGF is present in human cells as a single-copy cellular gene containing an undetermined number of introns (48). In a variety of human cells, including both normal and neoplastic cells, the TCGF gene did not show either polymorphism or rearrangements (48). The expression of the TCGF gene in cells was specifically correlated with the production of TCGF. Cells induced to produce TCGF showed abundant expression of TCGF mRNA, while no detectable mRNA was found in uninduced cells (48).

10. CONCLUDING REMARKS

The discovery of T-cell growth factor in 1976 has enabled significant progress in many biologic systems involved with the growth of T-cells. Relatively little is yet known, however, about the mechanism of action of TCGF or its regulation, and how both these processes may be altered in disease states. It seems certain that with the recent advances in the purification of the factor and its cloning, these more basic questions will soon be addressed. In the not so distant future a review on TCGF will undoubtedly include many clinicial applications of bacterial-derived human TCGF and will also deal with questions of the immune regulation and interaction of T-cells with other components of the hematopoietic system by means of the lymphokines they generate. We hope these future experiments will also have bearing on T-cell leukemogenesis and, in addition, will provide lessons of a more general nature for the growth factor field.

REFERENCES

1. Metcalf, D., *Hemopoietic Colonies: In Vitro Cloning of Normal and Leukemic Cells*, Springer-Verlag, Berlin, 1977.

2. Gerber, P., Whang-Peng, J., and Monroe, J. R., *Proc. Natl. Acad. Sci. USA*, **63**, 740 (1969).

3. Collins, S. J., Gallo, R. C., and Gallagher, R. E., *Nature*, **270**, 347 (1977).

4. Moore, G. E., and Minowada, J., *N. Engl. J. Med.*, **288**, 106 (1973).

5. Royston, I., Smith, R. W., Buell, D. N., Huang, E. S., and Pagano, J. S., *Nature*, **251**, 745 (1974).

6. Morgan, D. A., Ruscetti, F. W., and Gallo, R. C., *Science*, **193**, 1007 (1976).

7. Kasakura, S., and Lowenstein, L., *Nature*, **208**, 794 (1965).

8. Gordon, J., and Maclean, L. D., *Nature*, **208**, 795 (1965).

9. Oppenheim, J. J., Mizel, S. B., and Meltzer, M. S., in S. Cohen, E. Pick, and J. J. Oppenheim, Eds., *Biology of the Lymphokines*, Academic, New York, 1979.

10. Aarden, L. A., Brunner, T. K., Cerottini, J.-C., Dayer, J.-M., deWeck, A. L., Dinarello, C. A., Di Sabato, G., Farrar, J. J., Gery, I., Gillis, S., Handschumacher, R. E., Henney, C. S., Hoffman, M. K., Koopman, W. J., Krane, S. M., Lachman, L. B., Lefkowits, I., Mishell, R. I., Mizel, S. B., Oppenheim, J. J., Paetkau, V., Plate, J., Röllinghoff, M., Rosenstreich, D., Rosenthal, A. S., Rosenwasser, L. J., Schimpl, A., Shin, H. S., Simon, P. L., Smith, K. A., Wagner, H., Watson, J. D., Wecker, E., and Wood, D. D., *J. Immunol.*, **123**, 2928 (1979).

11. Ruscetti, F. W., Morgan, D. A., and Gallo, R. C., *J. Immunol.*, **119**, 131 (1977).

12. Gillis, S., and Smith, K. A., *Nature*, **268**, 154 (1977).

13. Ruscetti, F. W., and Gallo, R. C., *Blood*, **57**, 379 (1981).

14. Gillis, S., and Watson, J. *Immunol. Rev.*, **54**, 81 (1981).

15. Fleischer, B., *J. Immunol. Methods*, **47**, 191 (1981).

16. Bonnard, G. B., Yasaka, K., and Maca, R. D., *Cell. Immunol.*, **51**, 390 (1980).

17. Moretta, A., Colombatti, M., and Chapuis, B., *Clin. Exp. Immunol.*, **44**, 262 (1981).

18. Alvarez, J. M., de Landazuri, M. O., Bonnard, G. D., and Herberman, R. B., *J. Immunol.*, **121**, 1270 (1978).

19. Ruscetti, F. W., Mier, J. W., and Gallo, R. C., *J. Supramol. Struct.*, **13**, 229 (1980).

20. Schwartz, R. H., Yano, A., and Paul, W. E., *Immunol. Rev.*, **40**, 153 (1978).

21. Thomas, D. W., Yamashita, U., and Shevach, E. M., *Immunol. Rev.*, **35**, 116 (1977).

22. Coutinho, A., Larsson, E.-L., Gronuck, K. O., and Anderson, J., *Eur. J. Immunol.*, **9**, 587 (1979).

23. Bonnard, G. D., Yasaka, K., and Jacobson, D., *J. Immunol.*, **123**, 2704 (1979).

24. Gullberg, M., Ivars, F., Coutinho, A., and Larsson, E.-L., *J. Immunol.*, **127**, 407 (1981).

25. Flower, R. J., and Vane, J. R., *Biochem. Pharmacol.*, **23**, 1439 (1978).

26. Goodwin, J. S., Bankhurst, A. D., and Messner, R. P., *J. Exp. Med.*, **146**, 1719 (1977).

27. Goodwin, J. S., Messner, R. P., and Peake, G. T., *J. Clin. Invest.*, **62**, 753 (1978).

28. Tanaka, Y., Sugamura, K., and Hinuma, Y., *Microb. Immunol.*, **25**, 1077 (1981).

29. Inouye, H., Hank, J. A., Chardonsens, X., Segall, M., Alter, B. J., and Bach, F. H., *J. Exp. Med.*, **152**, 143s (1980).

30. Farrar, J. J., Mizel, S. B., Fuller-Farrar, J., Farrar, W. L., and Hilfiker, M. L., *J. Immunol.*, **125**, 793 (1980).

31. Fuller-Farrer, J., Hilfiker, M. L., Farrar, W. L., and Farrar, J. J., *Cell. Immunol.* **58**, 156 (1981).

32. Stadler, B., Farrar, J. J., and Oppenheim, J. J., *Behring Inst. Mitt.*, **67**, 245 (1980).

33. Rosenstreich, D. L., and Mizel, S. B., *J. Immunol.*, **123**, 1749 (1979).

34. Sando, J. J., Hilfiker, M. L., Salomon, D. S., and Farrar, J. J., *Proc. Natl. Acad. Sci. USA*, **78**, 1189 (1981).

35. Rosenstreich, D. L., and Mizel, S. B., *Immunol. Rev.*, **40**, 102 (1978).

36. Larsson, E. L., Iscove, N. N., and Coutinho, A., *Nature*, **283**, 664 (1980).

37. Smith, K. A., Lachman, L. B., Oppenheim, J. J., and Favata, M. F., *J. Exp. Med.*, **151**, 1551 (1980).

38. Epstein, L., in M. Stewart, Ed., *Interferons and Their Actions*, Cleveland, 1977.

39. Prival, J. T., Paran, M., Gallo, R. C., and Wu, A. M., *J. Natl. Cancer Inst.*, **53**, 1583 (1974).

40. Watson, J., Aarden, L. and Lefkovits, I., *J. Immunol.*, **122**, 209 (1979).

41. Blyden, G., and Hanschumacher, R. E., *J. Immunol.*, **118**, 1631 (1977).

42. Duncan, M. R., George, F. W., and Hadden, J. W., *J. Immunol.*, **129**, 56 (1982).

43. Schrader, J. W., *J. Immunol.*, **126**, 452 (1981).

44. Glasebrook, A. L., Kelso, A., Zubler, R. H., Ely, J. M., Prystowsky, M. B., and Fitch, F. W., in C. G. Fathman and F. W. Fitch, Eds., *Isolation, Characterization, and Utilization of T-Lymphocytes*, Academic, New York, 1983.

45. Schrader, J. W., and Clark-Lewis, I., *J. Immunol.*, **129**, 30 (1982).

46. Kelso, A., Glasebrook, A. L., Kanagawa, O., and Brunner, K. T., *J. Immunol.*, **129**, 550 (1982).

47. Taniguchi, T., Matsui, H., Fujita, T., Takaoka, C., Kashima, N., Yoshimoto, R., and Hamuro, J., *Nature*, **302**, 305 (1983).

48. Clark, S. C., Arya, S. K., Wong-Staal, F., Matsumoto-Kobayashi, M., Kay, R. B., Kaufman, R. J., Brown, E. L. Shoemaker, C., Copeland, T., Oroszlan, S., Smith, K., Sarngadharan, M. G., Lindner, S. G., and Gallo, R. C., Submitted.

49. Gillis, S., Scheid, M., and Watson, J., *J. Immunol.*, **125**, 2570 (1980).

50. Gillis, S., and Watson, J., *J. Exp. Med.*, **152**, 1709 (1980).

51. Schwenk, H.-U., and Schneider, U., *Blut*, **31**, 299 (1975).

52. Anderson, D. W., Hayward, A., and Jones, C., *Immunol. Commun.*, **10**, 697 (1981).

53. Rabin, H., Hopkins, R. F., III, Ruscetti, F. W., Neubauer, R. H., Brown, R. L., and Kawakami, T. G., *J. Immunol.*, **127**, 1852 (1981).

54. Kawakami, T. G., Huff, S. D., Buckley, P. M., Dungworth, D. C., Snyder, J. P., and Gilden, R. V., *Nature, New Biol.*, **235**, 170 (1972).

55. Markham, P. D., Ruscetti, F. W., Salahuddin, S. Z., Gallagher, R. E., and Gallo, R. C., *Int. J. Cancer*, **23**, 148 (1979).

56. Markham, P. D., Ruscetti, F. W., Kalyanaraman, V. S., Ceccherini-Nelli, L., Miller, N. R., Reitz, M. S., Salahuddin, S. Z., and Gallo, R. C., *Cancer Res.*, **41**, 2738 (1981).

57. Gootenberg, J. E., Ruscetti, F. W., Mier, J. W., Gazdar, A., and Gallo, R. C., *J. Exp. Med.*, **154**, 1403 (1981).

58. Poiesz, B. J., Ruscetti, F. W., Gazdar, A. F., Bunn, P. A., Minna, J. D., and Gallo, R. C., *Proc. Natl. Acad. Sci. USA*, **77**, 7415 (1980).

59. Poiesz, B. J., Ruscetti, F. W., Reitz, M. S., Kalyanaraman, V. S., and Gallo, R. C., *Nature*, **294**, 268 (1981).

60. Gallo, R. C., Mann, D., Broder, S., Ruscetti, F. W., Maeda, M., Kalyanaraman, V. S., Robert-Guroff, M., and Reitz, M. S., Jr., *Proc. Natl. Acad. Sci. USA*, **79**, 5680 (1982).

61. Popovic, M., Sarin, P. S., Robert-Guroff, M., Kalyanaraman, V. S., Mann, D., Minowada, J., and Gallo, R. C., *Science*, **219**, 856 (1983).

62. Kalyanaraman, V. S., Sarngadharan, M. G., Robert-Guroff, M., Miyoshi, I., Blayney, D., Golde, D., and Gallo, R. C., *Science*, **218**, 571 (1982).

63. Yoshida, M., Miyoshi, I., and Hinuma, Y., *Proc. Natl. Acad. Sci. USA*, **79**, 2031 (1982).

64. Haynes, B. F., Miller, S., Palker, T., Moore, J., Dunn, P., Bolognesi, D. and Metzgar, R., *Proc. Natl. Acad. Sci. USA*, **80**, 2054 (1983).

65. Stull, D., and Gillis, S., *J. Immunol.*, **126**, 1680 (1981).

66. Okada, M., Yoshimura, N., Kaieda, T., Yamamura, Y., and Kishimoto, T., *Proc. Natl. Acad. Sci. USA*, **78**, 7717 (1981).

67. Nabel, G., Greenberger, J. S., Sakakeeny, M. A., and Cantor, H., *Proc. Natl. Acad. Sci. USA*, **78**, 1157 (1981).

68. Bianchi, A. T. J., Hooijkaas, J., and Benner, R., *Nature*, **290**, 62 (1981).

69. Ely, J. M., Prystowsky, M. B., Eisenberg, L., Quintas, J., Goldwasser, E., Glasebrook, A. L., and Fitch, F. W., *J. Immunol.*, **127**, 2345 (1981).

70. Kaieda, T., Okada, M., Yoshimura, N., Kishimoto, S., Yamamura, Y., and Kishimoto, T., *J. Immunol.*, **129**, 46 (1982).

71. Gootenberg, J. E., Ruscetti, F. W. and Gallo, R. C., *J. Immunol.*, **129**, 1499 (1982).

72. Gillis, S., Baker, P. E., Union, N. A., and Smith, K. A., *J. Exp. Med.*, **149**, 1460 (1979).

73. Smith, K. A., Baker, P. E., Gillis, S., and Ruscetti, F. W., *Molec. Immunol.*, **17**, 579 (1980).

74. MacDonald, H., Lees, R. K., Glasebrook, A. L., and Sordat, B., *J. Immunol.*, **129**, 521 (1982).

75. Wagner, H., and Rollinghoff, M., *J. Exp. Med.*, **148**, 1523 (1978).

76. Meuer, S. C., Hussey, R. E., Penta, A. C., Fitzgerald, K. A., Stadler, B. M., Schlossman, S. F., and Reinherz, E. L., *J. Immunol.*, **129**, 1076 (1982).

77. Okada, M., and Henney, C. S., *J. Immunol.*, **125**, 300 (1980).

78. Engleman, E. G., Benike, C. J., Grumet, F. C., and Evans, R. L., *J. Immunol.*, **127**, 2124 (1981).

79. Mier, J. W., and Gallo, R. C., *Proc. Natl. Acad. Sci. USA*, **77**, 6134 (1980).

80. Watson, J. D., Gillis, S., Marbrook, J., Mochizuki, D., and Smith, K. A., *J. Exp. Med.*, **150**, 849 (1979).

81. Robb, R. J., and Smith, K. A., *Molec. Immunol.*, **18**, 1087 (1981).

82. Granelli-Piperno, A., Vassalli, J. D., and Reich, E., *J. Exp. Med.*, **154**, 422 (1981).

83. Welte, K., Wang, C. Y., Mertelsmann, R., Venuta, S., Feldman, S. P., and Moore, M. A. S., *J. Exp. Med.*, **156**, 454 (1982).

84. Zoon, K. C., Smith, M. E., Bridgen, P. A., zur Needen, D., and Anfinsen, C. B., *Proc. Natl. Acad. Sci. USA*, **76**, 5601 (1979).

85. Sarngadharan, M. G., Ting, R. C., and Gallo, R. C., in D. Barnes, Ed., *Methods in Molecular and Cell Biology*, Alan Liss, New York, in press.

86. Lotze, M. T., and Rosenberg, S. A., *J. Immunol.*, **124**, 2972 (1980).

87. Fagnani, R., and Braatz, J. A., *J. Immunol. Meth.*, **33**, 313 (1980).

88. Epstein, L. B., *Methods Enzymol.*, **78**, 147 (1981).

89. Wietzerbin, J., and Falcoff, E., *Methods Enzymol.*, **78**, 552 (1981).

90. Smith, K. A., in E. Moller and G. Moller, Eds., *Genetics of the Immune Response*, Plenum, New York, 1983.

91. Gillis, S., and Henry, C. S., *J. Immunol.*, **126**, 1978 (1981).

92. Stadler, B. M., Dougherty, S. F., Carter, C., Berenstein, E. H., Fox, P. C., Siraganian, R. P., and Oppenhein, J. J., in A. L. Goldstein and M. A. Chirigos, Eds., *Lymphokines and Thymic Hormones: Their Potential Utilization in Cancer Therapeutics*, Raven, New York, 1981.

93. Gillis, S., Ferm, M. M., Ou, W., and Smith, K. A., *J. Immunol.*, **120**, 2027 (1978).

94. Gallo, R. C., in H. S. Kaplan and S. A. Rosenberg, Eds., Third Annual Bristol-Myers Symposium on Cancer Research, Academic, New York, 1982.

95. Okada, M., Klimpel, G., Kuppers, R. C., and Henney, C. S., *J. Immunol.*, **122**, 2527 (1979).

96. Okada, M., and Henney, C. S., *J. Immunol.*, **125**, 850 (1980).

97. Wagner, H., Hardt, C., Heeg, K., Rollinghoff, M., and Pfizenmaier, K., *Nature*, **284**, 278 (1980).

98. Watson, J., Aarden, L. A., and Lefkovits, I., *J. Immunol.* **122**, 209 (1979).

99. Kern, D. E., Gillis, S., Okada, M., and Henney, C. S., *J. Immunol.*, **127**, 1323 (1981).

100. Männel, D. N., Falk, W., and Dröge, W., *J. Immunol.*, **130**, 2508 (1983).

101. Farrar, W. L., Johnson, H. M., and Farrar, J. J., *J. Immunol.*, **126**, 1120 (1981).

102. Torres, B. A., Farrar, W. L., and Johnson, H. M., *J. Immunol.*, **128**, 2217 (1982).

103. Palacios, R., and Moller, G., *J. Exp. Med.*, **153**, 1360 (1981).

104. Parker, D. C., *J. Immunol.*, **129**, 469 (1982).

105. Leibson, H., Marrack, P., and Kappler, J., *J. Exp. Med.*, **154**, 1681 (1981).

106. Swain, S., Dennert, G., Warner, J., and Dutton, R., *Proc. Natl. Acad. Sci. USA*, **78**, 2517 (1981).

107. Pickel, K., Hammerling, U., and Hoffman, M. K., *Nature*, **264**, 72 (1976).

108. Rosenberg, J. S., Gilman, S. C., and Feldman, J. D., *J. Immunol.*, **129**, 996 (1982).

109. Hilfiker, M. L., Moore, R. N., and Farrar, J. J., *J. Immunol.*, **127**, 1983 (1981).

110. Pure, E., Isakson, P. C., Paetkau, V., Caplan, B., Vitetta, E. S., and Kramer, P. H., *J. Immunol.*, **129**, 2420 (1982).

111. Howard, M., Kessler, S., Chused, T., and Paul, W. E., *Proc. Natl. Acad. Sci. USA*, **78**, 5788 (1981).

112. Nakanishi, K., Howard, M., Muraguchi, A., Farrar, J., Takatsu, K., Hamaoka, T., and Paul, W. E., *J. Immunol.*, **130**, 2219 (1983).

113. Robb, R. J., Munck, A., and Smith, K. A., *J. Exp. Med.*, **154**, 1455 (1981).

114. Robb, R. J., *Immunobiology*, **161**, 21 (1982).

115. Gillis, S., Crabtree, G. R., and Smith, K. A., *J. Immunol.*, **123**, 1624 (1979).

116. Smith, K. A., *Immunol. Rev.*, **51**, 337 (1980).

117. Baker, P. E., and Smith, K. A., *Fed. Proc.*, **39**, 803 (1980).

118. Cheever, M. A., Greenberg, P. D., Fefer, A., and Gillis, S., *J. Exp. Med.*, **155**, 968 (1982).

119. Donohue, J. H., and Rosenberg, S. A., *J. Immunol.*, **130**, 2203 (1983).

120. Flomenberg, N., Welte, K., Mertelsmann, R., Kernan, N., Ciobanu, N., Venuta, S., Feldman, S. P., Kruger, G., Kirkpatrick, D., Dupont, B., and O'Reilly, R., *J. Immunol.*, **130**, 2644 (1983).

121. Reitz, M. S., Poiesz, B. J., Ruscetti, F. W., and Gallo, R. C., *Proc. Natl. Acad. Sci. USA*, **78**, 1887 (1981).

122. Robert-Guroff, M., Nakao, Y., Notake, K., Ito, Y., Sliski, A., and Gallo, R. C., *Science*, **215**, 975 (1982).

123. Kalyanaraman, V. S., Sarngadharan, M. G., Nakao, Y., Ito, Y., Aoki, T., and Gallo, R. C., *Proc. Natl. Acad. Sci. USA*, **79**, 1653 (1982).

124. Blattner, W. A., Kalyanaraman, V. S., Robert-Guroff, M., Lister, T. A., Galton, D. A. G., Sarin, P., Crawford, M. H., Catovsky, D., Greaves, M., and Gallo, R. C., *Int. J. Cancer*, **30**, 257 (1982).

125. Robert-Guroff, M., Kalyanaraman, V. S., Blattner, W. A., Popovic, M., Sarngadharan, M. G., Maeda, M., Blayney, D., Catovsky, D., Bunn, P. A., Shibata, A., Nakao, Y., Ito, Y., Aoki, T., and Gallo, R. C., *J. Exp. Med.*, **157**, 248 (1983).

126. Gallo, R. C., Kalyanaraman, V. S., Sarngadharan, M. G., Sliski, A., Vonderheid, E. C., Maeda, M., Nakao, Y., Yamada, K., Ito, Y., Gutensohn, N., Murphy, S., Bunn, P. A., Jr., Catovsky, D., Greaves, M. F., Blayney, D. W., Blattner, W., Jarrett, W. F. H., zur Hausen, H., Seligmann, M., Brouet, J. C., Haynes, B. F., Jegasothy, B. V., Jaffe, E., Cossman, J., Broder, S., Fisher, R. I., Golde, D. W., and Robert-Guroff, M., *Cancer Res.*, **43**, 3892 (1983).

127. Ruscetti, F. W., Robert-Guroff, M., Ceccherini-Nelli, L., Minowada, J., Popovic, M., and Gallo, R. C., *Int. J. Cancer*, **31**, 171 (1983).

128. Miyoshi, I., Kubonishi, I., Yoshimoto, S., Akagi, T., Outsuki, Y., Shiraishi, Y., Nagata, K., and Hinuma, Y., *Nature* **294**, 770 (1981).

129. Markham, P. D., Salahuddin, S. Z., Kalyanaraman, V. S., Popovic, M., Sarin, P., and Gallo, R. C., *Int. J. Cancer*, **31**, 413 (1983).

130. Poiesz, B. J., Ruscetti, F. W., Mier, J. W., Woods, A. M., and Gallo, R. C., *Proc. Natl. Acad. Sci. USA*, **77**, 6815 (1980).

131. Gallo, R. C., Popovic, M., Ruscetti, F. W., Kalyanaraman, V. S., Reitz, M. S., Jr., Royston, I., Broder, S., and Robert-Guroff, M., in R. F. Revoltella, Pontieri, G. M.,

Basilico, C., Rovera, G., Gallo, R. C., and Subak-Sharpe, J. H., Eds., *Expression of Differentiated Functions in Cancer Cells*. Raven, New York, 1982.

132. Uchiyama, T., Broder, S., and Waldmann, T. A., *J. Immunol.*, **126**, 1393 (1981).

133. Uchiyama, T., Nelson, D. L., Fleisher, T. A., and Waldmann, T. A., *J. Immunol.*, **126**, 1398 (1981).

134. Leonard, W. J., Depper, J. M., Uchiyama, T., Smith, K. A., Waldmann, T. A., and Greene, W. C., *Nature*, **300**, 267 (1983).

135. Manzari, V., Wong-Staal, F., Franchini, G., Colombini, S., Gelmann, E. P., Oroszlan, S., Staal, S., and Gallo, R. C., *Proc. Natl. Acad. Sci. USA*, **80**, 1594 (1983).

136. Wong-Staal, F., Hahn, B., Manzari, V., Colombini, S., Franchini, G., Gelmann, E. P., and Gallo, R. C., *Nature*, **302**, 626 (1983).

137. Manzari, V., Gallo, R. C., Franchini, G., Westin, E., Ceccherini-Nelli, L., Popovic, M., and Wong-Staal, F., *Proc. Natl. Acad. Sci. USA*, **80**, 11 (1983).

138. Hizuka, N., Gordon, D., Lesniak, M. A., Van Obberghen, E., Carpentier, J.-L., and Orci, L., *J. Biol. Chem.*, **256**, 4591 (1981).

139. Gorden, P., Carpentier, J.-L., Freychet, P., and Orci, L., *Clin. Res.*, **27**, 485 (1979).

140. Gorden, P., Carpentier, J.-L. Cohen, S., and Orci, L., *Proc. Natl. Acad. Sci. USA*, **75**, 5025 (1978).

141. Scatchard, G., *Ann. N.Y. Acad. Sci.*, **51**, 660 (1949).

142. Greene, W. C., Wong-Staal, F., Depper, J. M., Leonard, W. J., Gallo, R. C., and Waldmann, T. A., Abstract presented at the Annual Meeting of the American Federation of Clinical Research, 1983.

143. Blaeckley, R. C., Caplan, B., Havele, C., Ritzel, R. G., Mosmann, T. R., Farrar, J. J., and Paetkau, V., *J. Immunol.*, **127**, 2432 (1981).

144. Lin, Y., Stadler, B. M., and Rabin, H., *J. Biol. Chem.*, **257**, 1587 (1982).

145. Gillis, S., Mochizuki, D. Y., Conlon, P. J., Hefeneider, S. H., Ramthun, C. A., Gillis, A. E., Frank, M. B., Henney, C. S., and Watson, J. D., *Immunol. Rev.*, **63**, 167 (1982).

146. Villa-Komaroff, L., Efstratiadis, A., Broome, S., Lomedico, P., Tizard, R., Naber, S. P., Chick, W. L., and Gilbert, W., *Proc. Natl. Acad. Sci. USA*, **75**, 3727 (1978).

AUTHOR INDEX

Numbers in parentheses are reference numbers and indicate that the authors' work is referred to although his name may not be mentioned in the text. Numbers in *italics* show the pages on which the complete references are listed.

SUBJECT INDEX